Co

and built

onments   155

data

51

List of maps

List of figures

Acknowledgments

This book and the accompanying datasets are the result of a team project, and the author wishes to thank the many people who contributed to its success.

Christopher Simeone, a San Francisco State University (SFSU) student with a bachelor of arts in geography, provided invaluable technical and cartographic support in developing the maps and exercises.

Myles Boylan and David MacArthur of the National Science Foundation (NSF) encouraged this project and set high professional standards for our work. The NSF Course, Curriculum, and Laboratory Improvement—Educational Materials Development (CCLI-EMD) grant program, which they ably manage, made this instructional module possible.

Dean Joel Kassiola of San Francisco State University's College of Behavioral and Social Sciences enthusiastically supported this project.

Christian Harder, publisher of ESRI Press, encouraged us at every stage. Judith Hawkins, managing editor of ESRI Press, oversaw the entire production process and helped resolve many issues along the way. Savitri Brant, a book designer at ESRI Press, designed the book and cover and provided invaluable assistance with graphics. Bo King, a cartographer at ESRI, reviewed maps and provided cartographic support, as did Michael Law, a cartographic specialist at ESRI Press. Brian Parr, workbook project manager, and Sally Swenson, education specialist, put the exercise data through rigorous testing. David Boyles edited the manuscript, and Tiffany Wilkerson copyedited the book. Lesley Downie provided helpful administrative support. Elizabeth Fredericks contributed proofreading support.

The project coprinciple investigator, Professor Ayse Pamuk of the San Francisco State University Urban Studies Program, helped obtain and administer the NSF grant. Ayse collaborated on identifying data sources; shared data; helped define concepts to teach; and helped work out the research design, review process, training, evaluation, and other aspects of the project. Professor Pamuk is completing a companion volume, *Mapping Global Cities: GIS Methods in Urban Analysis.*

John Landis of the University of California, Berkeley, Department of City and Regional Planning; Myron Orfield of the University of Minnesota Law School, Ameregis, and the Metropolitan Area Research Council (MARC); and Professor Keith Clarke of the University of California, Santa Barbara, Department of Geography critiqued the research design and provided feedback on the manuscript.

Professor Earl Bossard's pioneering work at San Jose State University on envisioning neighborhoods was an early inspiration for this project, and Earl's input enriched the symbology chapter of this book.

Portland State University professors Carl Abbott and Ethan Seltzer shared their knowledge of regional planning in the Portland metropolitan area and Metro's Regional Land Information System.

Michael Reilly, University of California, Berkeley, Department of City and Regional Planning PhD, and Monique Nakagawa and Lisel Blash of the San Francisco State University Public Research

Institute, provided invaluable assistance in gathering and cleaning data, developing exercises, and sharing their knowledge of GIS theory and ArcGIS® operations. Michael Reilly created the data graphics in chapters 4, 8, and 11.

Diane Godard of the San Francisco State University Public Research Institute developed the plan for evaluating this instructional module and evaluated a beta version of the module at San Francisco State and other universities.

Jody Littlehales and Aly Pennucci organized a summer training session for faculty from other universities who, along with the author and other SFSU faculty members, tested this instructional module at six U.S. universities in fall 2004.

San Francisco State University urban studies students Fredrick Schermer and Bridgette Carroll, along with Jody Littlehales and Aly Pennucci, tested all the exercises in draft form and read and marked up early versions of the book.

Many people were generous with permissions to use data they had assembled. Special thanks are due to Steve Ericksen and Richard Bolen at Metro (Portland, Oregon) and Myron Orfield at Ameregis. For their help in getting data together and granting permission to use it in this book, grateful appreciation is offered to Olson Lee at the San Francisco Redevelopment Agency, Bill Stewart at the California Fire and Resource Assessment Program (FRAP), Molly Penberth at the California Farmland Mapping and Monitoring Program (FMMP), Thomas Büttner at the United Nations Population Division, Patricia Schultz at Edwin Mellen Press, David M. Stoms at the UC Santa Barbara Biogeography Laboratory, and Simon Murphy of London's Transport Museum.

Several people beta tested this module during a 2004 summer workshop at San Francisco State University; they include Earl Bossard (San Jose State University's Department of Urban and Regional Planning); Francis Neely, Christopher Bettinger, Mai Nguyen, and XiaoHang Liu (San Francisco State University's Departments of Political Science, Sociology, Urban Studies, and Geography); John Flateau (Medgar Evers College's School of Business and Public Administration); Gianpaolo Baiocchi (University of Massachusetts, Amherst's Sociology Department); Mary Edwards (University of Illinois Champaign-Urbana's Department of Urban and Regional Planning); Xinhao Wang (University of Cincinnati); Sanda Kaufman (Cleveland State University's Levin College of Urban Affairs); and Haydar Kurban (Howard University's Economics Department). Professors Flateau, Nguyen, and Baiocchi also beta tested the module with students at their respective universities.

The following people deserve special thanks for going out of their way to search for appropriate photographs for the book: Brad Rovanpera, public information officer for the city of Walnut Creek; Sharon Koomler, curator of the Shaker Museum and Library in Old Chatham, New York; Stuart Shinske and Michael Schwartz of the *Courier-Post* newspaper in Cherry Hill, N.J.; and Simon Murphy of London's Transport Museum.

Andrew Roderick, Alex Keller, Vincent Cheung, Barry Nicols, Lena Deng, and the rest of the extraordinary SFSU College of Behavioral and Social Sciences technical support staff maintained the servers and networks and kept ArcGIS running smoothly in our offices and computer labs.

My wife, Joanne Fraser, and daughter, Courtney LeGates, supported long nights, busy days, and frequent trips away from home as the book came together.

Introduction

The premise of this book is that space is an important dimension in most real-world issues that concern social scientists and students of public policy. However, except for geographers, these scientists and students often neglect the spatial aspect of issues. Geographers are fond of saying that "spatial is special." Over the years, geographers and experts in fields closely related to geography have developed specialized knowledge useful for understanding physical space that is quite different from methodologies like descriptive or inferential statistics that apply across all the social science disciplines. This book introduces social scientists to this important material.

The book is designed as a month-long module for beginning social science and public policy research methods courses. The structured exercises are designed to be done in six hours of computer lab time. Students should be able to complete a final exercise from among four suggested at the end of the book to synthesize and apply the material in six hours of independent work.

This book is appropriate for students who have not completed a course in statistics or social science data analysis. It assumes only that students have basic computer skills. It does not assume familiarity with statistics or computerized statistical package(s) like the Statistical Package for the Social Sciences (SPSS®). A planned companion volume, *Mapping Global Cities: GIS Methods in Urban Analysis*, by Ayse Pamuk, will continue to develop spatial thinking using descriptive and inferential statistics encountered in upper division undergraduate social science statistics/data analysis courses.

Geographic information systems (GIS) software is now widely available and is becoming increasingly easy to use. GIS has begun to spill beyond the boundaries of geography into environmental studies, urban planning, business, and other curricula. A few innovative sociologists, political scientists, historians, and anthropologists now use GIS in their own research and are beginning to introduce their students to spatial analysis. But the great majority of all undergraduate research methods courses remain totally aspatial.

There is a scholarly literature on the theory and practice of constructing data graphics. William Cleveland at Bell Labs has written lucidly on the theory underlying conventional data graphics such as pie, bar, line, column, and area charts. Jacques Bertin, Edward Tufte, John Tukey, and others have written theoretically astute books on data visualization filled with examples of good and bad practice. Yet this important material is rarely taught in undergraduate research methods courses.

This is a topics-based book focusing on urban phenomena and urban issues. Cities are and have always been messy places with lots of problems. But they are also the loci of opportunity and generators of human culture and technological change with many assets (Hall 2002). Opportunities to make things better abound even in the worst areas of troubled cities. This book identifies urban assets and opportunities as well as urban problems. Students will learn how to see both urban problems and urban opportunities more clearly and they will learn strategies to overcome problems and capitalize on opportunities. This book encourages students to be visionary—even slightly utopian—in imagining better urban futures. "Vision," as Jonathan Swift said, "is the art of seeing things invisible."

The title of this book reveals two of the author's biases: the importance of placing all urban development in a global context and the need to address urban problems at the regional scale. Globalization has proceeded so far that no city, region, or nation state can be understood without a grasp of worldwide phenomena. Discussion, data, and exercises in this book constantly refer to the global scale and encourage students to think globally. Most people think of the place where they live as the norm; learning about places that are richer or poorer, more populous or more sparsely settled, more or less urbanized, growing more slowly or more rapidly than one's own community helps put local urban phenomena in context. When the sixteenth century Jesuit Mateo Ricci introduced the Ming Emperors to European maps of the world, they were distressed to see that the celestial kingdom was not at the center of the world.

Most cities in the United States and the rest of the world are parts of metropolitan areas. Individual cities have increased in population size and physical land area or have blended into neighboring cities to form a continuous band of urbanization. Accordingly, both urban problems and urban assets and opportunities are best viewed in a regional context today. Air and water pollution do not stop at the borders of any one city. Each city can contribute only its small part to solving the regional problem of air pollution. Traffic originating elsewhere flows through cities on highways and roads built and operated on a regional or statewide basis. Whether a city's streets are congested or not depends as much on what neighboring cities do as decisions the city itself makes. Metropolitan housing markets are also regional in nature. If some jurisdictions in a fast-growing region restrict the number of building permits they grant, population that would have settled within them spills over to neighboring cities. Cities that refuse to take their fair share of their region's affordable housing impose costs on their neighbors. These are important equity issues discussed in part III of the book. This book zooms in to some neighborhood-level issues and zooms out to the national and world scale. But most of the discussion and most of the exercises focus on metropolitan regions and encourage students to think and act regionally.

It is not just problems that are regional today. Many assets should be considered regional resources. If a spectacular stretch of ocean beach or an old growth redwood forest happens to fall within the boundaries of one city, the locals should not be the sole stewards for what are really regional (or even statewide or national) resources. Big infrastructure decisions, such as the decision to build an airport or mass transit system, affect all the jurisdictions in a region. The economic health of metropolitan areas depends on collective decision making to take advantage of opportunities the region presents.

While urban planning and management should be increasingly regional, with rare exceptions they are not. Metropolitan regions are fragmented into dozens or hundreds of small competing jurisdictions. Only a few states mandate serious regional planning. Metro, in the Portland, Oregon, region, is the only elected commission in the United States with authority to do regional planning. Metro is highlighted in the last chapter and final exercise.

The book stresses both theory and practice. Academic scholarship is important, and the chapters that follow place a heavy emphasis on enduring concepts in spatial analysis. But this book also has a very applied focus—a focus on action. Each part shows how theory can be put to work making the world a better place. In addition to encouraging students to undertake academic research, the material encourages students to put what they learn to use in solving problems.

Enthusiasts for computer-based learning stress the advantages of asynchronous learning—learning in which students can use a personal computer to proceed at their own pace at hours that best suit their schedules. While asynchronous learning has its place, there is a well-justified backlash against uncritical enthusiasm for asynchronous teaching. Thoughtful instructors are moving toward mixed models of instruction: plenty of good old-fashioned lecture–discussion sessions and laboratory work with the instructor or a teaching assistant present, as well as asynchronous learning. That is the approach in this book. Students can read the chapters about substantive regional problems, GIS concepts, and data graphics on their own schedule without an instructor present. Six of the twelve chapters are like that: chapters 1, 4, 5, 8, 11, and 12. Six other chapters—2, 3, 6, 7, 9, and 10—focus on GIS concepts and operations and are closely tied to the laboratory exercises at the end of the book. Students should read these chapters just before tackling computer labs when they are about to plunge into "learning by doing" or just after they emerge from the computer lab empowered by what they have learned but in need of verbal reinforcement of concepts they have just encountered.

This is a book about visualization—not only presenting information visually as the polished end product of analysis, but also "using vision to think." The best social science research often involves iterative exploratory data analysis. While research should be guided by theory, there is plenty of room for being playful in the research process. What researchers find out at intermediate stages in a research project should provoke new questions. Social science research should branch out to find answers to questions that empirical study recasts more clearly as the research proceeds. Visualization should both help crystallize knowledge and display analysis outcomes. This book encourages students to create lots of intermediate maps and data graphics as vehicles for clarifying their research as it proceeds.

Good visual display of analytic results is a powerful aid to both understanding and remembering. While conclusions may be expressed in words or statistical output, visual images are an important aid to thought. Matteo Ricci—who shook the Chinese Ming Emperors' worldview with his European maps—advocated building mental "memory palaces" constructed entirely of visual images of things to remember (Spence 1994). "To everything that we wish to remember," Ricci wrote, "we should give an image; and to every one of these images we should assign a position where it can repose peacefully until we are ready to claim it by an act of memory."

There is an aesthetic prejudice in this book—a strong emphasis on graphical minimalism. Landscape architect Andrew Jackson Downing said that functionalism is the American aesthetic (Downing 1844). Downing argued that design should be for use rather than for ornament. The theme of minimal functionalism is picked up in places as varied as Strunk and White's advice about how to cut excessive verbiage in *The Elements of Style* (Strunk and White 2000), the Shakers' principles for designing simple functional furniture, Mozart's musical theory, and Edward Tufte's idea that data graphics should maximize data-ink ratios (Tufte 2001).

Related to the idea of simple, functional visual communication is the idea of breaking down complex problems into simplified models of reality. Just as a physical model can use only selected elements of interest, scale them down, and permit scientists to observe how the model behaves under controlled circumstances, simplified digital representations of parts of urban reality can help observers better see how critical features like streets, streams, parks, and housing developments really work. The beauty of digital representations is that they can be easily and repeatedly changed and the consequences of alternative plans and policies endlessly examined. This book does not purport to introduce sophisticated spatial models—that is way beyond the author's competence and this book's intent. However, undergraduate students can grasp the idea of modeling physical and social reality. All of the maps in all of the exercises in this book are models of reality, and the text and exercises constantly remind students that they can build digital models.

● ● ●

Professor Michael Goodchild of the University of California, Santa Barbara, says that GIScience and GIS are technology-driven (Goodchild 1997). The kinds of inquiry that practitioners undertake are shaped by what GIS technology can do. While this comment is insightful about what does occur, this book argues that computer tools should not drive social science questions. Throughout, this book tries to let the kinds of analyses social scientists and public policy professionals really do drive the operational chapters and exercises. An example may make this clear. One of the things that current raster GIS technology does especially well is allow users to compute cost-weighted distance—the distance across a surface where there is impedance from things like difficult terrain, ground cover, or slippery soils. Most GIS textbooks devote a substantial amount of space to discussing this conceptually interesting topic and showing students how to create cost surfaces and do cost-weighted distance analysis. Like learning Latin, this is good for the students' minds. If they master the concepts and operations, they will better understand spatial analysis. However, few social scientists and public policy professionals will ever need to compute a cost-weighted distance surface in their own research or work. So this book touches only lightly on this topic. On the other hand, social scientists and public policy professionals work extensively with the spatial units the U.S. Census Bureau has developed such as blocks, block groups, census tracts, and Public Use Microdata Areas (PUMAs). They do a lot of thematic mapping of demographic and housing census data. Accordingly, this book devotes quite a bit of attention to thematic mapping of census data. The importance of a particular kind of analysis to social scientists and public policy professionals—not neat things the technology can do—drives the selection of the material included in this book.

This book emphasizes the way in which technology can empower people to act effectively in a principled way based on their values. Discussion of the topics incorporates the author's own values—implementing better planned responses to urbanization, achieving greater harmony between the built and natural environments, and increasing equity and spatial integration within metropolitan regions. Students need not agree with these values. The book encourages analysis based on what students consider to be important and provides plenty of opportunity for them to create models of futures that conform to their own values.

For purposes of clarity, a limited number of key variables are included in exercise datasets accompanying this book so that students will not be overwhelmed with information overload. But the maps and analyses throughout this book are true to reality, and students who explore with care will discover many surprises that will hopefully challenge their preconceptions and expose them to the subtlety of real-world phenomena. "The truth," Oscar Wilde wrote, "is rarely pure and never simple" (Wilde 1895). Students who think core cities are inhabited by low-income minority residents and suburbs by rich white people will discover in the maps and data in this book that the demographics of core cities and suburbs today are much more complicated than that. Students who think all prime farmland is vanishing at an alarming rate may be surprised to discover empirically more complex patterns about how much prime farmland is being lost, at what rate, and where. Environmental justice advocates may be surprised by some of the maps of contaminated sites in this book. While these sites are often located in low-income and minority neighborhoods, some sites are also located in middle- and upper-income, predominantly white neighborhoods.

Each of the three main parts in this book starts with a chapter describing an important urban-related topic—urbanization in chapter 1, conflicts between the natural and built environments in chapter 5, and regional equity issues in chapter 9. These initial chapters are followed by chapters on spatial analysis concepts and operations. The final chapters in each of the first three parts of the book describe data graphics. A final section contains a chapter describing how Metro in the Portland, Oregon, region brings together good regional planning practice and skillful GIS analysis. Exercises related to the four parts of *Think Globally, Act Regionally* are grouped together at the end of the book.

Students need to approach the material in this book differently from the way they would a novel in a general education course. In courses like that, students may be able to wing it by reading the material after the classroom lectures and cramming at the end of the course. That won't work with this material. Mastering the operational GIS material in this book is a multistage process. Students need to do the following:

- Read the topical chapters to get an introduction to substantive issues. The first chapters in each part of this book describe an important topic related to cities and regions. Students like topics-based courses in which theoretical and applied material is introduced through topical material that they relate to. Chapters 1, 5, and 9 cover topics related to cities and regions that students at San Francisco State and other universities, where the modules were tested, found interesting.
- Read the conceptual chapters to get an overview of spatial analysis concepts. The most important thing students can take away from an introduction to spatial analysis is an understanding of enduring concepts. Chapters 2, 3, 6, 7, and 10 describe spatial analysis concepts that will remain relevant for a very long time. Fundamental spatial relationships—proximity, adjacency, containment, clustering, and dispersion—do not change. Methods of classifying and querying data are well developed and will evolve slowly in the future. Theory that cartographers have developed over centuries has been seamlessly integrated into GIS and will change gradually over the coming decades. Theory about the proper visual representation of quantitative data, graphic semiology, and principles of map symbology, described in chapters 4, 8, and 11, evolve slowly. If students reread these chapters ten years from now, most of what they say will still be relevant. In contrast, in ten years, the description of GIS operations and the exercise material in this book will be very outdated.
- Read the GIS operations chapters just before doing the exercises. Chapters 2, 3, 6, 7, and 10 summarize the operations. These chapters won't teach students what computer keys to push. They are a bridge to the step-by-step exercises at the end of the book that teach students to do GIS operations. There is a lot of material in the operational chapters. Some material may be hard to understand before students have done the exercises and actually see what the operations do. The material will be clear on a second reading after they have completed the exercise related to the chapter.
- Do the step-by-step computer lab exercises that accompany the operational chapter. The best way to understand the theory and practice of spatial analysis is to do it. This book is based on learning by doing. Exercises at the end of the book accompany chapters in the book. The best way to start to do GIS is to follow step-by-step instructions to see how the software works. The first six exercises in this book teach the operational steps to do analysis that use the concepts described in the conceptual chapters.
- Do the "Your Turn" exercises at the end of the step-by-step exercises. There is a Your Turn section at the end of each of the exercises that requires students to repeat all of the operations they have just learned using different data and without step-by-step instructions. Students need to complete the Your Turn exercises to make sure they have mastered the operational GIS steps.

- Reread the conceptual and operational chapters. When students first read the conceptual and operational chapters, they are reading about a lot of material that they haven't seen before. Some concepts and operations will not be clear. There is a lot of new terminology. On a second reading, after they have seen the concepts and operations in practice in the step-by-step exercises, concepts and operations that may have been unclear before they did the exercise will make much more sense. So will the terminology. A glossary at the end of each chapter contains key terms.

- Complete the final project. Once students have read the entire book and completed the first six exercises, including the Your Turn material, they need to apply what they have learned to a topic of their own choosing. This will cement their confidence in their ability to do basic spatial analysis on their own. The last chapter in this book describes Metro—the Portland, Oregon, regional planning organization. A final project suggests how students can analyze Metro data on their own. The project exercise contains actual data from Metro for this analysis. In addition to pulling together all of the skills they have learned, the final project is an opportunity for students to be slightly utopian and to create models of the world that reflect their own values.

Richard LeGates
San Francisco, California
June 2005

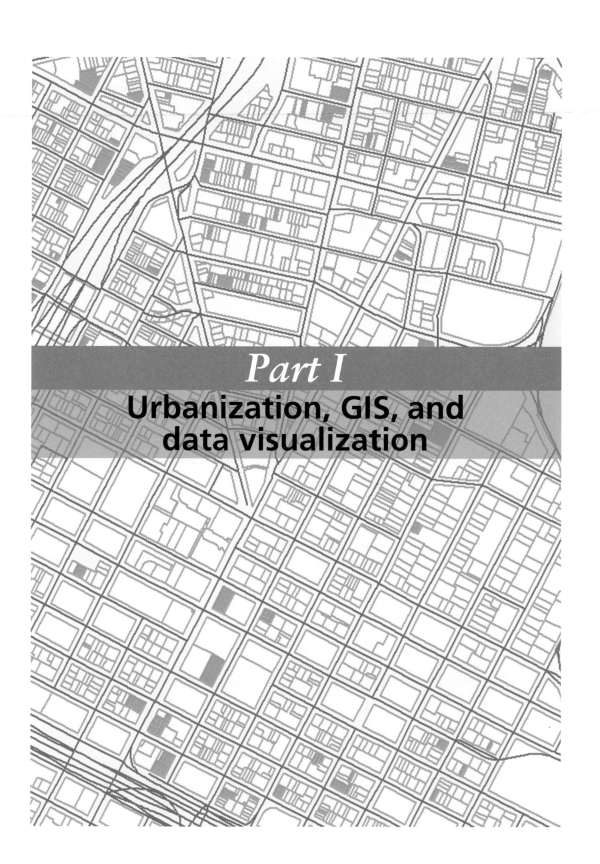

Part I
Urbanization, GIS, and data visualization

Chapter 1

Urbanization and its discontents

"Neither the historian nor the cartographer can ever reproduce the reality they are trying to communicate to the reader of books or maps; they can but give a plan, a series of indications, of this reality. There are contrasting schemes for choosing from enormous numbers of geographic details. You may have a map in which every feature that can be named . . . is crowded in . . . or you may have a map in which many details are omitted in the effort to show the reader the lay of the land. . . . Both kinds are useful, depending on the needs of the viewer."

Crane Brinton (1963)

Introduction

"Cities are inherently messy places," concluded the great British urbanist Sir Peter Hall in his magisterial history of great world cities, *Cities and Civilization* (Hall 2002). Cities are filled with both problems and opportunities.

One purpose of this book is to help social science and public policy students—in geography, sociology, political science, history, anthropology, environmental studies, urban studies, urban planning, public administration, and related disciplines and fields—identify and think clearly about urban problems in order to devise solutions. Another purpose of this book is to help students see the opportunities that urban areas present and to use spatial analysis and data visualization to better understand how to capitalize on the opportunities. Throughout the book there is an emphasis on analysis: using human intelligence (aided by information technology) to analyze conditions and then formulate policy to address problems and take advantage of opportunities, rather than to act based on imprecise and often erroneous impressions of the conditions.

Each section of this book focuses on one topic and primarily uses examples from one region. This section focuses on urbanization and the problems and opportunities urbanization presents. Many of the examples in this chapter are from the San Francisco Bay Area. You will not work with data from the Bay Area in exercise 1, but in exercise 2 you will learn GIS operations using Bay Area data on traffic congestion, the location of low-rent housing, and where foreign-born residents in the Bay Area live. Exercises 3 and 4 focus on impacts of urbanization on the environment in Contra Costa County—a county across San Francisco Bay from San Francisco.

Before proceeding with a discussion of urbanization and the problems and opportunities it creates, it is helpful to introduce this interesting and unique region.

Welcome to the San Francisco Bay Area

The San Francisco Bay Area is a beautiful and prosperous region. It is physically lovely, with beaches and mountains, ranches and agricultural land, forests and wetlands, mountains, lakes, and rivers. It has a dynamic, mixed economy driven by high-tech information and biotech firms. Incomes and home prices are among the highest in the world. Despite its advantages, the Bay Area has its share of problems, including urban poverty, congestion, pollution, and conflicts between the built and natural environments.

The Bay Area is usually defined as all of the land within nine counties that are members of the Association of Bay Area Governments (ABAG)—the regional **council of governments** (COG). There are 101 cities within the ABAG region. One of the cities—San Francisco—is a combined city and county, so there are a total of 109 separate local governments in the Bay Area.

The entire Bay Area covers about nine thousand square miles. Approximately 17 percent of the land is developed. Much of the remaining 83 percent is undevelopable because it is within a federal, state, or regional park, or is watershed land, land set aside for military use, or land whose topography makes it impossible to develop. Other land in the region might be developed in the future, but it is not presently serviced by roads and other infrastructure.

Most people read maps without much thought as to how they were constructed and exactly what they are really saying. Since this is a book about spatial analysis and data visualization, every map in this book requires a careful look. Map 1.1 is a map layout with one main and two smaller maps. The main map shows the nine Bay Area counties symbolized in a light green color and the 101 cities in orange outlined in gray. The Pacific Ocean is on the left (west) of the map. San Francisco is on the peninsula near the center of the map and is outlined in red and labeled for clarity. Contra Costa County is across the bay from San Francisco and is outlined in amethyst and also labeled. San Francisco Bay is the large bay between San Francisco and East Bay cities such as Oakland

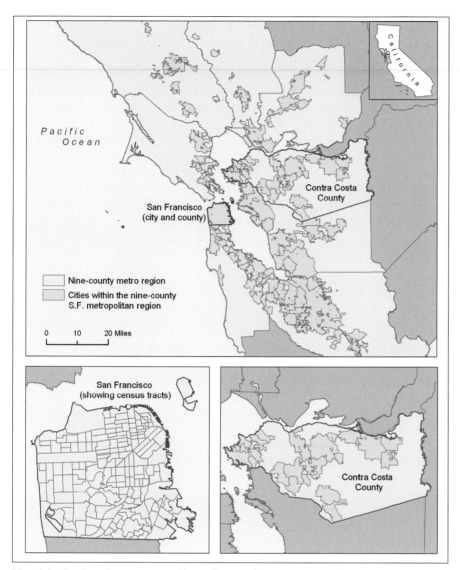

Map 1.1   San Francisco Bay Area with small maps of San Francisco and Contra Costa County.
Source: 2000 U.S. Census of Population and Housing

and Berkeley. One small map shows San Francisco in greater detail—including the outline of census tracts, geographic areas the U.S. Census Bureau uses for reporting demographic, housing, and other census information. The other small map shows unincorporated county land in Contra Costa County in light green and land within the nineteen cities in the county in orange outlined in gray. You will explore San Francisco census tract data in exercise 2 and learn more about conflicts between the built and natural environments in Contra Costa County in exercises 3 and 4.

The scale bar in the large map is included to help map readers understand distances in the map. A cartographic decision was made not to include scale bars in the two small maps because the scale is sufficiently clear from the scale bar in the large map. None of the maps include a north arrow or other map elements because these are not really necessary given the map context. You will learn how to create scale bars and other map elements in exercise 6.

The San Francisco Bay Area's population has grown steadily since the mid-1800s Gold Rush era (Scott 1985) and continues to grow (ABAG 2003). The U.S. Census reported 6,783,760 people living in the Bay Area in 2000 (U.S. Census 2000a).

Bay Area residents are a very diverse group. A little more than half the Bay Area population is white, followed by large numbers of Asians, Hispanics, African-Americans, and members of other racial and ethnic groups (U.S. Census 2000a). Hispanic and Asian immigration fuels much of the current Bay Area population growth.

Historically, San Francisco was the dominant city in the region. When the United States acquired California from Mexico in 1848 at the conclusion of the Mexican-American War, there were only a few hundred people in San Francisco. Just a year later, the Gold Rush changed all that. "The world rushed in" (Holliday 1981), and San Francisco became an instant city of several hundred thousand people (Barth 1988). The census reported San Francisco's population to be 776,773 in 2000.

San Francisco is the historical, financial, and cultural center of the Bay Area.
Source: Photodisc

San Francisco has only fifty square miles of area. It is surrounded on the north, west, and east by water. All of the land south of San Francisco lies in incorporated cities, so San Francisco cannot physically expand its land area by annexing unincorporated county land. Almost all of the land in San Francisco is developed. San Francisco's population is still increasing as infill lots are developed and parts of the city are redeveloped—usually at much higher densities.

Over the last thirty years, the Bay Area has grown by about one hundred thousand people a year (ABAG 2003). San Francisco can't accommodate more than a small fraction of this continuing population growth. Accordingly, development in the Bay Area has proceeded north and south along the Pacific Coast, across San Francisco Bay, inland along Highway 80 that goes to California's capital city of Sacramento, and in urban fringe areas like eastern Contra Costa County. You can see in map 1.1 that there now is a nearly continuous band of urbanization around San Francisco Bay.

The small map of Contra Costa County shows a pattern common to many suburban areas. There are nineteen cities in Contra Costa County covering about 27 percent of the county's land area. The rest of the land—73 percent—is unincorporated county land. Each of the nineteen cities governs itself and makes decisions about the land within its borders. The county government governs the remaining unincorporated areas.

Even though this is a book about urban issues, map 1.1 shows a metropolitan region. The exercises emphasize urban analysis at the regional scale. The reason for this emphasis is that urban planning and policy need to be based on regional considerations.

Urbanization

Since the beginning of the industrial revolution (about 1750), there has been a huge increase in the proportion of the world's population living in cities as opposed to small towns and rural areas (Davis 1965). We are still in the midst of a monumental shift in the nature and extent of human settlements. The combination of massive world population growth and urbanization has produced an exponential increase in the number of very large cities and huge urban agglomerations where multiple cities blend together.

In thinking about urbanization, there are three concepts to keep in mind: (a) increases in total population, (b) the proportions of the population in a region that are urban and nonurban, and (c) the physical size of a city or agglomeration. All three concepts are related and all three usually occur simultaneously, so it is easy to confuse them. A simplified set of graphics can help to illustrate these relationships.

City population size refers to the absolute city population. Figure 1.1a illustrates an increase in city population size from 100,000 people in 1950 to 250,000 people in 2000—a 150 percent population increase in fifty years.

Urbanization refers to the proportion of the population that lives in urban areas as opposed to nonurban areas like rural areas and small towns. Figure 1.1b illustrates two countries with different levels of urbanization. In the country on the left, half of the country's population is

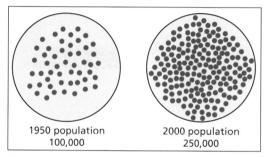

Figure 1.1a   Increase in city population.

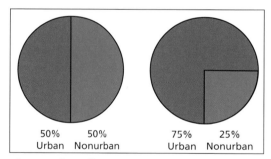

Figure 1.1b   Different levels of urbanization (two countries).

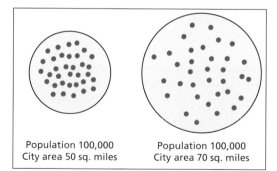

Figure 1.1c   Increase in city physical size (no increase in population).

urban, and half is nonurban. In the country on the right, three quarters (75 percent) of the country's population is urban, and 25 percent is nonurban. Urbanization is usually analyzed at the level of a large geographic area, such as a country.

City physical size refers to the area of a city measured in units like square miles. Cities with constant or declining populations usually stay the same physical size. So do cities like San Francisco, which are surrounded by already incorporated cities and natural barriers like the Pacific Ocean and San Francisco Bay. If a city can annex additional land, it is likely to add area as its population grows. In figure 1.1c, the physical size of a hypothetical city has grown from fifty square miles to seventy square miles while its population remained constant.

World urbanization

Demographers are social scientists who study the human population. The word demographer comes from the Greek word *demos* (people). Keeping track of the precise number of people on earth and specifying what percentage of the human population lives in urban areas is a difficult task. Data is unreliable for many countries. Countries' own definitions of what is and is not an urban area vary from country to country. Conditions are changing rapidly. The best existing estimates come from experts at the Population Division of the United Nations Department of Economic and Social Affairs. United Nations (UN) demographers estimate the world population to be 6.3 billion people (UN 2002). They estimate that a little less than half of this population (47 percent) lives in urban areas (UN 1999). According to the UN, most of the world's population—nearly five billion people—now live in less-developed regions of the planet.

The UN estimates that the world population is growing by about 77 million people a year. Demographers forecast that the world population will increase to 8.9 billion in 2050. The population of more developed regions—currently at 1.2 billion—is expected to remain about the same in 2050. Despite the AIDS epidemic, the population of less-developed regions is projected to rise from 4.9 billion today to 7.7 billion in 2050 (UN 2002). UN demographers also predict increasing urbanization. If their forecasts hold true, at some point in 2007 a baby born in a city or one new migrant to a city will tip the balance, so that more than half of the human population lives in urban areas (UN 1999).

Maps can help us see the global distribution of the world's population, different levels of urbanization in different countries, and the distribution and size of world cities. In the balance of part I and in exercise 1, you will learn more about the historical growth of world cities and urbanization and will create your own maps analyzing these important issues. But first a word of advice about reading maps.

Maps 1.2, 1.3a, and 1.3b show some critical information about world cities and about the extent of urbanization in different countries of the world. Social science research requires researchers to specify what exactly they are measuring—the unit of analysis. The unit of analysis in map 1.2 is different from the unit of analysis in maps 1.3a and 1.3b. Map 1.2 uses cities as the unit of analysis; maps 1.3a and 1.3b use countries as the unit of analysis. The symbology of the maps is also different. Map 1.2 represents cities as points; maps 1.3a and 1.3b represent countries as polygons. You will learn more about procedures like specifying units of analysis and the visual representation of spatial information with appropriate symbology in this book and accompanying exercises. For now, look critically at maps 1.2, 1.3a, and 1.3b, both for their content and the way in which they were constructed.

One of the vexing issues in urban analysis is how to define a city. The area of a legally incorporated city is often a poor descriptor of the urban area where the city is located because suburbs and other smaller jurisdictions are really part of the same urban area. The UN uses the term **agglomeration** to refer to a distinct urban area and provides past, current, and projected estimates of the population size of more than four hundred urban agglomerations (UN 2004). Most urban agglomerations consist of a well-know city and their adjacent urban area, such as the London agglomeration and the Paris agglomeration. But some agglomerations—such as the North Ruhr-Rhine agglomeration in Germany—include several large cities and the continuous band of urbanization between them.

Map 1.2 shows the location of urban agglomerations with more than five million people in 2000 as defined by the United Nations (UN 2004). Taking a careful look at map 1.2, you will see that each agglomeration is symbolized as a single point. All the points are the same size, even though the populations of these large agglomerations range from a little more than five million (the Madrid agglomeration) to nearly thirty-five million (the Tokyo agglomeration). We can't tell from this point data how urbanized the respective countries are.

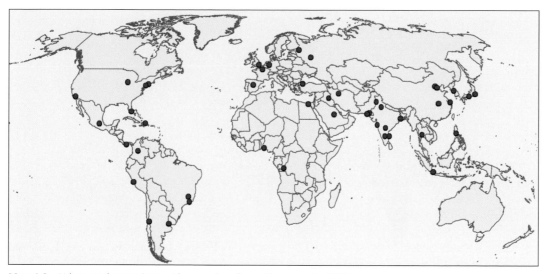

Map 1.2   Urban agglomerations with more than five million people, 2000.
Source: United Nations

In map 1.3a countries—not urban agglomerations—are the unit of analysis. Map 1.3a shows data from the World Bank on the percent of the population that was urban in different countries in 2003 (World Bank 2004). It presents the results of a cross-sectional analysis of conditions at one point in time. The countries in map 1.3a are colored different shades of orange to symbolize the percentage of their population that is urban: the most urbanized countries are dark orange, the least urbanized countries light orange. Map 1.3a tells us about the percentage of the population of a county that is urban, not the population size of individual urban agglomerations within the country. Rather than points, the countries are symbolized as polygons (enclosed shapes with many sides). Map 1.3a shows that in 2003 the United States, Canada, and most West European countries were more than 75 percent urban, as we might expect. So were many South American countries and the entire continent of Australia.

Some other highly urban countries in map 1.3a may come as more of a surprise. For example, countries with the highest percentages of their population urban include Saudi Arabia (mostly desert with a large percent of its population living in cities newly built with oil money). Almost all of the lightest orange areas in map 1.3a are in Africa and Southeast Asia: the least urbanized parts of the world today. Map 1.3a shows what percentage of the population is urban in different countries. It does not show how fast the urban population of cities is growing. Map 1.3b answers that important question.

Map 1.3b symbolizes the countries whose urban populations are growing most rapidly—over 4 percent a year—in dark orange and the countries whose urban populations are growing least rapidly—between 0 and 1 percent a year—in light orange. Countries that are losing population are symbolized in beige. Almost all of the countries that are urbanizing very rapidly (dark orange) are in Africa. Most eastern European countries are de-urbanizing (beige).

It would be interesting to see a data graphic comparing the variables mapped in maps 1.3a and 1.3b to see if there is a relationship between how fast the urban population of each country is growing and the percentage of each country's population that is urban. In chapter 8, you will see

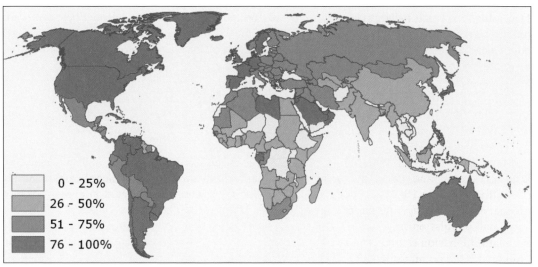

Map 1.3a   Percent of population urban by country, 2003.

Source: World Bank, World Development Indicators 2003

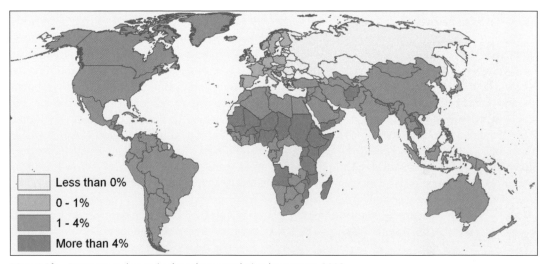

Map 1.3b   Percentage change in the urban population by country, 2003.

Source: World Bank, World Development Indicators 2003

how a kind of data graphic called a scattergram shows this relationship very clearly for selected countries.

The balance of this chapter sets the stage for what will follow by further describing population growth, urbanization, city size, and the problems and opportunities they present.

Urban problems: A new concern

At the beginning of the twenty-first century, it is difficult to imagine a world without cities. But there were no cities at all for most of human history. Until a few centuries ago almost all of the largest cities in the world today were smaller than Peoria, Illinois, which in 2000 had a population of about 113,000.

Social scientists do not agree on when human beings emerged or the first cities were built. Depending on which paleontologist you believe about which bone fragment qualifies as human, human beings have lived on earth for about 2.5 million years. Depending on which archaeologist you believe about which human settlement is big enough, dense enough, or has enough cultural attributes to qualify as a city, cities have existed for about 5,500 years: about 1/5 of 1 percent of human history.

Until the nineteenth century, very few people lived in cities. The great majority of the world's population lived in rural areas and small towns. What cities there were had small populations and covered little land area. Cities we think of as very important in the eighteenth century and before were very small.

Map 1.4 shows the population size of six of the biggest cities in Europe in 1750. The two largest, London and Paris, had populations of 676,000 and 560,000 people, respectively (Chandler and Fox 1974). Virtually all of the inhabitants were concentrated in core city areas. Vienna, Rome, Madrid, and Berlin had populations of fewer than 200,000 people each. These are very small population sizes compared to the populations of these cities today. The United Nations Population Division estimates the 2003 population of the Paris agglomeration (region) to be 9.8 million and the population of the London agglomeration to be 7.6 million people (UN 2004).

Population growth and urbanization

The U.S. Census Bureau's world population clock, described in box 1.1, estimates the population of the earth to be over 6.3 billion people and growing very rapidly. Until recently, the population

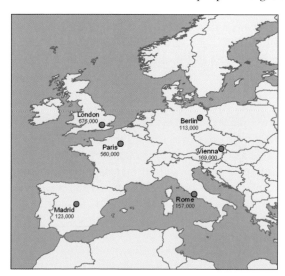

Map 1.4 Population size of selected European cities, 1750.

Source: Tertius Chandler and Gerald Fox, *3000 Years of Urban Growth*

Box 1.1   World population clock

The U.S. Census Bureau's world population clock on the World Wide Web at *www.census. gov/ipc/www/popclockworld.html* provides a continuously updated estimate of the world's population. As of 11:57 AM Eastern Standard Time on Saturday, November 30, 2004, the world population clock estimated the world's population to be 6,397,241,883 people. A minute later the estimate had risen to 6,397,242,017 people. Visit the population clock on the Web and you will see millions or tens of millions more people in the world depending on when you click on the site.

of the earth was much smaller and the rate of population growth also much less. What happened and why? What is happening now? Where might we be headed? Spatial analysis and data visualization about urbanization can help us answer these questions. Anyone doing such analyses needs to be careful because urban population data is not very reliable and different sources use different definitions.

Information on the current population of cities is abundant but conflicting and incomplete. A number of different government agencies estimate the current population of cities, countries, and the entire world. As mentioned, the U.S. Census Bureau's population clock provides a running estimate of the population of planet Earth. The UN estimates the population of over four hundred urban agglomerations with more than 750,000 people (UN 2004). The World Bank continuously updates estimates of countries' populations (World Bank 2004).

The U.S. Census has conducted a complete enumeration of the entire U.S. population every ten years since 1790 (U.S. Census 2002a). In the future, the U.S. Census will do annual studies of large samples of the U.S. population rather than a single decennial census (Peters and MacDonald 2004). The census provides demographic data grouped for the entire U.S., each state, every incorporated city (and other census designated places), and other census-defined areas such as consolidated metropolitan areas, Public Use Microdata Areas (PUMAs), census tracts, block groups, and blocks. State sources may provide up-to-date population estimates for counties and cities within the state.

Information on the population of cities in the past is contradictory and not very reliable. Only a few dedicated urban demographers have attempted to assemble historical city data. Kingsley Davis (1908–1996) carefully studied the size of European cities from the Middle Ages until the late twentieth century (Davis 1965). Davis concluded that the industrial revolution drove the rapid and massive urbanization of Europe. Beginning about 1750, advances in water- and then coal-powered machinery produced a revolutionary change in the way that material goods could be produced. Mechanization of agriculture meant that many fewer people were needed to produce enough food to sustain the rest of the population. More and more people left the land for cities and factory work.

Davis found that urbanization—the proportion of the population living in urban as opposed to nonurban areas—proceeded very slowly in England and other European countries until about 1750. When the industrial revolution occurred in England, urbanization increased rapidly, until England was predominantly urban, and then leveled off. Davis describes the pattern as an attenuated "S" curve beginning slowly, rising quickly as urbanization proceeded, and then diminishing as England became nearly fully urbanized. Shortly after England began to urbanize, Germany and other European countries followed the same trajectory: a process Davis describes as well represented by a family of "S" curves. The "S" curves that Davis discusses depict urbanization—the proportion of a society's population living in urban areas—not growth in the number or population

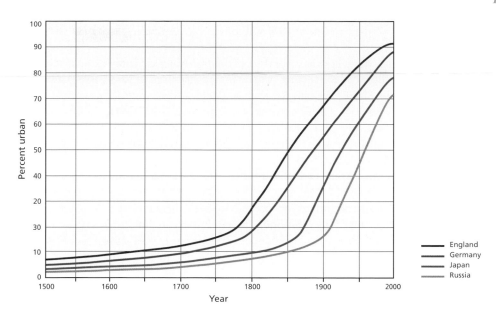

Figure 1.2 Kingsley Davis's family of "S" curves representing the urbanization of four countries over time.

Source: Based on Kingsley Davis, "The Urbanization of the Human Population," *Scientific American*

size of cities. Figure 1.2 illustrates Davis's notion of how a family of "S" curves describes the process of urbanization.

The most thorough studies of city population sizes at different times in history were compiled by Tertius Chandler and Gerald Fox (Chandler and Fox 1974) and in a second study by Tertius Chandler alone (Chandler 1987). These two remarkable books contain population estimates of world cities at different historical epochs with documentation of how the estimates were made.

Not everyone accepts Fox and Chandler's estimates of the populations of cities in the past, and more reliable estimates for some cities and some time periods are constantly being developed. But no one has attempted a comparable synthesis of population estimates for all cities through all of history. In exercises 1 and 5, you will work with Fox and Chandler's data to explore the population of world cities at different times. In exercise 1, you will also work with contemporary United Nations data on the population of urban agglomerations today and data on cities that scholars classify as global cities.

Immigration and the growth of cities

Cities' populations may grow as a result of combinations of different factors—including an increase in births over deaths, the blending together of formerly separate settlements to form a larger city, or from immigration from the same country or from foreign countries (Davis 1965).

In the United States, foreign immigration has been a driving force in urbanization since the first European colonists arrived in the early seventeenth century (Daniels 2002). The number of foreign immigrants and their countries of origin have changed over time. During the great Irish potato famine of 1848 a wave of Irish immigrants came to the United States (Golway 1997). Later in the nineteenth century, most immigrants to the United States came from southern and central Europe (Daniels 2002).

The 2000 U.S. Census found that 31.1 million people living in the United States in 2000 were foreign born (U.S. Census 2002b). A little over 40 percent of the foreign-born population were naturalized U.S. citizens in 2000. Between 1990 and 2000, the foreign-born population of the

United States increased by 57 percent from 19.8 million to 31.1 million people (U.S. Census 2002b).

Today, Hispanic immigrants from Mexico, South and Central America, and Asian immigrants from China and other Asian countries are fueling American urbanization. In 2000, over half of the foreign-born population in the United States—16 million people—were from South and Central America, Mexico, and the Caribbean. Thirty percent of the foreign population in 2000 was born in Mexico. Twenty-eight percent of the foreign-born were from Asia.

Map 1.5 is a thematic map showing the percent of the population in the San Francisco Bay Area who were born in foreign countries by census tract. In exercise 2, you will learn how to classify San Francisco Bay Area census tracts and create thematic maps with color ramps similar to map 1.5.

Immigrants and the descendents of immigrants contribute to the diversity of cities. In some San Francisco neighborhoods more than half the population in 2000 was foreign born. Maps 1.6a and 1.6b show the distribution of Asian/Pacific Islanders and Hispanic residents of San Francisco in 2000.

Specks in the wilderness

Just how dramatic world urbanization is can be well illustrated using an example from U.S. history. An examination of the size of cities in colonial America at the time of the American Revolution with comparably sized cities today illustrates just how tiny population sizes were a few centuries ago.

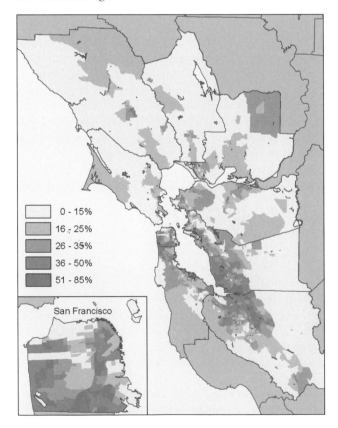

Map 1.5 Percent of the population foreign born, San Francisco Bay Area, 2000.

Source: 2000 U.S. Census of Population and Housing

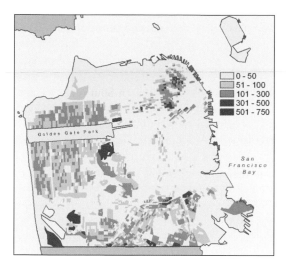

Map 1.6a Number of Asians/Pacific Islanders in San Francisco by census tract, 2000.

Source: 2000 U.S. Census of Population and Housing

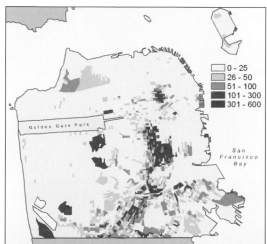

Map 1.6b Number of Hispanics in San Francisco by census tract, 2000.

Source: 2000 U.S. Census of Population and Housing

Immigrants add diversity and cultural richness to neighborhoods like San Francisco's Chinatown.

Source: Photodisc

For students of American colonial history, Philadelphia, New York, and Boston loom large. In the political and intellectual history of the United States they were indeed significant. But in population size and spatial extent, they were tiny. These and other colonial cities illustrated in map 1.7a were what urban historian Carl Bridenbaugh called "specks in the wilderness" (Bridenbaugh 1938). The largest cities in America at the time of the American Revolution—Philadelphia and New York—had only about 25,000 people each (Chudacoff and Smith 2005). Map 1.7b shows five U.S. cities with 2000 populations comparable to the five U.S. colonial cities with the largest populations at the time of the American Revolution. Never heard of North Attleborough Center, Valley Falls, or Hanahan? Well . . . that's the point.

The colonial cities were also small in physical extent. Because most residents had no other means of transportation than their feet, these walking cities could be traversed by foot in less than half an hour.

Map 1.7a   The five U.S. colonial cities with the largest populations in 1775.

Sources: Christopher Simeone, based on population estimates in Howard Chudacoff and Judith Smith, *The Evolution of American Urban Society 2nd ed.*

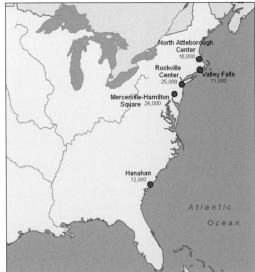

Map 1.7b   Five cities with populations in 2000 similar to the five largest U.S. colonial cities in 1775.

Source: 2000 U.S. Census of Population and Housing

Not only were the colonial cities of what was to become the United States small, the urban population of the colonial cities was also very small relative to the total population of the colonies. The first U.S. decennial census in 1790 found only one American in twenty living in cities—5 percent of the population (U.S. Census 2004).

Suburbanization and balkanization

The word suburb (from the Latin words "under" and "the city") was first applied to irregular settlements of merchants and traders outside the city walls of European cities. Since cities were often located on high ground for defensive reasons, these first suburbs were literally urban areas under (sub) the cities. These first suburbs grew up in the early Renaissance period beginning as early as the eleventh century. Later the word suburb came to refer to any human settlement on the fringe of existing cities.

Today most urban growth is occurring in suburbs on the urban fringe. Typically when enough population has grown up at a sufficient density, a suburban area is incorporated as a new legally incorporated city no longer governed by the county where the city is located and separate from other cities in the region.

Metropolitan regions of the United States are fragmented into many different government units—counties, cities, and special districts. Each city and county has its own separate government. Each regulates land use and makes decisions regarding the character of urbanization within its borders.

There are a large number of different local governments in most metropolitan areas. For example, metropolitan San Diego, California, has nineteen different local governments. As noted previously, the San Francisco Bay Area has 109. The Pittsburgh, Pennsylvania, metropolitan area has 418 different local governments (Orfield 2002).

A term commonly used to refer to this extreme fragmentation of authority is **balkanization**. The Balkan Peninsula—North of Greece and across the Adriatic Sea from Italy—has been characterized for most of the last two millennia by small nation states fighting with each other. Map 1.8 illustrates the balkanization of local government authority in the San Francisco Bay Area. It shows the nine Bay Area counties (light green) and 101 cities (orange with gray borders). Counties outside of the Bay Area are symbolized in gray.

There are only a few examples in North America of bold attempts to plan and govern regions in innovative new ways. In the Minneapolis–St. Paul, Minnesota, region, taxes are shared so that less affluent jurisdictions receive some additional money from wealthier jurisdictions (Miller 2002). In metropolitan Toronto, Canada, separate fringe jurisdictions have been fully consolidated into the city of Toronto itself. In the Portland, Oregon, region, Metro is a regional elected supergovernment that plans for the urban area of three counties and twenty-four cities and provides some services on a regional basis (Abbott 2001, Ozawa 2004). You will read more about the Portland area in chapter 12 and explore planning and policy issues in the Metro region in exercise 7.

Urban problems and opportunities

Urbanization can bring both problems and opportunities. Cities are incubators of technological change and culture. The growth of cities presents opportunities for economic development, modernization, and cultural advance. Urbanization can promote economic prosperity and higher standards of living, access to education and culture, and social mobility. But urbanization often also brings a host of problems including sprawl, congestion, and a loss of livability. Spatial analysis can show policy makers how to capitalize on opportunities that urbanization presents and how to cope with the problems it brings. This section describes some of the problems and opportunities

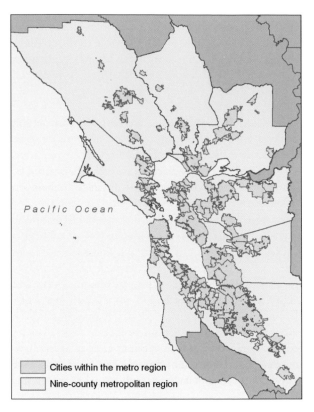

Map 1.8 Balkanization of San Francisco Bay Area local government.

Source: 2000 U.S. Census of Population and Housing

Legend:
- Cities within the metro region
- Nine-county metropolitan region

urbanization presents and how spatial analysis can help illuminate what they are and how to respond to them.

Urban areas growing too large, too fast

Concern with city size and growth rates focuses on three main issues: (a) the population size of some urban agglomerations is becoming unmanageably large, (b) the biggest cities in the world are becoming unmanageably spread out, and (c) growth rates in many urban areas are so fast that government cannot provide infrastructure fast enough to meet human needs.

Urbanists use different terminology to refer to large urban areas. Sometimes they use the word cities. As discussed earlier, the UN prefers the term urban agglomerations. A common term for the largest cities is megacities. The UN considers an urban agglomeration with more than ten million people a megacity. Many urbanists fear that the population of some cities is growing too large. The megacities of Tokyo, Mombai (Bombay), Delhi, Mexico City, and São Paolo, Brazil, already have populations exceeding twenty million (UN 2002). Urbanization at this scale strains the capacity of a region to provide resources to support the urban population.

Megacities may have dense cores, but most are surrounded by low-density development that covers large amounts of land. Huge, low-density development imposes long commutes. Traffic congestion and air pollution in most megacities are much worse than in even the largest cities in the developed world (Gilbert 1996, Lo and Yeung 1996, Rakodi 1997).

Some cities—regardless of their absolute size or how spread out they are—are growing too fast. Often their residents' need for urban services is outstripping the ability of government to provide services. Infrastructure is out of balance with development. In slum areas of cities in fast-growing developing countries, many residents have no indoor water, sewers, or electricity. In some booming U.S. suburbs, schools are on double session, wastewater goes untreated, and traffic congestion is a serious problem (Weitz 2000).

The growth of metropolitan fringe areas presents metropolitan regions with the opportunity to decentralize. Planned new communities can be built. Developers can build attractive, well-designed new developments that fit into the regional fabric. Moderate- and upper-income families may be able to buy single-family homes with yards. Modern office space can usually be built at lower costs than in central cities. There is a large literature on how to develop regions (Duany and Plater-Zyberk 2001, Calthorpe and Fulton 2001). But too often fringe development proceeds piecemeal—poorly planned and uncoordinated among jurisdictions.

Urbanization in metropolitan regions can take many different forms. Population may be concentrated in one or a few areas with most of the remaining area empty farmland and open space. Alternatively, uniform low-density development may cover large areas of a region.

Sprawl and density

In urban areas, density is measured by the number of people per unit of area. For example, if there are five houses on one acre of land, with three people living in each house, the density would be 15 people to the acre (5 houses x 3 people each = 15/1 acre): a moderate residential density. If there were four 20-story apartment buildings on an acre, each with 100 residents, the density would be 400 people per acre: a very high residential density.

From a planning perspective density is a two-edged sword. Development at very low densities consumes land and creates sprawl. Low-density development makes it economically impossible to support public transit systems and perpetuates auto dependency. On the other hand, many people don't like density. They would prefer to live in a low-density area—a suburb of single-family homes on individual lots.

The U.S. Census Bureau each year estimates both the population and the amount of urbanized land in the United States. The census estimates show that the average density of urban areas in the United States is decreasing. In the twenty-five largest metropolitan areas the population grew by 20 percent between 1970 and 1990, but the urbanized land area grew by 46 percent (Orfield 2002). Development at very low densities tends to snake out along transportation corridors and leapfrog some distance from the urban fringe. This creates patchy, low-density sprawl. Sprawl often uses up farmland and open space, increases infrastructure costs, requires more driving (with attendant air pollution), and may increase economic and racial segregation. Sprawling development may affect the fiscal structure of a metropolis. If new office development occurs in affluent edge cities, central cities and older suburbs will not get the property tax revenue the new development would generate if it occurred within their borders.

Most citizens and most policy makers believe that sprawl is bad (Weitz 2000). Sprawl development is arguably less efficient than compact, city-centered growth. New urbanist contrarians Peter Gordon and Harry Richardson at the University of Southern California dispute these common assumptions (Gordon and Richardson 2000). They argue that sprawl is a rational private market response that distributes population efficiently.

Statistics on sprawl are not nearly as effective as maps that visually show the extent and nature of sprawl. For example, map 1.9 depicts eastern Contra Costa County. It shows the area that was urban in 1984 in gray and the additional area that became urban between 1984 and 2000 in orange cross-hatching. Prime farmland as it existed in 1984 is in dark green. The cities of Brentwood, Oakley, and Antioch are indicated. Both land within incorporated cities and unincorporated county land at the urban fringe became urban during this sixteen-year period. The amount of prime farmland—a source of the best Bay Area corn, peaches, and other produce—has shrunk, particularly in and around the city of Brentwood.

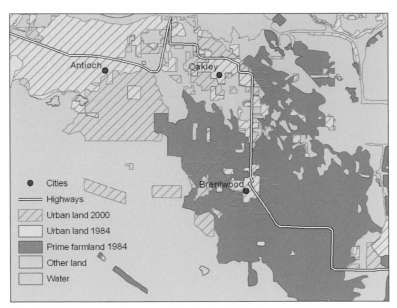

Map 1.9 Urban sprawl in eastern Contra Costa County.
Source: 2000 U.S. Census of Population and Housing

   Map 1.9 could show urban planners how much sprawl has occurred in eastern Contra Costa County and where. It could provide guidance to city and regional planners as to how to achieve more compact, efficient growth patterns that provide housing and also preserve prime farmland.

Mobility problems

Mobility in cities is a worldwide problem. It is often time-consuming and unpleasant to get from one place to another within cities—particularly by car. Traffic congestion is a major negative side effect of urbanization virtually everywhere in the world. It has many causes: population growth, increased per capita auto ownership, more miles driven on average by each driver, and individual desires to drive alone rather than carpool (Downs 1992). The near impossibility (physical and financial) of most governments everywhere in the world to build enough new roads to meet expanding need further compounds the problem.

   Maps 1.10a and 1.10b show geographical units called **census tracts** in the southern part of Santa Clara County—the most southerly of the San Francisco Bay Area counties. Census tracts are one of the most important and most widely used of all the geographic units for which the U.S. Census reports information. Each census tract contains about four thousand people—a large enough number of people that the Census is confident that releasing detailed information on attributes of the census tract will not compromise the privacy of any individual. Census tracts with more than one thousand people age 16 or older who reported in the 2000 Census that they drive to work alone are outlined with dark black borders. In map 1.10a the key census tracts outlined in black are labeled with the number of people who drive to work alone. In map 1.10b the key census tracts are labeled with the number of people who carpool to work. For visual clarity the other, less problematic, census tracts are not labeled.

   Maps 1.10a and 1.10b could suggest to transportation planners and local officials where it might make sense to organize carpools. Census tracts where there are a large number of people who drive to work alone are good candidates for programs to encourage carpooling. Further spatial and statistical analysis of the demographics and driving behavior of workers in these

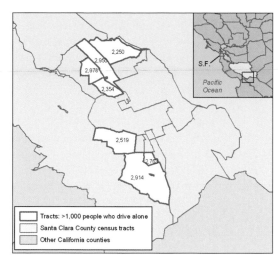

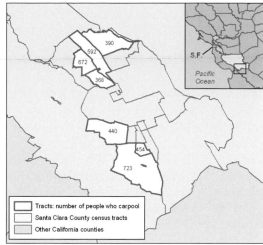

Map 1.10a Number of people age 16 and older who drive to work alone, selected Santa Clara County census tracts, 2000.

Source: 2000 U.S. Census of Population and Housing

Map 1.10b Number of people age 16 and older who carpool to work, selected Santa Clara County census tracts, 2000.

Source: 2000 U.S. Census of Population and Housing

Traffic congestion is a major negative product of urbanization.

Source: Photodisc

areas could help congestion management programs. In exercise 2, you will analyze carpooling in southern Santa Clara County. Chapter 8 includes a multicolumn chart showing data on driving behavior in these census tracts and a discussion of how data graphics can help policy makers see policy problems and opportunities.

The separation of jobs and housing

Jobs are essential for individuals to earn a living and for municipalities to generate revenue to pay for public services and to minimize welfare costs. But jobs are not evenly distributed in metropolitan areas. In most regions, jobs and job growth cluster in some areas and are sparse or almost entirely absent from others. Where the jobs are is often not where the people who want to fill the jobs arc. There is what economist John Kain calls a spatial mismatch between jobs and housing (Kain 1968). Jobs and housing are not in balance (Cervero 1991 and 1996).

Spatial mismatch between jobs and the workforce creates problems. Some middle- and upper-income homeowners now live in California's Central Valley where housing costs are comparatively low, and they commute two or more hours to work in high-tech Silicon Valley jobs where wages are comparatively high. According to the Job-Center Housing Coalition—a Northern California organization that advocates increased jobs-housing balance—in 2004 a registered nurse in San Jose earning $56,650 a year needed to make an additional $81,683 per year to afford the median-priced home in the Silicon Valley region (Job-Center Housing Coalition 2004).

People with low incomes and people without cars are particularly hurt by spatial mismatches between housing and jobs. Some low-income domestics and fast food restaurant workers reverse commute from inner city neighborhoods to work in the suburbs. In addition to imposing hardship on the workers involved, this kind of spatial mismatch adds to transportation congestion and air pollution from automobile emissions. GIS allows regional planners to see where spatial mismatches exist and help them develop strategies to improve the jobs-housing balance, a topic discussed in greater detail later in this chapter.

Livability

Urbanization creates problems of **livability**. Crowding, noise, long commutes, and poorly functioning public services make many large cities and rapidly urbanizing places much less livable than smaller, more stable communities. People living in these large cities and fast-growing places may have greater opportunities than people living in small towns and rural areas, and in some respects their quality of life is better. They may make more money than their rural counterparts and have access to educational, cultural, and other resources that big cities afford. But their day-to-day life is often less pleasant and sometimes more dangerous and less healthy than in rural areas and small towns.

Urban solutions

Solving urban problems is often difficult. Urban planning often takes place "in the face of conflict" (Forester 1987). There is rarely enough money to do things as well or as quickly as activists would like. But imaginative theory and solid examples of successful solutions abound (Downs 1994). Following is a discussion of how theorists propose to capitalize on opportunities urbanization creates and address issues of city population size, rapid growth rates, sprawl, traffic congestion, and livability. In addition to discussing theory, the following section provides examples of successful programs.

Urban growth management

Many cities have adopted **urban growth management** plans (Porter et al. 1996). These plans usually look far into the future—often to build out—and envision what should be built where. In fast-growing residential communities, comprehensive growth management ordinances usually have tempo control provisions that regulate the timing of when housing can be built. Many growth management plans require concurrency between population growth and infrastructure. Without concurrency, public infrastructure such as water and sewer services, schools, and firehouses may lag behind new housing units and new residents. As a result, there may be water shortages and sewage treatment problems, schools may be overcrowded, and response times for firefighters to get to fires may be unacceptably high. Tempo controls are one way to achieve concurrency. Careful capital budgeting with a capital improvement plan that matches infrastructure to growth is another way to achieve concurrency.

Petaluma, California, is an attractive small city north of San Francisco that has taken growth management seriously. The 1979 "Petaluma Plan" pioneered growth management. Once the white leghorn chicken capital of the world (according to Petaluma) and the seat of an annual arm-wrestling championship today, Petaluma retains small-town charm in an expanding metropolis. The best-known feature of the Petaluma Plan was a limit of five hundred on the number of residential building permits that would be granted each year. Petaluma used a point system whereby a committee ranked proposed residential development and assigned points for features of the development the city valued. The projects with the highest number of points were awarded building permits.

Economics 101 suggests that limiting housing supply in the face of high housing demand will increase housing prices. Strict growth management may cause development to spill over into other nearby communities. Some communities have deliberately or inadvertently created growth management systems that have greatly limited the supply of housing and deserve to be criticized for their exclusionary land-use practices (Downs 2004). Petaluma is often criticized for being exclusionary. In fact, Petaluma's growth management system was not nearly as restrictive as plans in many other cities (LeGates 1989). Petaluma zoned a larger amount of land for residential development than most Bay Area cities. Petaluma's 500 units per year limit on residential building permits did prevent some housing construction in boom times, but in the long term Petaluma permitted more residential building than comparable Bay Area cities. Petaluma provided some incentives for affordable housing. Today Petaluma is an attractive community with a compact form, a greenbelt surrounding most of the city, infill development on empty lots in the middle of the city, and balanced development in different parts of town. The 2000 U.S. Census reported 8,458 Latinos, 2,170 Asians, 606 African-Americans, and 2,085 other minorities among Petaluma's 60,000 residents (U.S. Census 2000a).

Distributing density

Most urban planners recognize that density is unpopular and sometimes problematic. But planners also know that higher densities are necessary to reduce sprawl and provide for efficient public services. The only way out of this dilemma is to increase average densities for a region but distribute the density in a sensible way. Quite high-density development is appropriate in some parts of a region, such as downtown central business districts. Low to moderate density may be appropriate in residential areas. Very low density is appropriate in agricultural areas.

Urban planners have identified ways to increase average density in regions and at the same time not overwhelm areas or alienate citizens. Quite high density is appropriate around light-rail stations and other major transit nodes. Residential density can be increased in cities by building more units on infill sites and by creative design such as building housing units in air rights over retail space. Relatively high-density commercial and office space is appropriate along main streets and transit corridors. Well-designed neighborhoods can be attractive despite relatively high densities. The same Americans who protest increased density in their own cities love the character of neighborhoods in Paris with four- and five-story attached apartment buildings.

Sensitive distribution of density requires careful analysis, collaborative planning to assure the support of neighbors, and good design. Done well, it can produce compact, efficient development that people like.

Garden cities, greenbelts, and urban limit lines

At the turn of the twentieth century, British social visionary Ebenezer Howard proposed **garden cities** of about 32,000 people, each surrounded by a permanent five-thousand-acre **greenbelt** devoted to agricultural and recreational use (Howard 1898). What is remarkable about Howard's vision is that people acted on it. Over a hundred years ago, an organization named the Garden City Association purchased land about fifty miles from London and built Letchworth as a garden city following Howard's principles (Hall 2002). Soon afterward, the Garden City Association began work on a second garden city named Welwyn. Both Letchworth and Welwyn are attractive, functional cities today that still serve as models of good urban planning.

Sprawl can be managed and sometimes eliminated altogether by drawing **urban limit lines** around cities and requiring all growth to take place within the limits. Many European cities have clear urban limit lines. In these cities lively, dense urban areas stop abruptly and fields begin rather than sprawling out through low-density tract homes and tacky fast food outlets.

Urban limit lines raise fundamental issues about the relationship between government and private property and fairness to property owners whose ability to use their land as they choose is limited. Proscribing what can be built where and when creates winners and losers among property owners. It may be good public policy to limit new development outside an urban limit line for as long as twenty years. But the owner of land just outside the urban limit line may see a huge drop in the value of the land. Many property owners who have been affected in this way, or fear that they will be, are involved in a powerful national property rights movement. Conversely, it may also be good public policy to rezone land near a light-rail stop to permit much higher density residential development than elsewhere in a neighborhood, but that regulatory decision will almost certainly greatly increase the value of the land and provide a windfall for the property owner. Defining all of the gains and losses and attempting to compensate landowners for all value lost as a result of regulation or capturing the unearned increment in land value that occurs as a result of regulation is virtually impossible. Defining when a regulation is so severe as to constitute a "taking" of land requiring government to pay just compensation to the owner has been the subject hundreds of lawsuits and a great many learned legal opinions. While this is not the appropriate place to review the takings issue and the property rights movement, it is important always to think of all of the parties affected by land-use regulation and work for the fairest possible regulations.

Infill development

A different approach to providing affordable housing involves infill housing on underutilized land in older neighborhoods. **Infill development** is often undertaken by community-based housing development corporations (HDCs) or community development corporations (CDCs). In addition to providing shelter, HDCs and CDCs can build human capital by involving residents themselves in planning and carrying out affordable housing projects. *Streets of Hope* (Medoff and Sklar 1994) is an excellent account of how Boston's Dudley Street Triangle neighborhood revitalized their own local area and got affordable infill housing built.

In Oakland, California—a city of 380,000 people across San Francisco Bay from San Francisco —Jerry Brown ran for mayor successfully in 1999 with a pledge to get enough housing units built in the down-at-the-heels center of Oakland to house ten thousand new residents: Brown's so-called 10K Downtown Housing Initiative (Oakland CEDA 2004). Brown reasoned that relatively high-density condo, apartment, and loft development would bring in enough new residents to pump up local businesses, create more cultural activity, and revitalize Oakland. In addition to streamlining building permits and providing economic incentives, members of Brown's adminis-tration used GIS to help fulfill this campaign pledge. Cities have records of landownership almost always accompanied by cadastral maps—maps showing the location and ownership of land par-cels. Planners in the Brown administration mapped vacant parcels in Oakland and made this information available to developers. Map 1.11 shows vacant parcels in downtown Oakland that were zoned for two to four residential units as of 2004.

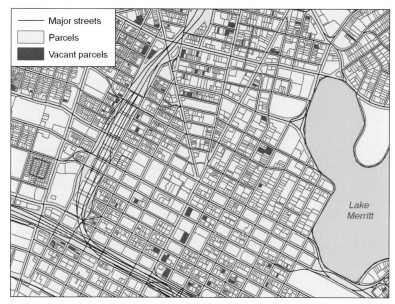

Map 1.11   Vacant lots in downtown Oakland, 2004.
Source: Oakland Office of Information Technology

The Brown administration succeeded in increasing housing construction in downtown Oakland, and GIS contributed to the program's success. According to the Oakland Community Economic Development Administration, as of July 2004, the 10K Downtown Housing Initiative had resulted in thirty-five residential projects with 4,969 housing units (Oakland CEDA 2004). Because hous-ing units house more than one person per unit on average, Oakland had nearly accomplished Brown's goal of providing housing for ten thousand new residents by 2004.

Unlocking gridlock

Oxford University geographer Colin Clark has termed transportation "the maker and breaker of cities" (Clark 1957). Increasingly, urban planners see good transportation planning linked to development as critical to successful cities. Most urban planners feel transportation options today are unbalanced—that people are forced to use automobiles because cities do not offer them enough options to walk, ride bicycles, or use light rail, buses, or other public transportation.

Increasing transportation choice is critical in unlocking gridlock. It is also an important key to creating more efficient and more livable communities.

Multimodal transportation

Overwhelmingly, the main mode of transportation in the United States today is the private automobile. If fewer people used automobiles or used them less frequently and for fewer miles, highways and streets would be less congested. In order to get people to switch from automobiles to other forms of transportation, there must be transportation options that people consider as good or better for some of their transportation needs.

Public transit systems include railroads, subways, and other forms of mass transit, buses, and light-rail systems. Mass-transit systems are very expensive. Railroads as a transit alternative pose financial and technological challenges. Bus systems in many American cities are poorly funded, unreliable, and unattractive. Often buses have become transportation of last resort, avoided by people with the money to afford other options. While reinvigorating and extending any of these transit options may be possible in a given situation, other modes of transportation appear to offer particular advantages.

Light-rail systems are less expensive to build and operate than mass-transit systems. Except in the very densest cities where very high-volume ridership can support the enormous cost, light-rail systems are a more realistic option for relatively high-volume public transit than subways and mass transit.

Bicycling and walking are much more widely used transportation options in Europe and other parts of the world (Beatley 2000). Efforts to increase bicycle use and promote pedestrian activity are important ways to increase mobility. The exercise they provide contributes to health.

Transit-oriented development

Land-use planning and transportation planning in the San Francisco Bay Area and elsewhere have often proceeded without any coordination at all. Zoning laws may limit the density of residential development in an area where a transit system is being built so that too few people live in the area to make the transit system financially feasible. In other areas, zoning may permit more development than the area's transportation system can handle.

There has been a movement among urban planners in the last ten years to better link transportation with housing and other development. **Transit-oriented development (TOD)** plans call for much greater residential densities around transit nodes such as light-rail stops (Bernick and Cervero 1997, Ditmar and Ohland 2003). Spatial analysis of transportation systems and land-use densities is very useful in transit-oriented development planning.

Balancing jobs and housing

One way to address the problem of spatial mismatch between areas where people live and where jobs are located involves improving **jobs-housing balance**. Urban planner Robert Cervero pioneered systematic analysis of the balance between jobs and housing (Cervero 1991 and 1996). Given the complexity of living and working patterns and the number of households with two or more wage earners, achieving a perfect balance between housing units and the workforce that lives in a single city is unrealistic. However, analyzing the nature and extent of imbalance and encouraging regional collaboration to achieve better balance can shorten commute times, relieve traffic congestion, and reduce air pollution.

California funds a number of interregional partnerships (IRPs) to encourage regions to plan together. The IRPs include cities and counties that do not ordinarily consider themselves part of the same region. Often members of an IRP have not collaborated in the past. Sometimes they have actively competed with each other. Working together as an IRP, these jurisdictions are encouraged to jointly develop strategies to increase jobs-housing balance in the extended region. The purpose of interregional partnership analyses is to promote development of new housing near jobs and new employment centers near housing. For example, an interregional partnership (IRP) has been created between some counties in the San Francisco Bay Area and adjacent counties to the east that are not part of the Bay Area. This IRP has used GIS to analyze jobs-housing balance in the extended region.

Similar projects in the San Diego and Santa Barbara regions are also using GIS to create interregional plans to achieve better jobs-housing balance. The partnerships identify, map, and analyze sites suitable for large new housing construction projects. They look for locations where jobs are plentiful and housing scarce. They conduct spatial analyses using GIS for areas covering more than one traditional region as defined by COG boundaries. Interregional partnerships do similar GIS analysis of sites suitable for new commercial and industrial development in areas that have few jobs, more affordable housing, and higher housing vacancy rates.

Making infrastructure work

Infrastructure—particularly transportation infrastructure—shapes urban development. Examples from two widely different locations—the city of Curitiba, Brazil, and the state of Maryland—show how infrastructure planning can shape growth.

Curitiba, in southern Brazil, has a population of more than 1.6 million people. Curitiba is remarkable for having made visionary decisions about its future urban form and developing appropriate infrastructure to govern its long-range growth (Rabinovitch 1996). Planners in Curitiba decided that as the city grew it would be essential to move very large numbers of people efficiently and economically to and from the city center. They decided that a high-volume bus system would be appropriate given Curitiba's financial resources, rather than a more expensive subway system. Accordingly, Curitiba laid out large radial streets served by very frequent, high-capacity buses specially built for the city by Volvo. The buses are designed to permit dozens of people to board and de-board at once. Curitiba is a much more functional and attractive city than many other cities of comparable size and resources.

Among U.S. states, Maryland has been a leader in concentrating infrastructure to promote compact, city-centered development (Porter, Dunphy, and Salvesen 2002). In the late 1990s and early twenty-first century, Maryland channeled all state infrastructure funding to areas where planners felt urban growth should occur—so-called "smart growth" areas—including existing municipalities, land inside the beltway between Baltimore and Washington, D.C., and fast-growing areas near existing developed municipalities. Many communities today have been inspired by Maryland's example and are pursuing smart growth strategies (Porter, Dunphy, and Salvesen 2002).

Despite many urban problems, there is reason to be optimistic about urban futures. We know a lot about problems of sprawl, traffic congestion, and spatial mismatch between jobs and housing. Theorists have developed ideas about how to tackle these problems and there are hundreds of excellent, successful examples of theory translated into practice making urban areas more efficient, less congested, and more livable.

One of the most promising new tools to help us diagnose problems and find opportunities to make urban areas better is GIS software. Chapter 2 introduces GIS.

Terms

agglomeration. A large urbanized area, including one or more cities, and the urbanized area around the city or cities. In some cases, an agglomeration may include urbanized land between two or more cities. The United Nations uses agglomerations as its unit of analysis to report on the population of large urban areas.

balkanization. Fragmentation of local government authority. Most metropolitan areas of the United States are governed by dozens or hundreds of separate county and city governments. These governments often plan and regulate development independently of or in competition with their neighbors. Like the little countries of the Balkan Peninsula, local governments tend to look out for their own self-interest rather than the common regional good.

census tract. An area defined by the U.S. Census Bureau within which demographic and other information collected by the census is reported. Census tracts usually contain about four thousand people. They vary in geographical extent. A great deal of urban spatial analysis uses census tracts as the unit of analysis.

council of governments (COG). A voluntary organization of the cities and counties in a metropolitan region. Member governments share the costs of the COG and in turn the COG provides data, helps coordinate development on a regional basis, and conducts region-wide projects. COGs don't have the power to impose their plans on member governments, but facilitate regional decision making.

garden city. An alternative to the large, sprawling cities and conurbations of nineteenth century England. Ebenezer Howard (1850–1928) proposed social cities of about thirty-two thousand people surrounded by greenbelts. The municipal corporation would own the land in a garden city and the increment in land value as land increased in value would be held in public trust for the citizens. Garden cities inspired by Howard were built in England and other countries and remain a powerful alternative to unplanned sprawl.

greenbelt. Ebenezer Howard proposed five-thousand-acre greenbelts of undeveloped land around garden cities devoted to agricultural and recreational use. Howard felt a greenbelt should serve as a natural boundary to keep the city a manageable size and create separation from other social cities. Howard also envisaged greenbelts as sources of homegrown produce and recreational opportunities. Many cities today have what they call greenbelts—undeveloped land at their fringe—though few are the size or perform all the functions that Howard envisioned.

infill development. A development on vacant or underused property in an already developed area. Many cities encourage infill development with modern land uses at appropriate densities. Infill development of affordable housing can promote equity.

jobs-housing balance. When there are enough housing units for the workforce in an area, the area has achieved jobs-housing balance. Often jobs and housing are out of balance. Jobs are located in some areas; housing in other areas. Some metropolitan areas are pursuing policies to balance jobs and housing. If jobs and housing are in better balance, people will have shorter commutes, and the metropolitan area will work more efficiently.

livability. The quality of being an attractive, pleasant place to live. Many urban areas concentrate on economic goals at the expense of livability. Today progressive cities are consciously pursuing policies that will make them more livable.

transit-oriented development (TOD). A type of development at relatively high density around a transit node such as a light-rail stop.

urban growth management. The idea of regulating the development of a community by specifying the timing and character of its development community-wide over a long period of time. Comprehensive growth management is different from permitting growth to proceed governed only by land-use regulations such as zoning, subdivision controls, and building codes.

urbanization. The process by which an area becomes urban. As a society urbanizes, a larger proportion of the total population lives in cities and a smaller proportion lives in rural areas and small towns. Very rural societies like Mali have not urbanized much; very urban societies like Denmark are nearly completely urbanized.

urban limit line. An urban limit line (sometime called an urban growth boundary) distinguishes land intended for development in the near future from land that will not be developed until some time in the future. Some cities establish urban limit lines in order to promote more compact growth and reduce sprawl.

Questions for further study

1. Historical urban demographer Kingsley Davis says that it is theoretically possible for the population of cities to grow as the country where the cities are located becomes less urban. Using Davis's definition of urbanization, explain this apparent paradox.

2. Usually, as the population of a region grows, the percentage of the region's population that is urban grows, the number of cities grows, the area of the cities grows, and the population of the largest city in the region grows. But these relationships are not necessarily true. Geographic barriers to expansion, war, technology, changing economies, and many other factors can affect population growth or decline, urbanization, city population size, and city size. For example, a depressed Welsh coal-mining town with little demand for coal, surrounded on all sides by other incorporated towns, in a prosperous region of Wales where high-tech businesses are booming in other nearby cities is likely to experience population decline and no change in the size of the city's land area at the same time that the region in which the city is located is urbanizing. Describe situations in which you believe it is likely that

   a. the population of a region is increasing, but the percentage of the population that is urban is decreasing;
   b. the population of a region is decreasing, but the percentage of the population that is urban is increasing;
   c. the population of a city is increasing, but the area of the city remains the same;
   d. the area of a city is increasing, but the population is decreasing.

3. Based on your own visit to the U.S. Census population clock at *www.census.gov/ipc/www/popclockworld.html*, what is the population of the earth now? How much has it changed since 11:57 AM Eastern Standard Time on Saturday, November 30, 2004, when the population estimate recorded on the clock was 6,397,241,883 people?

4. Identify a town near you with a population of about twenty-five thousand people. This was the size of the largest city in North America at the time of the American Revolution. How big is this city compared to the place where you live? The capital of your state?

5. How many different units of local government (cities and counties) are there in the metropolitan area you are most familiar with? Does it make sense to have this many different units of local government? How would you use maps and spatial analysis to identify areas where local governments need to work together on regional solutions in the region where you live?

Annotated bibliography

The classic definition of urbanization and description of how urbanization occurred in European history is Kingsley Davis's "The Urbanization of the Human Population," *Scientific American* (Davis 1965).

Tertius Chandler collected population figures on city population size at different times in human history in *Four Thousand Years of Urban Growth* (Chandler 1987) and, together with Gerald Fox, in *3000 Years of Urban Growth* (Chandler and Fox 1974).

The United Nations Population Division estimates the past, present, and projected future size of more than 400 urban agglomerations (United Nations 2004).

Anthony Downs's prolific writings on urban problems include *Stuck in Traffic* (Downs 1992), a readable account of traffic congestion. Downs has written widely on urban problems related to housing, race, and metropolitan development. Downs's essay titled "The Need for a New Vision of Metropolitan America," originally published for Salomon Brothers in 1989 and reprinted in Richard LeGates and Frederic Stout, *The City Reader,* third edition (LeGates and Stout 2003) is an excellent overview of metropolitan problems and prospects.

Peter Calthorpe, an architect and planner based in Berkeley, California, describes a new urbanist vision for the future in *The Next American Metropolis* (Calthorpe 1993). Calthorpe and California planner and journalist William Fulton apply new urbanist thinking to regional issues in *The Regional City* (Calthorpe and Fulton 2001).

Peter Medoff and Holly Sklar's *Streets of Hope* (Medoff and Sklar 1994) is a fascinating and inspirational account of how one lower-income Boston neighborhood took control of its own destiny and developed and successfully carried out a plan to redevelop the area.

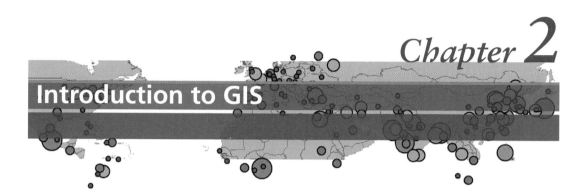

Chapter 2

Introduction to GIS

"*If we ask ourselves what is this wisdom which experience forces upon us, the answer must be that we discover the world is not constituted as we had supposed it to be. It is not that we learn more about its physical elements, or its geography, or the variety of its inhabitants . . . [it] has little to do with information about the names, the locations, and the sequence of facts; it is the acquiring of a different sense of life, a different kind of intuition about the nature of things.*"

Walter Lippmann (1929)

Introduction

Sometimes the problems confronting an urban region appear overwhelming and the opportunities to make positive change too complex to understand. Urban issues are complicated and regions face many choices. Analyzing information to solve urban problems and capitalize on opportunities is a fascinating enterprise. It is particularly exciting today as the digital revolution provides new tools to manage and understand information. Among the most powerful new technologies for understanding urban issues is geographic information systems (GIS) software. This chapter introduces GIS and shows how GIS can help explain urban phenomena and solve urban problems. Exercises at the end of the book will teach you to do GIS operations discussed in this chapter.

Digital thinking for interdisciplinary urban analysis

This book advocates thinking about urban issues in a new way, combining digital and interdisciplinary thinking. **Academic disciplines** concerned with cities provide a well-established body of theory and empirical information about cities. An academic discipline draws on a systematic body of knowledge and methods adopted by academics who define themselves as being members of an identifiable academic specialty such as geography, sociology, political science, economics, or history. There is a great deal of applied urban public policy research and writing about how to solve urban problems. Much of the best writing about cities is interdisciplinary—drawing on methods and substantive knowledge that cross academic disciplinary boundaries. This book encourages interdisciplinary applied thinking. It also encourages students to think digitally—to see the connection between urban phenomena and digital ways of representing and analyzing space.

Thinking digitally

Thinking digitally means being aware of the way in which computers represent reality. It requires an understanding of the limitations as well as the strengths of computer analysis. Because computer technology is advancing so fast and its power to extend understanding is so great, students must learn to think digitally to survive. But there is a danger in taking this approach too far. Social science analysis should remain an issue-driven enterprise that computerized tools can assist, rather than the other way around. Computer tools should not drive research questions.

Academic disciplines and interdisciplinary analysis

Beginning in the middle of the nineteenth century, social science disciplines began to partition human knowledge: sociologists staked out issues involving human society as their turf, political scientists issues of governance, and historians the past. In this rush to compartmentalize human knowledge, geographers claimed space—the location of physical, social, and cultural features—as their particular areas of expertise.

This artificial division of knowledge has had many benefits. Specialized social science disciplines developed rigorous theory and sophisticated methods to help analyze social phenomena. Both social science theory and social science methods are much more advanced today than they were a century and a half ago, before the rise and compartmentalization of social science disciplines. Economists have developed micro- and macroeconomic theory and rigorous quantitative methods for understanding the economic behavior of individuals and firms. Historians have developed methods for doing archival research quite different from the quantitative methods economists use. Each social science discipline has much to contribute to the understanding of urban and regional issues.

But compartmentalization of social science knowledge has also worked substantial mischief. Too often the peculiar way of dividing social science knowledge that has evolved at the beginning of the twenty-first century produces disciplinary determinism and blind spots in the way in which scholars see the world. Economists studying a topic tend to see economic factors as most important; sociologists feel sociological factors are paramount. But social and public policy issues great and small have multiple dimensions. The causes of urban sprawl are not just political, or economic, or social. Homelessness has historical, economic, social, spatial, and political dimensions.

Nowhere have disciplinary boundaries worked greater mischief or created bigger blind spots than with respect to spatial matters. By ceding the rigorous study of space to geographers and limiting themselves to aspatial analysis, social scientists from disciplines other than geography often leave the critical dimension of space out of their analyses.

The specialized knowledge that geographers have developed is fundamental to doing good spatial analysis. Spatial is special. The clearest example of this is with respect to the way in which the space of the earth (an oblate spheroid) is physically represented on two-dimensional maps. Over the centuries, geographers have developed sophisticated theory about geographic coordinate systems and map projections that few members of other social sciences understand. **Map projections** depict all or part of the earth's spherical three-dimensional structure on a flat two-dimensional map. Do-it-yourself pseudo-cartographers unfamiliar with map projections can easily create cartographic blunders that a trained geographer would not make (Monmonier 1996). Pushing buttons in a GIS makes it possible to make colossal blunders in the blink of an eye. This book introduces enough specialized geographical information to help beginning social science students do things right, understand their limits, and call for help when they confront conceptual or technical problems beyond their capacity.

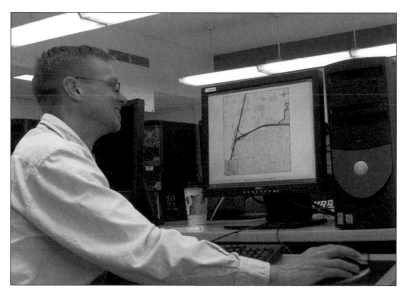

GIS software is now available for use on desktop computers.
Source: Elmer Tosta

Using vision to think

Urban planners, architects, and other professionals concerned with urban planning need to be visionary. Urban planners often engage in collaborative planning with all the stakeholders in a proposed plan. Architects and the public may jointly brainstorm about proposed buildings using design charettes. British visionary Thomas Moore (1478–1535) imagined an ideal society he called Utopia (Moore 1516), and the name has been applied to imagine ideal places ever since.

Many people scoff at utopian ideas for cities. Stuck in gritty reality with lots of urban problems and little money, they argue that visioning is a waste of time. In some cases, and for some kinds of visioning, they are right. Creating fanciful utopian plans that will never happen does not accomplish much. Historically, however, the best urban planning has been driven by visions of alternative futures that did not exist at the time and that many people thought folly. University of California, Berkeley, city and regional planning professor Jack Kent, who taught a generation of urban planning students beginning in 1949, was fond of telling his students good urban planning should be visionary—even utopian (Kent 1964). A huge marble temple on the Acropolis? We can't afford it, some Athenians told Pericles in the fifth century BCE. A canal running hundreds of miles from the Great Lakes to New York City? Impossible, said critics of New York Governor DeWitt Clinton's plans for the Erie Canal. Smokeless garden cities surrounded by greenbelts in early twentieth century England? Economic nonsense, said hardheaded businessmen of Ebenezer Howard's garden city vision. New affordable housing in the garbage-strewn vacant lots of the Dudley Street Triangle area in Boston's Roxbury neighborhood? Planned by untrained neighborhood residents themselves? Give me a break, said Bostonians in the late 1980s. But the Parthenon remains a wonder of the world, and the Erie Canal cemented New York's role as a world city. Ebenezer Howard spent his last days living in a garden city—surrounded by a greenbelt and built on his principles—north of London. And owners of affordable housing in the Dudley Street Triangle—a neighborhood where homes were planned by the residents themselves—are grateful that local residents answered the call of utopian visionaries.

The conventional wisdom is that visual images should be used to convey the results of thinking. The idea is to complete research first—then create good visual images as an artistic embellishment to make a good presentation. Communicating research findings is vital, and good data graphics, maps, line drawings, photographs, and other visual images often convey information more effectively than written or spoken words, numbers, and tables. But French semiologist Jacques Bertin argued that visualization in social research should do much more than effectively summarize the results of completed research (Bertin 1967). Bertin proposed turning the conventional view of how to use visual images in social research on its head. Bertin advocated "using vision to think." He believed that visual images should help researchers crystallize understanding as research proceeds. Bertin argued that research should be an iterative, exploratory process.

Princeton political science professor John Tukey elaborated an approach to social science research he called exploratory data analysis that used data visualization in the same way (Tukey 1977). Tukey encouraged his students to create visual representations of what they were finding as they explored data. Great explorers of the past—Magellan, Columbus, Lewis and Clark—approached the discovery of new territory with a plan for where they were going but changed direction and adapted their expeditions of discovery based on what they found as they proceeded on their journeys. Tukey infused this same spirit into social science and public policy research. Today information visualization is well advanced in some natural science applications—particularly medical imaging—but remains a neglected niche specialty in social science research methods. Too few social scientists heed Bertin and Tukey or use GIS maps and data graphics as tools to understand data as they conduct research.

Modeling the real world

The real world is complicated—sometimes overwhelming. To understand it and act effectively we need to break things down and simplify them. Models of reality are simplifications that help us see through the details to underlying aspects of reality that are important to us. By creating and manipulating models, we can understand reality better.

A physical analogy may help. A planner interested in sustainable urban development may be concerned about the long-term viability of the Yalu River in China. For millennia the Yalu River has provided water for farmers and served as a source of navigation for trade. Today, as parts of the river are dammed, dredged, and diverted, how much water goes where is changing fast. Scientific management of the river may provide more water to increase agricultural yields, generate clean hydroelectric power that China's industry badly needs, and supply better water-based transport. But will so much water be diverted upstream that farmers on the lower parts of the Yalu won't have enough water for their crops? Will diverting some water to serve the needs of a fast-growing new city make the river so shallow it will silt up downstream so that boats can't use it? What will hydroelectric dams do to the ecology of the river?

One way to approach these questions would be to build a physical scale model of the Yalu River, fill it with water, and conduct experiments by physically damming, diverting, and dredging parts of the model river. If a proposed dam has catastrophic hydrological effects downstream, the model could be modified. Models like this have been constructed for San Francisco Bay and the Mississippi River. A less costly, more flexible, and probably much more effective approach would be to build a digital model of the Yalu River and simulate the effects of the dam. Parameters of the model—such as the height of the dam—could be adjusted to see the consequences of different alternative scenarios.

Spatial analysis with GIS

Spatial analysis involves rigorous and systematic examination of physical space: analysis of what happens on the surface of the earth or a bit above and below it. GIS provides powerful tools that social scientists and public policy researchers can use to perform spatial analysis.

What is GIS?

Geographic information systems (GIS) has become the term of choice for computerized systems for managing, analyzing, and displaying spatial data. Geographic information science (GIScience) is a broader term used for the field of which GIS is part. GIScience extends beyond GIS to include the scientific study of all the hardware, software, and human systems involved in spatial information. There are a number of standard GIS texts (Bolstad 2002; Chrisman 2001; Clarke 2003; DeMers 2004; Heywood, Cornelius, and Carver 2002; Longley et al. 2005; Ormsby et al. 2004).

Because GIS has evolved very rapidly and borrowed from many different sources, definitions of GIS, according to UC Santa Barbara geography professor Keith Clarke "have sometimes been as clear as mud" (Clarke 2003). Box 2.1 summarizes five ways to define GIS that Clarke describes.

Why GIS matters to social scientists and public policy professionals

This book is designed for social science students for use in beginning social science research methods courses. If that describes you, a fair question to ask is why should spatial analysis and data visualization matter to you? Why not spend time reading Shakespeare, walking the dog, or listening to heavy metal music rather than reading this book and completing computer lab exercises?

While GIS is currently taught most frequently in geography departments, GIS is not just for geographers. Social scientists and public policy researchers should look to the specialized expertise people trained in geography bring to spatial analysis. However, understanding the spatial aspect of social phenomena is useful across all of the social sciences and related public policy disciplines like urban planning, public administration, and policy analysis. Sociologists often use census data to study race, income, gender, and other social issues. Social issues like this have a spatial dimension, and understanding how to use census data in a GIS can contribute to

---

Box 2.1   Five definitions of GIS

Toolbox definition. A GIS can be seen as a "toolbox" containing a set of computer tools for analyzing spatial data. Just as a carpenter takes a ruler out of her toolbox to measure a board she is working on, a social scientist using GIS may use a digital ruler to measure space on the computer screen.

Information system definition. The information system definition of GIS stresses that a GIS is a system for delivering answers to questions. This definition considers GIS a special type of information system—special because it links data to geographic coordinates.

GIScience definition. Michael Goodchild, a geography professor at the University of California, Santa Barbara, sees GIS as the product of revolutionary changes in the way in which data can be managed. In his view, a whole series of related innovations in the ways data can be manipulated electronically makes possible a new way of understanding the world. Goodchild coined the term GIScience to refer to the constellation of activities related to GIS.

Business definition. The business definition of GIS looks at GIS as a market phenomenon. It focuses on the rapid expansion and commercialization of the technology.

Societal definition. A final definition of GIS stresses the relationship between measurement and representation of geographical phenomena and society. Scholars interested in this definition of GIS focus on the way in which GIS fits into society.

Adapted from Keith C. Clarke, *Getting Started with Geographic Information Systems, 4th ed.* (2003)

---

sociological analysis (Brewer and Suchan 2001; Peters and MacDonald 2004). Patterns of kinship, religious belief, and other behaviors that interest anthropologists also often have a spatial dimension (Aldenderfer and Maschner 1996).

Political scientists can map voting outcomes and political attributes of countries, states, counties, precincts, and other geographical units and use GIS in redistricting (Ward and O'Loughlin 2002). Historians can use spatial analysis to analyze everything from where the people accused of being witches during the Salem witch trials lived to the route of the Lewis and Clark expedition (Knowles 2002). Local government officials and policy analysts often encounter spatial aspects of public policy issues (O'Looney 2000). City and regional planners deal with physical space. They must understand spatial relationships between land use and transportation in the cities and regions they are planning. Spatial analysis of planning issues can help them plan more effectively (Huxhold, Fowler, and Parr 2004). Planning support systems can inform their practice (Brail and Klosterman 2001).

Maps and attribute tables

Two essential parts of any GIS are the **map** itself and an **attribute table** that contains information about features on the map. A map is a simplified model of the earth or other geographical features. An attribute table consists of rows and columns. Each row in an attribute table contains information about one map feature. Each column consists of information about one attribute.

Map 2.1 shows affordable housing in San Francisco's South Bayshore neighborhood financially assisted by the San Francisco Redevelopment Agency. Below map 2.1 is part of the attribute table associated with it. An arrow runs from the point feature on the map showing the location of the Morgan Heights condominiums to information on the Morgan Heights condominiums in the attribute table.

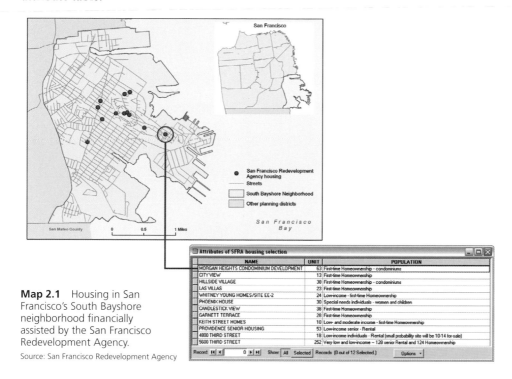

Map 2.1 Housing in San Francisco's South Bayshore neighborhood financially assisted by the San Francisco Redevelopment Agency.

Source: San Francisco Redevelopment Agency

GIS maps and attribute tables are linked so that a user can query the attribute table and see the results of the query on the map. For example, a user might formulate a query to look for all first-time homeownership units in the attribute table that accompanies map 2.1. These units will be highlighted on the map. Similarly, map features selected on the map will be highlighted in the attribute table.

Map layers

A second key aspect of a GIS is that it can contain multiple layers of information that can be analyzed together. A **map layer** is a set of map features related to a common theme. Map 2.2a shows a single map layer—San Francisco census tracts. Map 2.2b shows another map layer—San Francisco streets. Map 2.2c shows a layer of affordable housing units in San Francisco financially assisted by the San Francisco Redevelopment Agency. Map 2.2d shows all three layers together.

Looking at the spatial distribution of features in a single map layer to see if features are randomly distributed in space or related to each other in some systematic way is one important aspect of spatial analysis. Analysis of features in a single map layer can add value to aspatial analysis using a spreadsheet, statistical package, or other software. Even more powerful is overlay analysis looking at relationships among features in two or more different map layers. Overlay analysis may show spatial coincidence—that two or more features tend to exist in the same location. GIS software contains statistical tests to measure spatial coincidence using geospatial statistics that require advanced training (Mitchell 2005). But even by looking at relationships among layers, the beginning analyst may see important relationships.

Map 2.2a   San Francisco census tracts.
Source: 2000 U.S. Census of Population and Housing

Map 2.2b   San Francisco streets.
Source: 2000 U.S. Census TIGER® files

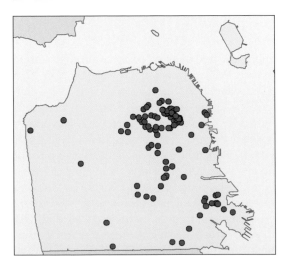

Map 2.2c   Affordable housing units financially
assisted by the San Francisco Redevelopment Agency.
Source: San Francisco Redevelopment Agency

Map 2.2d   Affordable housing units financially assisted by the San Francisco Redevelopment Agency, census tracts, and streets.

Sources: San Francisco Redevelopment Agency, 2000 U.S. Census of Population and Housing, and U.S. Census TIGER files

GIS data and metadata

Data can be distinguished from information. Data is the raw stuff from which information is constructed as the result of organization and analysis. High-quality geographic data collected by federal and state government agencies is available to the public for free. Other data is created by commercial firms and sold. Individual researchers may create their own spatial data. Sometimes they are happy to share their data; other times they will want to keep it to themselves.

Georeferencing

In order to qualify as geographic information, information must include a reference to a location in at least two-dimensional space and one or more attributes. Geographic information may include a third dimension (elevation), and it may reference time. A **georeference** is the term used to describe a location assigned to information (Longley et al. 2005).

To be useable, a georeference must be unique and agreed upon. Georeferences may change over time, but the less they do, the better in terms of possible error in using the geographic data. San Francisco's Army Street was renamed Cesar Chavez Way in the late 1990s. This implemented the community's will in honoring a great labor leader, but it caused confusion for people used to the old street name.

Some georeferences are unique. There is only one Greenwich, England. Other georeferences are unique only within an area or domain of the Earth's surface, and the same reference may occur elsewhere.

Place names may be helpful in locating a place, but they don't give enough detail for big areas (Asia, Russia) and when place names are too local, they may not be generally known. Postal addresses are quite precise—though a problem in Japan where many houses are numbered chronologically based on when they were built, rather than in relation to where they are on a street (Longley et al. 2005).

The best way to achieve agreed-upon definitions of where features are is to get an accurate, precise measurement of the earth that is universally accepted and a precise system for pinpointing the location of every geographical feature on it. Efforts to accurately measure the earth and to specify precise ways to represent the location of features on it have been going on for centuries. The specialized field of geodesy deals with the science of measuring the earth. Measurements of the size of the entire earth that are close to today's measurements were computed about one hundred and fifty years ago. There have been successively more accurate measurements of the size of the earth since that time.

While most people think of the earth as a perfectly round sphere, there is actually a small but significant difference between the distance around the earth pole to pole versus the distance around the equator. This means the earth is actually a form that scientists call an oblate ellipsoid or spheroid. An estimate of the ellipsoid is called a datum. Geographers use a datum to calculate the location (including elevation) of every place on earth (Clarke 2003).

There have been a number of slightly different datums used to map the earth, so it is important to be aware of which datum was used in map data you are using. The most widely used current measurement of the earth was completed in 1984 and is called the World Geodetic System 84 (WGS84) standard. A North American counterpart is the North American Datum of 1983 (NAD83).

The WGS84 and NAD83 standards are nearly universally accepted. Locations based on them can be specified with great precision. Earlier maps were based on slightly different measurements of the earth or measurements for countries or regions that depart slightly from the WGS84 and NAD83 standards. There are still many maps in existence based on an earlier North American datum: the North American Datum of 1927 (NAD27). Given the variety of datums, making sure map layers match requires care. If one layer of a map is based on the NAD83 standard and another layer is based on a different standard, features will not line up properly unless one of the layers is reprojected to match the other.

For social science and public policy analyses you need to pay attention to the coordinate systems and projections used in maps. The introductory exercises in this book don't require you to transform or reproject map data. The following discussion will introduce these issues.

Careful attention to map projections is essential for very precise mapping. For example, a small projection error in a map showing the precise location of an underground utility line could lead to catastrophic consequences. Someone relying on the map as a guide to where to dig a deep hole could sever the line.

The system of latitude and longitude is the most pervasive and important system of georeferencing. The location of every place on earth can be specified in terms of latitude (moving around the earth from east to west) and longitude (running north-south at right angles to latitude). The equator lies at 0 degree latitude. Distances from the equator to the North Pole are measured in 90 degrees going north and to the South Pole by another 90 degrees proceeding south. A slice through the earth at the Royal Observatory at Greenwich, England, measures 0 degrees longitude. Longitude moving east (toward Europe) is expressed in 180 degrees and west (toward America) in another 180 degrees—360 degrees in all. Locations may be specified in degrees, minutes (1/60 of a degree), and seconds (1/60 of a minute).

Most people are accustomed to working with two-dimensional maps—either on paper or computer screens. Map projections transform a position on the earth's surface identified by latitude and longitude into a position on a Cartesian coordinate system. Projections necessarily distort the earth. In order to move from a spherical surface to a two-dimensional Cartesian coordinate system, all maps distort some combination of area, shape, length, and direction. Box 2.2 lists some things to consider about map projections.

Primary and secondary data

Working with GIS may involve collecting original data, but frequently it involves analyzing data that a large government institution like the U.S. Census Bureau or a researcher with interests similar to your own has already collected. The first kind of data is called primary data; the second

---

Box 2.2   Map projection considerations

Check to see what geographic reference system your data uses. Most likely it will be based on either the World Geodetic System 84 (WGS84) or the North American Datum of 1983 (NAD83).

See if your data is projected and, if so, what the projection is. Be aware of the implications of how the projection distorts space.

Be aware that adding data in a different geographic coordinate system or map projection will likely cause a mismatch between areas. If you find that map layers in a GIS don't match, the problem may be caused by inconsistent coordinate systems or projections.

Remember that spatial data in one coordinate system can be transformed to match another coordinate system and that data projected one way can be re-projected to match a different projection. GIS software is making it ever easier to transform and re-project spatial data, but doing so properly requires both conceptual understanding and technical skill.

---

kind of data is called secondary data. A GIS project may involve using a combination of both primary and secondary data.

Imagine that you want to analyze the relationship between carpooling and traffic congestion in southern Santa Clara County, California. One efficient way to reduce data collection for a project like this might be to begin with existing secondary data from the U.S. Census on the number of workers in a census tract that carpool to work. This data has already been collected for you. It is reliable, free, public-domain data. You might collect your own primary data on traffic congestion in different census tracts based on your own field observations and construct a congestion index with "1" meaning least congested and "5" meaning most congested. This would take time and would be expensive if you paid workers to assist in the data collection. You would be responsible for the accuracy of the data and would need to check it carefully for errors. Once you had both the census data and your own primary data, you could combine the two sets of spatial data for analysis. For example, you could analyze whether congestion was lower in census tracts with a higher ratio of people carpooling compared to driving alone.

Relating and joining data in attribute tables

After collecting your own primary data on traffic congestion by census tract to analyze along with existing data on carpooling, you would have two separate files of attribute information that might look like tables 2.1a and 2.1b.

Each table has one common field—a field named FIRST_FIRS that uniquely identifies each census tract. A common field like this is called a join field. The existence of a join field makes it possible to join or relate the two tables.

When a GIS user joins two tables, the tables are physically combined into a new single table. In contrast, when a GIS user relates two tables, the first table is able to look up information in the second (physically separate) table and use it as if the two tables were physically joined, even though the tables remain separate.

In tables 2.1a and 2.1b, there is a one-to-one relationship between the two tables. For each record in the first table from the U.S. Census there is one, and only one, matching record in the second table of congestion index scores collected in the field. This is a good candidate for a join.

FIRST_FIRS	TOT_POP	DRVALONE	CARPOOL
06075010100	2879	578	61
06075010200	4288	1144	183
06075010300	4092	777	251
06075010400	4859	1064	207
06075010500	2278	339	55
06075010600	4218	499	190
06075010700	5634	418	123
06075010800	5130	777	393
06075010900	4506	1048	158
06075011000	5029	661	249
06075011100	5559	683	190
06075011200	3700	548	133
06075011300	3264	124	80
06075011400	3171	41	167

Table 2.1a   Attribute table using U.S. Census information on driving behavior in Santa Clara County census tracts.
Source: 2000 U.S. Census of Population and Housing

FIRST_FIRS	Congestion_Index
06075010100	1
06075010200	2
06075010300	1
06075010400	3
06075010500	3
06075010600	1
06075010700	4
06075010800	2
06075010900	5
06075011000	2
06075011100	3
06075011200	2
06075011300	1
06075011400	4

Table 2.1b   Table of congestion index scores for Santa Clara County census tracts based on field observation.

Source: Hypothetical data

In other situations one attribute table might contain information that applies to many different records in another table. For example, if table 2.1b contained block groups for every census tract, and you were relating the census tracts in table 2.1a, a one-to-many relationship between the two tables would exist. For each census tract in 2.1a, there would be many records in 2.1b.

GIS data functions

It is useful to think of a GIS as performing six essential data-related functions: (a) input, (b) storage, (c) management, (d) transformation, (e) analysis, and (f) display.

Data input is an essential first step. It involves acquiring information about geographic features and getting the information into digital format. Urban spatial and attribute data can be collected in different ways. Some urban data may be collected by doing survey research. That is how the U.S. Census collects data on the demographics of the U.S. population. Data may be collected in the field by recording feature locations with a global positioning system (GPS) receiver—a device that identifies the latitude and longitude of a location. For example, a sociology student interested in how liquor stores in East Oakland affect the community could physically go from liquor store to liquor store with a GPS receiver, press a button, and the receiver would automatically record the latitude and longitude of each liquor store. Spatial location data on each liquor store could be linked to information in an attribute table describing the store size, whether it just sold liquor or also other products, its ownership, and its patrons. Digital data may be created using a digitizing device—a device which allows the user to slide a puck (more similar to a computer mouse than a hockey puck) over features on a paper map and clicking to input data on feature coordinates into a database. Spatial data may also be extracted from satellite images.

Data storage is essential once data has been input or acquired. Once the data is in a form recognizable by the GIS, it can be stored in a folder and file structure for use. Attribute and spatial data need to be stored in a database management system (DBMS). Here GIS has borrowed from the parallel revolution that has occurred with computerized database management software. GIS companies create their own database software as one component of the GIS, or connect their software to existing databases like Microsoft® Access and Oracle®, or both. GIS data can be stored in many different computer file formats—ranging from common file formats like ASCII or Microsoft Word text files and Microsoft Excel spreadsheets to exotic satellite image formats. A part of a GIS must act as a gateway for data in different formats—making it possible for the GIS to use the data. At the software level, a robust GIS must contain routines to transform file formats and join different file formats to the mapping and analytic parts of the software.

As a GIS user, if you are working with data that is already in the proper file format you do not need to know about the complexities of different file formats. That is the case with all of the data in the exercises in this book. If you pursue GIS further and want to work with data from different sources, you will need to master intricacies of working with and transforming different kinds of data files. Experts in the software engineering end of GIScience spend a lot of time dealing with interoperability—making different file formats work together in GIS with the minimum of aggravation for users. Nonetheless, at the time this book was published in 2005, getting different file formats to work properly in GIS was still a significant challenge.

Data management is another important GIS data function. Data folders and files need to be added, deleted, renamed, and moved. Variables need to be added and deleted from data files, named, and perhaps moved around within the file. Data errors need to be corrected. Because GIS software uses a variety of files connected to each other, these data management functions are more complicated than just managing single files with Microsoft Windows®. If a GIS user accidentally moves or renames a file without moving related files, this may confuse the GIS, and it may not be able to find the data. GIS software includes specialized components for managing data.

Data transformation and reprojection are other GIS data functions. Because spatial data may be based on many different coordinate systems and projections, a robust GIS must permit users to reproject data so that data layers are in the same projection and will match each other. A GIS must permit users to reproject data in order to do a needed kind of analysis. If, for example, the task at hand involves accurately calculating and displaying the area of polygons, a map with an equal area projection would be necessary. If some GIS data is in a map projection that preserves direction at the expense of area, the data needs to be reprojected to an equal area projection.

Data analysis is the heart of a GIS. GIS software needs to let users query data, overlay different layers, create buffers, classify features, look for spatial coincidence, and do other spatial data analysis that you will learn in the exercises in this book.

Every GIS system needs to be able to display data in the form of maps using appropriate symbols, sizes, shapes, colors, and textures. Some GIS software includes routines to display data graphics created from data in the attribute table.

Data errors and data quality

The value of analytical output is only as good as the data that goes into it. If data is wrong to begin with or errors are introduced and propagated during the course of manipulating data, the output will be wrong—probably garbage.

Secondary data sources such as the U.S. Census and the U.S. Geological Survey (USGS) have highly trained experts. They are careful to assure a very high degree of accuracy in their data. Users can rely on these data sources. Data obtained by satellite imagery is professionally collected and carefully transformed and checked by trained experts. It is highly reliable. Secondary data from other sources varies in quality. Some organizations and individuals (well funded or not) produce excellent, reliable data. Others do not. Accordingly, it is very important to know the source of data and its reliability.

Data errors come from many different sources. Following is a list of some of the most important types of GIS-related data error and suggestions on how to avoid them.

Measurement error. Some data errors may be introduced at the time data is collected. If the instrumentation of a GPS receiver is wrong, or hills block satellite connections to the receiver, this may introduce errors in the location of features ranging from a few feet to many yards. This produces locational error where a feature is incorrectly located. Spatial analysis with wrong locations is flawed. Measurement errors can be reduced or eliminated by using high-quality measuring instruments and making sure they are functioning properly.

Data entry error. Data that is manually entered by typing values into a computer is subject to data entry error. A data entry person may type "100000000" instead of "10000000" into the city population field of an attribute table, creating the world's largest digital megacity. Errors can also be introduced as data is digitized or scanned. Failing to enclose a polygon or over- or undershooting a line that it is intended to end where it meets another line are common digitization errors. A squashed fly on a paper map may scan as a new city in Antarctica. Reporting that at an urban planning conference would really raise eyebrows!

Data entry errors can be reduced or eliminated by using skilled data-entry people and high-quality digitization and scanning technology, and checking data that has been entered for accuracy. Once attribute data is in a data table, aspatial or spatial analysis can identify impossible or improbable values. For example, if every census block in San Francisco has fewer than 100 very low-income households and one has 457, it is important to check that census block. Perhaps a data-entry person typed an extra digit on the end and the real value should be 45. Of course this may be an unusual block—perhaps one with a very large low-income housing project. You don't want to eliminate outliers—unusual values that fall outside the range of other values you are researching—because extreme values are often of particular policy significance. You will learn more about outliers in chapter 8. Looking carefully at attribute data after it has been entered—either by checking the numbers a second time or by looking at output for suspicious values—is called data cleaning. It is an essential step in getting data into shape for analysis.

Overlay errors. If map layers are very slightly different due to measurement errors or inconsistent projections, features of the layers will not line up precisely. One consequence of mismatched polygon overlay is what are called sliver polygons—skinny little polygons that show slight data inconsistencies rather than real geographical features. Overlay errors can be avoided by using map layers from identical sources and making sure that map layers are in the same coordinate system and projection.

Data obsolescence error. Data that was good when it was collected may be out of date. Standard metadata items include the date on which the data was collected and how frequently it is updated. If you have excellent road system data that was accurate when it was produced in 1972—but rely on it to map roads in a fast-growing suburb today—you will probably have serious errors.

Many new roads that did not exist in 1972 will not be on your map at all. Others may have been extended, moved, or eliminated altogether. Data obsolescence error can be reduced or eliminated by carefully checking metadata to make sure up-to-date data is used and updating features as necessary.

Error propogation. Data errors can propagate and magnify as incorrect data is processed with other data. Error propagation is best controlled by care in transforming data and checking output at each step in a multistep analysis before it is used in further analyses.

If you are conducting an analysis that involves complex selection or classification, two strategies to reduce error propagation are useful. One is to break a complex operation down into successive steps and to carefully check output after every step. A second strategy is to carefully examine selected features after the operation—particularly the highest and lowest values and values of features you are most familiar with—to make sure that the results of the analysis are correct.

Metadata

Map metadata is data that documents data. In order to use data correctly it is important for users to know what the data is, who produced it, how old it is, and technical information about the data such as its coordinate system and projection. Unfortunately, many people who produce spatial data do not adequately document their data. In the United States, federal agencies that produce geographic data are required to conform to standards prepared by the Federal Geographic Data Committee (FGDC). Many other organizations and individuals follow the FGDC standards, and you should get in the habit of creating good metadata to accompany any new GIS data you create. The FGDC standards require at a minimum that metadata accompanying a geographic dataset include the information in box 2.3 on the next page.

There are two principal models of GIS—vector GIS and raster GIS. The two different GIS models represent geographical space in fundamentally different ways. Both can perform many of the same functions, but there are some things one model can do that the other cannot and other things that the second model does better than the first model. The next two chapters introduce the vector GIS model. Chapters 6 and 7 introduce the raster GIS model.

Box 2.3   FGDC metadata standards

Section	Function
Identification information	Documents who produced the original data and when it was produced.
Data quality	A general assessment of the quality of the data. Indicates the scale at which the data was originally captured and the reliability of the data.
Spatial data organization	Provides a technical description of the mechanism used to represent spatial data in the dataset.
Spatial data reference	Records the type of projection the data is in and its coordinate system.
Attribute information	Defines the field names in the database and explains the words, numbers, or codes used in those fields.
Distribution information	Indicates who is distributing the data. The person or organization distributing the data can be different from who originally produced the data. Distribution information may include purchase costs and information on availability from either a Web site or CD-ROM.
Metadata reference information	A definition of what the dataset should be called.

Terms

academic discipline. A systematic body of knowledge and methods adopted by academics who define themselves as members of an identifiable academic specialty. Academic disciplines particularly relevant to the study of cities include geography, sociology, political science, economics, and history. Academic disciplines pride themselves on being based on basic knowledge about the world and differentiate themselves from interdisciplinary applied fields like urban studies and city and regional planning that draw on many different disciplines. Most members of academic disciplines today are housed in an academic department within a university.

attribute table. An attribute table consists of rows and columns with information about attributes of map features. Map features represented as points, lines, and polygons can be digitally linked to the attribute table, and the information can be analyzed by querying either the map or the attribute table. The city of Shanghai, China, represented as a point on a map could be linked to one row in an attribute table. Columns in the attribute table might contain information on attributes of Shanghai such as its population size, area, density, median income, and average temperature.

geographic information system (GIS). An information system used to capture, store, retrieve, analyze, and display spatial data. While technically a GIS can include any information system, whether or not it uses computers, today the term is virtually always used to refer to computer software.

georeference. Used as a verb, georeference means to specify the location of a feature. Georeferencing the location of a feature makes it possible to specify precisely where the feature is located. Used as a noun, a georeference is a specification of a feature location. A house address is an example of a georeference.

map. A simplified model of all or part of the earth or other geographic features. Historically most maps were two-dimensional representations of geographic reality reproduced on paper. Today map symbols may be geocoded and stored in a digital database for use by GIS software.

map layer. A set of map features related to a common theme. Modern GIS software permits users to create and analyze map data as digital layers. When a layer is coregistered with other layers, different aspects of the theme may be analyzed.

map projection. A depiction of all or part of the earth's three-dimensional structure on a flat, two-dimensional map. The earth is spherical, but humans usually work with two-dimensional flat maps. Map projections translate representation from the spherical earth to a flat map. All projections distort some combination of shape, area, distance, and direction.

metadata. Data about data. Users will often want to know information about a spatial dataset such as who created it and when, whether it is copyrighted, and who to contact for more information. They may also want to know the projection used for the data and other technical information. This kind of data about geographic data is metadata.

Questions for further study

1. Both urban problems and opportunities have multiple dimensions. Social scientists based in academic disciplines may be particularly well equipped to study some aspects of urban issues. Based on what you know about different social science disciplines, discuss what aspects of the following urban issues an economist, political scientist, geographer, and sociologist might be best equipped to study:

    a. homelessness
    b. bicycle-oriented transportation
    c. preserving an endangered wetlands area
    d. providing affordable housing

2. Most people think that visual images should be used to communicate the end results of analysis. How do Jacques Bertin and John Tukey turn this idea on its head?

3. What is a digital model of the real world? Why do we use digital models?

4. Would there be a one-to-one, one-to-many, or many-to-many relationship between each of the following pairs of data tables:

    a. a table of U.S. Census tract data and additional data collected in the field showing the number of pawn shops in each census tract

    b. a table showing the location of many crimes in a city and another table showing the criminal code section of different crimes

    c. a table with the addresses of farm owners in Contra Costa County, California, with a field indicating whether the soil type on each of thousands of farms is prime farmland, pastureland, or another of six types of farmland, and a small table with just the six types of farmland

5. If you want to combine National Oceanic and Atmospheric Administration (NOAA) data on marine life in San Francisco Bay with data you have collected on water pollution, which data source would be the primary data? Which would be the secondary data? Why might you want to combine the data?

Annotated bibliography

Introductory academic GIS texts include Paul A. Longley, Michael F. Goodchild, David J. Maguire, and David W. Rhind's *Geographic Information Systems and Science*, second edition (Longley et al. 2005), a lively, well-illustrated, and sophisticated introductory text by leaders in the field; Michael N. DeMers's professional and informative *Fundamentals of Geographic Information Systems*, third edition (DeMers 2004); Keith C. Clarke's readable elementary text *Getting Started with Geographic Information Systems*, fourth edition (Clarke 2003); Paul Bolstad's *GIS Fundamentals* (Bolstad 2002); Ian Heywood, Sarah Cornelius, and Steve Carver's *An Introduction to Geographical Information Systems*, second edition (Heywood, Cornelius, and Carver 2002); and Nicholas Chrisman's *Exploring Geographical Information Systems*, second edition (Chrisman 2001).

Getting to Know ArcGIS Desktop, second edition by Tim Ormsby, Eileen Napoleon, Robert Burke, Carolyn Groessl, and Laura Feaster (Ormsby et al. 2004) is an indispensable introduction to how to use ArcGIS. The work is a lively "how-to" book with step-by-step exercises that teach basic ArcGIS operations. Mixed in with the how-to-do-it material are lucid descriptions of GIS concepts introduced in this chapter.

Wilpen L. Gorr and Kristen S. Kurland's *GIS Tutorial: Workbook for ArcView 9* (Gorr and Kurland 2005) is a step-by-step introduction to ArcGIS that comes with exercise data on a CD-ROM.

Andy Mitchell's *The ESRI Guide to GIS Analysis, Volume 1: Geographic Patterns & Relationships* (Mitchell 1999) is a clearly written, thoughtful, and well-illustrated introduction to GIS analysis.

Chapter 3

Managing urbanization with vector GIS

"*Spatial analysis is in many ways the crux of GIS . . .. [It] is the process by which we turn raw data into useful information, in pursuit of scientific discovery, or more effective decision making.*"

Paul A. Longley, Michael F. Goodchild,
David J. Maguire, and David W. Rhind (2005)

Introduction

This chapter is where you begin learning how to use GIS. Chapter 1 described problems that cities and regions face today, opportunities that urbanization presents, and ways to address the problems and capitalize on the opportunities. Chapter 2 introduced GIS and provided an overview of how spatial analysis and data visualization can help social scientists and public policy professionals solve urban problems. This chapter provides a starter set of spatial analysis concepts and operational skills so that you can understand how to do urban spatial analysis. There is a reciprocal relationship between chapter 2 and this chapter and exercises 1 and 2. You need to master the concepts in order to understand the operations you will do in the first two exercises. The exercises illustrate the concepts and will help make them clearer. Additional material on GIS is available in standard GIS texts (Bolstad 2002; Chrisman 2001; Clarke 2003; DeMers 2004; Heywood, Cornelius, and Carver 2002; Longley et al. 2005; and Bernhardsen 2002).

Unless you are a geography major or have taken a GIS class, you have probably not used GIS software or even heard about GIS. While GIS has been around for more than thirty years, until the mid-1990s GIS software was very expensive, complex, and sometimes cranky. It was usually run on mainframe and mini computers. A handful of highly skilled experts used GIS to gain remarkable insights and produce stunning maps, but until very recently GIS was not for the faint-hearted. Software companies such as Environmental Systems Research Institute (ESRI®), MapInfo®, Intergraph®, and Autodesk® have created desktop GIS software products that run on personal computers. Exponential increases in personal computers' power and plummeting costs of hardware and software are making GIS increasingly accessible. You will learn spatial analysis skills by the end of this book that will empower you to do spatial analysis.

Getting started

Most of this chapter and most of exercises 1 and 2 involve analysis. But before you can analyze data, it is necessary to learn some basic GIS operations like opening GIS software, loading data, and moving around in digital space. The concepts and operations described in this chapter are software neutral to the extent that is possible. The exercises for this book are designed to be completed using **ArcMap**™—the mapping component of ESRI® ArcGIS®, the leading GIS software package in the world. Once you have mastered the concepts and operations in this book and learned how to implement them using ArcMap, you will be able to apply what you have learned to different GIS software and learn new GIS software as the technology evolves.

Opening GIS software and loading existing data

On the surface, GIS software works much like other software you have used. Like a word-processing program, you begin by opening ArcMap. Then you either load existing data or create your own. You will be using existing data in the exercises that accompany this book, rather than creating your own.

Finding and opening a GIS file is essentially the same as navigating to a folder and opening an existing Microsoft Word document or Microsoft Excel spreadsheet. The software manipulates the data in the file. Accordingly, you need to know how to navigate to the appropriate folder and load data.

Word-processing software allows the user to write a new text document such as a letter or a book report and save it to a computer hard drive, CD-ROM, or other storage device. Later, you can open the document and work on it again. The document is not part of the software—it exists separately from it. First-time users are sometimes confused about the relationship between GIS software and the data that the software operates on. They ask, "how many maps does the GIS software contain?" This is like confusing a word-processing program and the text of a report you write using the word-processing software. It is like asking "How many term papers does Microsoft Word contain?" GIS software allows a user to create maps and associated data and save them to a computer hard drive or other storage device. Later the user can reopen and reuse or modify the maps and attribute data in much the same way he or she opens a report written with a word-processor.

Most word-processor users work entirely with documents they create. In contrast, in GIS you will often use secondary data that has already been created by someone else such as the U.S. Census or the U.S. Geological Survey. You can learn how to create your own data within ArcMap from ESRI's introductory guide to ArcGIS: *Getting to Know ArcGIS*, second edition (Ormsby et al. 2004), other how-to GIS books (Gorr and Kurland 2005), or ESRI's online Virtual Campus courses *(campus.esri.com)*.

Once you have opened a GIS software program, the second step is to open a new, empty map, a template, or an existing map. You will learn how to open existing maps and add data to them in exercise 1.

Working with layers

In a word processor like Microsoft Word you work with the digital equivalent of one sheet of paper on your computer screen. In GIS you often work with multiple layers of data. Chapter 2 introduced the concept of map layers, but map layers are such an important feature of GIS that they merit more extended discussion.

It is helpful to think again of map layers as transparent sheets of plastic with map information on them. You might begin a GIS session analyzing world cities with just one map layer on the computer screen—perhaps the countries of the world in light green with thin gray borders *(map 3.1a)*. Then you might add a second layer showing urban agglomerations with between five and ten million people in 2000 symbolized as dark red point symbols with thin black borders *(map 3.1b)*, and then a third layer so that the map also shows megacities with populations in excess of ten million people in 2000 symbolized as yellow squares *(map 3.1c)*.

You may not be familiar with the map projection used in maps 3.1a, b, and c. Most primary and high school classroom maps still use the Mercator projection in which countries near the

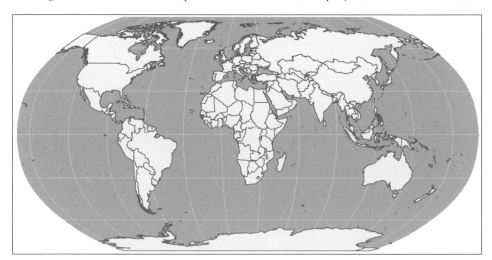

Map 3.1a Map with one layer (countries).
Source: ESRI Data and Maps 2003

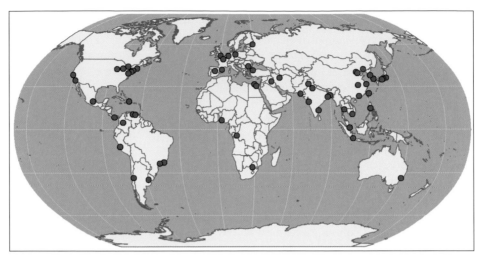

Map 3.1b   Map with two layers (countries and urban agglomerations with five to ten million people).
Sources: ESRI Data and Maps 2003 and United Nations

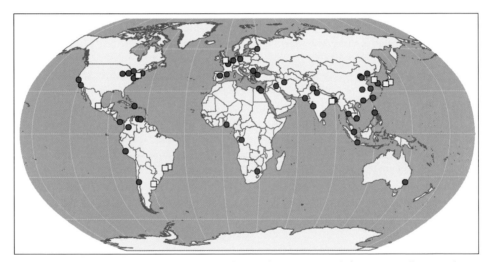

Map 3.1c   Map with three layers (countries, urban agglomerations with five to ten million people, and megacities with more than ten million people).
Sources: Source: ESRI Data and Maps 2003 and United Nations

north and south poles appear much larger than they are. Maps 3.1a, b, and c use the Robinson projection. You will learn more about technical aspects of map projection and about the politics of these two map projections in chapter 10.

Important GIS skills related to working with layers include learning how to add and remove layers, changing the order of layers so one layer does not hide features in other layer(s), and creating new layers that contain subsets of features by copying some or all of the features of existing layer(s) to a new map layer.

Locating spatial features

Geographical things are referred to as **features**. One data layer can contain many features. For example, a data layer showing the sites of toxic incidents might have forty different point features, each showing where a different toxic incident occurred. A beginning GIS skill is learning to locate spatial features on the digital map on your computer screen.

As you learned in chapter 2, GIS software contains information about map features in a database associated with the map. The software makes it possible for users to search the database based on attributes such as the feature's name. For example, from a map with thousands of Asian cities you could instruct the computer to find a specific city like Kuala Lumpur. Once the computer has found Kuala Lumpur in the attribute table, you can examine its attributes, or, since the attribute table is electronically linked to the map, see its location.

Zooming and panning

You can move around a digital map in different ways. Two basic operations are zooming and panning.

Zoom is an evocative word that gives a sense of the operation. Imagine yourself as a hawk looking down on a landscape searching for field mice. When you see a field mouse, you zoom down to grab it. Similarly, in a GIS you can look at a large area such as the entire world on your computer screen and then issue an appropriate command to zoom down to a specific feature such as the city of Camden, New Jersey. Then you can zoom back to the world scale. There are a number of different ways to zoom around. They are fun. You will learn them in exercise 1.

Map 3.2a shows the nine-county San Francisco Bay Area in green, with cities in light orange. This map is a small-scale map that is zoomed out to the full extent of the San Francisco Bay Area. At this scale the city names would be too small to read and do not appear on the map.

Map 3.2b is zoomed in to a portion of map 3.2a that includes San Francisco, part of San Francisco Bay, and several cities near San Francisco. At this (larger) scale the names of the cities appear.

There is a slight problem with map 3.2b. Only part of the East Bay cities of Oakland and Berkeley appear. The map would better display both San Francisco and the urbanized East Bay if the center of the map were pulled over to the left so that all of Oakland and Berkeley are on the map. You can take care of that problem by panning.

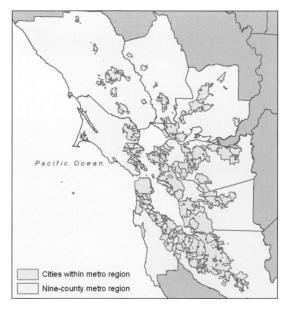

Pacific Ocean

☐ Cities within metro region
☐ Nine-county metro region

Map 3.2a   San Francisco Bay Area and Bay Area cities.

Source: 2000 U.S. Census of Population and Housing

Map 3.2b   San Francisco Bay Area zoomed to San Francisco County.
Source: 2000 U.S. Census of Population and Housing

Map 3.2c   San Francisco Bay Area zoomed out and panned left.
Source: 2000 U.S. Census of Population and Housing

If you **pan** around a digital map, you can position the map exactly where you want it on the computer screen. Hard-copy maps made from the computer map that appears on your computer screen will be positioned as they appear after you pan. Map 3.2c has been zoomed out slightly to a somewhat smaller scale and panned to the left so that the all of the East Bay cities of Oakland and Berkeley are visible.

Whenever a feature you are looking for on a digital map is just a little off the screen, as was the case in map 3.2b, you can pan the map display so that you can see the area that was previously off-screen. By zooming in or out and then panning right, left, up, or down you can get just the map extent you want. You will learn how to pan in exercise 1.

Finding geographical features and identifying their attributes

GIS maps are special because they may contain data on attributes of the features on the digital map. Often you want to find a specific feature—such as the city of Walnut Creek, California, or Highway 580. Once you have found a feature on a map, you may want to view the underlying data about it. For example, you may have found a site where a toxic incident occurred near an area you are considering for a red-legged frog habitat conservation area and now you want to know just what the toxic incident was. What was released? When? In what quantity? By whom? Has it been cleaned up? If this data is in the attribute table associated with a feature, you will want to learn how to take a look at it. These GIS operations—finding geographical features and identifying their attributes—are easy to do. Not only can you find an individual feature, you also can find subsets of features based on their attributes or locations.

Measuring geographic features

Maps have spatial extent. Things exist in relation to each other. They are of identifiable sizes. A common spatial analysis task is to measure geographical features. The most common measurement is the distance between two geographic features—for example, knowing the distance from an affordable housing project for low-income, elderly people with mobility problems and the nearest bus stop may be critical to assuring that project residents can shop and get medical attention on their own. But social scientists and policy analysts may also be interested in measuring area (how many acres is a proposed red-legged frog habitat conservation area?) or perimeter (how many feet is it around the lake?).

What maps can show

Once you know how to open a GIS software package, open an existing GIS file, find features, and pan so features are positioned where you want them on the computer screen, it is tempting to plunge right in and create maps. This is fun and a few commands will start the mapmaking process. A much better approach is to think first and map later. Picasso was too harsh when he said: "Computers are useless. They can only give you answers." But his hyperbole underlines the essential point that the key to good computer analysis is asking questions. Generating the answers is secondary. What is it that a map can show? What is the value added by the map? What does spatial understanding contribute to what you could learn from words or numbers? Once you have thought about these issues, you will be a more intelligent consumer of existing maps. You will also be better able to formulate questions for spatial analysis and to carry out your own mapping more intelligently.

Some important things maps can show are where features are (location), whether or not features are next to other features (adjacency), how close one feature is to another (proximity), whether features contain other features (containment), whether there are patterns to the way in which features are distributed in space (clustering, regularity, dispersion, density), and whether or not features vary over space or are changing over time (Mitchell 1999). Looking at multiple map layers in relation to each other can show you whether the locations of some features coincide with others (spatial coincidence). Just looking at maps is an important form of exploratory research that can help you understand phenomena. It may suggest why things are as they are (causation) and point you in the right direction for further research. Using spatial statistics built into GIS software or analyzing the data in the attribute table with a computerized statistical package can reveal much more about the map data (Mitchell 2005).

All maps are concerned with two central things: (a) location, and (b) attributes of geographical features in the real world. All maps exist at some scale. Every flat paper or digital map contains geometric transformations of spatial data. Every map uses symbols to represent reality. Despite these commonalities, maps that social scientists, planners, and public policy professionals use have a variety of different purposes. Being clear about the purpose of a map you propose to create is an essential first step in mapmaking.

Analog and digital maps

Cartography is the subfield in geography concerned with mapmaking (Robinson et al. 1995; Dent 1999). Historically, cartographers created a single end-state map. The purpose of mapmaking was to produce a finished map for end users. If the map was intelligently conceived and well executed, it served its purpose.

Today, when cartographers create digital GIS maps, they put location and attribute information together in a way that will do much more than create a single end-state map. A single map is often one, or even the only, intended product of a GIS mapmaking exercise. But today, once a digital map and its attribute table have been created, GIS permits mapmakers to make many variations quickly. Increasingly users themselves can modify digital maps based on their needs. By changing scale, zooming in on a particular feature, generalizing features, creating new map layers, and changing map symbology, a GIS user can quickly create a whole family of related maps. GIS maps provide the basis for analyses that can be displayed in map form or as statistical output, charts, or in other ways.

Map purposes

General reference maps are probably the type of maps you are most familiar with. Their purpose is to show where things are. An important kind of general reference map is a map designed to help people move around, such as a street map. Increasingly, digital street maps downloaded from the Web or on computerized navigation systems in cars are replacing paper maps. Airplane pilots and ship captains use similar reference maps to navigate.

Thematic maps concentrate on the spatial arrangement of one or more feature attributes. Map 3.3 shows the number of people in different parts of the San Francisco Bay Area age 16 and older who bicycle to work. It is an example of a thematic map. The data on commuting by bicycle is displayed for census tracts, but with the census tract borders dissolved so viewers will focus on the bicycle commuting behavior rather than the census tract borders. Three inset maps of the most urban areas—San Francisco, the East Bay, and the South Bay—provide greater detail on areas where the most people commute to work by bicycle. Notice the nice guidance map 3.3 gives to the map viewer. Each of the three key areas is outlined in black on the map and assigned a letter. The three inset maps repeat the map letter and are set off from the main map by a black border. The inset maps are at a larger scale, so they show the area in question in greater detail. A leading cartography text coauthored by Arthur Robinson (who invented the Robinson projection) calls thematic maps "a kind of graphic essay" (Robinson et al. 1995).

Cadastral maps depict landownership and attributes of individual land parcels. Map 3.4 is a portion of a cadastral map showing land parcels in Oakland, California. In addition to the parcel number, which appears on the map, the attribute table for map 3.4 contains the parcel area, owner's name, use, and other information about the parcel.

Analytic maps may tell us important things based on operations performed on the map data. Exploratory spatial data analysis is an iterative process. The results of intermediate analysis stimulate the researcher to ask more and better questions. One analytic map may become input for deeper analysis.

Policy analysts and planners analyze data from different sources in order to develop programs and plans. Elected officials frequently instruct analysts to do research that can help inform public policy. One issue that has been of concern in the last five years is fire danger from wildfires reaching urban areas. Aware of this concern, school district officials might call on policy analysts and planners to assess fire risk to elementary school students.

Map 3.5 is an example of an analytic map that could help government officials understand fire risk to elementary schools and set appropriate policy—such as requiring fire breaks around

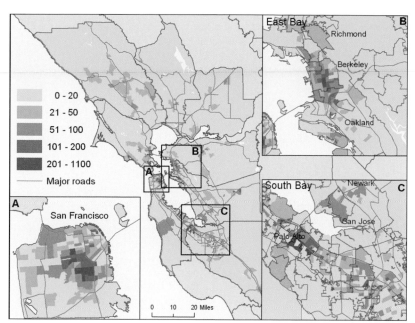

Map 3.3 San Francisco Bay Area residents age 16 and older who bicycled to work, 2000.

Source: 2000 U.S. Census of Population and Housing

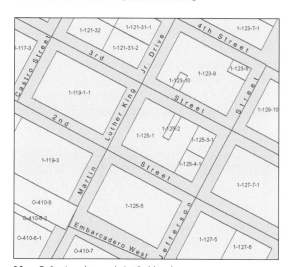

Map 3.4 Land parcels in Oakland.

Source: Oakland Office of Information Technology

PRINTPARCE	Use
1-127-5	Discount house
1-127-6	Exempt public agencies
0-410-7	Property owned by a public utility
1-123-7-1	Exempt public agencies
1-121-31-1	Warehouse
1-121-32	Warehouse
1-121-31-2	Warehouse
1-117-3	Light industrial
1-123-9	Warehouse
1-119-1-1	Warehouse
1-123-8	1 to 5-story offices
1-123-10	Light industrial
1-129-10	Light industrial
1-125-1	Warehouse
1-125-2	Vacant industrial land (may include miscellaneous
1-119-3	Property owned by a public utility
1-125-3-1	Parking lots
0-410-6-2	Property owned by a public utility
1-127-7-1	Store on first floor with offices or apartments or
1-125-4-1	Parking lots
0-410-9	Property owned by a public utility
1-125-5	Property owned by a public utility
0-410-6-1	Exempt public agencies

elementary schools that appear to be at risk or channeling funding for the construction of firehouses and purchase of new fire-fighting equipment to increase the ability of local fire-fighting units to respond to fire threats to the most vulnerable elementary schools. It draws on existing federal government data showing the location of schools and data developed by the California Department of Forestry on the location of large fires in the past. The power of GIS lies in the ability to combine these different data sources to produce an informative map. A decision maker could use map 3.5 to make decisions about fire safety for elementary schools.

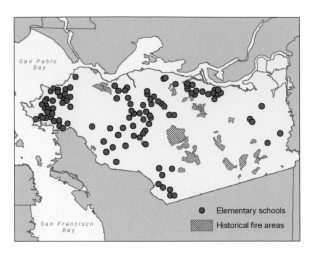

Map 3.5 Elementary schools and historic fire areas in Contra Costa County.

Sources: USGS Geographic Names Information System, and California Department of Forestry and Fire Protection's Fire and Resource Assessment Program

Location

Maps show where things are. You have undoubtedly used a map to find where a single feature is—perhaps the address of a friend you visited in an area you were not familiar with or a place of entertainment whose street address you found on a map. Looking at more than one feature or different kinds of features in relation to each other may tell you much more than looking at a single feature. Where are all the parcels of prime agricultural land? Where are the headquarters of global corporations with annual earnings of over $10 billion? Where do China-born individuals in San Francisco live? Do the China-born individuals live in the same areas as Mexico- or Philippines-born individuals, or in different areas?

Map 3.6a shows the location of a single feature—an affordable housing development named the Hamilton Family Center located in San Francisco's Western Addition neighborhood. Just a look at the map helps show a viewer where the feature is located. It expresses location more clearly than a written description of how to find the Hamilton Family Center.

Map 3.6a   Single feature: Hamilton Family Center.

Sources: 2000 U.S. Census of Population and Housing and San Francisco Redevelopment Agency

Map 3.6b shows the location of many features of the same kind—affordable housing in San Francisco financially assisted by the San Francisco Redevelopment Agency (SFRA). You can quickly see a number of things—that there are quite a few housing units assisted by the SFRA and that they appear to be clustered in certain parts of San Francisco.

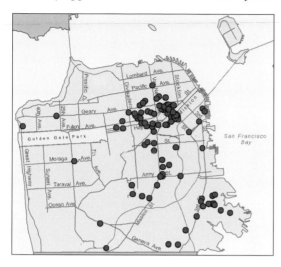

Map 3.6b Multiple features of the same type: housing financially assisted by the San Francisco Redevelopment Agency.

Sources: 2000 U.S. Census of Population and Housing and San Francisco Redevelopment Agency

In most parts of the United States housing is classified using standard U.S. Department of Housing and Urban Development definitions as affordable by very low-, low-, moderate-, and above-moderate-income households. Almost all housing financially assisted by federal, state, and local government is for very low- and low-income households. Because San Francisco residents have such a wide range of incomes, the San Francisco Redevelopment Agency (SFRA) divides the lowest income group into extremely low- and very low-income households. Some SFRA housing is built for people with AIDS/HIV or other special needs. Map 3.6c shows the same features as map 3.6b, affordable housing assisted by the SFRA, broken down by these SFRA definitions: (a) extremely low-income (red circles), (b) very low-income (orange circles), (c) low-income units (yellow circles), (d) special needs units (blue circles), and (e) other housing (gray circles). There are many features of each of the five different kinds of affordable housing.

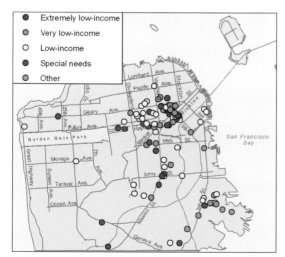

Map 3.6c Multiple features of different types: five kinds of affordable housing financially assisted by the San Francisco Redevelopment Agency.

Sources: 2000 U.S. Census of Population and Housing and San Francisco Redevelopment Agency

You may need to look at map 3.6c more carefully than the single feature map and the map of multiple features of a single kind. But if you do, you will be rewarded by seeing patterns that raise good public policy questions. Why are affordable housing units concentrated so heavily in downtown San Francisco and just a few other areas? Why are there no assisted housing units in the southwestern part of the city? Why are so many housing units the SFRA financially assists located in the South Bayshore neighborhood—a predominantly African-American neighborhood located at the lower right of the map?

Looking at features on a map can reveal where community assets and trouble spots are located. They can suggest where programs should be targeted to capitalize on the assets or to overcome the problems. Where are good sites for infill housing? The best habitats for red-legged frogs? Land appropriate for urban greenbelts? High-crime areas? Toxic-waste hot spots? Houses with lead-based paint that pose a health threat to young children? Vanishing wetlands?

Adjacency and proximity

Another thing to look for in a map is whether a geographical feature is adjacent (next to) another feature. Adjacency may be good or bad. It may be critical to single parents without cars that a day care center be adjacent to a workplace or bus stop. It may be equally critical for sustainable urban development that a toxic hazard site not be adjacent to a river where toxics may pollute the water.

Adjacency is the extreme case of a broader spatial property—proximity. Proximity describes how close features are to other features. Often in urban analyses it is important to know how close spatial features are to other spatial features. How many potential riders live within walking distance of a proposed light-rail station? How far is the nearest day care center from a major employment site? GIS locational queries permit users to select features within a specified distance of another feature.

Map 3.7 shows affordable housing units in San Francisco financially assisted by the San Francisco Redevelopment Agency that are located within one-quarter mile on either side of Mission Street. The units within one-quarter mile are symbolized in red; other assisted housing units are in blue. The green area in map 3.7 is a one-quarter mile buffer on either side of Mission Street (an area of half a mile around Mission Street altogether). A buffer like this makes it easy to see which features fall within a specified distance. There are many uses for buffers. You might draw a buffer around a toxic incident site and specify that no one can enter that area until tests confirm that it

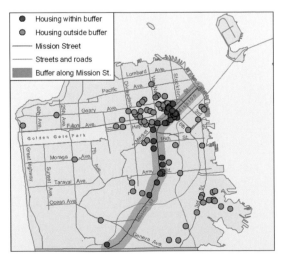

Map 3.7 Proximity: housing financially assisted by the San Francisco Redevelopment Agency within one-quarter mile of San Francisco's Mission Street.

Sources: San Francisco Redevelopment Agency, 2000 U.S. Census of Population and Housing, and U.S. Census TIGER files

is safe, or draw 500-foot buffers around streams where steelhead trout spawn to restrict logging that might disturb baby trout, or to show where a greenbelt around a rapidly growing city might be established.

Proximity is usually measured in standard distance units like miles or kilometers. Proximity can also be measured in more subtle conceptual units like travel time or travel cost. For example, it may be more costly to fly from San Francisco to a nearby city with a small airport such as San Luis Obispo, California, only two hundred miles away than to Chicago—a huge Midwestern airport hub where the volume of traffic makes it possible for airlines to offer low-cost flights. The cost of traveling from San Francisco to Chicago measured in dollars is less than the cost to travel from San Francisco to San Luis Obispo even though the straight line distance measured in miles is much greater. GIS—particularly raster GIS—is very good for calculating time- or cost-weighted distance. You will learn more about cost-weighted distance in part II.

Quantity

Just seeing where things are on a map is a good first step in many spatial analyses. But social scientific research usually requires researchers to measure and quantify phenomena to provide precise information beyond what appears just by looking. You may want to report that there were 11,419,832 people living in Northern California on census day 2000 rather than that there were "a lot of people" in Northern California at that time. Determining and specifying quantities adds important information to analyses.

Sometimes you just need a count of how many things are within a specified distance—for example, that there are six sites where San Francisco garter snakes live within half a mile of a park. Other times you need a list of all the features within a specified distance. For example, you might need the actual street addresses of twenty-six houses that are too close to an oil refinery in order to mail each individual resident a warning about a safety risk. Sometimes you need summary statistics like the total number of features or totals of one or more attributes of the features you are examining.

You do not have to go through the tedious process of counting points, lines, or polygons. GIS software can count, list, sum, and compute other summary statistics for vector GIS features. You will learn how to calculate summary statistics about a feature in exercise 2.

Features may be measurable at different **levels of measurement** according to a classification scheme proposed by Harvard psychology professor Stanley Smith Stevens in 1949 (Stevens 1949). Stevens distinguished between four levels of measurement: nominal, ordinal, interval, and ratio. His classification scheme is the foundation of many social science research methods and data analysis courses. Understanding what nominal-, ordinal-, interval-, and ratio-level measurements are and how to use them is important.

Nominal-level data just has a name associated with the feature, without numeric or quantitative significance. The word nominal comes from the Latin word for name. For example, if you are using U.S. Census data to map households by race you can use the categories of race that people have reported themselves to be—white, African-American, Asian/Pacific Islander, or combinations of races. Race is not numeric—it is just a name assigned to the attribute. Another example of a variable at the nominal level is religion. You might assign codes as follows: 1 Protestant, 2 Catholic, 3 Jewish, 4 Muslim, 5 Buddhist, 6 Hindu, and 7 Other. Calculating an average (mean) religion of 3.2 for a group sample would produce nonsense. It would not mean that the average person was a slightly Jewish Muslim!

Ordinal-level data is the name social scientists assign to data measured at a level that has order. The word ordinal comes from the Latin word for order. You might classify the condition of housing units in a redevelopment area as poor, fair, good, and excellent with ranks of 1, 2, 3, and 4. A

Box 3.1   Reporting what is contained within feature(s)

There are many different ways to report what is contained within a feature:

Lists simply report the attributes of each thing (such as the name). For example, the first four cities in a list of cities within Contra Costa County would begin
> Alamo
> Antioch
> Brentwood
> Concord

Counts summarize the total number of things. For example, a report might state that there are 114 affordable housing developments financially assisted by the San Francisco Redevelopment Agency in San Francisco.

Ratios describe a relationship between two different things. For example, the ratio of rental housing units to owned housing units within a census tract might be reported as a ratio of 260: 480.

Proportions are ratios expressed as percents. An example would be: 54 percent of the units in a census tract are rental units.

Summary statistics provide measures that summarize data. For example, instead of reporting the ages of five Cambodians living within a census block as 20, 23, 24, 28, and 30, reporting that the mean age of Cambodians was 25 would provide a summary statistic that would help a reader get an overview of the average age of Cambodians in the census block. Common statistics that researchers use to summarize the values of features contained within an area include the sum, mean, median, mode, range, and standard deviation.

---

house with a rank of 3 (good) is better than a house with a rank of 2 (fair), which is in turn better than a house with a rank of 1 (poor). Because the intervals may not be equal, you would not want to calculate an average rank or do other statistical procedures with the data that assumed equal intervals.

Interval-level data has equal intervals between values, but no absolute zero. Interval-level data is most commonly used in social science research to create indices and scales. The scale is relative, such as degrees Celsius or feet above sea level.

Ratio-level data is the name for numeric data that has a true zero so that dividing one number by another produces a meaningful ratio. An example of a variable measured at the ratio level is age. If you calculate an average (mean) age for a group of forty people, that has meaning. A 15-year-old is half as old as a 30-year-old; a 60-year-old is twice as old as a 30-year-old.

Containment

Often it is useful to know how many features are contained within one or more other features. How many affordable housing units are there within San Francisco's Mission District neighborhood? How many San Francisco garter snakes are there in eastern Contra Costa County?

You often want to know what is within an area in order to understand what is occurring there. You may also want to compare one area to another area. In which neighborhood, for example are there more or less affordable housing units, foreign-born residents, red-legged frogs, or fire stations? Knowing this kind of containment information can help government agencies target services. If you are identifying assets you might want to analyze things like the number of community-based organizations located within San Francisco's Mission District neighborhood.

While often you want to know what is within a single contiguous area—how many neighborhood health clinics there are in East Oakland—you may want to find out what is within several areas grouped as one (15 census tracts which approximate San Francisco's Mission District) or multiple areas that are not contiguous, like all of San Francisco's widely scattered parks. GIS allows you analyze containment in ways that would be very tedious without a computer.

Spatial patterns

Just looking at a map may show patterns in the way features are arrayed in geographical space. Sometimes patterns are clear; sometimes they are not. Everyday English has words to describe some patterns; others require a longer explanation in words or specialized summary statistical measures that are beyond the scope of this book (Mitchell 2005). Clustering, dispersal, randomness, and regularity are patterns that occur frequently in urban spatial analysis. Social science and public policy researchers also frequently analyze density.

Clustering

One spatial pattern is clustering, in which features are grouped together in one or more areas and appear less often or not at all in others.

Map 3.8a shows world cities with populations of 40,000 or more in 1850. You can see that at that time many of the largest cities in the world were clustered in Europe. There were also clusters in India and Asia.

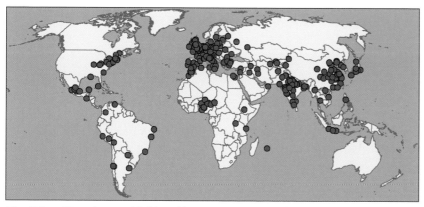

Map 3.8a   Clustering: world cities with 40,000 or more residents, 1850.
Source: Tertius Chandler and Gerald Fox, *3000 Years of Urban Growth*

Dispersal

A look at a map may reveal that features are dispersed, rather than clustered. Map 3.8b shows part of the area in map 3.8a. It shows that in 1850 cities with populations of 40,000 or more people in Asia were quite widely dispersed. The larger the scale (the closer to life size) the more dispersed features will appear: an example of a recurring issue geographers refer to as the modifiable area unit problem. You will learn more about the modifiable area unit problem in chapter 10.

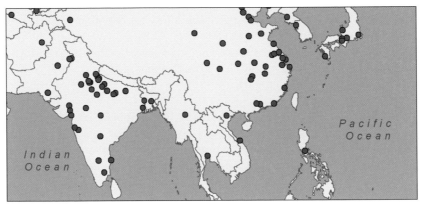

Map 3.8b   Dispersal: Asian cities with 40,000 or more residents, 1850.

Source: Tertius Chandler and Gerald Fox, *3000 Years of Urban Growth.*

Other patterns

Sometimes spatial patterns are regular. For example, many cities are laid out as grids with land parcels of identical dimensions. The distribution of spatial features may appear to be random, as in map 3.8c, which shows the location of cities in North and South America with 40,000 or more residents in 1850.

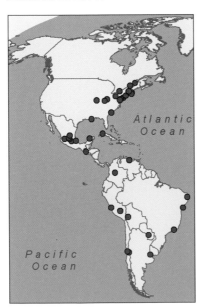

Map 3.8c   Apparently random pattern: cities in North and South America with 40,000 or more residents, 1850.

Source: ESRI Data and Maps 2003

Sometimes spatial patterns are neither clustered nor dispersed, but follow some other logic. For example, map 3.8d shows the location of cities in Contra Costa County, California. The cities are neither clustered nor dispersed, but they do show a regular pattern. They follow major highways.

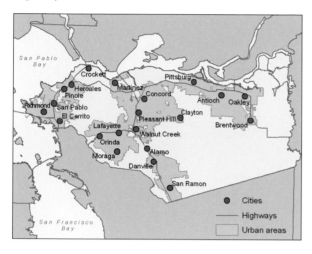

Map 3.8d Cities in Contra Costa County (ordered pattern following highways).
Source: 2000 U.S. Census of Housing and Population

Density

Density is an important concept in GIS analysis. Density measures how many features there are in proportion to an area. How many liquor stores are there per square mile? How many unwed mothers? Homeless heroin addicts? Potential commuters? In exercise 2, you will learn how to represent density with a color ramp in which darker colors represent more features in an area than light colors. Another way to represent density is with a dot density map.

A dot density map dot approximates density in two ways: (a) one dot represents some number of the features symbolized, not necessarily the actual number, and (b) the dot represents the approximate location of the feature symbolized. In map 3.9, for example, one dot represents one hundred African-American residents in the San Francisco Bay Area. The dots have been assigned randomly within census tracts. Because the map is intended to show the approximate location of African-Americans within the entire Bay Area, and the census tracts boundaries are not important to the map purpose, they have been dissolved. Don't confuse dots on a dot density map with point features in vector GIS. You can see from map 3.9 that one dot does not mean there is one variable represented exactly where the dot is located, as is the case with point features. You will learn more about dot density maps and how to create them in exercise 5.

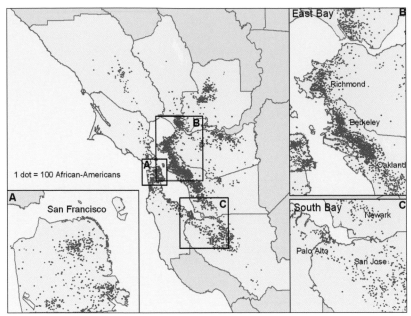

Map 3.9 Dot density map of San Francisco African-American population, 2000.
Source: 2000 U.S. Census of Population and Housing

Change

Features may change location and may change their attributes over time. Sometimes features change both their location and attributes at the same time. GIS can help identify and represent change. Sometimes features just move from one location to another. For example, several years ago Bank of America closed its corporate headquarters office in San Francisco and moved its headquarters to Charlotte, North Carolina. Sometimes things change in magnitude over time. California gained more than four million people between the 1990 and 2000 censuses.

Representing change in location over time on a map or maps is an art. It requires sensitivity to symbology. It may be possible to represent location change on a single map. In the case of the Bank of America headquarters, for example, simply labeling two points—"Bank of America old location" and "Bank of America new location," perhaps with an arrow showing the direction of the move, would do very nicely. A map to accompany historian Frederick Jackson Turner's thesis about the role of the frontier in American history could show the location of the American frontier at each decennial census moving gradually westward and then no longer discernible after 1890. Properly symbolized and labeled, a map like that would be a good addition to historical research.

Changes over time can be mapped in various ways. Sometimes they are mapped on a single map. A good example is the course of a hurricane moving from the Gulf of Mexico up along the East Coast of the United States. The eye of a hurricane could be mapped every hour and arrows or map annotations could make clear the location and other attributes of the hurricane such as wind velocity at different times and locations.

Learning to make great maps involves being aware of all these things that maps can show and putting the pieces together. Mapmaking is a creative process that involves having good ideas of important things to map, combined with aesthetic and technical skills to make the maps. One of the best ways to learn about how to make great maps is to look at examples.

A gallery of great maps

One good source is the series of *ESRI Map Books* (nineteen volumes at the time of this writing). Many GIS organizations post map galleries on the Web, so a Web search using the term "map gallery" will turn up examples of good maps—or at least maps the people who created them thought were good.

One way of defining a great map is based on the brilliance of the insight that underlies the map and the impact the map had, whether or not the map was cartographically excellent. Two famous great maps were produced by two very different nineteenth century Englishmen: William Smith and John Snow. Both maps had profound practical impacts: Smith's geological map of England and Wales (1820) defined that area's geology and literally fueled the industrial revolution by helping locate coal deposits (Winchester 2002). John Snow's map of cholera deaths in central London saved lives during an epidemic (Tufte 2001). More importantly, these seminal maps advanced two whole areas of enduring importance in spatial analysis: geological and epidemiological mapping.

Another way of defining a great map is based on the quality of the symbology underlying the map and the story the map tells. The third map in our gallery is the strikingly effective map of London's subway system produced by Harry Beck in 1933. The fourth map in our gallery of great maps, produced by Charles Joseph Minard in 1861, illustrates the fate of Napoleon's army in the catastrophic Russian campaign of 1812–1813. It is notable for the sophistication of the symbology and the compelling story it tells.

The fifth map in our gallery is the Greenbelt Alliance's "Region at Risk" map of threatened open space in the San Francisco Bay Area. It is notable both for its cartographic excellence and its polemical value as an advocacy tool.

The sixth and final map in our gallery qualifies as a great map on multiple counts. It summarizes the results of a five-year visioning process in the Portland, Oregon, region that produced a fifty-year plan for development of the region called the 2040 Growth Concept plan. Substantively, this is an important map that is shaping the Portland region and stands as a model for other regional planning efforts. It is cartographically excellent and shows what GIS can do. In chapter 12 you will learn more about how Metro, the Portland region's planning council, uses GIS to do regional planning.

Map 3.10   William Smith's geological map of England and Wales (1820).

William Smith was a humble Englishman who pursued a remarkable insight with superhuman dedication. Smith lived at the time that Charles Darwin theorized that plant and animal species and the earth itself had evolved over many millennia rather than being divinely created in a single week.

Descending to the bottom of a local coal mine, Smith noticed that the character of the rocks changed as one went down the mine shaft through different rock strata and so did the type of fossil shells embedded in the rocks. Visiting another mine in a different location he noted a similar pattern. Convinced that the earth had formed over many millennia and that mapping earth strata could help explain how the earth evolved, Smith devoted the rest of his life to producing an astonishingly accurate geological map of England and Wales *(map 3.10)*.

Smith pursued geological mapping from a fascination with understanding the world. His map attracted little interest at first. But in the nineteenth century the industrial revolution—and urbanization—was driven by coal. Coal-powered factories were a great technological breakthrough that made the rapid population increase of Manchester and other cities in the English Midlands possible. Understanding geological patterns proved the key to discovering where coal deposits were located. The dark, gray-black areas on his map are coal districts. Other colors represent shale, clay, and different types of limestone, among other types of geological deposits. People used Smith's map and his method—empirical study of geology—to locate the coal deposits. His map became "the map that changed the world" (Winchester 2002).

Map 3.11   A redrawing of John Snow's map of cholera in central London (1854).

Source: Edward Tufte, *The Visual Display of Quantitative Information*

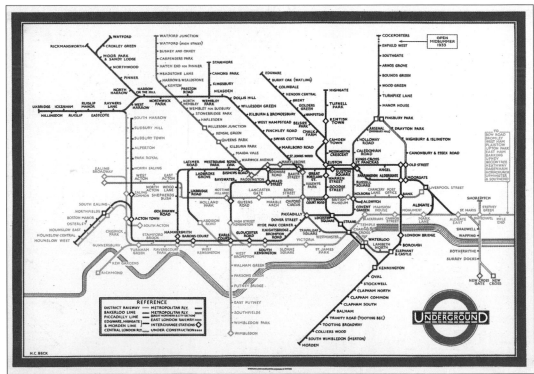

Map 3.12   The original London tube map created by Harry Beck (1933).

Source: London's Transport Museum

Unlike other doctors of the time who incorrectly believed that cholera was spread by unhealthy humors in the air, London physician John Snow correctly hypothesized that cholera was water-borne (Tufte 2001). Snow was looking for a way to stop the terrible cholera epidemic afflicting the impoverished London Broad Street neighborhood. When Snow plotted the locations where people died he notice that they were not random, but rather clustered within certain parts of the neighborhood. Few houses in this part of London had indoor drinking water at this time. Rather, people relied on public water pumps. Since he hypothesized that cholera might be waterborne, Snow mapped the location of public water pumps onto his map *(map 3.11)*.

Snow then saw that cholera deaths were disproportionately clustered near the Broad Street pump. Snow had the pump handle removed so no more water could be drawn from the pump. The cholera epidemic in the Broad Street neighborhood ended. Snow's map was not a cartographically elegant map, but it is a classic example of how exploratory spatial data analysis can generate important insights. A groundbreaking map often shows others the way to do related work. Snow's map encouraged the very important field of epidemiological mapping.

The London subway system or London Underground—lovingly known to Brits as "the tube"—is one of the most extensive and complex in the world. By the early 1930s, the network of underground trains was so complex that people had a hard time finding their way around the system. An electrical draughtsman named Harry Beck, who worked for the London Underground, produced a remarkably simple yet effective design for a map of the system. Map 3.12 is a reproduction of the original fold-out map the London Underground began distributing to riders in 1933. Beck based the map on the electrical circuit diagrams he drew for his regular job, reducing the sprawling tube network to its basic components. According to London's Transport Museum's Web site, "the result was an instantly clear and comprehensible chart that would become an essential guide to London—and a template for transport maps the world over" *(tube.tfl.gov.uk/content/history/map)*.

Beck's revolutionary design, with modifications, is still used for the London tube map today. Beck's design qualifies as a great map because of its simplicity, effectiveness, and elegance. It is a model of minimalist mapmaking. You will revisit the London tube map in greater detail in chapter 10, which discusses map symbology.

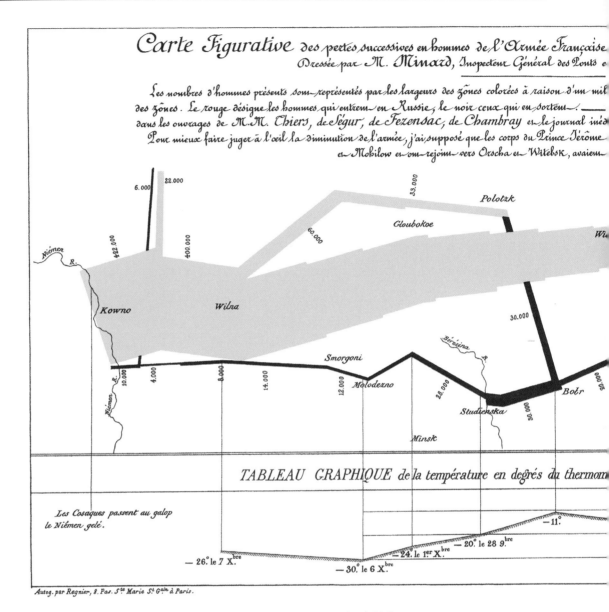

Map 3.13   Charles Joseph Minard's map of Napoleon's Russian campaign (1861).

Source: Edward Tufte, *The Visual Display of Quantitative Information*

Map 3.13, drawn by French cartographer Charles Joseph Minard in 1861, shows the fate of Napoleon's army in its catastrophic invasion of Russia in 1812. Edward Tufte, a Yale University professor emeritus and one of the most original and influential writers on data graphics, popularized this map (Tufte 2001). Map 3.13 is a fine example of adding a spatial dimension to time-series data, so that the data is moving over space as well as time. The map begins at the left with the French army massed on the Russian border near the Niemen River in June 1812. The gray line shows the army's advance into Russia. The thickness of the gray line symbolizes the number of men in the army—422,000 at the beginning of the invasion.

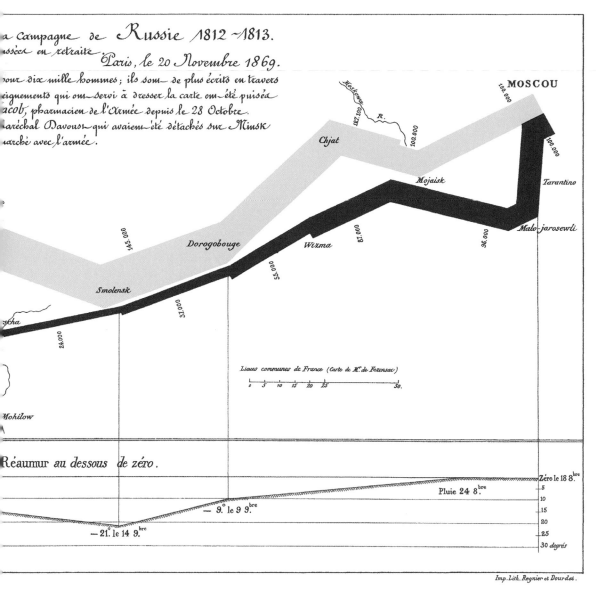

a Campagne de *Russie 1812 ~1813.*

ssée en retraite. *Paris, le 20 Novembre 1869.*

our dix mille hommes; ils son— de plus écrits en travers
eignements qui on—servi à dresser la carte on—été puisés
acob, pharmacien de l'Armée depuis le 28 Octobre.
aréchal Davoust qui avaien—'été détachés sur Minsk
arche avec l'armée.

Meskowa
1827.100.000

MOSCOU
100.000

Chjat

R.

100.000

100.000

Mojaisk

Tarantino

Malo-jarosewli

145.000

Dorogobouge

Wizma

87.000

36.000

Smolensk

55.000

37.000

cha

24.000

Lieues communes de France (Carte de M.ᶜ de Fezensac.)

0   5   10 15 20 25   50.

Mohilow

Réaumur au dessous de zéro.

Zéro le 18 8ᵇʳᵉ
5

Pluie 24 8ᵇʳᵉ
10

— 9.° le 9 9ᵇʳᵉ
15

20

— 21.° le 14 9ᵇʳᵉ
25

30 *degrés*

Imp. Lith. Regnier et Dourdet.

By September 1812, less than one quarter of the army (one hundred thousand men) reached Moscow, on the far right of the map. The Russians burned Moscow just before the French arrived and pursued a scorched earth policy. The French army turned back. The size of the army during the retreat from Moscow is symbolized in black. A temperature scale at the bottom of the map shows that the temperature was zero when the French army began their retreat from Moscow. By September 9, it was 21° below zero. On October 6, it was 30° below zero. By the end of the campaign only ten thousand soldiers—about 2 percent of the 422,000 who had set out—returned. Minard's map is notable for linking time (over the two-year period), location (of the army's march as it moved toward Moscow and back), size (of the army at different time in the campaign), and temperature to tell a compelling story.

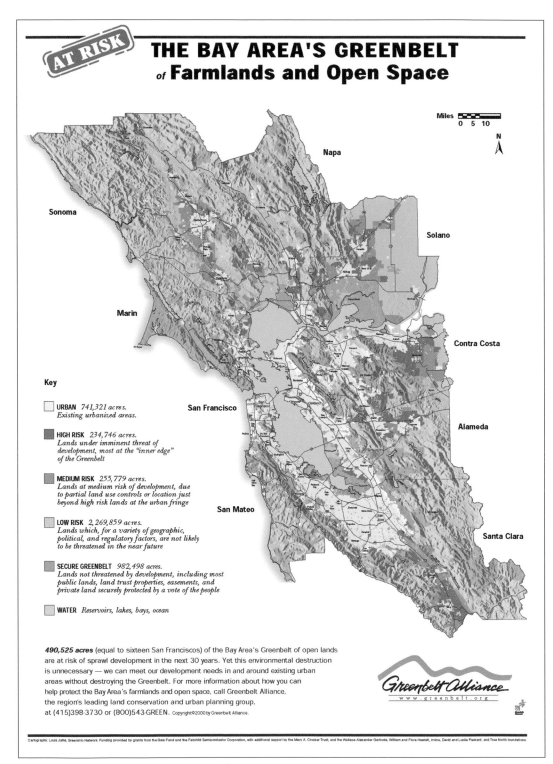

Map 3.14   Greenbelt Alliance "Region at Risk" map.

Source: Greenbelt Alliance

The Greenbelt Alliance is a remarkable environmental advocacy organization in the San Francisco Bay Area. From its origins as a tiny voluntary organization, the group has developed increasing sophistication, more members, and real political clout. The alliance is an advocacy organization and does not pretend to be neutral. It champions open space. In the political battles around development and conservation, the Greenbelt Alliance learned that maps are important vehicles to educate the public and to advance environmental causes. First on paper, then in progressively more sophisticated GIS formats, the alliance developed a map named "Region at Risk" to show what parts of the Bay Area are already urbanized, what parts are in protected open space, and—most importantly—what areas are at risk of being converted from open space to developed land *(map 3.14)*.

The alliance's "Region at Risk" map qualifies as a great map on the basis of how it is used. Variations of the map have been the centerpiece of the group's advocacy efforts for more than a decade. The map itself has become a Bay Area icon. It immediately conveys the alliance's twin messages: (a) Bay Area residents possess a unique and wonderful open space resource, and (b) Bay Area open space is threatened. Dark orange colorings draw attention to the areas the alliance considers at high risk. Today the Greenbelt Alliance makes available a Web-based GIS version of its "Region at Risk" map. Anyone can go to the Web site and see the map. Viewers can then zoom in to their region digitally to see details about land use and particularly land the Greenbelt Alliance considers to be in danger of being converted from open space use.

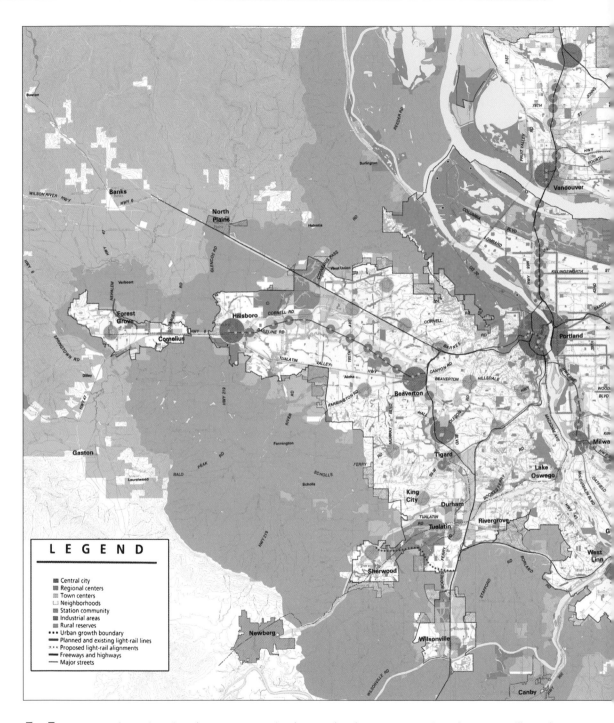

LEGEND

- Central city
- Regional centers
- Town centers
- Neighborhoods
- Station community
- Industrial areas
- Rural reserves
- Urban growth boundary
- Planned and existing light-rail lines
- Proposed light-rail alignments
- Freeways and highways
- Major streets

Metro—an elected regional government in the Portland, Oregon, region that you will read more about in chapter 12—was charged by voters in 1992 with creating a future vision for the region. After extensive GIS analysis and dozens of community meetings, Metro produced its vision. Map 3.15 summarizes thousands of hours of technical work and the collective wisdom that emerged from the public participation process.

Map 3.15 Metro's map of the Portland, Oregon, region 2040 Growth Concept (2004).

Source: Metro (Portland, Oregon)

Portland regional planners and citizens imagine a region in 2040 with compact, city-centered development, an efficient light-rail system, regional centers, abundant open space, and a clean division between the urbanized region and undeveloped land on the edge. Just as William Smith's geological map of England and Wales has been called "the map that changed the world," Portland area residents might call map 3.15 "the map that changed the region."

Querying maps

While looking carefully at a map is always important and sometimes sufficient, GIS provides important tools to answer questions about map data. Rather than counting the number of dots representing Asian households in San Francisco, California, it is much easier to ask the computer to do the counting.

It is also possible to instruct a computer to select features that meet certain conditions and then examine the attributes of the data selected in the attribute table or see the selected features on the map. Since GIS maps and attribute tables are linked, if a user selects features in an attribute table, the features will also be highlighted on the accompanying map, and vice versa.

By selecting subsets of data of particular interest, a GIS user may see patterns that are obscured by too much detail when looking at all the data in an attribute table. Queries allow users to select subsets of data for examination.

A **query** is a question posed to digital data using a query language with specified rules. The purpose of a GIS query is to extract useful information from the GIS attribute table—and often to display the results in map form.

Two different kinds of queries in GIS are attribute queries and spatial queries. Both kinds of queries use operators to find features that meet specified conditions. Three kinds of operators used in GIS software (and other computer programming languages) are arithmetic operators (+ - / and *), logical operators (= < > and <>), and Boolean operators (AND, OR, NOT). Combining operators and doing successive queries can produce very precise selections. Box 3.2 provides a quick look at the three kinds of operators for GIS queries.

Box 3.2   Operators for GIS queries

Arithmetic operators	Logical operators	Boolean operators
Addition +	Equals =	AND
Subtraction -	Greater than >	OR
Division /	Less than <	NOT
Multiplication *	Not equal to <>	

Attribute queries

An attribute query uses information in the attribute table to find features. Figure 3.1 is an attribute table with data about the population of the fifteen largest cities in the world at four historical times: 1800, 1850, 1900, and 1950. A striking feature of figure 3.1 is how rapidly the populations of all these cities have grown.

If you wanted to select from the 1900 population data in this table only cities with populations over 2,000,000 in 1900, you could use a logical operator to form a query in the following form:

Display for pop_1900 > 2,000,000

You might be interested in finding cities that meet the logical condition above (over 2,000,000 population in 1900), but also meet some other criterion—such as population less than 1,000,000 in 1850. You can use a Boolean operator to specify additional criteria as follows:

Display for pop_1900 > 2,000,000
AND pop_1850 < 1,000,000

NAME	1950_AD	1900_AD	1850_AD	1800_AD
St. Petersburg	2700000	1439000	5020000	220000
Glasgow	1320000	1015000	346000	85000
Belfast	0	0	99000	0
Leeds	575000	436000	184000	52000
Hamburg	1580000	895000	193000	130000
Manchester	2382000	1435000	404000	81000
Sheffield	730000	403000	141000	45000
Dublin	595000	382000	263000	165000
Berlin	3707000	2707000	446000	172000
Birmingham	2196000	1248000	294000	72000
Amsterdam	859000	510000	225000	201000
Warsaw	803000	724000	1630000	0
Rotterdam	803000	368000	111000	58000
London	8860000	6480000	2320000	861000
Leipzig	645000	532000	63000	32000

Record: 14 ◄   1 ► ►1   Show: All Selected   Records [0 out of 351

Figure 3.1 Historical city populations attribute table.
Source: Tertius Chandler and Gerald Fox, *3000 Years of Urban Growth*
(1800 and 1850); Tertius Chandler, *Four Thousand Years of Urban Growth*
(1900 and 1950)

By combining several Boolean operators you could pick out only geographic features that meet multiple criteria. For example, you might want to find cities with more than 2,000,000 population in 1900, less than 1,000,000 population in 1850, and which are not in Asia. A Boolean query to do that could be:

Display for pop_1900 > 2,000,000
AND pop_1850 < 1,000,000
NOT continent = Asia

One way to avoid mistakes in multipart queries is to do queries step by step. GIS allows users to perform a query that selects features and then do subsequent queries to select additional subsets. After the first step in the above multistep query, a user could examine the results of the query to make sure that the cities' populations were over 2,000,000 in 1900 as requested. After the second query a user could check to make sure that the cities selected met both criteria—1900 populations were greater than 2,000,000 and their 1850 populations were less than 1,000,000. Similarly, after the last step, a user could confirm that the cities in the final subset met both population size criteria and were also not in Asia. It is good practice to check output of multiple queries after each step to make sure the output is correct.

Spatial queries

In a GIS **spatial query**, the user selects features from one or more layers that meet specified geographical conditions. For example, the user may select a feature that is completely within another feature. Another common spatial query is to instruct the GIS software to find some type of features within a specified distance of a feature. For example, a user might instruct the GIS to find all affordable housing projects assisted by the San Francisco Redevelopment Agency within one-quarter mile of Mission Street. Like attribute queries, spatial queries can use combinations of arithmetic, logical, and Boolean operators. Spatial queries may also be performed sequentially, checking results after every step. You will practice attribute and spatial queries in exercise 2.

Classifying features

While sometimes GIS users are interested in individual features, often they are interested in classes of features. Rather than seeing a map of all cities, you may want to see a map showing cities divided into classes like megacities, global cities, and all other cities. This requires classifying features. Once similar features have been grouped into classes, appropriate symbology can be used to show the classes on a map.

Individual features and feature classes

Figure 3.2 shows the attribute table for a spatial database of South American cities. You can see in the attribute table that some South American cities have huge populations (over 10,000,000 in the case of Rio de Janeiro, Argentina). Others like Belem, Brazil (population 1,200,000) are smaller.

NAME	COUNTRY	POPULATION
Caracas	Venezuela	3600000
Medellin	Colombia	2095000
Bogota	Colombia	4260000
Cali	Colombia	1400000
Quito	Ecuador	1050000
Fortaleza	Brazil	1825000
Recife	Brazil	2625000
Brasilia	Brazil	1567709
Belo Horizonte	Brazil	2950000
Rio de Janeiro	Brazil	10150000
Sao Paulo	Brazil	15175000
Santos	Brazil	1065000
Curitiba	Brazil	1700000
Porto Alegre	Brazil	2600000
Cordoba	Argentina	1070000
Rosario	Argentina	1045000
Santiago	Chile	4100000
Buenos Aires	Argentina	10750000
Belem	Brazil	1200000

Figure 3.2 Attribute table of South American cities.
Source: ESRI Data and Maps 2003

Map 3.16a shows the cities as point symbols that are the same size. You can tell where the cities are but not how large their population size is relative to other cities.

Map 3.16b shows the cities classified by population size and symbolized using graduated point symbols. Different size circles symbolize different city population sizes. You can see that Buenos Aires, Argentina (the largest, southernmost circle on the Atlantic coast), and São Paulo and Rio de Janeiro, Brazil (the two large, overlapping circles about midway on the Atlantic coast), are much larger than cities like Belem and Cali that appear as small circles. You will learn to create graduated point symbols in exercise 5.

How many classes?

Determining an appropriate number of classes and where to place break points between classes is both an art and a science. Good classification depends on the nature of the data and the purpose of the map. In a study of cities, you might group all cities into just two classes—global cities that meet criteria scholars have set for a global city, and all other cities. In another context you might want to have three, five, or seven classes of cities. Maps displaying more than seven classes become difficult for the viewer to interpret.

Where to establish class boundaries

How do you classify features? The answer to this question is a bit like the answer to "where do you stash things in your home?" It really depends on the nature of the things themselves. It probably makes sense to store all of your Christmas decorations together and a husband's clothes

Map 3.16a   Uniform point symbols, South American cities.
Source: ESRI Data and Maps 2003

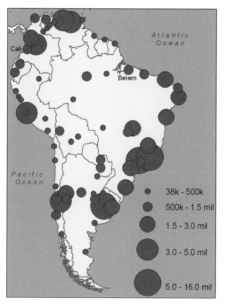

Map 3.16b   Graduated point symbols (five classes), South
American cities.
Source: ESRI Data and Maps 2003

separately from a wife's clothes. Pots and pans belong in the kitchen. But sometimes the choices
are not so clear. Should you put a ruler downstairs with the tools or upstairs in a drawer with the
scissors? In spatial analysis, GIS software tools make it easy to classify features in different ways.
It is very easy to misclassify features. There is no real substitute for thinking about how features
should be classified based on the features' characteristics.

Classification methods
There are a number of standard ways to classify geographical features. In exercises 4 and 5, you
will use the equal interval, quantile, and natural breaks (Jenks) classification methods. These and
other common methods are described below.

Map 3.17 shows California counties. Because the counties have been assigned different colors, it is easy to see where the counties are, but you can't tell which ones have large populations and which ones have small populations.

Map 3.17 California counties (unclassified).
Source: 2000 U.S. Census of Population and Housing

Urban planners need to know how the population of a geographical area such as the state of California is distributed in order to plan transportation systems, set aside land for parks, build infrastructure, plan new schools, and otherwise shape the future. Classifying California counties by population could help with a variety of urban and regional planning tasks.

On map 3.17, Modoc County at the very top right and Los Angeles County toward the bottom left look about the same size in land area. But a histogram of their population size shows that these two counties have very different populations. Histograms are the data graphic of choice to visually show the distribution of values of a single variable (there will be more about histograms in chapter 4). Figure 3.3 is a histogram showing the population of California counties. Blue lines divide the population of the fifty-eight different counties into five equal intervals.

The histogram of county populations shows that Los Angeles County has more than 9.5 million people. It is an outlier—with more than three times as many people as the next largest county (Orange County). In the smallest category of counties Modoc County has only 9,449 people, yet is classified in the same color as Yolo County with 168,000 people (nearly twenty times as many) and tiny Alpine County, which has only 1,208 people (only about one tenth as many people as Modoc County). Obviously California's population is not distributed evenly among counties. Map 3.18a, which classifies counties into equal intervals, does not reflect what the histogram shows about the population of California counties. It creates the erroneous impression that California counties in each class have about the same population for reasons described more fully below. This simple step—looking at how data values are distributed in a histogram—immediately tells you than a map classifying California counties using the equal intervals method would be misleading.

Understanding how to use four common methods for classifying spatial features in GIS correctly can help you create good maps that accurately represent the underlying data and avoid creating awful maps like map 3.18a that misrepresent the data. A good place to start is with a

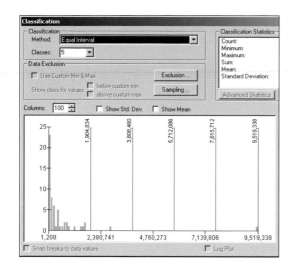

Figure 3.3 Histogram of California county populations classified in five equal intervals.

Source: 2000 U.S. Census of Housing and Population

method that is appropriate if data values are distributed evenly, but inappropriate for cases like the California county population example above where the data is not evenly distributed.

The *equal interval* method of classifying spatial data creates intervals of equal size. If you classify a group of numbers into five intervals using the equal interval method, the GIS software subtracts the smallest value from the largest value and divides the remainder by five to establish an interval size. It establishes a lower bound at the lowest value and sets five break points by adding the class size to the beginning value, then adding the class size to that value, and so on. All of the values that fall within the first interval—appear as gray columns within the class. All the values in the second class appear as gray columns in the second class, etc.

In the case of California counties, the software subtracts 1,208 (the population of tiny Alpine County) from 9,519,338 (the population of enormous Los Angeles County) and divides the remainder (9,518,130) by five, establishing an interval of 1,903,626 between the lowest and highest values in each of five classes. It sets the lower bound of the first interval at 1,208 (the population of the smallest county) and adds 1,903,626 to 1,208 to establish the boundary between the first and second interval, then adds 1,903,626 to that value to establish the boundary between the second and third interval, etc.

Figure 3.3 is a histogram of California counties classified into five classes by the equal interval method produced by ArcMap. Intervals are visually represented by the five vertical blue lines. You can see in figure 3.3 that almost all California counties have populations that fall in the first interval—between 0 and 1,904,834. In fact, fifty-five of California's fifty-eight counties fall in this first class. Only two counties (San Diego and Orange) have populations between 1,904,834 and 3,808,460 and fall within the second class. There are no counties at all in the next two classes. Los Angeles—with its huge population—is the only county in the fifth and final class.

In map 3.18a the values are visually represented just as you would expect. The fifty-five counties in the first interval are all symbolized with the same color (light orange); San Diego and Orange counties in the second interval are medium orange; no counties are symbolized as falling in the next two intervals; and Los Angeles County (dark orange) is all by itself in the interval representing counties with the highest population.

The *quantile* method of classifying spatial data divides data up so that an equal number of features falls into each quantile. Map 3.18b was created using the quantile method to classify California counties into five quantiles (fifths). It is not quite so awful as map 3.18a. It correctly suggests that California county populations vary quite a bit. But map 3.18b is still very misleading.

Looking just at map 3.18b you would think that a fifth of California counties had populations about as large as Los Angeles County, which you know from the histogram is not true.

The *natural breaks* method of classifying spatial data uses an algorithm to look at "natural" break points in the data—places that make sense given the distribution of the data—and divides the data into categories using these natural breaks. Map 3.18c was created by the natural breaks method of classification and then rounding the numbers. Map 3.18c shows a range of county populations with many counties with small populations in the north and east and a small number

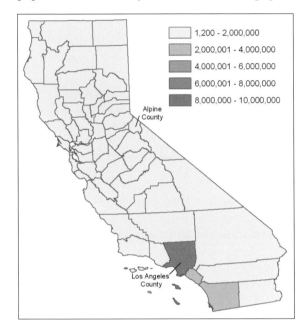

Legend:
1,200 - 2,000,000
2,000,001 - 4,000,000
4,000,001 - 6,000,000
6,000,001 - 8,000,000
8,000,000 - 10,000,000

Map 3.18a   Equal interval classification of California county populations, 2000.
Source: 2000 U.S. Census of Population and Housing

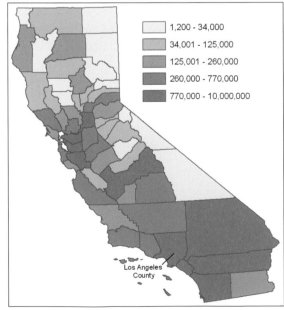

Legend:
1,200 - 34,000
34,001 - 125,000
125,001 - 260,000
260,000 - 770,000
770,000 - 10,000,000

Map 3.18b   Quantile classification of California county populations, 2000.
Source: 2000 U.S. Census of Population and Housing

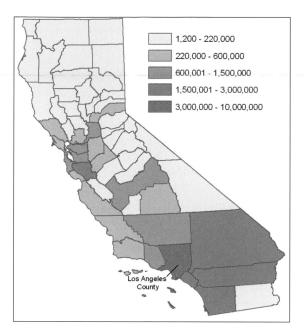

Map 3.18c Natural breaks classification of California county populations, 2000.
Source: 2000 U.S. Census of Population and Housing

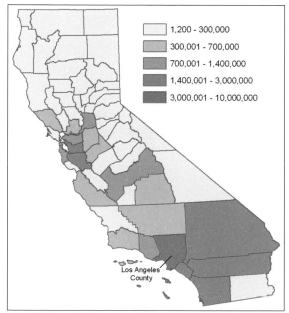

Map 3.18d Manual classification of California county populations, 2000.
Source: 2000 U.S. Census of Population and Housing

of counties with the highest populations in the south. This is a much more accurate representation of the way in which California's population is actually distributed than maps 3.18a or 3.18b.

Manual classification of spatial data allows users to create classes manually (by hand) with whatever break points they decide most accurately reflect important divisions in the data based on their examination of the data and the map purpose. A good example of using the manual classification method might be to represent census tracts where the median income was above or below the federal poverty line. None of the standard methods would be likely to divide the data right at that point, but dividing the data there manually makes sense from a policy perspective.

Classifying California counties using the natural breaks method and then manually changing the break points to place Los Angeles County in a separate class by itself is a good way to show the population of California counties. Map 3.18d does that.

Density

Density (a subject touched on in chapter 1 and earlier in this chapter) is important in urban and regional analysis. Density refers to the number of features (people, red-legged frogs, or houses) per unit of space (acre, square mile, hectare). Density is different from crowding, which refers to the number of people in a given area of living space. As the urban population grows, people must either live in denser settlement patterns or more spread out ones. In many cases, the negative effects of sprawl—loss of farmland, high infrastructure costs, long commutes, urban formlessness—are even more severe than the negative effects of density, particularly density distributed sensibly in relation to transportation nodes. Most city and regional planners feel that regions should contain a mix of densities. Central business districts and areas around transportation nodes like light-rail stops are appropriate for higher densities. Some residential areas are appropriate for quite low densities.

Density is calculated by taking the number of features and dividing it by the area in which they are located, for example: twelve housing units per one acre. You already know that a GIS can symbolize density in vector GIS with a color ramp and will do this yourself in exercise 2. You have read about dot density maps and seen examples of them already in this book. In exercises 2 and 5, you will create your own dot density maps. In chapter 6, you will learn about additional, more sophisticated, ways of representing density in raster GIS.

Vector GIS is a powerful tool for seeing the world more clearly. Exploring, querying, and classifying spatial data can illuminate conditions and suggest solutions to urban problems. Digital data has the great advantage over analog paper data in that once created, it can be used to quickly create additional maps that vary the number of layers used, scale, map projection, symbology, and other aspects. In the exercises to follow, you will learn how to zoom in and out, pan, resymbolize, and classify data to produce different maps. The data stored electronically in the attribute tables underlying GIS maps can be used in another way: to produce data graphics. You will be introduced to data graphics in the next chapter. But first, now that you have completed chapter 3, you are ready to do exercises 1 and 2, in that order. Exercise 1 will take about an hour and exercise 2 about 1 1/2 hours. After you are done with exercises 1 and 2, you will be ready to move on to chapter 4 and the material on data graphics.

Terms

ArcGIS. A leading desktop GIS software program produced by Environmental Systems Research Institute Inc. (ESRI), a private software company based in Redlands, California. ArcGIS contains a mapping component (ArcMap), a spatial data management component (ArcCatalog™), and a spatial data analysis and transformation component (ArcToolbox™). Extensions to ArcGIS permit spatial, geostatistical, network, 3D, and other types of analysis.

ArcMap. The core mapping component of ArcGIS. ArcMap is the software used to create and edit maps in ArcGIS.

attribute query. A GIS query that applies logical, arithmetic, or Boolean operators to data attributes in order to select features that meet specified conditions.

Boolean operator. Logical connections such as AND, OR, and NOT that can precisely select features that meet conditions specified by the operators. Named after the nineteenth century French mathematician George Boole who proposed them.

cartography. The subfield of geography concerned with the making and study of maps.

density. The number of people per unit of land. For example, if fifteen people live on an acre of land, the density would be fifteen people to the acre.

feature. A geographical element. In a GIS layer showing the location of affordable housing projects, each housing project would be one feature.

interval. A level of measurement with equal intervals between values but no true zero.

level of measurement. A property of an attribute based on how the attribute was measured. Levels of measurement are nominal, ordinal, interval, and ratio. Different analytic procedures are appropriate depending on the level of measurement.

nominal. A level of measurement that simply names data and does not express order or magnitude. For example, the codes representing Protestant (1), Catholic (2), Jewish (3), Muslim (4), Buddhist (5), Hindu (6), and Other (7) merely represent the names of the religions. The codes do not imply order and have no numerical significance.

ordinal. A level of measurement in which the things being measured fall into a meaningful order such as from smaller to bigger or lower to higher, but where the categories are not necessarily equal.

pan. To move to the right, left, up, or down. In GIS, panning permits the user to get the exact extent of the map desired on the computer screen.

query. A question posed to digital data. A query language can extract useful information from a GIS attribute table.

ratio. A level of measurement that is numeric and has a true zero. Ratios calculated with ratio-level data have meaning.

spatial query. A kind of query in which the user selects features from a GIS layer based on spatial attributes such as being contained within, completely containing, intersecting, or being within a specified distance of other feature(s).

zoom. To change the scale at which a map appears. In GIS it is possible to zoom in so that map features appear larger (and a smaller area is visible on the computer screen), or to zoom out so that features appear smaller (and a larger area is visible on the computer screen).

Questions for further study

1. Epidemiologists mapping the spread of the SARS (severe acute respiratory syndrome) epidemic identified clusters of SARS cases near major international airports. Does this prove that something found in airports causes SARS? Discuss why or why not.

2. Computerized mapping in the twenty-first century is essentially the same as mapping by hand in the nineteenth century. The tools are different, but the purpose is the same—to produce a map. Do you agree or disagree with this statement? Why?

3. On a map of the world all of the largest cities in colonial North America appear very close together. Would you say that they are clustered together? Discuss.

4. If you want to find all of the houses selling for less than $500,000 in a city, would you use a spatial or an attribute query? Or both?

5. Would the equal interval classification method be a good choice for classifying the populations of capital cities of countries in the world? Why or why not?

6. Light-rail systems need to have enough potential riders living close enough to transit stops to be economically viable. How could analyzing density help you plan a light-rail system? What exactly would you do?

7. The geographical boundaries of Walnut Creek, California, have expanded over time. How might you create a map or maps showing how Walnut Creek's boundaries have changed? What are alternative ways to show the change?

8. The histogram below shows the population of municipalities in Camden County, New Jersey. Would the quantile method be a good way to classify this data? Why or why not?

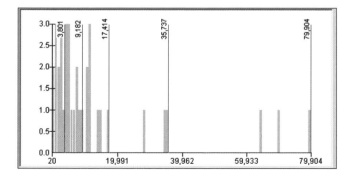

Annotated bibliography

GIS analysis is treated in chapter 13 "Geographic query and analysis: From data to information" and chapter 14 "Advanced spatial analysis" in Paul A. Longley, Michael F. Goodchild, David J. Maguire, and David W. Rhind's, *Geographic Information Systems and Science,* second edition (Longley et al. 2005).

Four chapters in Michael N. DeMers's *Fundamentals of Geographic Information Systems,* third edition (DeMers 2004) deal with topics covered in this chapter: chapter 7 "Elementary spatial analysis," chapter 8 "Measurement," chapter 9 "Classification," and chapter 11 "Spatial arrangement."

Four other GIS texts discuss GIS analysis: Keith C. Clarke's *Getting Started with Geographic Information Systems,* fourth edition (Clarke 2003), chapter 6, sections 6.6 "Spatial analysis" and 6.7 "GIS and spatial analysis"; Ian Heywood, Sarah Cornelius, and Steve Carver's *An Introduction to Geographical Information Systems* (Heywood, Cornelius, and Carver 2002), chapter 6 "Data analysis"; Paul Bolstad's *GIS Fundamentals* (Bolstad 2002), chapter 9 "Basic spatial analysis" and chapter 12 "Spatial models and modeling"; and Tor Bernhardsen's *Geographic Information Systems: An Introduction,* third edition (Bernhardsen 2002), chapter 14 "Basic spatial analysis" and chapter 15 "Advanced analysis."

Andy Mitchell's *The ESRI Guide to GIS Analysis, Volume I: Geographic Patterns and Relationships* (Mitchell 1999) is a readable, well-illustrated, and thoughtful introduction to GIS analysis.

Five chapters in Tim Ormsby, Eileen Napoleon, Robert Burke, Carolyn Groessl, and Laura Feaster's *Getting to Know ArcGIS Desktop,* second edition (Ormsby et al. 2004) describe ArcGIS analysis operations and include some narrative on analysis: chapter 3 "Exploring ArcMap," chapter 6 "Classifying features and rasters," chapter 8 "Querying data," chapter 10 "Selecting features by location," and chapter 12 "Analyzing spatial data."

Chapter 4

Visual images
and data graphics

"*Vision is the art of seeing things invisible.*"

Jonathan Swift (1711)

Introduction

Good visualization is a mixture of art and science. This book emphasizes graphical minimalism—a careful use of only the visual elements needed to convey information. Visual images and **data graphics**—visual representations of quantitative information about phenomena—help people see the world more clearly in much the same way that maps help people see spatial aspects of phenomena. Like the impact of GIS on maps, digital technologies for creating data graphics, taking and manipulating photographs, and creating line drawings are transforming the way in which researchers can see the world. These new technologies are also creating opportunities for much more effective communication of research findings.

This chapter discusses ways in which data graphics and digital visual images can be created and used to supplement other forms of communication such as oral briefings, written reports, and maps. The chapter discusses effective use of visual images and introduces data graphics commonly used to represent values of a single variable. Chapter 8 extends the discussion of data graphics to explore multivariate data graphics that show relationships among variables. Chapter 11 discusses theories of perception and principles of communicating information visually that extend the material in this chapter and chapter 8.

Visual images

Visual images—photographs and line drawings—can often convey information more effectively than words. We are in the midst of a revolution in the way in which visual images can be created, acquired, edited, and presented.

The Shakers were right (mostly)

In the early nineteenth century, a religious sect named the Shakers formed communities in the eastern United States. Like some Amish and Mennonite sects today, the Shakers rejected superfluous, unnecessary display and ostentation in material things. They valued spiritual over material goods and cultivated simple living. A strong aesthetic, grounded in their religious beliefs, eliminated unnecessary elements from everything the Shakers made. This produced a distinct style in Shaker furniture that is much admired today. Shaker furniture is minimalist and functional. Every part of a Shaker chair, cabinet, or bed serves a purpose; everything unnecessary is stripped away. Figure 4.1 is a photograph of Shaker chairs.

The Shakers had it almost right. Unfortunately, among the things of this world the Shakers believed to be unnecessary was sex! As a result, the Shaker communities died out.

What does a Shaker chair have to do with data visualization? The Shaker aesthetic is a fine example of focusing only on necessary things and consciously striving to eliminate the superfluous. Keep the image of a Shaker chair in your mind as you craft prose or prepare a map or data graphic. Strive to achieve the Shakers' spare, crisp, functional, minimalist style that strips away everything unnecessary. This will make it much easier for the people you are communicating with to understand information you are conveying.

In chapter 11, you will learn more about the theory and practice of data graphics. Chapter 11 describes theories of perception and principles of data graphics developed by Jacques Bertin, the French semiologist you encountered in chapter 2, and Edward Tufte, who was introduced briefly in chapter 3. In addition to providing examples of good and bad graphic practice, both Bertin and Tufte advance explanations of how people visually process representations of quantitative information and propose theories of how to communicate information effectively with visual images. Both Bertin and Tufte emphasize the importance of including only necessary elements in data graphics and stripping away superfluous material. If you keep the image of the Shaker chair in mind, the essential insight of both Bertin and Tufte will be familiar to you.

Figure 4.1 Shaker chairs: the epitome of minimalism.
Source: Shaker Museum and Library

The digital image revolution

As recently as 1995, digital cameras were rare and expensive. Even the best of them created images with mediocre resolution. There were few stores that could develop conventional film as digital images. Illustration software to create line drawings and other illustrations was expensive and hard to use. Almost no photographs and line art were on the World Wide Web, and search engines were not equipped to help people find images.

The digital revolution has changed all that. Almost every corner drugstore can develop digital images from any camera (including disposable point-and-shoot cameras) at the same cost as developing ordinary film. Millions of photographs and other visual images are on the Web and can be easily found through search engines like Google® and Yahoo!® Inexpensive, high-quality, flat-bed scanners can scan any image into high-resolution digital form as easily as photocopying a sheet of paper. Each year the quality of digital cameras improves as the prices of digital cameras decline.

Today anyone—including impoverished students with limited artistic or technical skills—can take their own digital photographs, scan images into digital format, and acquire images from the Web (with appropriate sensitivity to attribution and copyright issues).

Manipulating images is also becoming easier. Software products like Adobe® Photoshop® and a stripped down version of Photoshop named Photoshop Elements provide powerful digital tools to manipulate and enhance images.

In addition to photographs, line drawings may clarify a report. Microsoft Word and PowerPoint® contain simple drawing tools that allow users to create and manipulate shapes such as lines, circles, rectangles, polygons, and arrows; symbolize them with differing fill and line colors and line widths; move them anywhere on a page; move images in front or in back of other images; resize them; and crop (cut away) unwanted parts of an image. Simple schematic illustrations created with these drawing tools may enhance a report.

Sophisticated illustration software like Adobe Illustrator® and Macromedia® FreeHand® MX allows skilled users to draw high-quality illustrations. It requires technical skill and artistic talent to create digital illustrations.

The quality of printers is increasing rapidly, and their cost is dropping. The technology to print ever smaller pixels with ever-more colors keeps evolving rapidly. Even basic printers today print very good quality grayscale and color images satisfactory for written reports.

Digital images in the form of photographs and line drawings can be used to complement text and maps in several ways. The most straightforward involves free-standing digital images that illustrate features that appear in text or on a map. A report on open space in Contra Costa County could provide important information in the form of text, maps, data graphics, tables, and statistical output. However, an accompanying photograph showing the extraordinary beauty of open space in Contra Costa County can give a sense of what is at stake that is difficult to convey in any of these other ways. The photograph below of Contra Costa County open space by Brad Rovanpera, Walnut Creek's public affairs officer, conveys a sense of what open space in Contra Costa County is like that is difficult to capture in text or maps.

Figure 4.2 A photograph of Contra Costa County hiking trails shows open space in a way that text and maps cannot.

Source: Brad Rovanpera

Digital images can be used with GIS maps in two important ways: (a) inserting digital images into map layouts so that there is a visual representation of map features on the map itself, and (b) using digital orthophotos in a GIS.

Digital orthophotos

A **digital orthophoto** is an aerial photograph that has been rectified to remove terrain displacement; atmospheric effects; and roll, pitch, and yaw of the camera taking the photograph. Digital orthophotos can be aligned to GIS map layers so that the photographic image and digital representations of features exactly match. The digital orthophoto becomes a map layer. Digital orthophotos are commonly used as a base layer to provide context for other map layers laid over them. Sometimes they are taken at a relatively low altitude by airplanes. They may also be taken from satellites in space. For example, a digital orthophoto of an area of Portland, Oregon *(figure 4.3)* is an actual photographic image of the Willamette River, bridges, buildings, and other physical features. This is the digital orthophoto of Portland you will use in exercise 7 as a background layer with features like watersheds, bicycle paths, and point symbols representing residential building

Figure 4.3 Digital orthophoto of Portland, Oregon.

Source: Metro Data Resource Center (Portland, Oregon)

Figure 4.4 Bicycle routes superimposed over a digital orthophoto of Portland, Oregon.

Source: Metro Data Resource Center (Portland, Oregon)

permits as overlays. Figure 4.3 is at a relatively coarse resolution. Aerial photos and satellite images can be much sharper.

Figure 4.4 shows a vector GIS layer of bicycle paths superimposed over the digital orthophoto of Portland, Oregon, in figure 4.3. This combination of a digital orthophoto for context and other layers for analysis is extremely potent, not only for bicycle route planning, but for many other planning and public policy applications.

While you can zoom in and out and pan around digital orthophotos, measure them, and otherwise extract information from them, most GIS analysis tools do not work on digital orthophotos. For example, you cannot use the querying and classification commands you learned in chapter 3 on digital orthophotos because digital orthophotos are not composed of points, lines, or polygons.

Univariate data graphics

Information—aspatial or spatial—may be symbolized in data graphics. Data graphics may convey information about a single variable, two variables at once, or many variables. The simplest type of data graphic is a **univariate data graphic,** which conveys quantitative information about a single attribute of a variable. Aspects of geographic features that can vary are called variables. For example, countries have different names, so "country name" is a variable. Countries' populations, mean annual rainfall, and gross national products also differ from one country to another. All of these are variables. In GIS, each variable is stored in a separate field of an attribute table. Among GIS users, the term *field* is often used to mean *variable*. Once you understand the function of univariate data graphics and the terminology that applies to them, it is easy to delve deeper. Chapter 8 introduces bi- and multivariate data graphics. Specialized books discuss data graphing concepts (Cleveland 1994) and provide detailed guidance on how to construct them (Harris 1996).

Since data graphics are often used to accompany oral presentations, they are sometimes called presentation graphics. This difference in terminology is more than semantic: calling data graphics presentation graphics reflects the old-fashioned view that graphics should only be used to present the results of analysis rather than the more modern view pioneered by Bertin (Bertin 1967) and Tukey (Tukey 1977) that data graphics should also be used in exploratory data analysis. Data graphics should play two distinct roles in social science and public policy research: as tools during analysis itself and as devices to communicate the results of analysis.

GIS software such as ArcGIS, spreadsheet programs such as Microsoft Excel, statistical package software such as the Statistical Package for the Social Sciences (SPSS), SAS®, STATA®, and MINITAB® all include tools to create single and multiple pie, bar, column, area, and line charts, histograms, scattergrams, and other data graphics. All of these software applications can read data from GIS attribute tables either directly or with some conversion. These applications are well suited to iteratively create data graphics during exploratory data analysis. With practice and patience, working data graphics generated by these programs can be polished into presentable data graphics to communicate the results of analysis. Specialized illustration software is more costly and more complicated to use but produces superior polished final data graphics.

One strategy for creating data graphics is to use relatively unsophisticated data graphics tools built into analytic and mapping software during exploratory data analysis to create successive working data graphics, and then when you have decided on exactly which data graphics to use in a final report, you can create polished versions of them using professional illustration programs. The data graphics in this book were created that way—using Microsoft Excel to generate rough versions of data graphics based on data in the attribute tables accompanying maps in this book and Adobe Illustrator for the final data graphics.

There are many different kinds of univariate data graphics and many variations on different ones (Harris 1996). The most commonly used are pie, bar, column, and line charts, and histograms.

Pie charts

Pie charts are a common data graphic well suited to communicate percentages of a total. Each wedge of the pie chart visually represents the percentage of the total the wedge represents. The greater the percent is, the larger the wedge. Figure 4.5 is a pie chart created from U.S. Census data that shows the race and ethnicity of San Francisco residents in 2000. This pie chart communicates the essential information that San Francisco is a very diverse city. It gives viewers an immediate visual snapshot of San Francisco demographics.

Pie charts like figure 4.5 would be useful in planning for fair-share housing. They could help planners decide where to locate affordable housing to provide minority households greater opportunity to live, attend school, and work in affluent communities, which may make available to them a higher quality of life, better schools, and more plentiful and higher paying jobs. A planner or policy analyst looking at a series of pie charts showing the racial composition of all 101 Bay Area cities could quickly see where minorities are concentrated and which cities are nearly all white.

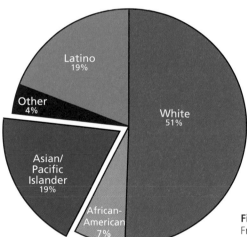

Figure 4.5 Pie chart showing race and ethnicity of San Francisco Bay Area residents, 2000.
Source: 2000 U.S. Census of Population and Housing

Pie charts—indeed all charts—should always have a title. In figure 4.5 the title "Pie chart showing race and ethnicity of San Francisco Bay Area residents, 2000" is sufficient to tell the reader what the pie chart shows independent of surrounding text. It is good practice to include a reference to the source from which the information comes. The data for this pie chart came from the 2000 U.S. Census of Population and Housing.

Particular values in a pie chart may be emphasized by exploding one or more wedges—pulling the wedge out from the rest of the pie chart. The wedge of the pie chart showing the percentage of Asians and Pacific Islanders in San Francisco in figure 4.5 has been exploded. This would be appropriate in a report on San Francisco's Asian and Pacific Islander population.

A data label is a textual explanation of a data element in a data graphic. In a pie chart, names and percentage labels may be added to the wedges for clarity. Notice that the wedges in figure 4.5 are labeled—White, African-American, Latino, Asian/Pacific Islander, and Other—and percentages have been added to them.

The pie chart wedges must be distinguishable from each other. In colored pie charts this can be done by assigning contrasting colors to the wedges. In grayscale pie charts, wedges can be assigned different shades of gray to make them distinguishable. Whether originally produced in color or grayscale, pie wedges must remain distinguishable if the charts are photocopied or reproduced in some other way.

Pie charts are best for representing variables with more than two and eight or fewer values. A pie chart showing the percentage of a variable with only two values (e.g., men and women in a census tract) is similar to a bar chart with only two bars. It conveys a very small amount of information relative to the space it takes up. Edward Tufte uses the concept of data density in evaluating the utility of a data graphic based on the following formula:

$$\text{Data density of a graphic} = \frac{\text{number of entries in a data matrix}}{\text{area of a data graphic}}$$

In Tufte's view, charts with just two values have a very low data density and usually should be avoided.

A pie chart showing the respective percentages that fall into fifteen different income categories of households within a census tract would be too cluttered. The viewer can't easily grasp the meaning of any pie chart with more than eight wedges. Effectively representing variables with more than eight values visually requires a different kind of data graphic: a bar chart or a column chart.

Bar and column charts

Bar charts use horizontal bars—running from left to right—to represent values of a variable. The human eye can grasp many bars—particularly if they are sorted in ascending or descending order. This means that bar charts are not limited to showing eight or fewer values. Charts similar to bar charts, but using vertical bars, are called column charts because the bars look like columns in a building. Single bar charts are a good type of data graphic to show differences in values of a single variable with more than eight values.

Figure 4.6 is a bar chart showing the per capita property tax capacity for selected New Jersey municipalities. It is easy to understand the data graphic even though twelve different municipalities are represented. Two municipalities of interest—Camden and Mount Laurel—are highlighted in red. You can see in figure 4.6 that Camden has much less per capita tax capacity than Mount Laurel.

Tax capacity is a measure of how much revenue a municipality can raise. Since municipalities vary greatly in size, it would be hard to get a sense of which municipalities have greater or less ability to pay for services their residents need just by looking at the absolute tax capacity of the municipality. Dividing tax capacity by the population of the municipality yields per capita tax capacity—a better measure of a jurisdiction's ability to raise revenue in relation to its population size.

Data in figure 4.6 is arrayed along two axes. The horizontal **axis** in figure 4.6 runs from left to right across the graphic and shows dollars per capita of property tax revenue available to the municipality. The horizontal axis in this and any two-dimensional data graphic is referred to as the x-axis. The vertical axis is referred to as the y-axis. In figure 4.6 the y-axis displays the names of different municipalities. The municipalities are sorted in descending order from the municipality with the highest per capita property tax revenue (Moorestown) to the municipality with the lowest (Audubon Park). The two municipalities highlighted in red—Camden and Mount Laurel—figure prominently in the discussion of equality in part III of this book.

Part III of this book is concerned with spatial equality and regional integration. In part III, you will learn more about measures of inequality, including differences in local property taxes.

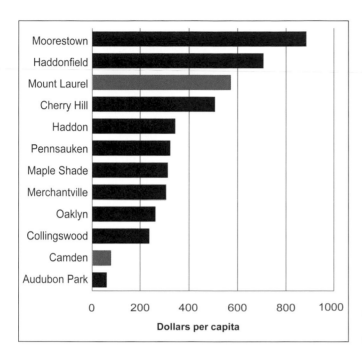

Figure 4.6 Bar chart showing tax capacity per capita: selected southern New Jersey municipalities, 2000.
Source: Ameregis

In exercise 6, you will do spatial analysis on per capita taxes in southern New Jersey. The output will be a map showing the spatial distribution of per capita taxes by municipality classified and displayed as a color ramp.

In addition to showing the values of a single variable, bar charts can also show values of two or more variables. In chapter 8, you will see how multiple bar charts can show values of multiple variables at the same time.

Histograms

Histograms are like bar charts. They show the distribution of values for a variable. You already encountered a histogram showing the population of California counties in chapter 3. Figure 4.7 is a histogram showing the population size of world cities with populations over 11,000 people in 1800. It was created using ArcGIS from Tertius Chandler and Gerald Fox's data on the population size of world cities at different times in history (Chandler and Fox 1974). You began to explore Chandler and Fox's historical city population data yourself in exercise 1 and will work more with

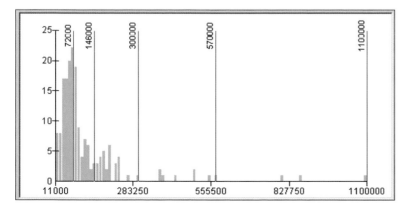

Figure 4.7 Histogram showing city population sizes in 1800 for world cities with populations of more than 11,000.

Source: Tertius Chandler and Gerald Fox, *3000 Years of Urban Growth*

this data in exercise 5. The histogram in figure 4.7 is divided into five classes using the natural breaks classification method you used in exercise 2. You can see that most of the world cities in 1800 had populations under 72,000 people. Only three cities in the world at that time had populations of more than 570,000. These three cities (Bejing, London, and Canton) fell into the largest class. Three small, gray, vertical bars on the far right of the figure represent these cities.

Line charts

Line charts connect data values horizontally from left to right to create a continuous line. Line charts are particularly useful for longitudinal studies showing change over time.

Figure 4.8 is a line chart showing the population of London, England, every fifty years beginning in 1750. You can see that the population of London grew only slightly between 1750 and 1800 and then began to rise rapidly. A **tick mark** is a small line at a right angle to the x-axis, indicating where a value lies. For example, there are tick marks indicating where the years fall along the x-axis in figure 4.8 and tick marks along the y-axis indicating population values. These tick marks help orient the viewer to the meaning of the data.

You worked with data on historic world city populations in exercise 1 and you will again in exercise 5. These exercises involve mapping city size in different parts of the world at different times in history. A line chart showing the population of a city at different times in a single visual image would nicely complement maps showing population change over time.

Line charts are a poor choice to represent fewer than four values. In that case, the values are usually best summarized in words.

Like multibar charts, multiline charts can show relationships between two or more variables over time. For example, a multiline chart could plot the populations of Paris and Rome at different time periods on the same chart with the population of London. This would show not only how the population of each city changed over time, but also allows the viewer to compare the populations of the three different cities at different times. Chapter 8 discusses multiline data graphics

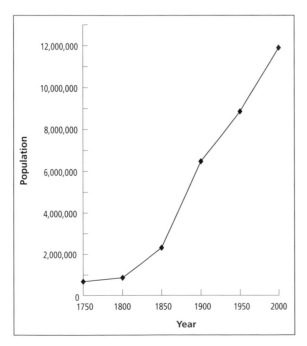

Figure 4.8 Line chart showing population size of London, England, 1750–2000.

Sources: Tertius Chandler and Gerald Fox, *3000 Years of Urban Growth* (1750, 1800, and 1850); Tertius Chandler, *Four Thousand Years of Urban Growth* (1900 and 1950); United Nations (2000)

in greater detail and contains a multiline graph of the populations of London, Paris, and Rome from 1750 to 2000.

Photographs, line drawings, and data graphics may enhance and complement map information and sometimes communicate information more effectively than text or maps. Data graphics can help researchers understand data during the course of exploratory data analysis. The digital revolution has made it much easier to create, acquire, edit, and display these kinds of images. It is possible to integrate photographs into a GIS map layout. Moreover, digital orthophotos can be used as an actual map layer.

Digital images are stored electronically in a format that is different from vector GIS points, lines, and polygons. A photograph from a digital camera is composed of thousands of tiny dots called pixels. A digital photographic image is like nineteenth-century French painter Georges Seurat's famous pointillist painting, "A Sunday Afternoon on the Island of La Grande Jatte." Seurat's work is composed entirely of small colored dots. Seen from a distance, the painting is an image of elegant Parisians in a park setting. Up close, a viewer sees only colored dots. Similarly, a digital photograph up close ceases to look like a photograph and appears simply as a collection of dots.

Raster GIS—the second main GIS model in addition to vector GIS—represents the world in a way similar to a pointillist painting. Rather than using points, lines, and polygons as in vector GIS, a raster map is composed of thousands of pixels of information. Computers manipulate rasters in fundamentally different ways than they manipulate vector graphic data.

Raster GIS is particularly useful for analyzing conflicts between the built and natural environment, which is the focus of the next part of this book. After an introduction to conflicts between the built and natural environments in chapter 5, two chapters in the next section introduce raster GIS and show how it can be used to analyze how to balance the built and natural environments. The final chapter in part II picks up the discussion of data graphics this chapter began and extends it to data graphics that show relationships between two or more variables.

Terms

axis. The horizontal or vertical orientation of a data graphic. Most data graphics have two axes—a horizontal x-axis and a vertical y-axis at a right angle to the horizontal axis. In three-dimensional data graphics, a third axis—the z-axis—represents height.

data graphic. A visual image that symbolizes data. Common data graphics include pie, bar, column, and line charts.

data label. A data label is a textual explanation of a data element in a data graphic. For example, in a pie chart showing the racial breakdown of a region, data labels such as "White," "African-American," and "Asian/Pacific Islander" might be placed on different wedges.

digital orthophoto. A digital orthophoto is an aerial photograph that has been rectified to remove terrain displacement; atmospheric effects; and roll, pitch, and yaw of the camera taking the photograph. Digital orthophotos may be used in a GIS as background for other map layers.

tick mark. A tick mark in a data graphic is a small line at a right angle to an axis indicating where a value lies. Tick marks help orient the viewer to the meaning of the data.

univariate data graphic. A data graphic that shows the value of a single variable. Pie charts are univariate data graphics because they always show values of only a single variable. Bar and column charts with only one set of bars or columns are univariate data graphics.

Questions for further study

1. How have changes in digital technology made it much cheaper and easier to acquire high-quality digital photographs in each of the following ways:

    a. taking pictures with a digital camera
    b. getting your own digital photos if you do not own a digital camera
    c. scanning digital images
    d. getting digital images from the World Wide Web

2. If you find and download digital photographs of San Francisco from the Web, what ethical and legal issues should you consider before using the images?

3. Which type of data graphic would be most appropriate to represent each of the following kinds of data:

    a. information on median house prices in the San Francisco Bay Area each year from 1970 to 2005
    b. the percentage breakdown by academic major of students in a general education class with students from many different majors
    c. the population of each of the nineteen cities in Contra Costa County

Annotated bibliography

William Cleveland's *The Elements of Graphing Data,* revised edition (Cleveland 1994) is a clear and scholarly introduction to the principles and practice of data graphing.

Robert L. Harris's book *Information Graphics: A Comprehensive Illustrated Reference* (Harris 1996) is an encyclopedic reference to data graphics. Each of the types of data graphic discussed in this book is included in *Information Graphics* along with many others. *Information Graphics* discusses and provides examples of thousands of variations on data graphics to effectively communicate information.

The Visual Display of Quantitative Information, second edition (Tufte 2001) is Edward Tufte's seminal work on the theory and practice of visually communicating information. Tufte includes examples of good and bad data graphics and articulates a minimalist approach.

John Wilder Tukey's *Exploratory Data Analysis* (Tukey 1977) is an influential book that pioneered the modern approach to using data graphics in research described in this book. Rather than seeing data graphics as just vehicles to communicate final research findings, Tukey argued that researchers should continually create new data graphics as they explored information. The data graphics could help researchers see patterns in the data. Tukey invented many of the standard ways of visually representing statistical information used today.

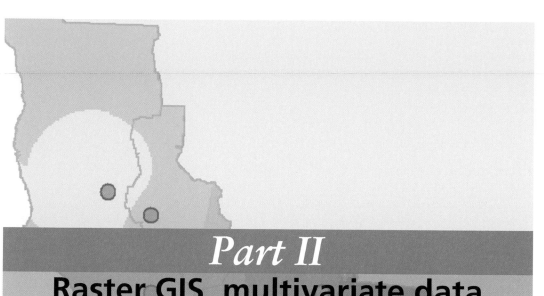

Part II
Raster GIS, multivariate data graphics, and balancing the natural and built environments

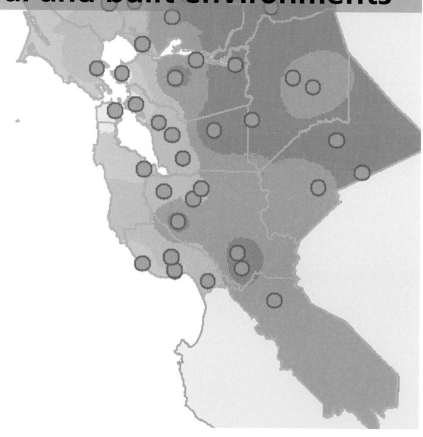

Chapter 5

Urbanization in harmony with the earth

"*The more clearly we can focus our attention on the wonders and realities of the universe about us, the less taste we shall have for destruction.*"

Rachel Carson (1962)

Introduction

Traveling through Kentucky in 1813, the great ornithologist, John James Audubon, compared the sights and sounds of a huge flock of passenger pigeons landing in the trees around him to a violent storm shaking the rigging of a ship at sea. When another flock blotted out the sun, Audubon thought he was experiencing a solar eclipse. Just over a century later, in 1914, the last passenger pigeon on earth, Martha, died in the Cincinnati Zoo.

Preserving biodiversity to save species like the passenger pigeon is an important part of protecting the environment. Part II of *Think Globally, Act Regionally* focuses on this and other issues related to urban growth: loss of prime farmland, air pollution, fire risk, and toxic releases. It explains how spatial analysis and data visualization can help social scientists and policy makers understand these conflicts and develop appropriate policy to better balance the natural and built environments.

This chapter describes the kinds of damage to the natural environment that urbanization can cause. It is a long and gloomy list. This chapter also contains much good news. It describes theoretical approaches to creating harmony between the built and natural environments and many positive things that people have done to make things better.

Chapter 6 introduces a second model of GIS—raster GIS—and many more useful concepts to help urban planners and policy makers design programs to save prime farmland, reduce air pollution, find suitable sites for habitat conservation areas and otherwise preserve the natural environment from the negative impacts of urbanization.

Chapter 7 describes GIS raster operations useful for resolving the kinds of conflicts described in this chapter. Exercises 3 and 4, to be completed after you read chapters 5, 6, and 7, will teach you how to do raster GIS analyses of human–natural environment relationships using ArcGIS.

Urbanization and the natural environment

Urbanization stresses the natural environment. A number of scholars and activists have documented the impact that poorly conceived urbanization has had (Carson 1962, Cronon 1992, Reisner 1993). Unplanned urbanization proceeding without thought for the impact on the natural environment is a destructive process everywhere on earth. A handful of prescient conservationists, like California-based naturalist John Muir, advocated stewardship of the environment in the nineteenth and early twentieth centuries. However, it was the huge global surge in concern for the environment in the 1960s that fueled most of the theory and practices we can look to today. Approaches overlap, but four main strands provide a good introduction to current thinking about how to rebalance the natural and human environments: sustainable urban development, design with nature, ecological design, and green urbanism.

Sustainable urban development

In 1983, the United Nations General Assembly established the World Commission on Environment and Development. Former Norwegian Prime Minister Gro Harlem Brundtland chaired this commission of leading citizens from twenty-one countries. The Brundtland Commission held public hearings on five continents, received ten thousand pages of testimony, sought advice from numerous experts and advisory panels, and commissioned more than seventy-five studies and reports (Wheeler 2004). The final commission report—*The Report of the World Commission on Environment and Development*—was widely distributed as a trade paperback under the name *Our Common Future* (World Commision on Environment and Development 1987). The commission defined sustainable development as "development that meets the needs of the present without jeopardizing the ability of future generations to meet their own needs" and emphasized the need for all nations to cooperate to do this. The commission argued that we are living beyond our means and must develop new consumption standards within the bounds of the ecologically possible.

The Brundtland Commission was critical of unsustainable development in both rich and poor nations. They bluntly stated that much environmental stress results from the high living standards of relatively affluent nations that use a disproportionate share of the earth's scarce resources and generate most of the world's pollution. But they also noted that some developing countries were destroying globally significant rainforests and other natural resources. While sympathetic to the pressing economic needs that poor countries face, the Brundtland Commission did not condone this shortsighted approach to development in developing countries, however impoverished. Rich or poor, developed or developing, market-oriented or centrally planned, the commission urged all nations to define economic and social goals in terms of sustainability.

While the sustainable development movement initially focused largely on agricultural and natural resource practices, urbanists inspired by the Brundtland Commission quickly developed a body of theory advocating sustainable urban development to meet the needs of present day city-dwellers without jeopardizing the needs of future generations who will live in cities (Beatley and Wheeler 2004). This is a worthy goal. Like apple pie, everyone likes the idea of sustainable urban development in principle. Translating the goal into action that affects the economic and political interests of nation states, corporations, and private individuals has proven to be a difficult task.

Recent world conferences—the Earth Summit in Rio de Janeiro in 1992 and the Habitat II conference in Istanbul, Turkey, in 1996—have further refined thinking on sustainability and sustainable urban development. In 2000, the United Nations established millennium goals calling for improvement in many areas, including sustainable urban development.

Design with nature

Design with nature, using principles developed by landscape architect Ian McHarg, is a particularly attractive approach to members of the design professions such as architects and landscape architects. McHarg's book, *Design with Nature* (McHarg 1969) established a new approach to design and a specific methodology to harmonize the built and natural environments. McHarg was a humanist, appalled by the destructive impact of industrial development on the natural beauty of his native Scotland. Trained in landscape architecture at Harvard University, McHarg became a professor of landscape architecture at the University of Pennsylvania.

McHarg argued that all human building should be preceded by careful study of the natural systems where the building will occur—soils, water, air, habitat, and species. He urged designing the built environment where the most precious resources of the natural environment were not located.

McHargian planning put ecologically critical areas off-limits to development. His analysis led naturally to the conclusion that virtually no development should occur in areas that are vital to refreshing an area's aquifer, supporting critical plant or animal communities, holding soil in place, or refreshing air basins. As more and more candidate areas for development are put off-limits for ecological reasons, a small number of buildable sites emerge as top candidates for development in a McHargian analysis. This sensible approach was revolutionary at a time when most highway engineers rammed highways from point a to point b to move traffic as fast as possible without any thought to soil, air, water, plants, animals, or anything other than highway engineering efficiency. McHarg wrote in an era when many developers constructed new sprawling subdivisions where land was cheap and building easy, and the U.S. Army Corps of Engineers was "reclaiming" (filling) wetlands without any regard to the environmental functions they served.

Ecological design

Ecological design is any form of design of the built environment that minimizes environmentally destructive impacts by integrating itself with living processes (Van der Ryn and Cowan 1996). Berkeley, California-based architect Sim Van der Ryn and Davis, California-based developer Stuart Cowan define ecological design as the effective adaptation to and integration with nature's processes.

Van der Ryn and Cowan draw an analogy between the environment and a fund of money. Today, they argue, we are using up our "natural capital" (quality soil, clean air and water, life-sustaining land and oceans, diverse varieties of plant and animal life) and imperiling our ability to reproduce succeeding generations of plants and animals. Ecological design encourages the use of only "natural interest" lumber, fish, and crops, leaving what these theorists term "natural capital" (uncut forest land, breeding stocks of fish and animals, and fertile soil) to assure that future generations will be able to harvest more "natural interest" indefinitely.

Van der Ryn and Cowan distinguish among three different strategies for the preservation of irreplaceable natural resources: conservation, regeneration, and stewardship. Conservation involves paying attention to using fewer natural resources and minimizing waste. Regeneration involves repairing and renewing the environment. Like the Brundtland Commission, Van der Ryn and Cowan believe humans should be stewards and hold the natural environment in trust for future generations.

Van der Ryn and Cowan suggest that architects think ecologically about building materials used in the construction of the built environment. Architects can avoid using materials that are in short supply or difficult to reproduce such as rare woods from slow-growing trees and instead use materials like plywood that can be produced from trees that are much more abundant and grow much faster.

Green urbanism

Green urbanism is a worldwide political movement to implement green concepts similar to design with nature and ecological design. Green political parties exist in many countries. While green politics is still a fringe political movement in most places, greens have achieved political power in some European cities and political influence in many others. Timothy Beatley, a professor of urban and environmental planning at the University of Virginia, has studied green urbanism in Europe and the lessons it holds for the United States (Beatley 2000).

European countries tax gasoline much more heavily than the United States, so fewer people own cars and those who do usually drive them less. Accordingly, there is a large enough ridership to support extensive mass public transit systems in most European cities. Unlike the United States, where bus systems are increasingly the transportation of last resort for poor people who have no cars, the Paris metro, the London tube, Italian bullet trains, and Barcelona's light-rail and bus system provide good transportation used by virtually everyone. With fewer cars and better public transportation, European cities are often more compact than American cities. There is less sprawl, a sharper division between city and countryside, and more agricultural land and open space near most European cities than in most metropolitan areas of the United States. Energetic European green policy makers are building paths to make bicycling a viable alternative, housing developments that rely on solar heating, and ingenious systems for recycling wastewater (Beatley 2000).

Theory and practice are linked. Many of the theorists writing about sustainable urban development, design with nature, ecological design, and green urbanism are also practicing architects, planners, designers, and engineers who incorporate their theories into their professional practice. In order to better understand the connection between theory and practice, it is useful to look at a concrete example. Specifics of one region also illustrate how spatial analysis and data visualization can help show the relationship between the built and natural environments and help planners and policy makers develop solutions.

Moderately messy regions

A moderately messy region with both problems and assets is a good setting for a close look at the issues described above. Locating such regions is not difficult. Almost every metropolitan region everywhere in the world qualifies.

A moderately messy region usually contains prime farmland but has lost a substantial amount of it recently and stands to lose more in the future. Incorporated cities probably cover a substantial and growing part of the region, but most of the region still consists of land that is not governed by cities (unincorporated county land in the United States). Much of the urbanized area of the region is within incorporated city boundaries, but some urbanization spills beyond the boundaries of incorporated cities. Highways make it possible to move around the region—but they are congested and people get stuck in traffic during the morning and evening commute hours and at choke points other times of the day. There are other kinds of problems—natural areas that have burned and may burn again, wetlands that have been dredged and filled, and forests that have been clear-cut. There are sites where toxic incidents occur and toxic substances are released into the air or water as the result of industrial accidents or corporate misfeasance. Toxic waste has been dumped and still not cleaned up, leaving undevelopable—perhaps dangerous—brownfield areas.

The region we are talking about still has a variety of plants and animals and some remaining habitat for them—but the mammals, birds, amphibians, and reptiles that were once there are fewer than they were and the habitat is disappearing. Some plants and animals that were once in the region have become extinct. Others are on national or state registers of threatened or endangered species and may become extinct if their habitats are not conserved and strong measures to protect them are not devised and enforced.

Welcome to Contra Costa County, California

In chapters 1 and 3, you learned a little about Contra Costa County—a county across San Francisco Bay from San Francisco. Contra Costa County qualifies as a moderately messy region, and the balance of this chapter focuses on the challenges Contra Costa County faces and how spatial analysis can help planners and policy makers understand the conflicts and devise solutions to them. Before moving into this material, some more background on Contra Costa County is in order.

In 1775, when Spanish missionaries first settled on the peninsula that is now the city and county of San Francisco, they could look east across San Francisco Bay to the lovely rolling hills of the *contra costa*—"the coast across." Until the California gold rush in 1849, only a handful of Europeans had settled on enormous ranchos on the "contra costa" side of San Francisco Bay. In 1850 California's constitutional convention mapped county boundaries and assigned them names. The constitutional convention named the county on the east of the bay Contra Costa. New cities of Oakland, Berkeley, and Alameda sprang up in Contra Costa County in the early 1850s (Scott 1985), and in 1853 a new county named Alameda County was created from the southern part of Contra Costa County and the northern part of Santa Clara County.

Contra Costa County has more regional assets, fewer regional problems, and better planning and management of the natural and built environments than many regions of the United States. There is still productive agricultural land in Contra Costa County, including the Brentwood area where the world's best peaches grow on Frog Hollow Farm. Contra Costa County has beautiful and productive grazing land, a pretty good highway system that clogs only some of the time and, in some places, attractive residential communities and economically prosperous cities. There is plenty of plant and animal life to enjoy in Contra Costa County. If you are lucky, you can still spot a red-legged frog, though this and some other animals and plants in Contra Costa County are endangered.

As a moderately messy region with problems typical of most regions—lots of examples of good things that have been done within the county and some problems that should have been avoided or need to be dealt with now—Contra Costa County is a good window into how spatial analysis and data visualization can help social scientists and public policy professionals understand and ameliorate conflicts between the built and natural environments. It is an excellent laboratory to show how regions can capitalize on their natural assets. Map 5.1 shows key features of Contra Costa County that will be discussed in greater detail in the balance of this chapter and that you will explore in exercises 3 and 4.

Contra Costa County has some problems to correct and many regional assets to preserve.

Source: Brad Rovanpera

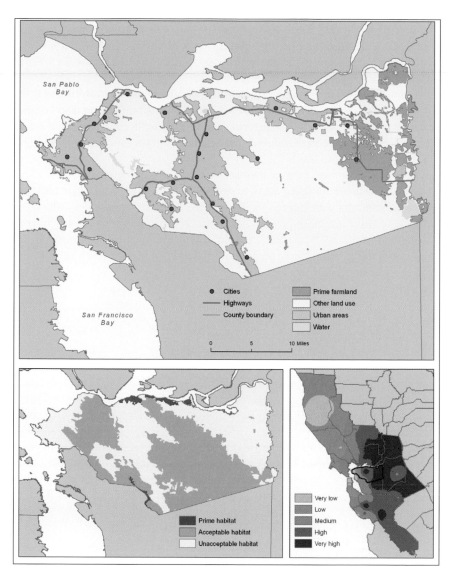

Map 5.1 Three views of Contra Costa County and environs: land use (main map); red-legged frog habitat (bottom left); regional ozone pollution (bottom right).

Sources: 2000 U.S. Census of Population and Housing (county and city boundaries); U.S. Census TIGER files (highways); California Air Resources Board (ozone); California Gap Analysis Project (red-legged frog habitat)

Urbanization and the natural environment

Urbanization impacts the natural environment in many different ways. Fortunately, social scientists, planners, and policy makers have developed a range of responses to the growth of cities. Following is a description of critical problems urbanization can cause and a discussion of responses to them.

Saving precious natural resources

Many people are concerned about the loss of natural resources. They feel that there are "limits to growth" (Meadows et al. 1972) as the earth's population grows, cities develop, and humans more aggressively exploit the earth. They fear that the development patterns of the twentieth century are unsustainable and cannot be continued far into the future without devastating impacts on the earth's ability to feed the human population and provide a minimum quality of life (World Commission on Environment and Development 1987).

The earth's resources most important to human beings are not evenly distributed around the globe. Barren deserts and frozen northern environments hold a special fascination and contain many natural resources. But most critical to human survival is land with good soil, water, and temperate climates for agriculture; good rangelands that can provide grass for ranches; and parts of the ocean particularly rich in fish and shellfish.

Farmland—particularly prime farmland—is a shrinking resource. Cities and towns are often founded on or near prime farmland. As these small farming communities grow, their need for food increases. At the same time, the development of houses, roads, offices, and stores consumes prime farmland. Increasingly, there are more people to feed and less prime farmland on which to grow crops close to population centers. That is the case with many communities in Contra Costa County that began as small farming towns built on prime farmland in the nineteenth century but today have become cities covering significant land area.

Map 5.2 shows a developing area in the eastern part of Contra Costa County. The incorporated city limits of Oakley, Antioch, and Brentwood are outlined in red with a fill consisting of red cross-hatching. Urban land is light orange and prime farmland is dark green. Other land in the area is symbolized light green and other counties are shown as gray.

While a common perception is that cities consist entirely of urban land and no unincorporated county land is urban, that is not necessarily true. Whether or not land is considered urban depends upon the actual development (or lack of it) on the land, not its legal status as part of an incorporated city or not. If you look closely at map 5.2, you will see that more than half of the land in each of these three cities is not yet classified as urban. You will also notice a number of patches of urban land in the unincorporated county land outside of the boundaries of the three cities. Patches of urban land on the fringe of the fully urbanized part of Antioch are examples of leapfrog development in which building has jumped over patches of undeveloped rural land. Most urban planners are critical of a development pattern with urban land as fragmented as the land in map 5.2. They feel that this kind of development makes it expensive and difficult to provide water, sewer, and other urban services. This kind of patchy development may result in very low average densities—too low, for example, for cost-effective public transit.

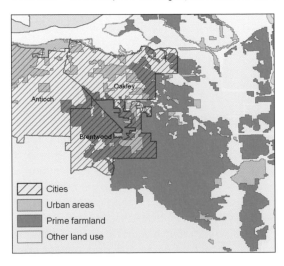

Cities
Urban areas
Prime farmland
Other land use

Map 5.2 Urbanization and prime farmland in eastern Contra Costa County, 2000.

Sources: 2000 Census of Population and Housing (city boundaries); California Department of Conservation Farmland Mapping and Monitoring Project (farmland in 1984 and 2000)

In addition to prime farmland, urbanization can destroy forestlands that provide high-quality timber, good rangeland for raising cattle, and wetlands well suited for shellfish or migratory bird flyways.

Open space near population centers isn't only useful for farming. Enough watershed land needs to remain free from development (particularly from toxic waste disposal) so that underground aquifers can be recharged to supply enough uncontaminated water for the urban population.

City dwellers value recreational open space land and deplore its loss. As population grows, more people use wilderness areas, public parks, lakes, streams, and unique regional treasures like San Francisco Bay. As the urban population becomes more affluent, more people hike, bike, canoe, hang-glide, ski, snowboard, and otherwise enjoy the natural environment.

As the urban population grows, city dwellers value land like this Contra Costa County open space.
Source: Brad Rovanpera

Wetlands have been dredged and filled to provide more land for urban and agricultural uses. Only in the last thirty years have ecologists discovered the vital role wetlands play in ecosystems: providing nutrient-rich habitats for plant and animal communities critical to the food chain. Wetlands cleanse the air, cool excessive heat, and provide other valuable functions for the quality of life in a region.

Ocean and marine resources are being depleted through over-fishing, the damming of rivers where salmon and other ocean-going fish spawn, and pollution. Some coastal areas are so polluted that fish eggs do not hatch, young fish die, or mature fish contain dangerous levels of heavy metals.

Cultural and historical resources may also be threatened by urbanization. Some development destroys natural or man-made features of historic or cultural value. Land sacred to Native Americans, and historic landmark buildings and districts are often far more valuable for their development potential than preserved as they are. Too often they are destroyed.

Maintaining clean air and water

Pollution is perhaps the most visible and one of the most important negative impacts humans have on the natural environment. Air and water pollution are huge problems in metropolitan areas everywhere in the world (Ortolano 1997).

Air pollution comes from stationary **point sources** like factories and **nonpoint sources** such as automobile emissions. At the global level, emissions of carbon dioxide (CO_2) into the atmosphere appear to be creating global warming and pose a serious planetary risk. In northeastern China, Eastern Europe, parts of the American Midwest, and elsewhere, acid rain from sulphur dioxide in the air destroys crops, damages property, and can cause serious physical and health problems in humans.

Air pollution is addressed at the state and regional levels. Large states like California have a state air resources board and regional air quality boards in the major metropolitan regions of the state. The boards collect air samples and subject them to laboratory analysis to determine the type and amount of pollution in the air on different days of the year under different conditions. Once air quality samples are collected and analyzed, the results can be modeled using GIS, and the output can be visually displayed in maps.

In the San Francisco Bay Area, about 350 staff of the Bay Area Air Quality Management District (BAAQMD) monitor and regulate air quality in a six-thousand-square-mile air basin roughly—but not exactly—coterminous with the nine-county San Francisco Bay Area region. Contra Costa County is entirely within the BAAQMD.

The BAAQMD is concerned with pollution from stationary sources like factories and mobile sources like automobiles. One of the BAAQMD's big concerns is with ozone, particularly during periods of peak pollution such as morning and evening commute hours and during heat inversions when ozone doesn't disperse. The district has twenty-two monitoring stations to measure ozone and a plan to reduce ozone.

The BAAQMD calculates population-weighted and area-weighted indices of exposure to ozone and has developed measures to reduce the amount of ozone and the risk ozone poses to humans. The BAAQMD is largely in compliance with federal and state air quality standards.

How might spatial analysis help the BAAQMD to monitor and regulate ozone emissions into the air? Map 5.3 illustrates the power of spatial analysis to help in air pollution control.

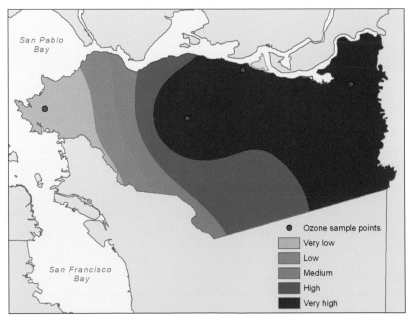

Map 5.3 Ozone pollution in Contra Costa County.
Source: California Air Resources Board

Map 5.3 is a raster GIS map that shows areas of low and high ozone concentration in Contra Costa County with colored contour lines. The map was created by classifying grid cells based on the number of parts per million of ozone in air samples measured on a specific day in 2001 extracted from the California Air Resources Board's ambient air quality databases CD. The air samples were grouped into five classes and symbolized with a color ramp ranging from yellow (very low) to dark purple (very high). Map 5.3 shows that there is more ozone pollution in the western part of Contra Costa County than the east, particularly near San Francisco Bay, where the bay winds help bring in cleaner air. This is a raster statistical surface. The surface was created by estimating the levels of ozone from measured samples. You will learn more about classifying grid cells and how GIS interpolates values from measured samples in chapter 6 and will create a statistical surface of ozone pollution yourself in exercise 3.

Water is another key resource under threat in metropolitan areas. **Watersheds** are geographic areas in which water systems are related; water in a watershed flows to its lowest part. Watersheds are important in regional water quality planning and efforts to deal with pollution.

Water pollution is caused by industrial, household, agricultural, and other waste in water systems. Sometimes this involves humans directly dumping pollutants into streams and rivers where particulates remain suspended in the water and move as the water flows. Water pollution can also involve contaminants that leech into underground water. Groundwater contamination may spread unseen through aquifers critical to maintaining safe drinking water for humans.

Federal and state clean water standards roughly parallel air quality standards. Clean water laws were passed after clean air laws and modeled on them. Regional **water quality control boards** monitor water samples and study the nature of the water pollution problem, develop plans to reduce water pollution from point and nonpoint sources, impose regulations and, where necessary, levy fines to achieve better water quality.

Dealing with toxic waste

Industrial economies are characterized by manufacturing processes that produce huge quantities of industrial waste. Beginning during the industrial revolution of the late eighteenth and early nineteenth centuries, industrial production grew rapidly—first in England, soon after in the rest of Europe and the United States, and now almost everywhere in the world. Until the last twenty-five years or so, the negative environmental impacts of different kinds of toxics were poorly understood.

Toxic waste produced at a factory must be stored or disposed of in some way. Often solid waste is stored on-site temporarily, in piles or containers. Liquid waste may be temporarily stored on-site in holding tanks or barrels. Eventually, though, most toxic waste is disposed of off-site. Depending on the nature of the toxic, it can be expensive to transport and dispose of such waste in a way that assures it will not harm the environment.

Until passage of the Comprehensive Environmental Response, Compensation, and Liability Act of 1980 (CERCLA) also referred to as the **Superfund,** companies in the United States dumped waste without making sure that the toxics were safely sealed. Because of ignorance about the negative impacts toxic waste could have and a desire to dispose of waste cheaply, airborne and liquid toxic waste was often disposed of simply by discharging it into the air or dumping it into nearby rivers, streams, lakes, or the ocean. Solid waste was often transported to dump sites or landfills and dumped without making sure that the toxics were safely sealed. Without laws clearly establishing legal liability for the harm toxic waste disposal causes, companies had little incentive to consider the health-related and other impacts toxics could cause.

In the United States, most developed countries, and increasingly in developing countries, concern for managing toxic waste has grown rapidly in the last twenty-five years. CERCLA provides billions of dollars to clean up toxic waste sites. The law regarding liability for toxics has developed rapidly. Storage and transport of toxic wastes is now carefully regulated.

To effectively regulate toxics it is necessary to know what is where. Inventorying, analyzing, and mapping toxics are important. So is identifying sources of "toxic incidents" where industries release toxic substances into the environment.

Today the **U.S. Environmental Protection Agency (EPA)** and counterpart state EPAs and similar agencies in other countries study and map toxic sites and struggle to clean them up or establish liability for the polluters to clean them up.

The federal EPA monitors toxic releases and publishes a Toxic Release Inventory (TRI) describing the location and attributes of every toxic release that qualifies as a toxic incident using its definitions. State counterparts of the federal EPA also inventory, map, and monitor contaminated sites and have their own remediation programs.

The EPA is a model for a goal many seek in government—transparency. Many public administrators argue that if private organizations and government regulatory agencies disclose information about matters of importance to the public, wrongdoers will be forced to change their ways. Potential wrongdoers—fearing the impact of disclosure—will be much more careful to avoid wrongdoing.

One of the most effective examples of using information technology to make spatial information widely available involves the EPA's information on CERCLA Superfund sites, air and water pollution, and toxic releases. Any citizen can go to the Internet, open the EPA's Enviromapper program *(maps.epa.gov/enviromapper)* and navigate to their state and then to the county, city, and even the neighborhood where they live. They can open map layers showing geographical features such as streets, schools, and churches to orient themselves. Using commands similar to the ArcMap commands you learned in exercise 1, Enviromapper users can add map layers showing CERCLA Superfund sites, sites where hazardous waste is handled, sites of toxic releases, and locations where pollutants have been discharged into the air or water. Enviromapper has tools allowing users to zoom in or out and pan to position the map. Maps can be printed out or saved in electronic format to e-mail or use in reports and presentations. Using a tool similar to ArcMap's *Identify* tool, users can click on any site of interest (maybe next door!) and see a description of the site. The geographical data in Enviromapper is linked to EPA databases with detailed data on these environmental features and events. Any citizen can follow these links and obtain detailed information about any site. Another EPA site takes Internet users to a similar Web-based GIS program for EPA's Toxic Release Inventory—TRI Explorer *(www.epa.gov/triexplorer)*. TRI Explorer permits dynamic mapping similar to Enviromapper. It allows users to zoom to their state and county and examine map layers showing the location and attributes of toxic releases and to obtain detailed data about individual toxic releases from EPA databases. Some states have similar inventories and make data accessible to the public on the Web. In exercise 5, you will work with data from New Jersey's inventory of known contaminated sites on the state's site remediation program (SRP) comprehensive site list where groundwater contamination has been identified.

Map 5.4 shows EPA Toxic Release Inventory data on the location of sites in part of Contra Costa County along the San Joaquin River where one or more toxic releases occurred in 2003. This is an area where oil refineries and heavy industry are located.

Note choices made in creating map 5.4. This is a relatively large-scale map focusing on just part of Contra Costa County where toxic incidents are most problematic. The toxic release sites are identified by red circles with black borders and are labeled with names of companies so that map viewers can see exactly who was polluting where in 2003. The names of the companies on the map are not real, but map 5.4 is based on Toxic Release Inventory categories and data on toxic releases that occurred in Contra Costa County in 2003.

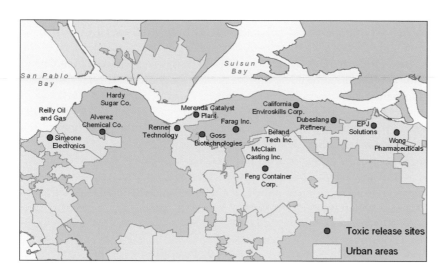

Attributes of Toxic Release Sites

FACILITY	CITY	CHEMICAL_N	UNITS	QUANTITY
FENG CONTAINER CORP.	CONCORD	LEAD COMPOUNDS	Pounds	656
SIMEONE ELECTRONICS	PINOLE	LEAD COMPOUNDS	Pounds	5.1
OREILLY OIL AND GAS	HERCULES	NITRIC ACID	Pounds	0
FAR-EAST PETROLEUM	CROCKETT	NITRATE COMPOUNDS	Pounds	296071
HARDY SUGAR CO.	HERCULES	COPPER	Pounds	30
RENNER TECHNOLOGY	MARTINEZ	SULFURIC ACID (1994 AND AFTER "ACID A	Pounds	15
MERENDA CATALYST PLANT	MARTINEZ	VANADIUM COMPOUNDS	Pounds	370
ABC DIE CASTING	MARTINEZ	ETHYLENE	Pounds	0
PACIFIC POWER	MARTINEZ	PROPYLENE	Pounds	0
BELAND TECH INC.	CONCORD	1,3-BUTADIENE	Pounds	24
MCCLAIN CASTING INC.	CONCORD	TOLUENE	Pounds	13000
CALIFORNIA ENVIROSKILS CORP.	PITTSBURG	PHENOL	Pounds	200
DUBESLANG REFINERY	PITTSBURG	N-HEXANE	Pounds	8300
EPJ SOLUTIONS	PITTSBURG	CYCLOHEXANE	Pounds	2100
WONG PHARMACEUTICALS	PITTSBURG	DIETHANOLAMINE	Pounds	850
GOSS BIOTECHNOLOGIES	ANTIOCH	PROPYLENE	Pounds	3800
FARAG INC.	RODEO	ANTHRACENE	Pounds	1
ALVEREZ CHEMICAL CO.	RICHMOND	TETRACHLOROETHYLENE	Pounds	61
ENVIRONMENTAL ANTIGEN SYSTEMS	RICHMOND	MOLYBDENUM TRIOXIDE	Pounds	1
PATSOXRULE INC.	CONCORD	CRESOL (MIXED ISOMERS)	Pounds	170

Record: 1   Show: All Selected Records (0 out of 175 Selected.)   Options ▾

Map 5.4 Toxic release incidents in Contra Costa County.

Source: Hypothetical data based on 2003 U.S. Environmental Protection Agency Toxic Release Inventory data

Information on the toxic releases in the attribute table linked to the map describes the nature of toxics released and how many pounds were released. The combination of map and attribute data helps government and environmental regulators control toxic incidents.

In addition to posing health threats to human beings, decreasing the quality of life for residents in the area, and requiring spending for regulation and cleanup, toxic incidents may also injure plant and animal species. Together with urbanization, exploitation of natural resources, and hunting, toxic incidents and toxic waste disposal contribute to a loss of biodiversity.

Preserving biodiversity

The United States has approximately two hundred thousand plant and animal species, more than 10 percent of all species known on earth (Stein, Kutner, and Adams 2000). From the redwood forests of the West Coast to the Gulf Stream waters of the south, from Alaska's arctic tundra to Florida's mangrove swamps, the varied habitats of the United States still have the most species of mammals and the richest flora of any temperate country in the world. This "precious heritage" extends over 120 degrees of longitude and 50 degrees of latitude, with 3.5 million square miles of land and 12,000 miles of coastline. That's the good news. The bad news is that no passenger pigeon is left of the flocks that Audubon described blocking out the sun and shaking trees in the

Kentucky forests. Hundreds of other plant and animal species also have vanished over the past two hundred years.

A critical concept in conservation analysis and policy is **biodiversity**—the variety of plants and animals. Preserving biodiversity has become a key goal of conservationists. Biodiversity involves diversity of species, ecological systems, and landscapes. Species diversity may be measured in terms of absolute numbers of species, the number of different species in an area, and how rapidly the variety of species varies over space. Ecological diversity refers to the higher-level organization of different species into natural communities and the interplay between these communities and the physical environment that forms ecosystems. Interactions such as those between predator and prey or pollinators and flowers are key to ecological diversity. Landscape diversity—the geography of different ecosystems across a large area and the connections among them—is critical to ecological and species diversity, which changes in response to climate, soils, elevation, and related characteristics of the landscape.

Protecting endangered and threatened plant and animal species

As species are killed off and suitable habitats destroyed, some species are threatened with extinction. The United States passed an **Endangered Species Act (ESA)** with teeth in 1973 (U.S. ESA 1973) and has periodically reauthorized and revised the ESA. The ESA seeks to protect endangered plant and animal species by identifying them, prohibiting actions that further threaten them, and developing recovery plans specifying goals and actions needed to promote recovery of the species. Numerous U.S. states and many other countries have passed legislation modeled on the United States' ESA.

In the United States, the federal law provides for plant and animal species that are in trouble to be classified as either **endangered species** or **threatened species**. The ESA defines an endangered species as "any species that is in danger of extinction throughout all or a significant portion of its range." The act defines a threatened species as "any species which is likely to become an endangered species within the foreseeable future throughout all or a significant portion of its range" (ESA 1973). Endangered species are accorded special protection and efforts are made to assure their survival. Threatened species are offered significant protection, but less than endangered species.

Two federal agencies—the U.S. Fish and Wildlife Service (USFWS) and the National Marine Fisheries Service (NMFS)—are responsible for placing land and marine species on the endangered and threatened species lists. Species may also be classified as candidate species, pending a full study and determination whether to list them or not. Several thousand species are being studied as candidates for listing at the present time.

Federal agencies must consult with the USFWS or NMFS before proceeding with federal projects that threaten listed species. These oversight agencies have the power to prevent projects they feel will jeopardize species. They may allow projects to proceed if appropriate mitigation measures are adopted.

Section 9 of the ESA prohibits **taking** endangered species. Taking is defined to include harassing, harming, pursuing, hunting, shooting, wounding, killing, trapping, capturing, or collecting. The prohibition against taking endangered species has generated the greatest controversy of any aspect of the ESA. Landowners stand to lose millions of dollars in development value if their activities are defined as harming or harassing endangered species.

An alternative approach to the essentially impossible task of locating individual endangered plants and animals is to classify habitat in a county in terms of its suitability for one or more endangered species. For example, Contra Costa County might develop a program to preserve enough habitat to assure that red-legged frogs can survive—particularly prime habitat like emergent wetlands where red-legged frogs thrive.

Analyses of endangered and threatened species often start by inventorying species and classifying them as endangered or threatened. Biological inventories seek to quantify how many members there are of different species and where. This makes it possible to "protect the last of the least and the best of the rest," as a Nature Conservancy slogan advocates. The inventory can include information on the distribution of species, population trends, vegetation structure and composition, and ecological relationships. Of course, inventorying species and determining their status is a complicated and subjective enterprise. Definitions differ and experts disagree on how to evaluate the evidence of how many and which plant and animal species are threatened. Lists of extinct species also differ. The International Conservation Monitoring Centre Web site *(www. wcmc.org.uk/species/data/index.html)* contains links to the most reputable inventories of extinct, endangered, and threatened species. One of the most thorough lists is the "red list" compiled by the Cambridge, England-based International Union for the Conservation of Nature and Natural Resources. A Web-based version of the IUCN red list is constantly updated (IUCN 2004). Of more than a million and a half plant and animal species in the world, the IUCN classified 38,046 as endangered as of December 2, 2004.

Once an inventory is as complete as the difficult nature of the task permits, it is possible to rank species and ecological communities in terms of their importance and threat levels.

California and the San Francisco Bay Area are hotspots for endangered species. There are conflicts between a huge range of species and urbanization pressures. Contra Costa County has habitat for a number of endangered species, including the California towhee, San Francisco garter snake, the California vole, and the red-legged frog. Spatial analysis of the distribution of these species and of the habitat that supports them is vital for plans and policies to protect them.

Finding all of Contra Costa County's red-legged frogs would be impossible. We joked about sending a research assistant out to inventory frogs. Instead, we convinced ourselves that since this is an academic exercise and frogs hop around anyway, that we would put some hypothetical point data in exercise 4 in plausible frog locations. Forgive us—that's one of the few instances of made-up data in this book.

Classification of species and identification of the habitat where they reside is serious business. From the point of view of environmentalists, failure to classify a species as rare or endangered when it is at the borderline places the species at risk. From the point of view of property owners, an incorrect classification that results in land-use regulations that keep landowners from using their land in ways they want can be a costly and unjustified intrusion on their property rights. Private property owners who are prevented from using their land in ways that are most profitable in order to protect endangered and threatened species are likely to carefully scrutinize the data and assumptions underlying regulation of their land. They are likely to be in an adversarial relationship with regulating agencies. Thousands of lawsuits challenging the application of environmental regulations that reduce private property owners' rights to use land as they want are filed each year. Public policy professionals need to measure species and habitats carefully and map them precisely. Their classifications are almost always controversial and subjected to scrutiny. GIS can help with this kind of a classification.

Preserving critical habitat

In exceptional cases, environmentalists identify and track all the individual remaining members of an endangered species—increasingly by tagging them with monitoring devices that can be read by a GPS receiver and mapped using GIS so that the location of every individual member of the species can be constantly monitored. Usually, though, tracking every individual member of a threatened or endangered species is too expensive and too difficult.

An alternative approach to protecting endangered and threatened species is to study **habitat** appropriate to the species. The theory behind habitat conservation is that if there is enough suitable habitat for a species, the species is likely to survive. If there is not enough suitable habitat, the species is likely to become extinct. Conserving habitat in order to conserve the species becomes a key policy concern. In 1982, the ESA was amended to permit the U.S. Fish and Wildlife Service (USFWS) to issue incidental take permits allowing development to proceed where developers and landowners have prepared satisfactory **habitat conservation plans**. There are now many examples of habitat conservation plans that have succeeded in identifying appropriate habitat for endangered species and getting enough of it set aside to reasonably ensure survival of the species (Beatley 1994). You will learn how to use raster GIS to create a proposed habitat conservation area in exercise 4.

Protecting grassland habitat from encroaching urbanization could help save endangered species such as the California vole from extinction.
Source: Brad Rovanpera

Habitat varies depending on elevation, temperature, soil, precipitation, the presence or absence of other plant and animal species, the extent of human development in the area, and other factors. Ecologists know a great deal about the kinds of habitat that must be present for species to survive. An endangered bird species like the California towhee cannot live in habitat that is at too high an elevation, too arid, or too cold. If existing habitat is too patchy it may not provide enough food for towhees to eat or cover for their nests. If predators are forced into the limited habitat available for the towhees, those natural enemies may exterminate the birds.

Gap analysis is a procedure designed to identify gaps in current efforts to preserve plant and animal species and habitat areas of the world (Scott et al. 1993). The gap analysis approach divides an area into thousands of similar-sized polygons and classifies each in terms of habitat suitability. **The U.S. Geological Survey (USGS)**—a federal agency that studies and maps geological and other phenomena throughout the United States—is conducting a national gap analysis program for all the United States. As part of the national effort, in California, a statewide habitat gap analysis project—CA-GAP—at the University of California, Santa Barbara, has classified the suitability of every part of California for different species. Maps in this chapter and some of the data in exercise 4 come from the CA-GAP program.

California voles (an endangered mouse-like creature) particularly like grasslands; can live in coastal shrub, croplands, and coastal oak woodlands; but can't survive in barren, riverine, or estuarine habitats. The CA-GAP program has divided the state of California into thousands of polygons and assigned data regarding the habitat found there and its suitability for different species to the polygons. Map 5.5 uses CA-GAP data to show the location of prime California vole habitat in Contra Costa County. A program to conserve California voles would protect enough of this habitat to give the voles a high probability of surviving.

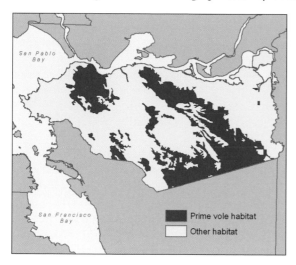

Map 5.5 Prime California vole habitat in Contra Costa County.

Source: California Gap Analysis Project

The ESA requires that critical habitat for endangered or threatened species be designated at the same time a species is officially listed as endangered or threatened. Critical habitat is defined as areas that contain "physical or biological features (I) essential to the conservation of the species, and (II) which may require special management considerations or protection" (U.S. ESA 1973).

Protecting environmentally sensitive areas is similar to protecting habitat for endangered and threatened plant and animal species. In this case, the emphasis is on protecting an environment that is particularly fragile or particularly valued regardless of whether or not that will preserve threatened or endangered species.

Preserving environmentally sensitive areas

In addition to general-purpose governments (states, counties, and cities) some specialized governmental agencies have been set up to plan and manage environmentally sensitive areas. The best example involves coastal management (Kay and Alder 1999; Beatley, Brower, and Schwab 2002). People value coastal land. Citizens like to have access to beaches and boat ramps. They want to enjoy coastal areas without seeing tacky human development. They increasingly value coastal wetlands, and the unique plant and animal communities that flourish by the ocean. Coastal states like North Carolina and California have created specialized government agencies to plan and manage coastal land (Beatley, Brower, and Schwab 2002). The San Francisco Bay Conservation and Development Commission (BCDC) has broad power to plan land use on the shore of San Francisco Bay and to regulate (prevent!) bay fill. Similar special government entities have been set up to regulate other environmentally fragile natural resources like the Florida Everglades.

Minimizing natural risks to human settlements

An important aspect of the human-natural environment relationship involves efforts to protect human settlements from the destructive forces of nature. Forest fires, earthquakes, tsunamis, floods, landslides, hurricanes, avalanches, and other natural forces can destroy property and injure or kill humans. In many cases, these dangers can be reduced or eliminated by studying the nature of the risks and planning to minimize them. Spatial analysis is critical to these studies. For example, in California the Alquist-Priola Act requires all earthquake fault lines to be mapped. Many local governments prohibit building of any kind directly on earthquake fault lines and will not allow facilities such as schools and hospitals to be located near them. Based on scientific studies of the probabilities of shaking and liquefaction, governments may require special building materials and techniques to minimize the risk of buildings collapsing. Areas at risk from landslides, avalanches, unstable soils, and related natural features can be analyzed and mapped to reduce risks to the built environment.

Historically, many towns and cities have been located in dangerous places. Some neighborhoods or individual homes within cities risk destruction because of where they are located. In particularly risky areas, local land-use regulations may require special building standards or prohibit building altogether. Special insurance requirements may be established to help insure people against catastrophic losses.

Cities near forested areas have been a source of particular concern to firefighters, citizens, and local elected officials. Forest fires can leap from forested areas into urban areas and cause enormous damage.

Maps analyzing forest cover and fuel load near cities and process models based on the type of vegetation, prevailing winds, and what is known about how forest fires spread, permit analysts to map urban forest fire risk. Based on this kind of analysis, programs to reduce fire risk can be developed such as clearing fire breaks, requiring fire-retardant building materials, and increasing the response time of firefighters in areas at greatest risk.

The California Department of Forestry and Fire Protection uses GIS in its Fire and Resource Assessment Program (FRAP) to identify areas of fire risk and monitor their conditions. One of the items in FRAP is information on the location and attributes of historic fires. A look at Contra Costa County illustrates how GIS can help public officials understand fire risk.

Map 5.6 shows the location of historic fires—areas where a single large fire has occurred—in Contra Costa County from the FRAP database. The urban areas of Contra Costa County are indicated in light orange. The location where fires have occurred in the past are indicated in dark orange.

In chapter 2, you learned that a critical aspect of GIS is that information in attribute tables is in an electronic database and can easily be summarized. It is possible to determine from the attribute table associated with map 5.6, for example, what some of the fire causes were and how many acres were burned as a result of each cause. "Unknown" is listed as the cause of most of the fires accounting for most of the burned area (eighty-five fires that burned about fifty-four thousand acres, or about 60 percent of the total burned area). Eleven fires were caused by arson and six were deliberately set to train firefighters.

Flooding is another recurring issue in conflicts between the natural and built environments. Floodplains are areas near rivers and other water sources that may flood (Bedient and Huber 2002; Hoggan 1996). Based on rainfall, hydrological, and other data, statisticians can estimate areas that will likely experience at least one flood sometime in a one-hundred-year period. National legislation requires the U.S. Federal Emergency Management Agency (FEMA) to map **one-hundred-year floodplains**. FEMA has mapped floodplains throughout the United States. FEMA deems structures built outside of the one-hundred-year floodplain safe from flooding. It is probable that

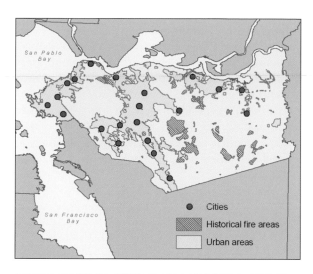

OID	CAUSE	Count_CAUSE	Sum_ACRES_CALC
0	Arson	11	6146
1	Firefighter Training	6	1723
2	Lightning	5	2432
3	Miscellaneous	7	1225
4	Railroad	4	7283
5	Unknown	85	53965

Map 5.6   Historic fire areas in Contra Costa County.

Source: California Department of Forestry and Fire Protection, Fire and Resource Assessment Program

they will never be flooded even during the worst storm of a century. FEMA considers buildings within the one-hundred-year floodplain to be at risk of flooding. Statistically it is probable that any site within a one-hundred-year floodplain will be flooded at least once every hundred years. Homeowners in one-hundred-year floodplains may be eligible for special federal flood insurance.

Spatial analysis of forest fire dangers and floodplain risks illustrate the way in which GIS can help identify areas at risk and assist public administrators implement regulatory policies to protect lives and property.

Metropolitan planning

One of the most important activities in the United States related to protection of the environment on a regional basis involves the day-to-day work of councils of government (COGs). COGs exist in almost every metropolitan area. COGs oversee regional collaboration and broker agreements among cities and counties in their region as a condition of receiving federal funding. Because COGs are voluntary associations of member governments, they cannot politically afford to upset their members very much. Accordingly, COGs tend to shy away from tough decisions. Most COGs perform valuable functions in providing information and getting local governments to talk to each other. COGs like San Diego, California's SANDAG (San Diego Association of Governments) have developed excellent GIS models of their region and use spatial analysis and data visualization extensively in their regional planning.

Transportation is fundamental to how regions develop. Transportation planning is by its very nature regional. Highways, light-rail systems, railroad lines, and airports must be planned on a regional basis. **Regional transportation planning agencies (RTPAs)** in metropolitan areas serve as conduits for federal transportation funding and oversee transportation planning on a regional basis.

Because transportation infrastructure is very costly, RTPAs usually have much more money than COGs. Some spineless RTPAs just dole out transportation money in response to local political pressures. More sophisticated and visionary RTPAs use their position and their federal money to encourage progressive planning for transit-oriented development and other programs to increase modal choice and reduce dependence on automobiles.

There are good reasons to be concerned about the impact of urbanization on the natural environment. At the same time there is a well-developed body of theory and many examples of good practice to harmonize the natural and built environments. GIS can play an important role both in understanding and dealing with the problems and implementing good theory about solutions.

You could use many of the concepts you learned in part I of this book to apply vector GIS analysis to solving environmental problems. But a second model of GIS—the raster GIS model—is more appropriate for many kinds of environmental analysis and for analyses of the relationship between the built and natural environments. Chapter 7 describes how a number of powerful raster GIS operations can help. But before you can move too deeply into how specific raster GIS operations can be used, you need some background on what raster GIS is, how it operates, and its strengths and weaknesses. Chapter 6 addresses these concerns.

Terms

biodiversity. The number of different plant and animal species in an area. Biodiversity is greatest in some undisturbed jungle areas that provide good habitat for many different mammals, birds, reptiles, amphibians, insects, and plants; it is least in some desert and frigid climates. Natural and social scientists have inventoried many species and developed measures of the habitat that can support them.

design with nature. An approach to design of the built (human) environment developed by landscape architect Ian McHarg that takes into consideration values in the natural environment. The approach is described in McHarg's classic 1969 book *Design with Nature*. Using precomputer technology, McHarg mapped layers of the natural environment onto transparent Mylar® sheets and overlaid them to identify areas of particular environmental value. Today, GIS, particularly raster GIS, and wide availability of high-quality digital environmental data, make it much easier to do McHargian analyses.

ecological design. Any form of design of the built environment that minimizes environmentally destructive impacts by integrating itself with living processes.

endangered species. As defined by the U.S. Endangered Species Act of 1973, an endangered species is "any species which is in danger of extinction throughout all or a significant portion of its range."

Endangered Species Act (ESA). In the United States, the federal Endangered Species Act of 1973 requires the U.S. Fish and Wildlife Service (USFWS) and the National Marine Fisheries Service (NMFS) to list endangered and threatened species and prohibits anyone from taking them.

gap analysis. A type of analysis designed to identify gaps in current efforts to preserve plant and animal species and habitat areas of the world. Gap analysis predicts the distribution of species based on mapped habitat variables. The gap analysis approach divides an area into thousands of similar-sized polygons and classifies each in terms of habitat suitability. The U.S. Geological Survey is conducting a national gap analysis program to apply the principles of gap analysis to all of the United States.

green urbanism. Green urbanism is a worldwide political movement to implement green concepts similar to design with nature and ecological design.

habitat. The natural environment in which a species lives, including all of the plants and animals in the area. Habitat is affected by elevation, temperature, soil, and many other variables, including the extent of human building in the area. Habitat is critical to the survival of plant and animal species.

habitat conservation plan. A plan to conserve the natural environment in which a species lives for one or more endangered species. Habitat conservation plans are developed locally and approved by the U.S. Fish and Wildlife Service. Landowners may be permitted to take endangered species under the incidental take provisions of the Endangered Species Act if they have an approved habitat conservation plan that will conserve enough habitat for the species.

nonpoint source. A source of air or water pollution coming from movable sources like automobiles or runoff of fertilizer from agricultural land into a river. All but special nonpolluting automobiles create some air pollution, but where the pollution occurs depends upon where the car is at a specific time. Thus, air pollution may be much greater along a major freeway during the morning and evening commute hours when larger numbers of cars are traveling on the highway than in other locations or on the same highway at other times when fewer cars are on the road.

one-hundred-year floodplains. Area that the U.S. Federal Emergency Management Agency (FEMA) has determined will probably flood at least once during a one-hundred-year period. FEMA has mapped all floodplains in the United States. FEMA considers buildings within one-hundred-year floodplains to be at risk of flooding.

point source. A source of air or water pollution coming from one specific location like a factory or toxic dump as opposed to nonpoint source pollution like runoff of fertilizer from many different parcels of agricultural land into a river.

regional transportation planning agency (RTPA). An agency at the metropolitan level responsible for regional transportation planning. The U.S. Department of Transportation requires RTPAs and disperses federal transportation funding to them. RTPAs in turn distribute federal transportation funds to local transportation service providers such as light-rail systems and bus companies.

Superfund. A federal fund used to clean up toxic waste sites. The Superfund was created by the Comprehensive Environmental Response, Compensation, and Liability Act of 1980. It is also referred to as CERCLA after the first letters in the name of the federal law that created the fund.

sustainable urban development. An approach to urban development that takes the long view and seeks to minimize depletion of natural resources. The World Commission on Environment and Development (The Brundtland Commission) put sustainable urban development on the world's agenda with an important 1987 report emphasizing that current development patterns could not continue for very long.

taking (endangered species). The U.S. Endangered Species Act prohibits taking endangered species. Taking is defined to include harassing, harming, pursuing, hunting, shooting, wounding, killing, trapping, capturing, or collecting the species.

threatened species. A plant or animal species that is at risk of becoming endangered.

U.S. Environmental Protection Agency (EPA). The federal agency with overall responsibility for protecting the natural environment. There are counterpart state EPAs in many states, and many other countries have their own EPAs. Among other duties, the EPA monitors releases of toxics and publishes a Toxic Release Inventory describing the location and attributes of every release of toxics that qualifies as a toxic incident using their definitions.

U.S. Geological Survey (USGS). A federal agency that studies and maps geological and other phenomena throughout the United States. Many of the agency's maps have been digitized and are widely available for public use in a form that can be analyzed using GIS.

water quality control board. A regional organization charged with monitoring and regulating water-related issues in a region. Regional water quality control boards typically sample water quality in rivers, lakes, streams, wetlands, and underground aquifers in their jurisdiction and develop plans and implement programs to clean up water pollution and prevent additional pollution in the future.

watershed. A geographic area in which water systems are related. All of the water in a watershed flows to the lowest part of the watershed. Watersheds are important in regional water quality planning and efforts to deal with water pollution.

Questions for further study

1. What are different types of natural resources that are being used up today? In your opinion, which are the most important to protect?

2. The Brundtland Commission report was critical of the failure of countries in both developing and developed countries to pursue sustainable development patterns for quite different reasons. What was the Brundtland Commission's criticism of practices in many developing countries? In the developed world?

3. Sustainable urban development, design with nature, ecological design, and green urbanism are all approaches to better balancing the natural and the built environments. Describe each approach and how it differs from the others.

4. Why do environmentalists emphasize the importance of preserving habitats appropriate for endangered and threatened species rather than just trying to save the species themselves?

5. How might you use GIS to identify land appropriate for a habitat conservation area for an endangered species?

Annotated bibliography

The destructive effects of urbanization on the natural environment are well described in Rachel Carson's 1962 classic *Silent Spring*, reprinted in 2002 (Carson 2002), William Cronon's *Nature's Metropolis: Chicago and the Great West* (Cronon 1992), and Marc Reisner's *Cadillac Desert: The American West and Its Disappearing Water* (Reisner 1993).

Sustainable urban development is described in Timothy Beatley and Stephen Wheeler's *The Sustainable Urban Development Reader* (Beatley and Wheeler 2004)—an excellent anthology of readings that contains excerpts from all the key writings on sustainable urban development. The influential report that put sustainability on the world agenda is the World Commission on Environment and Development, *Our Common Future* (World Commission on Environment and Development 1987), commonly referred to as The Brundtland Report.

Ian McHarg's *Design with Nature* (McHarg 1969) is a classic book on designing the built environment in harmony with the natural environment. Harvard professor Anne Whiston Spirn's *The Granite Garden: Urban Nature and Human Design* (Spirn 1985) describes nature in cities themselves.

Sim Van der Ryn and Stuart Cowan's *Ecological Design* (Van der Ryn and Cowan 1996) is a comprehensive statement of the ecological design philosophy.

Timothy Beatley's *Green Urbanism: Learning from European Cities* (Beatley 2000) describes both the theory of green urbanism and the practice of green urbanism in Europe.

Biodiversity and endangered species issues are well described in Bruce A. Stein, Lynn S. Kutner, and Jonathan S. Adams (eds), *Precious Heritage: The Status of Biodiversity in the United States* (Stein, Kutner, and Adams 2000). *Precious Heritage* presents factual information on the status of plant and animal species in the United States with particular emphasis on rare and endangered species. In addition to its objectivity and professional excellence, *Precious Heritage* is beautifully designed and contains excellent illustrations.

Habitat conservation planning is described in Timothy Beatley's *Habitat Conservation Planning: Endangered Species and Urban Growth* (Beatley 1994). Beatley describes the background and concepts of habitat conservation planning and case studies of habitat conservation areas.

Leonard Ortolano's textbook on environmental policy, *Environmental Regulation and Impact Assessment* (Ortolano 1997), describes the theoretical basis for, evolution of, and current approaches to controlling air and water pollution; controlling and cleaning up toxic waste; and other approaches to protecting the natural environment.

Chapter 6

Introduction to raster GIS

"The totality of our so-called knowledge or beliefs, from the most casual matters of geography and history to the profoundest laws of atomic physics or even of pure mathematics and logic, is a man-made fabric which impinges on experience only along the edges."

Willard Van Orman Quine (1951)

Introduction

In addition to the vector model of geographic space you learned about in part I, there is a second model of geographic space called the raster model. Raster GIS lends itself particularly well to studying the natural environment. This chapter describes raster GIS concepts. It is the most challenging chapter in this book. You may find yourself struggling to see how abstract concepts such as grid cell size, neighborhood analysis, and representation models can help provide solutions to urban problems. Maps in this chapter may help sustain your faith that mastering the concepts will empower you to do analyses that are extremely helpful for exactly that purpose. Three good books describing raster GIS concepts and operations provide the following: an introduction to how rasters can be symbolized and classified (Ormsby et al. 2004); an excellent overview (McCoy and Johnston 2001); and an in-depth discussion (DeMers 2001).

Raster GIS

Raster GIS represents physical reality as a matrix (grid) of cells arranged in rows and columns. Each cell contains a single pixel. Color symbology may be assigned to cells based on the values in the grid cells, just as colors may be assigned to points, lines, and polygons in vector GIS. Comparing vector and raster representations of the same area helps show the difference between the ways in which the two models represent space.

Maps 6.1a and 6.1b both show land on the urban fringe near Walnut Creek in Contra Costa County. Land uses in the area are classified by the California State Department of Conservation Farmland Mapping and Monitoring Program (FMMP). The program classifies farmland throughout California. Because the classification scheme is broad and maps 6.1a and 6.1b show only a small part of the state, there are only four kinds of areas on the map: urban land, grazing land, other land, and water. You will work with FMMP data for all of Contra Costa County in exercise 3. At that scale you will see additional land uses, including prime farmland.

Map 6.1a is a vector GIS representation of the area. The four different land uses are represented as polygons. Notice that the borders of the areas in map 6.1a are smooth. This is characteristic of vector GIS polygon representations of space.

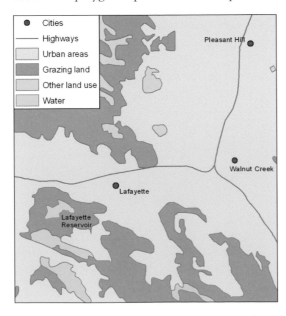

Map 6.1a   Vector image of land near Walnut Creek, California.

Source: California Department of Conservation Farmland Mapping and Monitoring Program

Map 6.1b is a raster GIS representation of the same area depicted in map 6.1a. Although you do not see numbers on the map, every grid cell where there is urban land has been coded with the value 1, grazing land with the value 2, other land uses with the value 3, and water with the value 4. You will learn more about the way in which values are assigned to grid cells later in this chapter. You will assign values to raster datasets yourself in exercises 3 and 4.

In map 6.1b, the color orange has been assigned to all cells with the value 1 (urban land), dark green to the cells with the value 2 (grazing land), light green to the cells with the value 3 (other land), and blue to cells with the value 4 (water). At this scale, you can see that map 6.1b is composed of hundreds of rectangular grid cells.

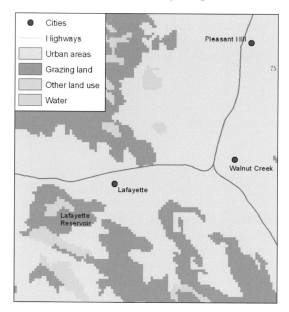

Map 6.1b Raster image of land near Walnut Creek, California.

Source: California Department of Conservation Farmland Mapping and Monitoring Program

Discrete features

A **discrete feature** in GIS has definite boundaries. For example, since the boundary of the city of Walnut Creek is legally defined and very specific, it qualifies as a discrete feature. If you stand inside the city limits of Walnut Creek, you are in Walnut Creek. If you step a foot across the border, you are not in Walnut Creek. While discrete features can be represented in raster GIS, they are usually represented with polygons in vector GIS.

Continuous features (surfaces)

A **continuous feature** in GIS does not have clear boundaries. Air temperature is a good example. If you sit in a café in downtown Walnut Creek on a pleasant June day, the air temperature measured to four decimal places where you are sitting may be 63.1257°. Across the street the air temperature will be just about the same—perhaps 63.5378°. But if you drive a mile east, it may be 70.0986°. If you climb Mount Diablo (the largest mountain in Contra Costa County), the temperature may be 40.1753°. Features like air temperature have continuous, not discrete, values. In GIS, a representation of a continuous feature is referred to as a surface or field. Some surfaces, such as elevation, are physical surfaces. There is another kind of **surface**—a statistical surface that is an abstract representation of reality. You will work with both kinds of surfaces in exercises 3 and 4.

Raster datasets

Raster data is stored in a **raster dataset**. Another name for a raster dataset is a grid. A raster dataset represents the location and characteristics of features in geographical space. Each raster dataset represents a single theme. Overlays of multiple raster datasets are necessary to represent the complexity of reality. For example, essential features of Contra Costa County might be represented by raster datasets of highways, cities, land use, and rivers.

Maps 6.2a and 6.2b and figure 6.1 are raster dataset images showing the suitability of habitat for red-legged frogs in Contra Costa County at three different scales.

Map 6.2a shows habitat suitability for the entire county. At this scale, different parts of the raster dataset appear as areas of solid color with smooth edges like vector GIS polygons. Notice the area of detail in the south central part of the county enclosed in a black square.

Map 6.2b zooms in to the area of detail. At the level of detail in map 6.2b, the image is less smooth. It is apparent that the image is composed of rectangular cells. Now notice another black square in the south central part of this map.

Figure 6.1 zooms in much further on just nine cells in the area of detail indicated in map 6.2b. Figure 6.1 is a grid with nine equal-sized rectangular cells. The cells are arranged in rows (across) and columns (down). Here the grids reveal different values: prime habitat (in red) has a cell value of 1; acceptable habitat (in green) has a cell value of 5; and unacceptable habitat (in light orange or tan) has a cell value of 10.

Cells

Raster datasets are made up of cells. A **cell** in a raster dataset is a square (in specialized raster datasets, cells are sometimes rectangles or hexagons). Each cell represents the smallest unit of area on the raster dataset map. Users may assign any cell size they want to a raster dataset, but once a cell size has been assigned, then all cells in the raster dataset have the same cell size.

For a map of the world it may be appropriate to have each cell represent one hundred square miles of the earth's surface. For a detailed map of part of the red-legged frog habitat in Contra Costa County, it might be appropriate for a cell to represent just sixteen square feet. Since a cell is a digital representation of reality, and cell size is variable, how precisely a cell actually represents a geographical feature varies too. Very small cells can more precisely depict reality than large cells.

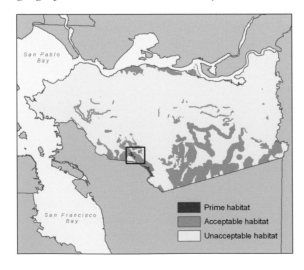

Map 6.2a   Suitability of Contra Costa County habitat for red-legged frogs.

Source: California Gap Analysis Project

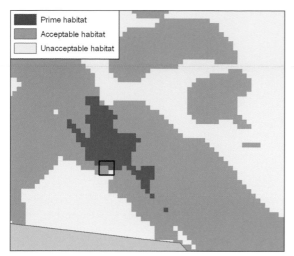

Map 6.2b Area of detail.
Source: California Gap Analysis Project

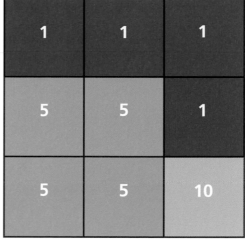

Figure 6.1 Zoomed view of nine cells in a raster
dataset grid representing area of detail in map 6.2b.
Source: California Gap Analysis Project

A cell size finer than the input resolution of a raster dataset will not produce more fine-grained data than the input data. Output rasters should be at the same or coarser resolution than the input data.

The larger the number of grid cells in a raster dataset, the more time it takes a computer to process the data. Rasters covering large areas with very small cells can take a long time to process, particularly on desktop computers.

Cells in different raster datasets do not need to be stored in the same resolution (the same size), but when processing multiple datasets together, the cell resolution must be the same. It is possible to resample rasters to change their resolution. Some modern GIS software can automatically resample rasters on the fly so the user does not have to do the resampling. In other cases, software tools allow users to resample rasters from a graphical user interface. Resampling is mathematically complex, but modern GIS tools reduce the operation of resampling to a few mouse clicks, so getting rasters to be in the same resolution in order to analyze them together is not a technical problem.

Rows and columns

Raster dataset cells are arrayed in a matrix of rows and columns. Each row runs horizontally (across); each column runs vertically (up and down). By convention, the horizontal (row) axis is called the x-axis; the vertical (column) axis the y-axis. Each cell has a unique row and column address. All locations in the extent of the raster dataset are covered by the matrix. The grid in figure 6.2 has three rows and two columns of cells with two different values.

Values

Each cell in a raster dataset is assigned a value (a number), unless data for the cell is missing. The number can represent different kinds of things. Some raster dataset cell values specify quantities with a numeric measure. For example, a cell may contain a numeric measure of elevation (500 feet above sea level) or ozone in the atmosphere (.0877 parts per million). Other raster dataset cell values represent categories the cell belongs to, based on scientific measurement or human judgment. As noted earlier, urban land might be assigned the cell value 1, prime farmland the cell value 2, and

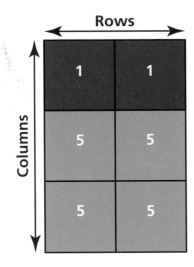

Figure 6.2 Rows and columns in a raster dataset grid.

grazing land the cell value 3. Where a value in a raster represents a category, the value is a code for the attribute, not a number representing an actual measured value.

There is usually a one-to-many relationship between cell values and the number of cells assigned to that code. For example, the value 1 representing prime farmland in Contra Costa County may have 4,382 cells in a raster dataset.

Another use of cell values involves digital images like satellite images and scanned photographs. In the case of images, raster dataset cell values may refer to precise colors that can be used to digitally construct the image.

NoData

Sometimes no data is available for a cell. In raster datasets, NoData (sometimes called *null*) values are treated differently from other values. Missing data occurs for many different reasons. At the global level, officials in the impoverished and war-torn country of Somalia may be unable to supply the United Nations with data about natural parks in Somalia, and the UN may in turn indicate in a table summarizing natural park areas by country that there is no data for Somalia.

Contra Costa County land records may have a small error involving a parcel, making it impossible for a researcher to tell if one small patch of land is in public or private ownership. The researcher would have to code that patch NoData.

NoData also occurs because of human error or malfunctioning data collection equipment. A field researcher sampling water quality every fifty feet along a stream may forget to take a sample because of a momentary distraction. A GPS receiver being used in the field to register the location of red-legged frogs may fail to record an observation because it is blocked by a hill or vegetation. Clouds may make a satellite record an incorrect value for a few pixels in a satellite image of ground cover in Contra Costa County that might have to be coded NoData.

A value of NoData can be entered for a raster dataset cell wherever data is missing or has been deliberately removed because of data errors like the ones described in the previous paragraph. A GIS can produce output where it encounters NoData cells in a mathematical operation on multiple cells in different ways: (a) it can assign all of the cells the value NoData, or (b) it can ignore the NoData cells and assign values based only on the values that do exist, or (c) it can estimate the NoData values based on the known values and use the estimates in output. It is important to understand which operation makes sense in a given context and check to see if the default operation produced the output you want or, alternatively, to instruct the GIS software to perform the desired calculation.

Zones

Cells with the same value in a raster dataset form a **zone**. A zone must contain at least two cells, but usually contains many more. The cells need not be contiguous. Map 6.3a shows Contra Costa County land classified into two zones as public (brown) and private (green). All land falls into one or the other of these two zones. Note that the cells in the public and private landownership zones in map 6.3a are not contiguous. There are many brown zones of different sizes that do not touch other brown zones. Raster GIS contains software tools to analyze zones. One part of the public land zone in map 6.3a is circled. It is a region.

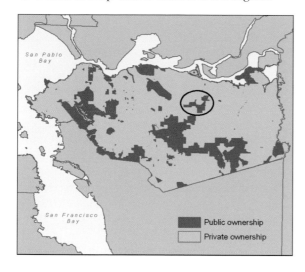

Map 6.3a   Raster dataset zones.

Source: California Resources Agency Legacy Project, Public and Conservation Lands (2003)

Regions

Contiguous cells in a zone form a **region** or patch. Map 6.3b is a close-up of the zone of contiguous cells circled in black in map 6.3a. Because the cells are contiguous, this area qualifies as a region. Raster GIS contains software tools to analyze regions.

Integer and floating-point raster datasets

There is a distinction between integer raster datasets and floating-point raster datasets. Values in an integer raster dataset are whole number integers, such as 1, 5, 27, and 345. In a floating-point raster dataset, the numbers have a decimal point and may have decimal values of varying lengths such as 1.5, 2.76, and 5.8648. Since discrete data is well represented by whole numbers, integer raster datasets are appropriate and usually used to represent discrete data, like the boundary of the city of Walnut Creek. Continuous data is usually represented by floating point raster datasets because finely differentiated values like the temperature at different places in Contra Costa County don't fit into categories.

The distinction between integer and floating-point raster datasets makes an important difference with respect to attribute tables. You learned in chapter 2 that vector GIS features (points, lines, and polygons) can be associated with attribute tables. The attribute table stores information about attributes of the features.

An integer raster dataset can have an attribute table. A raster attribute table is called a **value attribute table** or **VAT**. A floating-point raster dataset cannot have an attribute table.

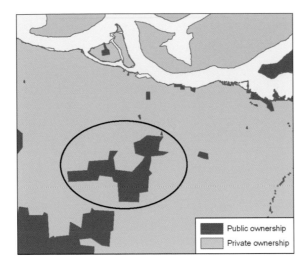

Map 6.3b   Raster dataset region.

Source: California Resources Agency Legacy Project, Public and Conservation Lands (2003)

Legend:
- Public ownership
- Private ownership

If you think about what kind of data different types of raster datasets are representing, it makes sense that integer rasters can have VATs and floating-point ones cannot. A discrete feature like a point representing the location of a red-legged frog sighting, a line representing a road, or a polygon representing a census tract can have attributes like frog size, highway number, or number of Hispanic households, respectively. A continuous feature like air temperature does not have such sharply differentiated attributes, because at every location the air temperature is slightly different: 63.1257° at the café in Walnut Creek described earlier, 63.5378° across the street, and 40.1753° on top of Mount Diablo. It does not make sense to have a table with value attributes attached to thousands of grid cells, each with slightly different air temperatures.

All raster dataset VATs have two mandatory columns of information. The first item in every VAT is named value and indicates the value assigned to each zone in the raster dataset. The second mandatory item in the VAT is named count and stores the count of the number of cells in the VAT with that value.

The third dimension

In addition to values stored in grid cells formed by horizontal (x) and vertical (y) axes, raster datasets may (but do not need to) contain z values representing height. This is easiest to understand in terms of the elevation in a physical surface, but z values may also represent quantities of something (registered voters, people with SARS, San Francisco garter snakes) present at locations represented on a statistical surface.

The most common use of z values is in a **digital elevation model (DEM)**. DEMs show elevation as well as the location of features in two-dimensional space. Map 6.4 is a digital elevation model of San Francisco. Hillshade has been symbolized to represent elevation. Note that map 6.4 also shows the negative elevation of water under San Francisco Bay and in the Pacific Ocean. This is an example of bathymetry—the scientific measurement of the depth of large bodies of water. Bathymetric maps are widely used in the natural sciences to study marine biology, coastal upwelling, and other issues of interest. Bathymetric maps of San Francisco Bay are important to the San Francisco Bay Conservation and Development Commission (BCDC)—a regional governmental body charged with regulating development in and on the shores of the San Francisco Bay. For example, understanding the depth of the bay helps BCDC decide if and when to issue permits for dredging and filling parts of the bay.

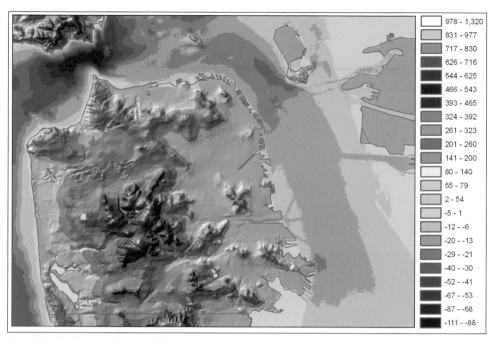

Map 6.4   Digital elevation model (DEM) of San Francisco.

Source: 2000 U.S. Census of Population and Housing

Raster operators, expressions, and functions

Most raster GIS analysis involves inputting expressions using operators and functions to create new raster datasets. Procedurally, writing computer expressions to create new raster datasets is not difficult, because modern GIS software has preprogrammed functions and easy-to-understand graphical user interfaces to guide users. Conceptually, inputting expressions to create new raster datasets takes thought.

Operators used in a raster environment are the same arithmetic, logical, and Boolean operators you learned about in chapter 3.

A raster **expression** is a statement combining rasters, functions, and operators following rules built into the software. An expression operates on a raster to produce a new raster output layer with cell values created by the expression. For example, an expression for creating a red-legged frog habitat conservation area might calculate a grid showing potential frog habitat conservation areas based on habitat suitability, proximity to rivers, absence of toxics, and affordability of land. The expression would look like this:

Frog_HCA = ([frog_habitat] + [near_river] +
[no_toxics]) NOT [price] > 100,000

The expression uses several different rasters, an arithmetic operator (+), and a logical operator (NOT). You may want to refer back to box 3.2 and accompanying text in chapter 3 for a summary of arithmetic, logical, and Boolean operators. You will have an opportunity to use what you have learned in exercise 3.

When a raster GIS expression is evaluated, the GIS software first creates a new grid and then populates the cells of the grid with values based on the expression. The extent and cell size of the new grid are based on the analysis environment. Processing usually starts at the lower-left cell (cell row 0; column 0) and moves sequentially through the columns within a row. When processing for one row is complete, processing proceeds to the next row. The computer uses the expression's arguments, functions, and values of the input raster dataset to determine an appropriate value to enter into each cell of the output raster dataset. Processing continues until every cell in the new raster dataset is filled in. Functions are critical to the process of creating new raster datasets. There are four main types of functions in raster GIS: local, focal, zonal, and global. Each is described below. You will see how they work in exercises 3 and 4.

Local functions

A **local function** (also called a per-cell function) computes a new output raster dataset where the value at each location is a function of the values associated with that location in one or more of the input raster datasets.

Maps 6.5a and 6.5b show habitat suitability for two endangered animals found in Contra Costa County—San Francisco garter snakes and California towhees (a small bird a little larger than a sparrow). Like map 6.2a, which showed habitat suitability for red-legged frogs, habitat suitability in each of the maps is classified into three categories: red areas are prime areas, green areas are acceptable, and beige areas are unacceptable. Suitability patterns for the two species are different. The red (prime) areas overlap in some places, indicating that the area is prime habitat for both San Francisco garter snakes and California towhees.

In addition to red-legged frogs (whose habitat is illustrated in map 6.2a), San Francisco garter snakes, and California towhees, Contra Costa County also is home to endangered California voles (a mouse-like creature). You could create a habitat suitability raster for the California voles similar to maps 6.2a, 6.5a, and 6.5b.

You may want to identify areas of the county that are acceptable or prime habitat for two or more of the four endangered species. You could start by creating rasters for habitat for each of the four endangered species coded 1 for prime habitat, 2 for acceptable habitat, and 3 for unacceptable habitat. If you then add the four rasters together, the resulting map might have up to 12 different types of areas (4 layers x 3 types of areas = 12 possible types of areas). If there was any land in Contra Costa County that was prime habitat for all four species, it would receive a 4 (4 x 1). Land that was unacceptable for all four species would receive a 12 (4 x 3). If the county wanted to acquire land that would be most attractive to the greatest variety of endangered species, land with the lowest values would be best.

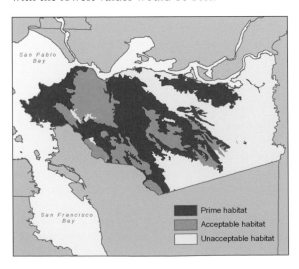

Map 6.5a   Habitat suitability for San Francisco garter snake.

Source: California Gap Analysis Project

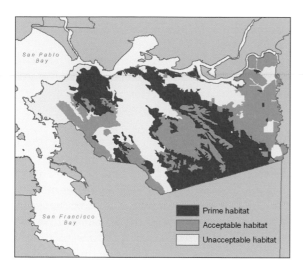

Map 6.5b Habitat suitability for California towhee.

Source: California Gap Analysis Project

Performing the overlay analysis described above, we discovered that no land in the new raster received a score of 4 (prime for all four endangered species) or a 5 (prime for three species and acceptable for the fourth). Cell values ranged from a low of 6 to a high of 12. Grouping these values into three categories produced map 6.6. The red areas are prime for at least one endangered species and at least acceptable for two others. We labeled this land "best." Environmentalists in Contra Costa County could use this map to search for land in the red areas to set aside as habitat conservation areas.

In this example, the local statistic calculated is the sum of the values of each individual raster dataset. It is also possible to use local functions to calculate the minimum, maximum, range, majority, minority, or variety of values on a cell-by-cell basis. For example, if you instructed the computer to calculate the minimum value of cells in a raster with values of 1, 3, 3, 3, 6, 6, the computer would select 1, because it is the lowest (minimum) value. If you instructed it to calculate the maximum value, it would select 6 (the highest value). The range of these four values is 5: the difference between the lowest value (1) and the highest value (6). The minority is 1, because there are three cells with the value 3, two with the value 6, but only 1 cell with the value 1. The majority

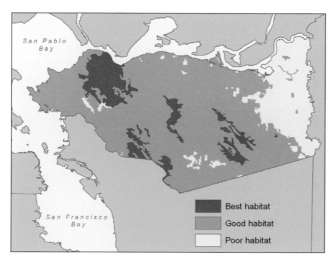

Map 6.6 Areas of Contra Costa County with habitat most suitable for two or more of four endangered species.

Source: California Gap Analysis Project

is 3, because that is the number that occurs most frequently. The variety is 3, because there are three different values in the six cells.

Local functions are useful in overlay analysis comparing multiple rasters. In exercise 4, you will sum grid cells from four different layers to create a map showing the suitability of land in Contra Costa County for red-legged frog habitat conservation areas.

Focal functions

A focal function (also called a neighborhood function) produces an output raster dataset in which the output value at each location is a function of the input value at the location and the values of the cells in a specified neighborhood around that location.

Map 6.7 is a raster GIS map of Contra Costa County showing urban land, agricultural land, and four broad categories of vegetation types: woodlands, grasslands, wetlands, and chaparral. The vegetation types were created by classifying twenty-one vegetation types identified in the California Gap Analysis Project (CA-GAP) into these six categories.

Map 6.8 also is concerned with vegetation in Contra Costa County, but it is a more abstract map that was created from the CA-GAP data by doing a focal analysis with a 5 x 5 grid cell radius. The computer started at a cell and searched the cells in its neighborhood. If all the cells had the same value, the computer would enter the number 1, indicating that only one type of cell was in the neighborhood. If it found even one cell with a different value, it would enter 2. If it found cells with six different values somewhere in the neighborhood, it would enter the value 6. Then it would move to the next cell and repeat this process. The resulting raster was symbolized so that areas with very low variety of vegetation types were colored light green; areas with a very high variety of vegetation types were colored with dark green. Area 1—a part of Contra Costa County with a lot of vegetation variety around rivers—is dark green, reflecting the substantial variety of cells within the area. In contrast, Area 2 is light green, showing very little variety in the vegetation in that area. Areas with a variety of vegetation types are of particular interest to ecologists for their potential to sustain many different kinds of plants and animals. A map like map 6.8 would be useful in studies to preserve biodiversity in Contra Costa County.

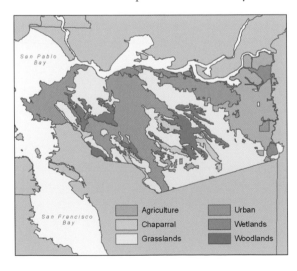

Map 6.7 Vegetation types in Contra Costa County.
Source: California Gap Analysis Project

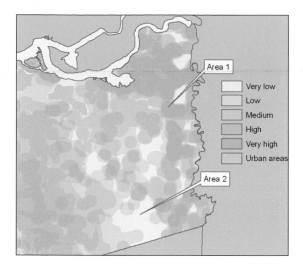

Map 6.8　Variety of vegetation types in eastern
Contra Costa County.

Source: California Gap Analysis Project

Zonal functions

A **zonal function** computes an output raster dataset where the output value for each cell depends on the zone where the cell is located. Remember, a raster GIS zone is defined as all cells in a raster dataset with the same value, whether or not they are contiguous.

Each of the areas in map 6.9 is one of sixty-one watersheds in Contra Costa County. Watersheds are areas where the hydrology is functionally related. Streams drain into the watershed. Each watershed is one raster zone. The watershed with the greatest variety of vegetation types in map 6.9—the Coyote Creek watershed—is indicated in red.

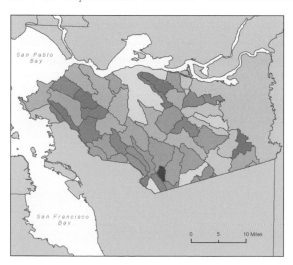

Map 6.9　Contra Costa County watersheds.

Source: California Department of Forestry and Fire Protection, Fire
and Resource Assessment Program

Figure 6.3 is a column chart illustrating output from a zonal analysis of the sixty-one watersheds. Each watershed is represented as a single column along the x-axis. The y-axis of figure 6.3 shows the variety of different vegetation types in each watershed. The highest column (labeled and indicated) is the Coyote Creek watershed.

Zonal analysis of the variety of vegetation types can be extremely useful to ecologists and public policy professionals studying the natural environment in order to promote species conservation and sustainable urban development practices. Zonal analysis can be used to analyze

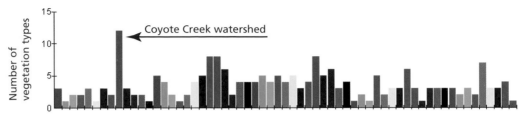

Figure 6.3 Variety of vegetation types in sixty-one Contra Costa County watersheds.
Source: California Department of Forestry and Fire Protection, California Fire and Resource Assessment Program

features of interest in many kinds of zones, such as immigrant clusters in urban neighborhoods, toxic sites in a city, and affordable housing in redevelopment areas.

Global functions

A **global function** (also called per-raster function) creates an output raster dataset in which the output value of each cell is potentially a function of all the cells in the input raster dataset. In exercise 3, you will learn how to compute distance for an entire raster surface using the global straight line distance function.

Raster GIS represents the world in a different way than vector GIS. Now that you understand some fundamentals about raster GIS, you are ready to learn more about typical raster GIS operations and how they help show conflicts between the natural and built environments.

In the next chapter, you will learn how to set up an environment to conduct raster analysis, how to convert data between vector and raster GIS, and how to reclassify raster data. Chapter 7 describes key raster operations such as analyzing distance, density, and surfaces; interpolating unknown values from known measured values; and using map algebra to create new rasters. A great strength of raster GIS is how suitable it is for building digital models of the world. Chapter 7 discusses some common types of models that raster GIS can help you build: representation models and suitability models. With the background in this chapter and chapter 7, you will be ready to tackle exercises 3 and 4, where you will learn a starter set of raster GIS skills.

Terms

cell. A rectangular area in a raster dataset created by the intersection of columns and rows. Cells are also referred to as grid cells or pixels. Raster dataset cells store numeric values. Raster analysis can be performed on individual cells, cell neighborhoods, zones, regions, or on all the cells within a raster dataset.

continuous feature. A geographic feature that varies continuously across space. Air temperature is a good example, as there is a temperature everywhere and the temperature changes gradually over space. Continuous features are distinguished from discrete features in which there are clearly defined boundaries between features.

digital elevation model (DEM). A three-dimensional raster model showing the elevation (z-coordinate) as well as two-dimensional space.

discrete feature. A geographic feature that has clearly defined boundaries. A census tract is a good example of a discrete feature, as census tracts have boundaries that are clearly defined by the U.S. Census Bureau. Discrete features are distinguished from continuous features that vary continuously across space.

expression. A computer statement used to combine raster datasets, constants, operators, and functions to perform analysis and create a new raster dataset.

focal function. Focal functions produce an output raster dataset in which the output value at each location is a function of the input value at the location and the values of the cells in a specified neighborhood around that location. Also called a neighborhood function.

function. In GIS, a function is a spatial or mathematical operation that returns new values.

global function. A function in raster GIS that potentially uses every cell in a raster to calculate the value of a cell in a new raster dataset.

local function. A function in raster GIS that computes an output raster dataset where the output value at each location is a function of the values of cells at that location on all the input rasters. Also called a per-cell function.

raster dataset. A grid of pixels representing geographic space. The pixels are arrayed in columns and rows.

raster GIS. A model for representing space that uses a grid of cells. Each cell in a raster is one pixel. Values stored in the cells can be used to perform analysis and to symbolize the cells. New rasters can be computed by performing operations on raster layers using functions and operators.

region. A group of contiguous cells with the same value in a raster dataset.

surface. In raster GIS, a surface is a raster in which values may vary continuously. Features such as air and water temperature, levels of ozone pollution, and annual rainfall are best modeled as surfaces. Physical surfaces represent physical phenomena. Statistical surfaces represent statistical values.

value attribute table (VAT). A table containing values of a variable related to discrete data in an integer raster, similar to a vector GIS attribute table. It is not possible to have VATs with floating-point rasters that contain continuous data.

zonal function. A function that computes an output raster dataset where the output value for each cell depends on the zone where the cell is located. Zonal functions operate on grid cells whether or not they are contiguous.

zone. All cells with the same value in a raster dataset. Cells in a zone do not have to be contiguous.

Questions for further study

1. If you are interested in the way ozone concentrations affect people in different census tracts, which GIS model—vector or raster—would you use for the census data? Which for the ozone data? Explain your choices.

2. You are creating two maps—one showing endangered California towhee habitats for the state of California and one showing endangered California towhee habitats for the Mount Diablo region of Contra Costa County. Which map should have the larger cell size? Why? What are the implications?

3. Would a raster dataset showing ozone concentration be an integer grid or a floating-point grid? Could you have a VAT with it? Why or why not?

4. Describe a representation model you might create using raster GIS to depict farmland in Contra Costa County at different time periods—1984, 1992, and 2000?

5. Describe a process model showing the impact of urbanization on farmland in Contra Costa County. You don't have to describe how you would create the model—just what it would be like.

Annotated bibliography

The initial chapters of Michael N. DeMers's *GIS Modeling in Raster* (DeMers 2001) introduce basic raster concepts and operations. Later chapters cover more advanced raster topics appropriate to specialized GIS courses.

Jill McCoy and Kevin Johnston's *Using ArcGIS Spatial Analyst* (McCoy and Johnston 2001) provides a good introduction to raster concepts and step-by-step instruction on how to use the Spatial Analyst extension to ArcGIS to perform raster GIS operations.

ESRI Press's basic introductory book on ArcGIS—Tim Ormsby, Eileen Napoleon, Robert Burke, Carolyn Groessl, and Laura Feaster's *Getting to Know ArcGIS Desktop,* second edition (Ormsby et al. 2004)—describes how raster data can be symbolized and classified by ArcGIS in chapters 5 ("Symbolizing features and rasters") and 6 ("Classifying features and rasters").

Chapter 7

Using raster GIS to resolve conflicts between the natural and built environments

"Let's see the very thing and nothing else.
Let's see it with the hottest fire of sight.
Burn everything not part of it to ash."

Wallace Stevens (1990)

Introduction

Resolving conflicts between the natural and built environments is important as the population of the earth increases and the number and size of human settlements continues to grow. Raster GIS is a powerful tool to help social scientists, urban planners, and policy makers understand and resolve these conflicts.

Many environmental features such as air, water, and soil don't have the kind of precise boundaries that countries, counties, cities, and census tracts do. They are continuous features without sharp, discrete boundaries. These kinds of features are particularly well represented as surfaces. Since the raster GIS model works well with surfaces, it is particularly effective in analyzing these environmental features. Being able to do overlay analysis quickly and flexibly—particular strengths of the raster GIS model—is also a big help in environmental analyses. You can represent aspects of the natural and built environments in vector GIS and use distance measurements, queries, classification, and other skills from part I and exercises 1 and 2 to analyze areas where urbanization is affecting the environment. But understanding how to use raster GIS will greatly increase your ability to do this kind of analysis. Now that chapter 5 has introduced different dimensions of the problem growing cities pose for the environment, and chapter 6 has introduced raster GIS, it is time to learn more raster GIS concepts and operations and how they can help harmonize nature and human settlements in this chapter and exercises 3 and 4. Two books cover material in this chapter and additional raster GIS concepts and operations (McCoy and Johnston 2001) and DeMers (2001).

Getting ready for raster GIS analysis

Before doing raster GIS analysis, you need to set up the digital environment in which to work. Getting ready for raster GIS analysis requires attention to the nature of the data you will be working with and making choices about how the analysis will proceed. This involves some mechanical details such as specifying the spatial extent of the analysis, the size of grid cells, folders where temporary and permanent rasters you create during the analysis will be physically stored on the computer, and perhaps creating an analysis mask to specify which area of a raster to include in an analysis.

A first step in setting up a raster environment involves specifying a spatial extent for the analysis. A raster analysis extent is always a rectangle. The rectangle needs to be big enough to include all

Microcomputers are now able to handle GIS software for raster analysis.
Source: Richard LeGates

of the geographical area you will be analyzing. One way to define the rectangle is to specify geographic coordinates. For example, if you were analyzing Contra Costa County, you could specify latitude and longitude that would define a rectangular area big enough to include the entire county. The rectangle will also include some additional land between the county boundaries and the borders of the rectangle. If you already have a map layer with an appropriate extent, you may also define a geographical extent by referencing the extent of the layer. For example, after you have created a Contra Costa County, layer with an extent rectangle large enough to encompass the entire county, you might instruct the GIS software to use the spatial extent of the Contra Costa County layer for a new layer of Contra Costa County farmland.

Before you begin a raster analysis, you need to specify the size of grid cells. The cell size can be set to any dimensions from very small (such as one inch on a side) to very large (such as one thousand miles on a side). Deciding on cell size begins with a common-sense judgment about the size of the area being studied. If you were analyzing stream erosion that has been precisely measured for a fifty-foot section of stream, a very small cell size would be appropriate. It would be silly (and physically impossible on a personal computer) to set a cell size of one inch for an analysis with the whole world as the extent.

There is a second consideration in setting the cell size if you are using two or more data layers and want cells to match so that you can do analysis involving all the layers. You want to set the cell size of all the layers to be the same. However, you need to be careful. Data collected at a level of detail like thirty feet on a side can be converted to a *coarser* level like ninety feet on a side. The resulting raster will accurately represent the level of precision in the data. While data collected at a level like ninety feet on a side can be physically reclassified into a level like thirty feet on a side, such a reclassification would be misleading. The data is still only precise to the level of ninety feet on a side; it does not gain in precision by being reclassified to a smaller cell size. Accordingly, a common convention for setting cell size is to set the cell size identical to the layer with the coarsest data.

Another preliminary step before beginning a raster analysis involves specifying where newly created rasters will be stored. As you will see in exercises 3 and 4, raster analysis involves creating new raster layers. Often as you do exploratory data analysis, you will want to create a succession of new temporary raster layers, look at each, think of improvements, and then create successively more refined temporary raster layers. You need a folder on your computer in which to store the temporary rasters. When you have just the raster layer you want, you can permanently save it, perhaps in a different folder.

An optional step before beginning analysis may be to set an **analysis mask**. An analysis mask specifies what part of a geographical extent will be used for analysis. For example, from a larger rectangular extent that extends from the farthest northern, southern, eastern, and western points of a rectangle large enough for Contra Costa County to fit inside, a mask might specify that analysis is only to occur in an area that follows the irregular shape of Contra Costa County itself. If you are analyzing the amount of farmland in Contra Costa County, you may want to create an analysis mask that includes only land and excludes cells representing lakes and rivers so that their land area is not included in your calculations. A common mistake beginners make is to fail to exclude grid cells that should not be included in an analysis and perform raster calculations on an area of interest plus additional grid cells making up the rectangle that includes the area. This produces wrong results.

Converting data between vector and raster GIS

The physical format of raster data is different from the physical format of vector data. Sometimes you may want to convert data from one format to another. In ArcGIS and other modern GIS software, it is easy to do this. The operation simply involves identifying layers to convert and clicking the right buttons.

You know from part I that vector GIS data is stored as points, lines, and polygons. Under the covers there is quite a bit of complexity to the way in which these features are physically stored in the computer. You learned in chapter 6 that raster GIS data is stored as pixels in a matrix of grid cells. When you instruct GIS software to convert spatial data in vector format to raster format, the software creates a grid and populates it with numbers representing the vector data.

Converting raster data to vector is just the flip side of converting vector data to raster. The software itself constructs points, lines, and polygons from raster grid cells. Complex physical transformations of data are required at the level that data is stored in the computer, but the operations a user must know to convert raster data to vector data just involve pointing and clicking.

Analyzing distance

In exercise 2, you learned to measure distance in a vector GIS environment with a software tool that looked like a ruler. Raster GIS permits more sophisticated distance calculations and representations.

Raster GIS permits users to specify a source and then use a function to replace the value in each cell of the raster grid with a number representing the distance from the source to the cell. Once cells have a distance value, the distance may be symbolized with color.

Straight line distance

In everyday usage, distance means the shortest distance between two points. This is referred to as **straight line distance**. Straight line distance is also called Euclidean distance. Raster GIS can quickly calculate straight line distance.

Figure 7.1 shows a source—the red cell in the center labeled "elementary school." It is a symbolic representation of one Contra Costa County elementary school. Other cells have numbers representing the distance to the school. The gray rectangle of four grid cells in the top left shows an area where a fire occurred. If the cell size for this raster had been set to one mile, the number 1 would represent one mile, the number 2 would represent two miles, and so on. If you calculate straight line distance from the school to the fire, you would find that the fire came within about a mile of the school and the outer edge of the fire was about three miles from the school. The distances would be measured diagonally from the center of the grid cells. In exercise 3, you will measure straight line distance from libraries in Contra Costa County.

GIS analysis of the straight line distance from a highway to different plant communities could help an environmental scientist understand the impacts the highway could have on the plants and develop effective ways to mitigate potential harm.

Map 7.1 shows straight line distance around highways in part of Contra Costa County. Unlike more representational thematic maps, map 7.1 takes the form of a symbolic abstraction of reality illustrating straight line distance. The highways are represented as gray lines. The closest areas (within two miles of a highway) are yellow, the next closest (from two to four miles of a highway) light orange, all the way to an area southeast of the city of Clayton colored blue that is about nine miles from the nearest highway. Sensitive plant communities might be threatened by emissions from automobiles on the highways in the first two color bands closest to the highways, more hardy plant communities only in the light orange color band closest to the highways, and no plants in the other color bands.

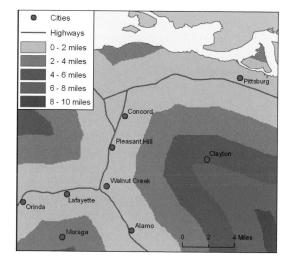

4	3	3	3	3
3	2	2	2	3
2	1	1	1	2
2	1	Elementary School	1	2
3	1	1	1	3
3	2	2	2	3
4	3	3	3	3

Figure 7.1 Raster cells with a source and straight line distance values.

Map 7.1 Straight line distance from Contra Costa County highways.

Source: 2000 U.S. Census TIGER files

On a computer, it is possible to determine the exact distance to a highway from any point in the digital map with a mouse click. The value in the grid cell where you click (the distance) will appear on the computer screen.

Raster GIS can also help social scientists and public policy professionals solve urban problems using more complex conceptual measures of distance. The next section explains some more sophisticated conceptual measures of distance that raster GIS can generate: cost-weighted distance and distance allocation. Finally, it describes the shortest path between two points considering the travel cost across a surface.

Thiessen polygons (distance allocation)

An extremely useful GIS function for social scientists and public policy professionals places a value in each cell of an output raster allocating the cell to a polygon that shows the shortest distance to a specified source. This is referred to as **distance allocation,** and the output is a **Thiessen polygon,** named after Reinhardt Thiessen (1867–1938), a pioneering coal petrologist who devised them.

Thiessen polygons are built from an input layer containing a set of points. Thiessen polygons are created by growing polygons around each point, generating regions that impinge on each other. The resulting output layer contains polygons in which every point within a polygon is closer to the point enclosed than to any other point in the extent.

The way Thiessen polygons are created is a good illustration of the way in which the vector and raster GIS models can work together. Conceptually, as polygons, Thiessen polygons are like vector polygon features. In the software used in this book for raster analysis—ArcMap, with the Spatial Analyst extension—Thiessen polygons are created in raster GIS as rasters around vector point features. In exercise 3, you will see how easy it is to create Thiessen polygons. Theoretical data model issues aside, distance allocation is extremely useful in defining service areas of facilities and in siting new facilities. An example will help make this clear.

California's Integrated Waste Management Board, which is charged with developing policy on disposal of waste in the state, is concerned that too many car owners who change their own engine oil dispose of the used motor oil improperly. Some bury it in their back yards. Others pour it into storm drains, where it may flow into streams, ponds, lakes, or the ocean. The board may want to set up sites where people can dispose of used motor oil properly, without contaminating the environment. The board might know that people are willing to travel up to four miles to dispose of used oil, but if the sites are farther than four miles, many people will not use them. One logical solution would be to have one used oil disposal site in each city at the locations indicated in map 7.2. But will that work? A public administrator working for the Integrated Waste Management Board could create Thiessen polygons that would help answer that question. Map 7.2 shows Thiessen polygons created around hypothetical used oil disposal sites in each Contra Costa County city as vector GIS points symbolized as red circles. Each site has a Thiessen polygon around it. For all the cells in each polygon, the site is the closest used oil disposal site.

Map 7.2 shows that used oil sites located as proposed will be within four miles of many people in Contra Costa County. Just looking at the Thiessen polygons and the scale bar, it is apparent that people living at the center of the map in Pleasant Hill and Walnut Creek do not have to travel more than four miles to get to a proposed used oil disposal site. If used oil disposal centers were established at these sites, people could reach them without having to travel too far. In contrast, people living at the northern border of the Thiessen polygon around Orinda would have to travel

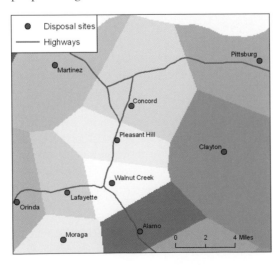

Map 7.2 Thiessen polygons around Contra Costa County cities.
Source: 2000 U.S. Census of Population and Housing

more than four miles to get to the Orinda site and even farther to get to the Martinez or Lafayette sites. While some people in Clayton live within four miles of the Clayton site, people at the bottom right of the map would have to travel over seven miles to get to the Clayton site. Whether a program that just located used oil disposal sites at these locations would work for these areas is problematic. A researcher doing exploratory spatial analysis for the California Integrated Waste Management Board could experiment with moving site locations or adding more sites and doing additional analysis with Thiessen polygons. The researcher could then propose a site location strategy to the board that would locate sites close enough to where people live so that everyone in the county could reach a used oil disposal site without traveling more than four miles.

Cost-weighted distance

Straight line distance is measured as the crow flies. It assumes that it is equally easy to travel everywhere. This is rarely the case. It is harder to travel up steep hills, across swamps, and on slippery soils. Sometimes physical barriers like a steep cliff or legal barriers like an off-limits military testing site present absolute barriers. From a road builder's perspective the shortest straight line distance between two points may be a very expensive way to build a road if she has to dig a tunnel or blast a mountain. A measure of distance that takes these kinds of considerations into account is called **cost-weighted distance**. Costs—as measured by money or difficulty—are considered in addition to measured distance. Instead of simply measuring the straight line distance from one point to another, the computer calculates the accumulated cost of traveling from each cell to the source, considering the greater cost of traveling across some cells.

There are many uses for cost-weighted distance. For example, an urban planner could use a cost-weighted distance function to create cells in a raster with values representing the cost of building a road between two points considering not only the distance between the two points, but also land acquisition costs, the difficulty of excavating different types of soil, costs of digging tunnels and building bridges, and costs of mitigating environmental damage the highway could cause.

Figure 7.2 illustrates cost-weighted distance. It is a diagram representing the urban planner's problem described above: what is the most cost-effective way to locate a highway between two points—labeled "start" and "end" in the diagram. While a straight line drawn at an angle between start and end would be shorter in distance, the computer selects the cell with the lowest impedance value moving toward the destination at each step from start to end. The path won't cross the

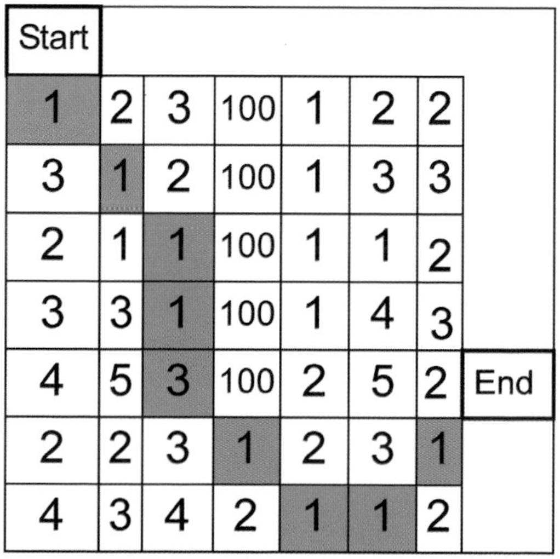

Figure 7.2   Cost-weighted distance raster.

barrier represented by cell values of 100. Confronted with a choice of moving by a longer route with a low-impedance value like 1 rather than a shorter route with a high-impedance value like 4, the computer chooses the least-cost solution. The sum of the values in the cells selected will be the lowest possible number. A line along them will represent the shortest path considering travel costs.

Shortest path distance

Raster GIS analysis often involves using the output of one process to create additional output. A cost-weighted distance raster can be used to produce a further useful kind of raster output: a map showing the **shortest path distance** between two points considering travel cost.

Mapping density

Density measures the number of features or the sum of values in an area divided by the area. In a vector GIS density calculation, a value assigned to a polygon divided by the area of the polygon yields the density. For example, if there are 200 housing units in land parcel number 1-125-5 in a cadastral map of Oakland land parcels, and the area of parcel 1-125-5 is 2 acres, there would be 100 houses to the acre (200 units/2 acres = 100 housing units per acre). The most common way to represent density in vector GIS is to divide the value of each polygon by the size of the polygon and classify the resulting values into a color ramp.

Raster GIS can create a statistical surface showing the density of points, lines, or polygons in an area. Density is a relative concept—how dense housing in an area is, for example, depends on how you define the area. Since raster GIS is analyzing a grid of many small cells rather than pre-defined vector polygons, it is much more flexible in how large the search radius it uses to define density can be. If you defined the search to include all of the parcels within one-half mile of Oakland parcel 1-125-5, and there were 1,000 housing units in that area, you would define the density of housing in the area as 1,000 housing units/0.5 miles = 2,000 housing units per square mile. Raster density analysis involves defining a search radius that makes sense in the context of the data and creating a new density raster. It is easy to repeat this operation and see different definitions of density.

Raster GIS also makes it possible to use a more sophisticated measure of density. Kernel density weighs values closest to a feature of interest more heavily than ones farther away. This creates a density surface that highlights areas where features are particularly concentrated.

Map 7.3 illustrates the density of red-legged frogs in Contra Costa County based on (hypothetical) frog sightings. It was created by instructing a GIS to conduct a kernel density search with a search radius of 10,000 square feet. It is easy to identify areas within the county where frogs are particularly dense. They are the areas of darkest purple.

Analyzing surfaces

One group of raster GIS functions involves **surface analysis**. This is a conceptually and cartographically interesting topic and is important enough to social scientists and public policy professionals to introduce briefly here. Attributes of surfaces that are commonly analyzed in raster GIS include contour, slope, aspect, hillshade, and viewshed.

A **contour map** is usually used to represent elevation. All of the area within one elevation range is enclosed by one contour line. Contour lines that are close together indicate that elevation is rapidly changing. Contour lines that are far apart indicate that elevation is changing slowly.

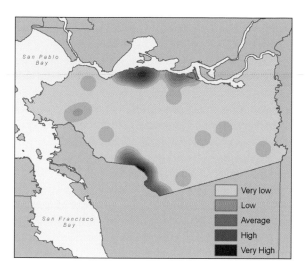

Map 7.3   Kernel density of red-legged frogs in Contra Costa County.
Source: Hypothetical data

Slope represents the change in elevation moving from one raster grid cell to an adjacent cell. Slope may be important in physical planning because areas that are too steep may be unbuildable. It is important in hazard planning to prevent floods and landslides.

Aspect is the orientation of an area in relation to the sun. In specialized planning applications—such as determining where to locate solar panels in a sustainable housing development—knowing aspect may be important.

Hillshade visually depicts where light and shadow fall in a geographical area. Including a hillshade layer beneath a semitransparent layer symbolized to represent elevation improves the cartographic appearance of maps. Map 6.4, the digital elevation model of San Francisco in the previous chapter, was created in this way.

A **viewshed** is an area that can be seen from a specified location. Raster GIS can calculate viewsheds from a single location or multiple locations. In Contra Costa County and other areas that have experienced destructive wildfires, viewshed analysis may be useful in showing where to locate fire observation towers. It may also help planners looking to purchase scenic easements that will preserve the aesthetic character of an area.

Interpolation

Raster GIS is particularly good at representing surfaces—physical surfaces like elevation, temperature, and air pollution and more abstract statistical surfaces that symbolize the distribution of features.

The noted California geographer Waldo Tobler formulated **Tobler's first law of geography**— that things close to each other are more likely to be similar than things farther away. An environmental researcher in a city with serious air pollution problems charged with implementing a system to measure air quality might propose taking air samples at different points across the city. One approach would be to draw a (paper or digital) grid with cells one thousand feet on a side, superimpose the grid on a map of the city, and then take air samples at the center of each grid cell on successive days. You would expect air quality adjacent to your sample point to be very similar to the value measured in a cell where a sample is taken. Depending on factors such as pollutant sources, wind direction, and trees that absorb pollution, an air pollution measurement in a raster cell might be somewhat more or somewhat less polluted than its neighbor. You could either enter a precise measurement of pollutants in the air as parts per million (ppm) or enter a pollution score as a single integer number such as 1 for "not polluted at all" to 10 for "very polluted."

You would probably find a pattern of air pollution: high air pollution in areas near factories and lower air pollution in residential areas. Remember, you are only actually taking measurements at selected sample locations. You would expect the cells in between the sampled points to fall somewhere between the values measured at the sample points. If your sample points were not regularly spaced, you would expect points to be most heavily influenced by the cells closest to them and less by values of the cells farther away.

Calculating how much different values at different locations would probably affect a given cell moves quickly into conceptual and statistical complexity. Clever geostatisticians have developed algorithms to do these kinds of calculations, and clever computer programmers have written computer code to perform the calculations correctly once a user inputs data correctly. Mastering the specialized field of spatial interpolation is beyond the scope of this book, but interpolation is important and will be covered shortly. More advanced GIS texts provide in-depth discussion of interpolation (Longley et al. 2005; DeMers 2001).

Air quality provides a good example of how interpolation works and why it is helpful in improving the relationship between humans and the environment.

Creating a surface from sample points

One of the most harmful forms of air pollution is ozone produced by automobile emissions and other sources. You learned in chapter 5 that the Bay Area Air Quality Management Direct (BAAQMD) analyzes air samples to determine the amount of ozone in the air at different locations within their jurisdiction. The monitoring stations are not located in a uniform grid. Their placement has been determined by geography and known sources of air pollution in order to best measure air pollution with sufficient precision to establish policy, but within budget constraints. Other air quality districts also take air samples to measure the amount of ozone.

0.0877		0.0810					0.0580
	0.0837						
	0.0816		0.0606			0.0580	
0.0847							
							0.0500
		0.0599			0.0500		
				0.0499			
0.0465							
				0.0466			
							0.0465
0.0462			0.0463				

Figure 7.3 Hypothetical distribution of Bay Area Air Quality Management District ozone field monitoring sites.

Figure 7.3 shows the hypothetical location of ozone-monitoring sites in an area and the average maximum daily amount of ozone found there during 2001 measured in parts per million (ppm). In the empty cells there are no field-monitoring stations.

Ozone can be represented as a surface—there is some level of ozone pollution, however slight, almost everywhere in the San Francisco Bay Area and surrounding areas. Within the degree of precision of the recording instruments, the actual amount of ozone is known at sample sites. The trick is to use these known values to estimate the ozone at every other point. Now you will see how to use inverse distance weighted interpolation to do this.

Inverse distance weighted interpolation

The most frequently used method to interpolate a surface from sample points is called **inverse distance weighted (IDW) interpolation**. The best way to understand IDW interpolation is to revisit the raster grid of sample values from the BAAQMD in figure 7.3. Using that grid, a computer could move from cell to cell. At the first cell, in the top left hand corner, there is already a value for the average maximum daily amount of ozone found in air quality samples at the location during 2001 measured in parts per million (ppm). In the next cell there is no value. Probably the value of this cell is similar to cells around it. If the computer searched one cell in each direction, it would find three values—.0877, .0837, and .0810. Adding them up and dividing by 3, the computer might reasonably conclude that the probable value in the cell is .0841. The calculation would be: .0877 + .0837 + .0810/3 = .0841. If it searched over a larger number of cells (a larger search radius) it would have more numbers to add up and would reach a similar, but probably slightly different, result.

IDW interpolation works like the above example, but with a significant improvement: it weighs values based on proximity. The closest values contribute more to the number assigned to a cell with an unknown value than ones farther away.

Just using the BAAQMD data to understand ozone in Contra Costa County presents a problem. There are only four sample sites in Contra Costa County—too few for accurate interpolation. The BAAQMD jurisdiction ends at eastern Contra Costa County. It is essential to have data from other air quality districts farther east. Many more sample points from sites to the north, south, and west of Contra Costa County would increase analysts' confidence that they could accurately interpolate a statistical surface of ozone pollution for the region that includes Contra Costa County. A solution is to create a statistical surface of ozone concentrations in a much larger area using many sample points and then cut out just Contra Costa County using a GIS operation called clipping. Clipping works like a cookie cutter—in this case cutting out just Contra Costa County. Think of cutting out Christmas cookies from a large sheet of cookie dough, but with a cookie cutter shaped like Contra Costa County rather than a Christmas tree.

Map 7.4 shows the location of forty-two air quality monitoring sites where ozone samples are taken—four sites in Contra Costa County and thirty-eight additional sites in surrounding counties.

At these sites, we know exactly the average concentration of ozone measured in parts per million (ppm) during the time period when the samples were taken. If, for example, the amount of ozone measured in an air quality sample taken at the site in the top right was .0877 parts per million, we can be reasonably sure that the ozone concentration very close to the site at the same time was .0877 parts per million, plus or minus a small amount. We are less sure about areas farther away.

Map 7.5 illustrates the way in which the map of the ozone concentrations in Contra Costa County *(map 5.3, in chapter 5)* was created. It is a statistical surface showing concentrations of ozone in seventeen northern California counties, including Contra Costa County. It was created using IDW interpolation from the forty-two sample sites shown in map 7.4.

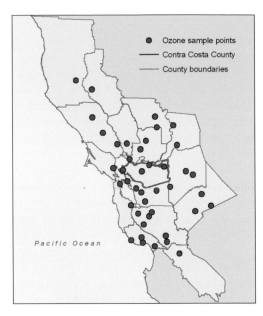

Map 7.4 Ozone sample sites.
Source: California Air Resources Board

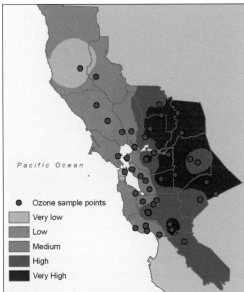

Map 7.5 Statistical surface of interpolated ozone levels for Contra Costa County.
Source: California Air Resources Board

Advanced interpolation

The physical world presents many different distributions of values, and geostatisticians have developed many ways to interpolate surfaces to best approximate observed conditions. An important example is where there is a sharp change in the landscape. Vegetation samples on top of a mountain may all be similar to each other, but characteristics of the vegetation may change abruptly on a cliff face. There may be one type of vegetation on one side of a stream and a quite different type of vegetation just a short distance away on the other side of the stream. Advanced interpolation allows users to insert these kinds of barriers into the data or weigh observations to best approximate what is not known based on what is known.

A particularly sophisticated interpolation method is called **kriging**. Kriging is named after the South African mining engineer (Danie G. Krige) who invented the method. Kriging uses all the values in every cell of a raster and complex, iterative mathematics to interpolate missing values.

Reclassifying raster data

In chapter 3 and exercise 1, you learned how to classify vector data and why classification is often useful. Sometimes you want to reclassify raster data for similar purposes. When you reclassify raster data, you substitute different values in some or all of the cells. A common reason to do this is to create a common scale to show how suitable the area is for some purpose. A raster suitability model is created by summing raster layers that have been classified to a similar scale to determine the most- and least-suitable areas for an activity. You will create a suitability model for evaluating land for an endangered red-legged frog habitat conservation area in exercise 4.

Map algebra

Raster analysis is performed using **map algebra**. The good news for the mathematically challenged is that modern GIS software presents users with a graphical user interface that makes it easy to instruct the software to perform map algebra calculations. Lurking behind the good news is the reality that performing incorrect, even meaningless, map algebra operations is as easy as performing correct analysis. There is no substitute for understanding what you are instructing the computer to do.

The following discussion introduces core map algebra concepts and gives examples of how map algebra is used to solve conflicts between natural and human environments. Exercises 3 and 4 will teach you how to use the core concepts to produce useful analytic output in the form of raster GIS maps. This is one of the hardest sections of this book and will require careful reading and reflection on what you are doing. If you master this section and the operations in exercises 3 and 4, you will accomplish the following: (a) you will understand map algebra and have a foundation on which to build in more advanced GIS courses or to learn GIS software on your own, (b) you will know how to use enough very powerful map manipulation commands to perform some powerful GIS analyses.

What is map algebra?

Algebra is a set of logical and mathematical rules that operate on numbers. You have probably used a hand calculator to do algebraic calculations—typing in numbers, functions, operators, and logical expressions and pressing a button to have the calculator do the math and return an answer. If you understood what you were doing and typed in the right information, the calculator gave you a right answer. If you made errors in the logic you used or careless errors, you got a wrong answer.

Some GIS software uses the calculator metaphor to present GIS users with a user-friendly interface. Figure 7.4 shows the ArcGIS **raster calculator**.

To split the bill for five people's dinners at a restaurant equally you would type the following expression into the calculator:

($12 + $14 + $17 + $11 + $20)/5

The calculator will faithfully execute the command you enter. First it would add up all the values within the parentheses to the sum of $74. Then it would divide by 5. The above expression is logically correct. Unless you enter a wrong value for one of the dinner prices, the calculator will

Figure 7.4 ArcGIS Spatial Analyst Raster Calculator.

return a correct new value—the average (mean) dinner price of $14.80—so you can split the total cost evenly. But let's say you tried to figure out how much everyone should pay using an incorrect formula:

$$\$12 + \$14 + \$17 + \$11 + (\$20/5)$$

The calculator would faithfully execute your command. First it would divide $20 by 5, yielding $4. Then it would add all of the values and conclude that each person owed $58.

The same is true with map algebra calculations in GIS. If you make logical or arithmetic errors, you will get incorrect results.

Armed with this understanding of why it is worthwhile to learn map algebra, you are ready to proceed with the rest of this section. You'll probably need to read this section several times, and it will make more sense after you have completed exercises 3 and 4. Rest assured that the material is not too difficult and that the operations in the exercise will produce astonishingly powerful output that is useful to social scientists and public policy professionals.

Map algebra can be used to analyze conflicting demands for land between the built and the natural environments. As the population of a region grows and the region urbanizes, land is needed for the built human environment and must be taken away from land in the natural environment or agricultural land. In addition to threatening habitats, land conversion can reduce available farmland. Prime farmland—the land where the highest yield can be grown most easily—is particularly important to preserve for sustainable urban development. A cross-sectional representation model of land use in Contra Costa County at one point in time can show how much land is devoted to each use, including prime farmland. A cross-sectional representation model of land use at some past time will show how much land was in what use at that time. Comparison of the two can show how land use has changed, including how much prime farmland has been lost.

Maps 7.6a and 7.6b display data from the California Department of Conservation's Farmland Mapping and Monitoring Program (FMMP). They show how raster analysis can represent prime farmland at different times. Map 7.6c shows how raster analysis can show loss of prime farmland over time. Maps 7.6a and 7.6b are cross-sectional maps showing urbanization and prime farmland at two points in time: 1984 and 2000. You can see that the proportion of all Contra Costa County land that is urban increased between 1984 and 2000. The amount of prime farmland in 2000 is less than it was in 1984. Prime farmland is being lost. Map 7.6c is a raster created by using logical operators to show land which was prime farmland in 1984 and was not prime farmland in 2000 using the information in maps 7.6a and 7.6b. It shows prime farmland that was lost during the sixteen years between 1984 and 2000 in black. The farmland that was lost is highly concentrated in the Brentwood area. It is possible to see that a substantial amount of prime farmland was

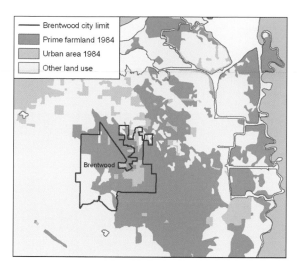

Map 7.6a Prime Contra Costa County farmland, 1984.

Source: California Department of Conservation Farmland Mapping and Monitoring Program

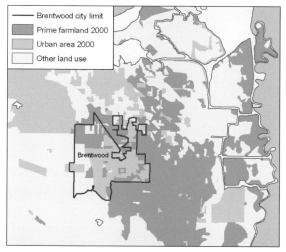

Map 7.6b Prime Contra Costa County farmland, 2000.

Source: California Department of Conservation Farmland Mapping and Monitoring Program

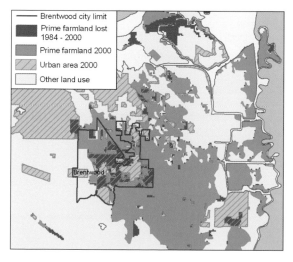

Map 7.6c Prime Contra Costa County farmland lost between 1984–2000.

Source: California Department of Conservation Farmland Mapping and Monitoring Program

lost between these two time periods. Raster GIS permits more precise calculations as described in the following paragraphs and box 7.1

It is possible to calculate the amount of farmland that was lost between 1984 and 2000 from data in the value attribute tables (VATs) associated with map 7.6c and to compare it with how much prime farmland there was in 1984 from data in the VAT associated with map 7.6a.

Box 7.1 Calculating loss of prime farmland in Contra Costa County 1984–2000

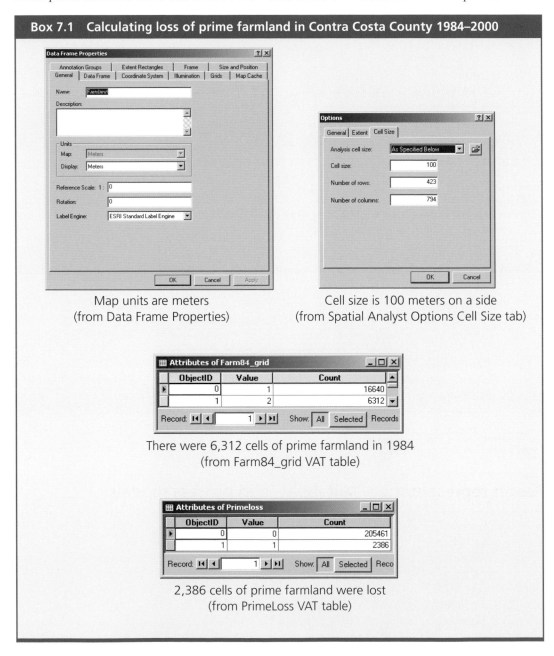

Map units are meters
(from Data Frame Properties)

Cell size is 100 meters on a side
(from Spatial Analyst Options Cell Size tab)

There were 6,312 cells of prime farmland in 1984
(from Farm84_grid VAT table)

2,386 cells of prime farmland were lost
(from PrimeLoss VAT table)

The total area of any value depicted in a raster can be calculated from information in the raster. Box 7.1 illustrates how to use information in the GIS to determine the total area of prime farmland in Contra Costa County in 1984 and how much was lost between 1984 and 2000.

Every VAT contains the number of cells for each value. If you know what value a code in the VAT represents, the map units used, and the cell size it is, then it is possible to multiply these three values together to determine the total area the value represents. Box 7.1 shows that the map units used in maps 7.6a and 7.6c are meters. Cell size was set to one hundred meters on each side. Thus each cell represents ten thousand square meters (100 meters x 100 meters = 10,000 meters). Ten thousand meters is one hectare of land.

Box 7.1 shows that 6,312 cells were coded as prime farmland in 1984 (value 1 in a raster named farm84_grid), so the total prime farmland at that time was 6,312 hectares. The PrimeLoss VAT in box 7.1 shows that 2,386 cells were coded with the value 1—representing prime farmland lost between 1984 and 2000. This shows that 2,386 hectares of prime farmland were lost during this time. Is this a little or a lot? Should we be alarmed or not worry? The amount of prime farmland lost in these sixteen years is about 38 percent of the total prime farmland that existed in 1984. Prime farmland was lost at the rate of about 2.4 percent a year.

The raster analysis provides precise and concrete quantitative and visual information that helps policy makers focus on the facts. It allows citizens arguing with government officials to "speak truth to power." Some people might feel that a loss of 2.4 percent of the county's prime farmland a year is unacceptable. Others might disagree. In any event, a precise analysis like this can raise the level of discourse from conjectures and ideological sparring to tough-minded disagreement over the meaning of facts. The above information provides fodder for both sides arguing about preserving prime farmland.

What if someone at a public meeting questioned the above data on the grounds that relatively little prime farmland was lost between 1984 and 1992 and most of the loss for the sixteen-year period between 1984 and 2000 occurred only in the last eight years? That might change the whole course of the debate. California's Farmland Mapping and Monitoring Project collects longitudinal data that permits exactly that kind of analysis. Maps showing the loss of prime farmland in Contra Costa County between 1984 and 1992 and between 1992 and 2000 could show local officials, policy makers, and citizens whether or not more prime farmland had been lost in recent years than earlier and where the loss was occurring. It is unlikely that the maps would get everyone to agree on the extent of the problem or what public policies to pursue, but more refined empirical evidence would raise the level of discourse still more.

Raster representation, suitability, and process models

You learned in chapter 1 that every GIS map is a model of the real world. You already worked with vector models in part I. Raster GIS provides powerful new ways to model the world. Well-funded experts have created very sophisticated raster GIS models from mountains of data and years of work to describe weather, the hydrology of river systems, the impact of oil spills on sea otters, the effects of a nuclear warhead striking San Francisco, the flooding a hurricane will cause in Florida, the spread of AIDS along highway corridors in Africa, and the way a forest fire will likely spread in at-risk forest areas. Courses and books on raster GIS modeling describe these advanced models and how to create them in detail (DeMers 2001, Tomlin 1990).

You can build simple raster models yourself. In exercise 3, you will build raster representation models useful for understanding urbanization, saving prime agricultural land, and determining sites to dispose of used motor oil. Once you see how this kind of raster modeling is done, you will be able to extend it to many areas of your own interest. In exercise 4, you will construct a raster suitability model for siting a habitat conservation area for red-legged frogs. Once you have mastered the logic and operations of building this suitability model, you will be able to build suitability models for other purposes—an extremely valuable skill.

Raster models may be subdivided into three main types: representation models, suitability models, and process models. The focus on exercises 3 and 4 is on the first two types.

A raster **representation model** simply describes reality. Representation models are the most common type of raster model. Creating raster representation models requires understanding how to use map algebra to create new rasters. By adding, subtracting, multiplying, and dividing, subjecting multiple rasters to logical tests, and learning your way around functions, you can create your own models to represent reality.

A raster **suitability model** describes how suitable different geographical locations are for some use or activity, such as a habitat conservation area, school site, or highway right-of-way. Suitability models are widely used in urban planning and public policy decision making. Deriving a suitability model involves determining the suitability of one or more sites for some activity. Whatever kind of activity you want to locate somewhere will work well in some areas and not others. If you want to build a job-training center to teach unemployed people job skills, it would be foolish to locate the job center in sparsely populated agricultural land, away from public transportation. Rather, you would want to look for sites that are near concentrations of unemployed people and near public transportation. If a team of urban planners wants to build a high-density transit village, they might brainstorm the necessary or desirable locational features—such as being near major public transit nodes with available land in an area where moderate- to high-density residential uses will be permitted. Every suitability analysis follows a similar analytic process:

- identifying what geographic features to study
- ranking attributes of the features in terms of their desirability
- creating rasters for each feature coded in the same ranking scheme
- combining the raster layers together (perhaps weighing them differently)

A basic raster suitability model could have just two layers, each with just two values—"suitable" and "unsuitable." Combining the two layers produces just three possible cell values: 0 (unsuitable on both criteria), 1 (suitable on one criterion, but not both), and 2 (suitable on both criteria). Creating such a model is useful in understanding the concept of suitability modeling. But most suitability models go further in two respects: (a) there are more than just two values in the ranking scheme, and (b) some factors are weighted more heavily than others.

Rather than just classifying cells in a suitability model as either 1 ("suitable") or 2 ("unsuitable"), ranking them with ordinal values produces more subtle results. You could build a suitability model from multiple rasters representing different features ranked with values based on how good or bad the feature is with respect to the purpose at hand. For example, if you were trying to determine the best area to purchase for a red-legged frog habitat conservation area, you might assign prime habitat a value of 1, acceptable habitat a value of 5, and unacceptable habitat a value of 10. The low value of 1 would contribute to a low (very good) overall score when combined with other rasters; a medium value of 5 would contribute to a significantly higher score in the new raster; and a high value of 10 would assure the score in the new raster would be so high the land would not be considered for the habitat conservation area.

Rather than just summing raster layers, giving each the same importance, you could assign the layers different weights based on their importance. For example, for a red-legged frog habitat conservation area, you might determine that very expensive land should be assigned a very high weight (very undesirable), because it will be very difficult to purchase, but that land located away from a river should be assigned only a modestly high weight (somewhat undesirable) because it will still do reasonably well for a frog habitat conservation area.

Figure 7.5 is a visual representation of a model that considers five different characteristics of a potential frog habitat: how far the land is from a toxic site (farther away is more desirable); how far it is from a river (closer is more desirable); how far it is from a highway (farther away is more desirable); how much the land costs (cheaper is better); and how much frogs like the habitat (prime habitat is much better, acceptable habitat okay, and unacceptable habitat so bad that if land is classified that way it will not be selected). The flowchart in figure 7.5 shows new rasters created by reclassifying values in rasters showing distance from toxics, rivers, and highways. These rasters are then combined with values on land cost and habitat suitability in a weighted overlay. You will learn how to build this model in exercise 4 using a feature of ArcGIS named ModelBuilder™.

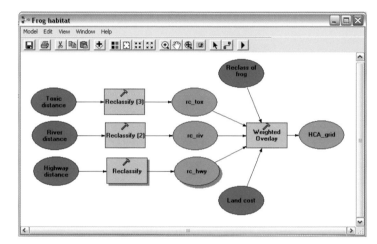

Figure 7.5 Red-legged frog habitat suitability model.
Source: Christopher Simeone

A **process model** is a more complex type of model beyond the scope of this book. Process models describe the way in which phenomena behave over both space and time. Given wind direction and velocity, ocean currents, and island barriers, how will an oil slick spread throughout Prince Rupert Sound in Alaska? Based on direction and wind speed, will a major hurricane still have hurricane force winds when it hits Cape Hatteras, North Carolina? Given the size of a Southern California forest, the fuel load of the ground cover, and the location of towns, will a forest fire burn houses in the city of Rancho Cucamonga? These, and similar questions, involve processes. GIS models to analyze them are process models.

Raster GIS provides a different way of seeing the world than vector GIS and a set of operations that work particularly well to analyze surfaces and certain kinds of natural environment phenomena.

Just as a set of more sophisticated tools can extend your capacity to do spatial analysis, additional data graphics showing multiple values of variables and relationships among variables can extend your capacity to create good data visualizations introduced in chapter 4. The following chapter describes multivariate data graphics.

But first, exercises 3 and 4 will teach you how to do raster GIS analyses of conflicts between the built and natural environments. Do exercises 3 and 4 now. Afterward, proceed to chapter 8.

Terms

analysis mask. An analysis mask specifies grid cells to be included in a raster analysis. It is an optional step in setting a raster analysis environment. For example, in a grid of Contra Costa County farmland that contains grid cells that represent both productive farmland and barren land, a user might specify that only the cells representing productive farmland are to be included in the analysis mask. Since cells representing barren land are not included in the analysis mask, in a calculation of the total acres of farmland the output would not include the barren land.

contour map. Contour maps are usually used to represent elevation. All of the elevation within one elevation range is enclosed by one contour line. Contour lines that are close together indicate that elevation is changing rapidly. Contour lines that are far apart indicate that elevation is changing gradually.

cost-weighted distance. A way of measuring distance that considers the financial or other cost of crossing the distance. For example, the cost-weighted distance of traveling one mile across steep brushy terrain might be as great as traveling ten miles across an open meadow.

distance allocation. An operation within raster GIS that assigns a distance value to each cell of the raster. Distance allocation produces Thiessen polygons.

inverse distance weighted (IDW) interpolation. The most commonly used method to estimate an unknown value at a location based on known values of surrounding locations. GIS will look at known values near a location and estimate the unknown value by assigning different weights to the known values. The closer a known value is to the value that is being estimated, the more weight it will have. The farther away it is, the less weight it will have.

kriging. An advanced interpolation technique in which the value of each cell in a statistical surface is estimated using all of the cells in a raster.

map algebra. A type of mathematics that operates on the cells of a raster grid.

process model. A model that describes the way in which phenomena behave over both time and space.

raster calculator. In ArcGIS, a calculator whose graphical user interface looks like a hand calculator that permits users to compute new values for cells in a raster using arithmetic, logical, and Boolean operators.

representation model. A type of digital model that represents spatial reality. Every raster GIS layer is a representation model. A representation model is different from a process model that describes processes rather than just showing reality at one point in time. It is also different from application models, used for specialized purposes such as a hydrological model describing water flow.

shortest path distance. A measure of distance between two points considering the difficulty of moving between the two points. Unlike straight line or Euclidean distance that considers only the measured distance, shortest path distance factors in the difficulty of traveling across some areas or the impact of barriers.

straight line distance. The distance between two points on a raster assuming that the cost (difficulty) of traveling is the same everywhere. Straight line distance is different from cost-weighted distance that factors in impedance values and barriers. Straight line distance is also called Euclidean distance.

suitability model. A model used to determine how suitable different areas are for a use or activity. For example, a suitability model might map the most suitable area for locating red-legged frog habitat conservation areas using different layers of information about how desirable different areas are for frogs.

surface analysis. Analysis of the characteristics of a surface. Usually performed using raster GIS. Analyses of contour, slope, aspect, hillshade, and viewshed are examples of surface analysis.

Thiessen polygon. A polygon created to allocate space to the nearest point. An input layer contains a set of points. The operation to build Thiessen polygons begins at each point and moves outward until it reaches the border of an adjacent polygon moving out from other point(s). The resulting output layer contains polygons whose boundaries are lines of equal distance between two points. Thiessen polygons are very useful in calculating the service area of facilities and in siting new facilities.

Tobler's first law of geography. A law of geography formulated by UC Santa Barbara geographer Waldo Tobler stating that geographic features are most likely to be like nearby features.

viewshed. The area visible from a specific location, taking into account that some features may be blocked by others. Viewshed analysis is a type of surface analysis.

Questions for further study

1. How messy is the region where you live? Thinking in terms of how vector and raster GIS represent the world, if you were creating a map of the region where you live, which features of the built and natural environments would you represent using vector GIS? Which using raster GIS? Why? You may consider any of the features discussed in this chapter and any others that you consider important for the region where you live.

2. How might creating Thiessen polygons help school district planners decide on appropriate school district boundaries?

3. Identify a service delivery issue that is important to you. Describe how distance allocation would be helpful in planning the service delivery.

4. If you wanted to create a statistical surface representing soil suitability for Contra Costa County, how would you go about it? What data collection strategy would you use? Once you had collected data, what steps would you follow to create the statistical surface?

5. What is the difference between an expression and a function?

6. You have been asked to create a suitability model to determine the best locations for a new bicycle path. Identify four layers that you think would be useful to create the bicycle path model. How might you weight each of the four layers? What factors would lead you to rank areas in each of the four layers good or bad?

7. Identify a site suitability issue that is important to you. What kind of facility are you trying to site? What factors would be desirable to be near the site? What features would you want the site to be away from? How would you weigh the factors in the suitability model?

Annotated bibliography

Two of the texts described in the annotated bibliography for chapter 6 describe the raster GIS concepts and operations discussed in this chapter: Michael N. DeMers's *GIS Modeling in Raster* (DeMers 2001) and Jill McCoy and Kevin Johnston's *Using ArcGIS Spatial Analyst* (McCoy and Johnston 2001).

C. Dana Tomlin's book, *Geographic Information Systems and Cartographic Modeling* (Tomlin 1990) is the basic source of information on map algebra.

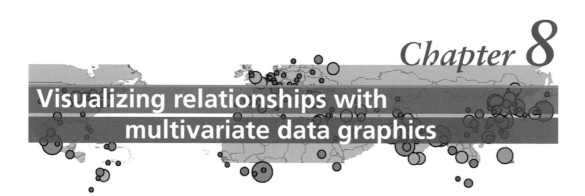

Chapter 8

Visualizing relationships with multivariate data graphics

"A rock pile ceases to be a rock pile the moment a single man contemplates it, bearing within him the image of a cathedral."

Antoine de Saint-Exupery, French writer (1900–1944)

Introduction

A data graphic that shows values of two or more variables on the same graphic—a **multivariate data graphic**—can visually illuminate relationships among the variables. This chapter builds on the univariate data graphics introduced in chapter 2. It shows multivariate data graphics that illustrate data underlying maps in this book, discusses the purpose of the different types of multivariate data graphics, and describes how to construct them correctly. Data graphics explained in this chapter are described in greater detail in two standard references (Cleveland 1994; Harris 1996).

Seeing relationships through data graphics

In chapter 2, you learned to see information through data graphics. That section described how they can be used as tools during research and as vehicles to communicate the results of analyses. It described data graphics commonly used to show values of a single variable—the results of univariate analysis.

This chapter extends the discussion in chapter 2 by showing how data graphics can reveal relationships among variables. For example, a column chart showing: (a) the percent of a country's population that is already urban in a given year, and (b) the percentage rate at which the country's urban population is growing in that year, makes it possible to see if the urban populations of countries that are less urbanized are growing faster or slower than the urban populations of countries that are already urbanized. A line chart showing the population size not just of London, but also of Paris and Rome every fifty years since 1750 makes it possible to see how each of these important European cities grew in population over time.

This section describes how data graphics you learned about in chapter 2—bar, column, and line charts—can be used to display information about values of two or more variables at once. It introduces a new kind of data graphic—the area chart. It doesn't say more about pie charts because they can only be used to show the results of univariate analysis. It also introduces another visual representation of data that is frequently used in social science and public policy research—the scattergram.

Multibar and multicolumn charts

You recall from chapter 2 that bar and column charts are very similar. In a bar chart, bars representing the values of a variable are displayed horizontally (across). In a column chart columns are displayed running vertically (up and down).

It is possible to include bars or columns in a bar or column chart representing two or more variables. A bar chart with two or more bars is called a **multibar chart**. A column chart with two or more columns is called a **multicolumn chart**. Figure 8.1 shows two variables: (a) the number of people age 16 and older who drove to work alone, and (b) the number of people age 16 and older who carpooled to work in each of twelve census tracts in southern Santa Clara County in 2000. This is the same area of southern Santa Clara County in maps 1.10a and 1.10b, but figure 8.1 shows data on some census tracts where a low percentage of people drive to work alone and some where a high percentage do. The two variables (drive alone and carpool) are columns originating on the horizontal x-axis. Values of these two variables—the number of drivers—are plotted on the vertical y-axis. For clarity, the columns are labeled with the number of people who drive alone or carpool, respectively. Each pair of columns represents one census tract. The census tract number is centered below the pair of columns. The black columns on the left in each pair represent the number of people age 16 and older who drive to work alone. The gray columns on the right in each pair represent the number of people age 16 and older who carpool to work. The pair of columns farthest to the left shows that about six hundred people drive to work alone and fewer than a hundred carpool in census tract 101. In census tract 102—represented by the second pair of columns—almost twelve hundred people drive to work alone and fewer than two hundred carpool. Most of the columns show a similar pattern—lots of people who drive to work alone and comparatively few who carpool to work. This pattern is different for census tracts 113 and 114. In census tract 113, relatively few people drive to work and a substantial number of those who do are carpoolers. In tract 114, carpoolers outnumber solo drivers about 4–1.

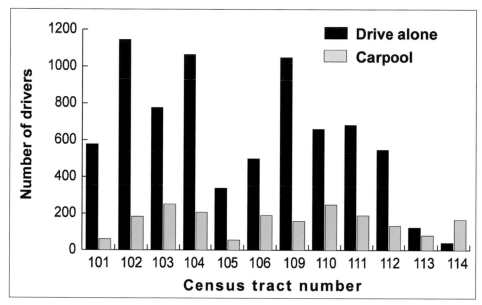

Figure 8.1 Driving alone and carpooling in twelve southern Santa Clara County census tracts, 2000.
Source: 2000 U.S. Census of Population and Housing

If you were working on developing a ride-sharing program for southern Santa Clara County, you might capitalize on the opportunity that census tracts 113 and 114 present. A campaign to inform residents in these census tracts that many carpools are available in their area might further increase carpooling. You also would likely focus attention on census tracts such as 101, 102, 104, and 109. In those tracts, lots of people drive to work alone and few people carpool. Perhaps designating carpool pick-up points and conducting a campaign to encourage more carpooling is needed for these problem tracts.

Figure 8.1 is an example of using vision to think. During exploratory research, a rough column chart generated by ArcMap or Microsoft Excel would disclose the important differences in driving behavior among these twelve census tracts. A polished data graphic like figure 8.1 (created in Adobe Illustrator) would be an effective accompaniment to maps illustrating how people commute to work in a final report. By seeing the information on commuting behavior in data graphics and maps, transportation planners, local elected officials, and citizens could formulate sound public policy to reduce traffic congestion by reducing the number of people who drive alone and increase the number who carpool.

Multiline charts

In chapter 4, you saw a line chart of the population of London from 1750 to 2000 at fifty-year time periods. This was a single-line chart—a visual representation of a univariate analysis.

More than one line can be drawn on a line chart, creating a **multiline chart**. That's the way stockbrokers graph prices of two or more stocks so that investors can tell in a single glance how well different stocks have performed in relation to each other over time. Why not draw multiple lines showing the population of two or more cities over time? Figure 8.2 is a multiline chart showing the population of London, Paris, and Rome from 1750–2000. In a multiline chart showing change over time like figure 8.2, time is plotted along the horizontal x-axis; the other variable (population in figure 8.2) is plotted along the vertical y-axis. Symbols like circles, triangles, diamonds, and squares may be inserted to help the viewer see exactly where the years fall. In figure 8.2, diamonds are used.

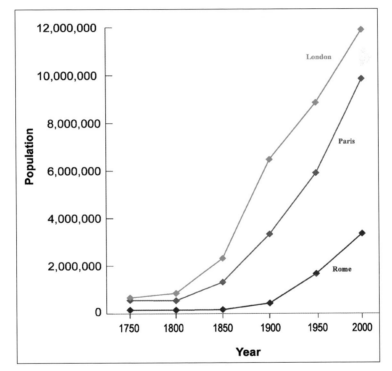

Figure 8.2 City population size: London, Paris, and Rome, 1750–2000.

Sources: Tertius Chandler and Gerald Fox, *3000 Years of Urban Growth* (1700–1800); Tertius Chandler, *Four Thousand Years of Urban Growth* (1900); United Nations (2000)

Figure 8.2 shows that as the industrial revolution began in England, London's population increased slightly between 1750 and 1800 while the populations of Paris and Rome stayed about the same. After 1800, London's population began to rise dramatically. The populations of both Paris and Rome began to rise somewhat later than London's. In all three cities, the 2000 population is much greater than the 1750 population.

Scattergrams

A **scattergram** shows the relationship between two variables. Often social scientists hypothesize that one variable explains or causes another. The variable that they seek to explain is called a **dependent variable**. The variable that they hypothesize might explain it is called an **independent variable**. Values of the two variables can be plotted against each other. The convention is to plot the dependent variable on the y-axis (vertical) and the independent variable on the x-axis (horizontal). The values form a scatter.

By looking at the pattern in the scatter, it is possible to see if the two variables are related, the strength of the relationship, and whether the relationship between the two values is positive or negative. If the values are positively related to each other, as one value increases the other also increases. A positive relationship does not necessarily mean that change in one variable causes a change in the other variable. A scattergram of London and Paris populations over time would show that the two are positively related. Generally as London's population increased, so did the population of Paris. The scatter would slope up. But growth in London's population did not cause an increase in the population of Paris.

A scattergram might show a negative relationship between two values. Many of the countries with rapidly increasing urban populations today are poor countries in Africa and Southeast Asia, and many of the countries whose urban populations are increasing slowly are wealthy countries in Europe and North America. A scattergram of urbanization rates and per capita income would show a negative relationship between these two variables. In general, the richer a country is, the less likely it is to be rapidly urbanizing. The scatter would slope down. This is because most countries with well-developed economies have already passed through their period of most rapid urbanization, while most less-developed countries are currently passing through a period of rapid urbanization. Values in a scattergram that are way above, below, or to the left or right of the other points in a scatter are called outliers.

Scattergrams also show how strongly two variables are related to each other. If the two variables are strongly related, the scatter is tight, with little distance between points and few points that depart very far from an imaginary regression line drawn through the center of the scatter. If the relationship is weak, the scatter is dispersed. In statistics, correlation and regression analysis produce precise estimates of the probability that relationships like the ones depicted in scattergrams occur by chance. If there is a very low probability that an observed relationship would have occurred by chance, the relationship is termed statistically significant and the level of significance is reported. For example, if there is less than a 5-percent chance that the relationship between the percent of a country's population that is urban and the country's current urbanization rate in figure 8.3 occurred by chance, the relationship would be reported as statistically significant at the .05 level. Regression analysis produces mathematical equations for estimating unknown values based on known values.

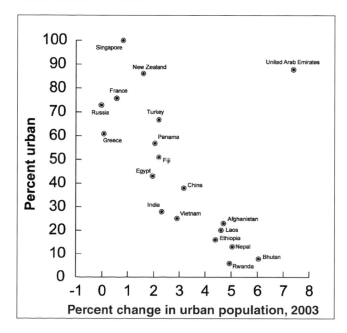

Figure 8.3 The relationship between percent urban and percent change in urban population for selected countries, 2003.

Source: World Bank

Figure 8.3 is a scattergram using the data underlying maps 1.3a and 1.3b that shows the percentage of a country's population that is urban and the percentage change in the country's urban population in 2003. Remember in maps 1.3a and 1.3b, you saw that the fastest percentage changes in urban populations are occurring in the least urbanized countries of Africa and Asia, so you would expect a scattergram to show a negative relationship between these two variables: the less urbanized a country is, the more likely it is that its urban population will be growing rapidly. The scattergram in figure 8.3 corroborates this expectation.

Relationships between variables in the messy real world are seldom as perfect as theoretical models. Some countries that are not very urban are not experiencing growth in their urban populations as rapidly as others. The United Arab Emirates (UAE) is a wealthy county at a relatively advanced stage of economic development whose urban population grew rapidly in 2003. The UAE is an outlier in figure 8.3 because the country is already quite urbanized but its urban population grew rapidly in 2003, unlike other countries. Looking at the overall pattern in figure 8.3 and variations within the patterns raises interesting questions about urbanization and percentage changes in urban population for further exploratory data analysis.

Stacked bar charts

Geographic units like countries, states, counties, cities, and census tracts have different attributes. Social scientists and public policy professionals are often interested in percentage breakdowns of an attribute among a number of different geographic units. For example, they may want to compare the population distribution by race within different census tracts. A good kind of data graphic to provide a rough comparison of the breakdown within different geographic units of the same type is a **stacked bar chart**.

You could create a series of stacked bar charts of different census tracts showing the percentage of the residents of each race in each census tract. By lining up a number of different census tracts it is possible to quickly get an idea of the racial breakdown of different census tracts and to spot tracts where there are particular patterns of interest. Because it is difficult for the human brain to translate the length of different segments of the bar into precise percentages, stacked bar charts don't allow a reader to quickly see precise percentages.

Figure 8.4 (next page) is a stacked bar chart that shows the racial breakdown of five San Francisco census tracts in 2000. Four census tracts represent places where members of one race are particularly concentrated. The fifth bar shows a tract where racial groups are more evenly distributed. The map below figure 8.4 shows the location of the five census tracts. More than 90 percent of the residents of the first census tract—tract 114—located in the heart of Chinatown are Asian or Pacific Islanders. About 75 percent of the residents in census tract 231.02 in the South Bayshore District are black, and about 70 percent of the residents of census tract 229.01 in the Mission District are Hispanic. About 85 percent of the residents of census tract 132 in the exclusive Sea Cliff neighborhood are white. The census tract with the racial composition that best reflects the diversity of San Francisco is census tract 254.03—located in San Francisco's rapidly changing Visitacion Valley neighborhood.

You could use stacked bar charts like figure 8.4 to show the different mix of modes of transportation to work in southern Santa Clara County, how many native-born and foreign-born residents there are in Bay Area census tracts, and to illustrate many other phenomena that appear in the maps in this book and in the exercises.

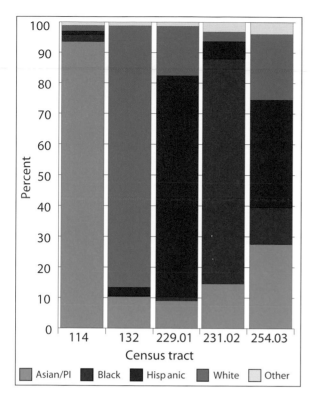

Asian/PI ■ Black ■ Hispanic ■ White □ Other

Figure 8.4 Demographics of five San Francisco census tracts, 2000.

Source: 2000 U.S. Census of Population and Housing

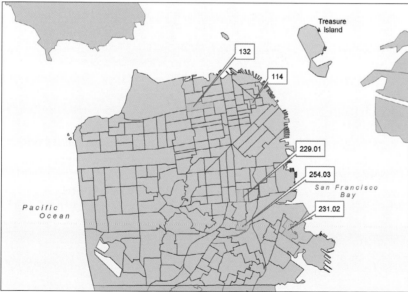

Area charts

Often analysts want to show the relative shares different variables contribute to a total number or percent. An **area chart** is a good way to do that. Figure 8.5 is an area chart presenting information on the population of five global cities at fifty-year increments between 1800 and 2000. You can see that in 1800, near the intercept of the x- and y-axes, the total population of four of the cities

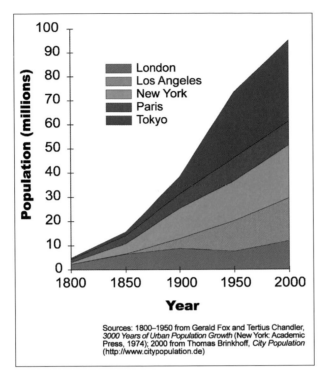

Figure 8.5   Area chart showing population of five global cities.

Sources: Tertius Chandler and Gerald Fox, *3000 Years of Urban Growth* (1700–1800); *Tertius Chandler, Four Thousand Years of Urban Growth* (1900); United Nations (2000)

was only about five million people. At that time, Tokyo's population was tiny, and Los Angeles (founded in 1791) consisted of just a handful of adobe houses. In 2000—at the right edge of the area chart—the combined population of these five global cities was nearly 100 million people. The chart shows how the cities grew at different rates over the same time period.

Part II of this book has built upon the introduction to GIS and data graphics in part I by introducing a second GIS model—raster GIS—and extending the initial discussion of data graphics to include multivariate data graphics. Part II also delved into new substantive material concerning conflicts between the natural and built environments.

Part III takes the discussion of urban issues, GIS, and data visualization even further and deals with the important issues of equity and spatial integration. The GIS material in part III describes how to symbolize maps and create effective map layouts. Finally, part III describes some important theory about data visualization and provides guidance on the role that maps and data graphics should play in communicating information.

Terms

area chart. A data graphic that plots the values of different variables along the x- and y-axes and displays results as an area. An area chart is similar to a line chart but has been colored in between the lines, creating an area. Area charts are good for displaying the trend of values over time or categories.

dependent variable. In the examination of causation in a relationship between two or more variables, the dependent variable is the variable a researcher hypothesizes might be explained by values of one or more independent variables.

independent variable. In the examination of causation in a relationship between two or more variables, an independent variable is a variable that a researcher hypothesizes may help explain values of the dependent variable.

multibar chart. A data graphic using two or more sets of horizontal bars to represent values of two or more variables. Each set of bars represents values of one variable.

multicolumn chart. A data graphic using two or more vertical columns to represent values of two or more variables. Each set of columns represents values of one variable.

multiline chart. A data graphic using two or more lines to represent values of two or more variables over time. Each line represents values of one variable. The lines start near the intercept of the x- and y-axes and should be read horizontally, from left to right.

multivariate data graphic. A data graphic illustrating two or more variables.

scattergram. A data graphic that visually displays the relationship between two variables. Values of one variable are plotted horizontally, in relation to the x-axis of the scattergram. Values of the other variable are plotted vertically in relation to the y-axis. A scattergram helps researchers see whether there is a relationship between two variables, and if so, whether the relationship is positive or negative, strong or weak, statistically significant or not.

stacked bar chart. A data graphic that looks like a single vertical column divided into segments. Each segment in a stacked bar chart is proportional to and represents a percentage of the entire height of the bar. Stacked bar charts are particularly useful for showing differences in the composition of similar features. For example, four stacked bar charts showing the percentage of the housing stock consisting of single-family homes, condominiums, apartments, and other types of units in four different census tracts would allow the viewer to immediately see differences in the mix of housing in the five tracts.

Questions for further study

1. You hypothesize that high birth rates cause countries to urbanize. If you had data on the number of live births per one thousand population and the percentage of the country's population that was urban, how would you construct a scattergram to show this relationship? Which would be the dependent variable? Which would be the independent variable? What would you expect the scatter to look like? Sketch it.

2. You plan to use stacked bar charts to show the religious affiliations of people in five countries with quite different mixes of religious belief. Using the categories Protestant, Catholic, Jewish, Muslim, Hindu, Buddhist, and other, sketch stacked bar charts for the five countries.

3. How would you construct a multibar chart to illustrate the number of people age 16 and older who work at home, walk to work, or bicycle to work in ten world cities? What would be the x-axis of your chart? The y-axis? How many variables would there be in each group of bars?

4. If you want to illustrate the volume of personal communications that occur by landline telephone, cell phone, and e-mail, what kind of multivariate data graphic would you use?

Annotated bibliography

William Cleveland's *The Elements of Graphing Data*, revised edition (Cleveland 1994), discussed in chapter 4, describes the theory and practice of creating multivariate data graphics.

Robert L. Harris's *Information Graphics: A Comprehensive Illustrated Reference* (Harris 1996) discusses and provides examples of thousands of multivariate data graphics to effectively communicate information.

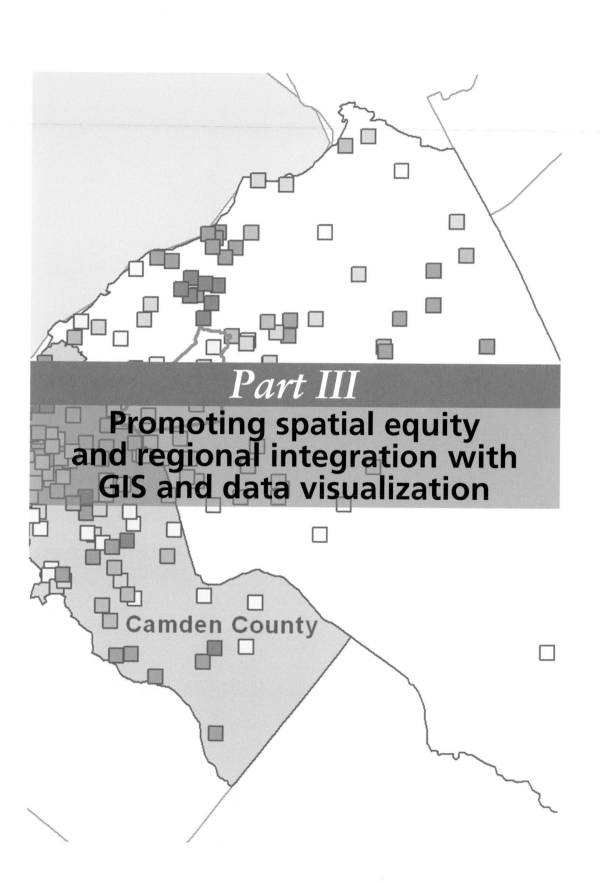

Part III

Promoting spatial equity and regional integration with GIS and data visualization

Camden County

Chapter 9

Spatial equity and regional integration

"... the test of our progress is not whether we add more to the abundance of those who have much; it is whether we provide enough for those who have little."

Franklin Delano Roosevelt (1937)

Introduction

Social justice and equality of opportunity—particularly for young people—are ideals nearly everywhere in the world. But most societies are not just. Opportunities often depend on a person's family income, race, religion, and gender (Marger 2001; Harvey 1973). Equality and opportunity are often related to geographical space. People in some countries, regions, cities, and neighborhoods within cities have better services and greater educational, cultural, and employment opportunities than others. De facto geographic segregation based on income and race remains widespread. Educational opportunity depends largely on the school district where children live. Inequality in education helps perpetuate inequality from generation to generation. Many children who receive an inferior education are unable to compete economically.

Most analyses of equality are aspatial; they look at things like income differentials between men and women, or how likely it is that Hispanic high school graduates will complete college compared to white high school students with the same grades. But there are spatial dimensions to equality, such as differentials in the amount of spending per student in different school districts.

Policies to promote greater spatial equality may be at any scale, but they are often best planned and implemented at the regional scale. Visionary thinkers like Anthony Downs (Downs 1973) and Myron Orfield (Orfield 1999 and 2002) argue persuasively that promoting spatial equality and regional integration at the metropolitan regional level is an important key to a healthy society.

This chapter discusses what spatial equality and regional integration mean, the spatial nature of segregation and inequality in metropolitan regions today, and ways in which spatial analysis and data visualization can help suggest strategies to promote spatial equality and regional integration.

Chapter 10 describes map symbology and how to create map layouts. It uses examples based on the material in this chapter.

Chapter 11 focuses on theory about data visualization and how to create data graphics. It uses material on spatial equality and regional integration to illustrate how text, maps, data graphics, tables, photographs, PowerPoint presentations, and the output from spreadsheets and statistical packages can be used together to communicate effectively.

Exercises 5 and 6 will teach you GIS operations to produce maps to see inequality clearly and to devise plans and policies for social change. They will show how to use GIS analyses to devise policies to create greater regional income and racial integration, fairer distribution of tax burdens and public service benefits, better environmental conditions for low-income and minority neighborhoods, and greater equality of educational opportunity for primary school children.

There is a wealth of good theory about spatial equality and regional integration. There are excellent models of specific programs to put theory into practice. Following is a review of some of the best theoretical writing about how to promote spatial equality and regional integration. The balance of this chapter describes how theory about increasing spatial integration and regional equality can be put into practice.

Theories of regional equality

A number of theorists have written about approaches to increasing regional equality. Among the most important theoretical approaches are Myron Orfield's ideas about metropolicy, Norman Krumholz's theory of equity planning, Paul Davidoff's approach to advocacy planning, and Anthony Downs's ideas about opening up the suburbs.

Metropolicy

Minnesota law school professor Myron Orfield is a theorist and activist. In his books and research reports, Orfield analyzes what he calls "metropatterns" of inequality in the economic, fiscal, and social situations of different types of communities in metropolitan areas (Orfield 1999 and 2002; Orfield and Luce 2003). His *American Metropolitics* (Orfield 2002) classified American metropolitan areas today into seven categories. Based on his spatial and statistical analysis, Orfield concluded that three kinds of "at-risk" jurisdictions have much in common with central cities: at-risk segregated jurisdictions, at-risk older jurisdictions, and at-risk developing jurisdictions. Orfield notes that if these three kinds of jurisdictions vote together as a bloc, they have a majority of votes in most state legislatures.

Based on his findings, Orfield proposes a metropolitics agenda designed to promote metropolitan health by reducing inequality. If they join forces, Orfield argues, coalitions of core cities and the three types of at-risk jurisdictions have the political power to redistribute tax burdens and benefits more fairly, improve urban services in poor jurisdictions, equalize school funding, and reduce school segregation. As a former Minnesota state assemblyman and current state senator, Orfield built coalitions between the core cities of Minneapolis and St. Paul and at-risk jurisdictions in the region where he lives. He has achieved some significant success in his metropolitics agenda. Orfield is continuing his analysis and also his coalition building as a state senator and a national advocate for reforming local government to produce greater regional equality.

Equity planning

Norman Krumholz, a professor of urban planning at Cleveland State University and the former planning director of Cleveland, Ohio, is another scholar and activist who has thought deeply about equality and worked hard to implement programs to improve equity.

During his tenure as Cleveland's planning director, Krumholz made equity the central focus of the city planning department's policy. Decisions about transportation, housing, infrastructure, and the environment were tested against the question "how will the plans and policies we develop promote social equity?" In his coauthored books *Making Equity Planning* Work (Krumholz and Forester 1990) and *Reinventing Cities: Equity Planners Tell Their Stories* (Krumholz and Clavel 1994), Krumholz develops a theory of **equity planning** and provides concrete examples of equity planning in action. Although Krumholz was the planning director of a single city, not a regional planner, many of the policies he and other equity planners have pursued are intended to promote regional equity.

Paul Davidoff, a lawyer and planner active in affordable housing programs to economically and racially integrate suburbs in the 1960s, developed a model of city planning called **advocacy planning** (Davidoff 1965). Davidoff envisaged some urban planners acting like lawyers, advocating the interests of their groups in presentations before planning commissions. For example, an urban planner speaking for low-income and minority residents of a poor inner city neighborhood might represent his clients before the planning commission of a neighboring suburb, urging the commission to include plans for more affordable housing in their community. This is exactly the kind of advocacy planning Davidoff himself practiced.

One of the earliest analyses of regional inequality remains one of the clearest and most provocative. In *Opening Up the Suburbs*, Brookings Institution policy analyst Anthony Downs argued that the way to halt America's slide into two unequal societies was national policy to promote racial integration on a regional basis (Downs 1973). Downs is a hard-nosed policy analyst who cuts to the heart of urban problems and proposes structural solutions. Downs argued that bettering the condition of low-income urban African-Americans could be accomplished by a number of strategies. One, sometimes called "gilding the ghetto," would be to promote economic and social development in poor African-American neighborhoods. Other possible strategies that Downs identified were models of regional integration—either dispersed integration or consciously creating what

Downs called mini-ghettos throughout metropolitan regions rather than in old core cities. Downs merely identified possible alternatives. He did not recommend creating mini-ghettos.

The best way to learn about how theories of spatial equality and regional integration can be applied and what policies are possible is by taking a close look at one region. Part III of this book focuses on two adjacent counties in New Jersey—Camden and Burlington—and particularly the city of Camden in Camden County and Mount Laurel Township in Burlington County.

Welcome to Camden and Burlington counties, New Jersey

Map 9.1 shows the location of Camden and Burlington counties with three smaller maps showing the two counties and the city of Camden and Mount Laurel in greater detail.

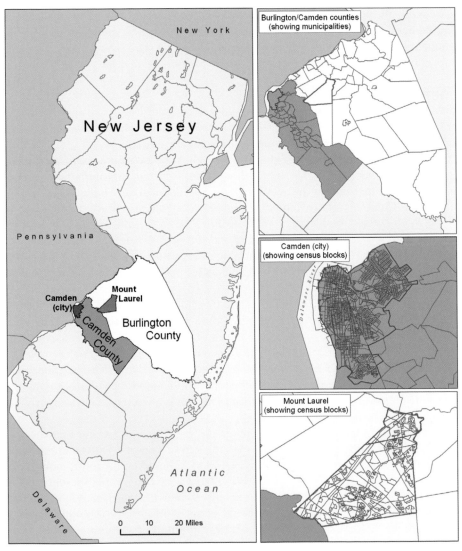

Map 9.1   Camden and Burlington counties, Camden (city), and Mount Laurel, New Jersey.

Source: 2000 U.S. Census of Population and Housing

Camden is a poor, old central city with a long history. It was once the prosperous headquarters of the RCA Victor phonograph company and the Campbell Soup Company. But after World War II, Camden's economy faded. RCA Victor and Campbell moved out. New freeways provided quick access between Camden and suburbs north and east of the city. Many upper- and middle-income households moved out of Camden to the suburbs. New migrants into Camden were disproportionately poor African-Americans, Puerto Ricans, and foreign immigrants. Banks stopped lending in some Camden neighborhoods. The city's old housing stock deteriorated.

Today much of Camden's population is poor, and prospects are that Camden will become even poorer. Since participation in the federal free-school-lunch program is limited to children from low-income households, the percentage of school children participating in the free-lunch program is an important indicator of poverty. All of the twenty-one highest-poverty schools in southern New Jersey ranked by rates of free lunch eligibility in 2000 are in Camden (Orfield and Luce 2003). Nearly half of southern New Jersey schools with free-lunch rates greater than 50 percent are located in Camden. The lowest poverty rate at any Camden public school in 2000 was 65 percent.

In contrast, Mount Laurel is a growing bedroom community close to Camden. At the time of the American Revolution, Mount Laurel was already a prosperous farm community. Most Mount Laurel residents at that time were Quaker farmers.

Mount Laurel has a long-standing African-American community. African-American slaves in Mount Laurel were freed during the Revolutionary War. After the revolution, more freed African-Americans from other locations settled in Mount Laurel. There is an African-American church built in 1820 in Mount Laurel. Some African-American families in Mount Laurel still own the manumission papers freeing their ancestors.

Mount Laurel's character changed slowly for nearly two centuries. Only after World War II did new highways, population growth, and changes in the regional economy begin to transform Mount Laurel. In addition to farming, Mount Laurel became a bedroom commuter suburb for Camden and Philadelphia and an employment center in its own right. Subdivisions and office parks replaced many of Mount Laurel's farms.

There are many other contrasts between Camden and Mount Laurel. The demographics, economies, housing, fiscal situation, number of contaminated sites, and student profile of the two communities are very different.

Camden's population—79,904 in 2000—is about twice as large as Mount Laurel's population of 40,221 (U.S. Census 2000a). Mount Laurel's population grew by 25 percent between 1990 and 2000, while Camden's population dropped 10 percent during the same period. Eighty-seven percent of Mount Laurel's population in 2000 was white. Only 17 percent of Camden's population was white in 2000. Camden's population density is more than four times as great as Mount Laurel's: 7,684 people per square mile in Camden compared to 1,832 in Mount Laurel.

There are still a substantial number of jobs in Camden, though the ratio of jobs to residents is much lower than in Mount Laurel. In 1999, the number of people employed in Camden—31,671—was only slightly larger than the number employed in Mount Laurel—30,237—though Camden has almost twice as many residents (Orfield and Luce 2003). Most new job growth in the region is taking place in Mount Laurel and other suburbs, not in Camden (Orfield and Luce 2003).

Camden has a mix of single-family homes, row houses, apartment houses, low-rent public housing projects, and other subsidized housing. Most of the housing in Mount Laurel consists of single-family detached privately owned homes built within the last thirty years. Some farms and historic older housing remain in Mount Laurel. There are a small number of affordable housing units forced upon the community by notable New Jersey state Supreme Court decisions and the New Jersey statewide Council on Affordable Housing. Housing sale prices and rents are much lower in Camden than in Mount Laurel.

Much of the housing in Camden is older, multifamily homes.
Source: *Courier-Post* (Cherry Hill, N.J.)

In Mount Laurel, most of the housing consists of single-family homes built in the last thirty years.
Source: *Courier-Post* (Cherry Hill, N.J.)

Camden has a much lower per capita tax capacity than Mount Laurel. It has a higher tax rate than Mount Laurel, but still generates less tax revenue per capita than Mount Laurel (Orfield and Luce 2003). Police, fire, library, park, and other public services are much better in Mount Laurel than in Camden.

There are a few sites in Mount Laurel that are contaminated with toxic substances from Mount Laurel's relatively few industries. In contrast, Camden has many contaminated sites (NJDEP 2001).

Students in Mount Laurel's public primary and high schools are predominantly white. Students in Camden's public primary and high schools are predominantly non-Asian minorities (Orfield and Luce 2003).

Regional integration: income, race, and education

Regional integration is a spatial issue. It involves bringing different kinds of people together on a regional basis. It is helpful to think of three different dimensions of regional integration.

Income integration

Sociologists use the term **social stratification** to refer to differences in social classes. The analogy is to geology where some strata of rocks are at one level, others at another. Sociologists disagree about exactly how to measure social strata that accurately capture the class structure of modern society. But they agree that wealth and income are important dimensions of social class. There are differences in earned income (how much money households receive from employment), other income (from sources such as stock dividends and rent), and wealth—everything of value that an individual has accumulated or inherited. Sociologists such as C. Wright Mills (Mills 1956), political scientists such as Paul Domhoff (Domhoff 1967), and others have studied the distribution of income and wealth in America. They conclude that a small percent of very rich individuals own a disproportionate share of the nation's wealth, middle-class households own almost all of the rest, and large numbers of poor people own only a tiny sliver of the nation's total wealth.

Household income varies widely. Wealthy doctors, lawyers, and business people have large earned income. In addition, they and other wealthy people may receive income from investments, rent, and other sources. Schoolteachers, policemen, and librarians earn less money than well-paid professionals and usually get less supplemental income from other sources. People employed full time in minimum wage jobs as retail clerks and farm laborers earn low incomes and rarely receive any supplemental income at all. People who are unable to work because of age, physical or mental disabilities, or lack of jobs where they live may rely only on meager monthly welfare checks. Within regions, rich and poor households are distributed very unevenly. In some cities, many households have earnings below the federal poverty threshold. In other cities, almost no household is that poor.

Maps are excellent vehicles to visually represent segregation. Percentages of the total population of a geographic area can be classified and represented by a choropleth map. Absolute numbers of individuals or households of a specific race or income can be represented in a dot density map.

Map 9.2 is a dot density map of Camden and Burlington counties. It shows the number of children under age 5 who are below the federal poverty threshold. It is easy to see from map 9.2 that within Camden and Burlington counties poor young children are heavily concentrated in the city of Camden. You will learn how to create dot density maps like map 9.2 in exercise 5.

Poor people whose income forces them to live in poor communities generally have a worse living environment than people who live in more affluent communities. They may have access to inferior housing, worn out infrastructure, fewer and less-well-maintained parks and libraries, fewer police and firefighters, and inferior public health care. As jobs vanish in poor areas, the low-income people who are left have fewer opportunities to find work and face longer commutes—the problem of spatial mismatch.

Income segregation affects moderate-income households too. In some communities police officers, firefighters, teachers, and librarians can't afford housing and no longer live where they work. Better off households often recognize the problem of housing affordability when their own children cannot afford to live where they grew up.

The group hardest hit by income segregation is school-aged children. Education is critical to their future, and the quality of schools varies enormously between rich and poor school districts.

Within cities there are also differences in where rich and poor people live. Income data at the census tract level is readily available from the U.S. Census Bureau. The most commonly used income measure is household income rather than individual income, because members of a household such as a husband, wife, and children living at home generally pool their resources. Wealth is much harder to define than income, and there is no agreed upon source of information on the distribution of wealth in America. The balance of this section focuses on income disparities.

Statisticians use the term *central tendency* for measures that describe the most common value in a group of values. The measure of central tendency usually used to summarize income is median household income. The median household income for an area is the amount that falls in the middle of the income distribution for households in the area. Half of all households in the

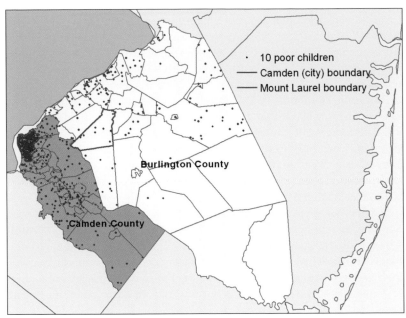

Map 9.2   Poor children under age 5 in Camden and Burlington counties.
Source: Myron Orfield and Thomas Luce, *New Jersey Metropatterns*

area have less than the median household income; half have more. Most analysts feel the median is a better measure to use in describing income distributions than the mean. The mean income for an area is calculated by adding all household incomes and dividing by the number of households. A very few rich outliers (extreme cases) in an income distribution will pull the mean income up. Saying that the mean annual household income in the census tract where Microsoft Corporation founder Bill Gates lives is $7,000,000 may be correct, but it does not accurately reflect the true average income in the census tract because Gates's enormous income pulls the mean way up. Saying that the median income for the census tract is $87,000 (with Gates's very large income just one value lying above the median) would more accurately reflect the true income distribution of the census tract where most of the approximately four-thousand other households may be earning between $40,000 and $120,000 a year.

One approach to analyzing metropolitan income disparities is to compare the median income of one city like Mount Laurel with another city like Camden. In this kind of analysis, cities are the unit of analysis. Based on such an analysis, a social scientist would conclude that median household income is much higher in Mount Laurel than in Camden.

A second approach to analyzing metropolitan income inequality is to look at the percent of households falling within each of the census' income categories. A community with much higher percentages of its population falling in the census categories $0 to $15,000, and $15,000 to $25,000, has a higher percentage of poor people than one with lower percentages falling in these two lowest categories. Dividing the number of poor people by the total population of a city produces the percentage of the city's population that is poor. Percentages like this make it possible to compare poverty among cities.

A third approach to analyzing metropolitan income inequality focuses on poverty. The U.S. Bureau of Labor Statistics computes a poverty threshold adjusted for family size and regional differences in the cost of living (Orshansky 1963 and 1965). Using this approach, a social scientist could describe the number of households falling below the federal poverty threshold in different cities.

Analysis of the income distribution among jurisdictions in metropolitan areas in the United States today using any one of the above methods shows great variation. Classifying the jurisdictions into classes using techniques you learned in chapter 3 allows income comparison among jurisdictions. Mapping the disparities is revealing and also helpful in devising strategies to increase equality.

Map 9.3 is a vector GIS choropleth map showing median income of cities in Burlington and Camden counties classified into five classes using the natural breaks method of classification described in chapter 3. Map 9.3 is symbolized with a monochromatic color ramp. Lighter values represent lower median household income; darker values represent higher median household income. Map 9.3 shows that median household income in the city of Camden is much lower than median household income in Mount Laurel.

There are many different approaches to increasing income integration within regions, and all of them can benefit from spatial analysis using GIS.

One approach is to bring new economic development and employment opportunities to distressed communities with high unemployment rates. Federal and state enterprise zone legislation, the federal empowerment zone/enterprise community program, and urban redevelopment program are examples of programs that revitalize distressed areas. If, for example, a major corporation is willing to build a new factory on vacant land within an empowerment zone because of tax breaks and other incentives, unemployed people in the area may get jobs in the factory. Their incomes will go up. Economic inequality within the region will be reduced. The successful efforts by residents of Boston's impoverished Dudley Street Triangle area to redevelop their neighborhood are described in Peter Medoff and Holly Sklar's *Streets of Hope* (1994). Chester Hartman has chronicled the struggles of San Francisco's South of Market area residents to make redevelopment of their neighborhood more responsive to them (Hartman 2002).

Another approach to regional income integration is to increase the affordable housing within affluent communities. This will make it possible for some low- and moderate-income households to live in communities they could not otherwise afford.

A third approach to increasing income equality within regions is to provide intergovernmental transfers so that poor jurisdictions have more money to pay for services for their residents. For example, if the federal government provides the poor city of Camden with a $300,000 community

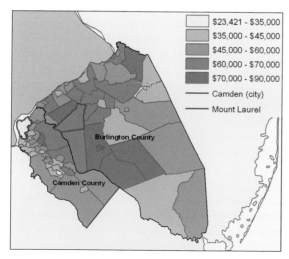

Map 9.3 Median income: Camden and Burlington counties cities, 2000.

Source: Myron Orfield and Thomas Luce, *New Jersey Metropatterns*

development block grant that can be used for a new senior center serving mainly low-income elderly people, the costs of the center do not have to come from the seniors' incomes or from local government sources.

Racial integration

In the not-too-distant past, segregation based on race or religion was legal in the United States. Homeowners could legally refuse to sell to African-Americans and Jews and could even include racially restrictive covenants in their house deeds forbidding whites who bought their houses to sell to "Negroes or people of the Jewish faith." African-American students went to segregated schools for African-Americans only and white students went to all-white schools. In many parts of the United States, African-Americans could not stay in the same hotels as whites, sit in the same sections of busses, or be served at whites-only lunch counters. They had to drink from segregated water fountains and use separate restrooms.

Harvard sociologist William Julius Wilson draws a sharp distinction between this kind of legally sanctioned **historical racism** and what he terms **contemporary racism** (Wilson 1987). Historical racism was open, acknowledged, and legal. Contemporary racism is disguised, denied, and illegal.

Where people of different racial and ethnic backgrounds live often differs greatly among cities within the same region and between neighborhoods within the same city. In some cases, this ethnic clustering is by choice. Members of an ethnic group may enjoy the familiar culture, language, and support systems of ethnic neighborhoods. Immigrant clusters can provide social support systems and cultural diversity. *Mapping Global Cities: GIS Methods in Urban Analysis*, by Ayse Pamuk (scheduled for publication by ESRI Press in 2006), will describe immigrant clusters in detail and include exercises to teach spatial data analysis skills using immigrant cluster data from San Francisco, Los Angeles, New York, and Washington D.C.

In other cases, clustering by race is the legacy of racial discrimination perpetuated by contemporary racism. Very low-income households living in segregated urban ghetto areas face what sociologist Wilson terms a tangle of pathologies including high unemployment rates, crime, drug dependency, and teen pregnancy as well as inferior housing, bad schools, and inadequate social services (Wilson 1996). Some social scientists, including Wilson, use the controversial term **underclass** to refer to people in the very bottom stratum of society.

Map 9.4 is a dot density map showing the location of African-Americans in Mount Laurel. Each dot represents ten African-Americans. The census enumerated 2,467 African-Americans in Mount Laurel in 2000 out of the total population of 40,221, about 6 percent of the population. Map 9.4 shows that Mount Laurel's African-American population was not dispersed evenly throughout the township in 2000. Most of Mount Laurel's African-American households lived in the northeast part of the city at that time. In chapter 10 you will learn more about how to symbolize the geographic distribution of populations in maps like map 9.4.

Increasing racial balance among different jurisdictions in a region is related to increasing income integration. Because racial minorities tend to have lower incomes than whites, they are likely to particularly benefit from construction of new affordable housing in high-income communities.

Enforcing laws against discrimination is still necessary to increase racial integration. Lawsuits related to employment and housing discrimination continue to play a major role in opening up suburbs to greater diversity.

School integration

Of all locally delivered services, public education is the most important. The quality of a person's primary and secondary education has an enormous impact on their life chances. People who are poorly educated often can't compete for college or good jobs. People who are well educated can.

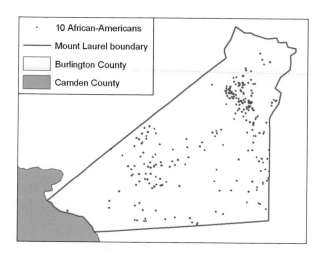

Map 9.4 African-Americans in Mount Laurel.
Source: Myron Orfield and Thomas Luce, *New Jersey Metropatterns*

Unless they are wealthy enough to afford private schooling for their children, families with school-aged children typically rely on public schools. The quality of public schools where they live is fundamental to their children's futures. Pleasant, well-maintained schools, with small class sizes, well-trained and well-paid teachers, extracurricular activities, parents involved in the school, and motivated peers produce a stimulating environment where children can learn. Old, decrepit schools with large class sizes, poorly trained and poorly paid teachers, few extracurricular activities, apathetic parents, and many disruptive and alienated students make it hard for even the most dedicated teacher to teach effectively or for the most talented child to succeed academically (Kozol 1992).

Public schools in the United States remain highly segregated by race a half century after the landmark U.S. Supreme Court case of *Brown vs. Board of Education* declared segregated schools unconstitutional. One important study concludes that racial segregation in schools has increased since the height of the civil rights movement (Orfield and Yun 1999).

GIS is an excellent tool for analyzing racial imbalance in schools on a regional level. Map 9.5 shows the percentage of non-Asian minority students in elementary schools in Camden and Burlington counties in 2000. Schools, not individuals, are the unit of analysis, and points are symbolized to show differences in the percentage of non-Asian minority students in the schools. The concentration of darkest blue squares (over 60 percent non-Asian minority students) in the city of Camden shows the high concentration of non-Asian minority students in elementary schools in the city. In 2000, more than 95 percent of the students in twenty-six Camden elementary schools were non-Asian minorities. In contrast, four of the squares in Mount Laurel are the lightest shade of blue (less than 10 percent non-Asian minorities in 2000), and one is the second lightest shade of blue (11 to 20 percent non-Asian minorities in 2000).

GIS can also illustrate school segregation by race at the community level. Map 9.6 contains the same layer representing the location of African-Americans in Mount Laurel as map 9.4 with one dot representing ten African-Americans. It contains a second overlay layer showing the location of Mount Laurel's five primary schools represented as red points. While there are more African-Americans living in Mount Laurel in 2000 than in the past, and African-American households live in many different Mount Laurel neighborhoods, there is still substantial clustering in the northeastern part of the township, where two of the schools are located.

There are many different approaches to improving educational equality. Spatial analysis can contribute to many of them.

Drawing the boundaries of school districts and determining which students will go to which schools will have a major impact on the composition of the student body in the schools. Boundaries

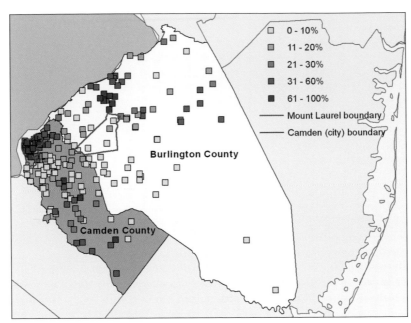

Map 9.5   Percentage of non-Asian minority students in Camden and Burlington counties elementary schools, 2000.

Source: Myron Orfield and Thomas Luce, *New Jersey Metropatterns*

that are drawn tightly around an area where low-income minorities are concentrated will lead to a student body consisting disproportionately of low-income minority students. Drawing boundaries to include a mix of incomes and races will produce schools with more diverse student bodies. From your reading in this book and the exercises, you can see how doing overlay analyses of school district boundaries compared to census data on race and income can help school districts draw boundaries that will promote school integration.

At the state level, New Jersey and many other states provide state education **equalization aid** so that poor school districts receive state money to help bring their per student funding levels up closer to those of more affluent school districts. Determining how to allocate state education equalization aid is greatly facilitated by spatial analysis of school district boundaries, student demographics, and the fiscal capacity of jurisdictions.

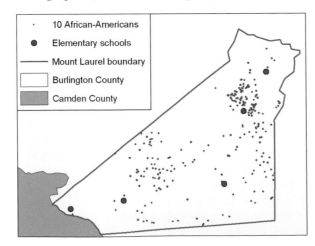

Map 9.6   African-Americans and primary schools in Mount Laurel.

Source: Myron Orfield and Thomas Luce, *New Jersey Metropatterns*

Housing policies for regional integration

Housing theorists see housing as a bundle of goods and services beyond the physical structure itself. Place matters a great deal to the quality of life a household experiences. Being able to live in a decent, safe, and sanitary house in a good neighborhood is very important. The neighborhood in which housing units are located is as important to the quality of residents' lives as the physical units themselves. An apartment in a crime-infested neighborhood or a house in an area with no jobs may be more problematic than a physically deteriorated unit.

People can live in a community only if there is housing available and affordable to them. A common rule of thumb is that a household can afford to pay one-third of pre-tax income for shelter. For homeowners the accepted rule is that the costs of Principle, Interest, property Taxes, and hazard Insurance (**PITI payments**) should not exceed one-third of their pre-tax income. For renters, monthly contract rent should not exceed one-third of their income.

There are a great variety of types and costs of housing appropriate to different households with different incomes. There is housing that is owned or rented; single-family or multifamily; with 0, 1, 2, 3, 4, or more bedrooms; and representing a wide range of sizes, conditions, and prices.

Types of housing are not equally distributed spatially. In most regions, some cities consist almost entirely of very expensive single-family homes; others have a mix of modest homes and rental units; still others consist primarily of relatively inexpensive single-family homes, condominiums, mobile homes, rental units, and government-assisted affordable housing units.

Local governments exercise a powerful indirect control over what is built in their communities. While most housing is built by the private sector and privately owned, local governments influence the type of housing in their community through zoning and other land-use regulations. If a community zones almost all its land for single-family homes on large (expensive) lots, the community will have quite a different character than if it sets aside a significant amount of land for single-family homes on small lots (which will be relatively affordable) and zones some land for condominiums, apartment houses, and mobile homes which are likely to be even more affordable. The community can assure an even greater variety of household types if it practices inclusionary housing policies and promotes construction of affordable housing. Efforts to promote inclusionary housing polices have been particularly important in New Jersey. Two New Jersey Supreme Court cases held that Mount Laurel's exclusionary land-use practices violated the state constitution and required Mount Laurel to change its land-use regulations so that developers could build affordable housing. The legal and political battles that these landmark court cases unleashed are well described in David Kirp's book, *Our Town: Race, Housing, and the Soul of Suburbia* (1995).

The 1949 Housing Act—the fundamental law that has defined federal housing policy for over half a century—declared a national goal of providing every American household with "decent, safe, and sanitary housing at rents and prices they can afford" (U.S. Housing Act of 1949). While the United States is still far from meeting the 1949 goal, the idea of providing housing to meet every household's needs remains a powerful vision. Progress toward this goal requires providing more housing choices for low- and moderate-income households—particularly in suburbs and other high-cost areas.

Ability to afford housing is usually determined by comparing household income to shelter costs. Using our New Jersey example, since the number of Camden residents with very low incomes is much greater than in Mount Laurel, you might expect that more people in Camden cannot afford housing than in Mount Laurel. However, since much of Camden's housing stock is old and in poor physical condition, house prices and rents are much lower in Camden than in Mount Laurel. Spatial analysis reveals that more people are able to afford housing in Camden than in Mount Laurel.

There are many approaches to increasing housing opportunities to promote regional integration. Among the most important are greenlining, inclusionary housing policies, and fair-share housing policies.

Greenlining

Housing inequalities are affected both by the behavior of private market lenders and the land-use policies of local governments. Whether or not banks make mortgage credit available in an area will have a large impact on house values and the ability of homeowners to maintain them.

Redlining is the systematic exclusion of entire neighborhoods from mortgage and other credit (Parzen and Kieschnick 1992). Imagine a senior vice president for mortgage lending looking at a map of low-income and minority neighborhoods and, after deciding the areas are in decline economically, circling the areas with a red, felt-tipped pen. That in turn puts the areas off-limits to the bank's residential mortgage lending. Thereafter, all homeowners in the redlined area—regardless of whether they have a nice house, stable job, and unblemished credit history—will be unable to get a mortgage from the bank. Without access to credit to maintain their houses, homeowners will see their houses deteriorate over time. If all the homeowners in the neighborhood lack access to loans to maintain their houses, all the houses in the neighborhood will deteriorate. New homebuyers, unable to get mortgages and aware of neighborhood decline, won't buy houses in the redlined area or will only be willing to pay much less for them, so property values will decline. Redlining thus becomes a self-fulfilling prophecy.

It is easy to stereotype banks that redline as irresponsible, and sometimes that is justified. But redlining raises difficult issues about who should pay the costs of social interventions such as providing mortgage loans in high-risk areas. According to one study of mortgage lending in low-income communities (Parzen and Kieschnick 1993), some banks have pursued socially responsible policies of carefully screening loan applicants and loaning money to qualified applicants in poor areas. Some banks consciously devote a portion of their portfolios to high-risk loans from a sense of public responsibility or in response to community and regulatory pressure.

Federal government policy regarding mortgage credit in high-risk areas has varied widely over the last fifty years. Politically conservative administrations have pursued a laissez-faire approach, allowing banks to decide where to lend and with what underwriting criteria. Liberal administrations have required banks to do some mortgage lending in high-risk areas, but provided federal mortgage guarantees so that the federal government covers banks' losses in the case of defaults. Spatial analysis with maps linked to attributes of mortgage lending such as property values, loan-to-value ratios, and numbers of defaults can help government formulate sound policies.

Greenlining turns redlining on its head—it is the process of actively making credit available to marginal neighborhoods. Chicago's South Shore Bank and other community banks, economic development corporations, and housing development corporations have programs to extend mortgage credit (Parzen and Kieschnick 1993).

Inclusionary housing policies

Metropolitan regions are fragmented into dozens or hundreds of separate jurisdictions. Understandably, if regrettably, each jurisdiction looks out for its own interests. Each jurisdiction usually promotes polices to assure that new housing is as expensive as possible in order to maintain (indeed increase) property values. Municipalities generally want to avoid the costs and problems they perceive coming from lower-income residents. Accordingly, many jurisdictions do not want much affordable housing, if any, in their community. They are leery of outsiders who do not currently reside in the community—particularly if they are very low-income minority families. Acronyms have come to describe some of the players in these situations: NIMBYs ("Not In My

Back Yard") are people who don't want affordable housing near them, and NIMEYs ("Not In My Election Year") are local elected officials who won't vote to approve affordable housing in the year in which they will stand for election.

An **exclusionary land-use practice** is a practice a local government pursues to keep a **locally unwanted land use (LULU)** such as low-income housing out of their community. Exclusionary land-use practices can include zoning land into large lots so that only expensive housing can be built, prohibiting multifamily housing such as apartments and condominiums so that only single-family homes can be built, and prohibiting mobile home parks. Communities can also keep affordable housing out of their communities by failing to seek out government-assisted housing funding and imposing regulations that make it difficult or impossible for nonprofit or for-profit housing developers to build affordable housing within their borders. Restrictive building codes, subdivision ordinances that make the cost of a development expensive, and growth management ordinances that limit the number of units that can be built can contribute to a jurisdiction's exclusiveness.

An **inclusionary land-use policy** is aimed at reversing exclusionary practices. Inclusionary policies are intended to allow more low- and moderate-income housing suitable for a greater variety of household types to be built in a community.

Local governments decide how to zone their jurisdictions and zoning in turn affects what kind of housing (single- or multifamily, and at what density) can be built and where. **Upzoning** is the process of increasing the permitted intensity of use in a zone. Upzoning to permit more multifamily housing at greater densities and smaller in size can make it possible for developers to build housing for a greater variety of households. Upzoning can make it possible for low- and moderate-income households—who can afford to purchase only modest starter homes or condominiums, rent inexpensive apartments, or live in government-assisted affordable housing units—to live, work, and educate their children in the same communities as households who can afford moderate- and upper-income housing in the private market.

Some communities require developers to set aside some percent of units in new development as affordable housing. For example, a community can require a developer building one hundred new condominiums that would sell in the private market for $250,000 to make 15 percent (fifteen units) available to low- and moderate-income households who would pay no more than 30 percent of their income for PITI payments. These units (identical to others in the building) might sell at a deeply discounted price like $175,000. This kind of inclusionary housing will assure at least a mix of moderate-income households (police officers, teachers, librarians) among wealthier households. Few inclusionary housing programs require deep subsidies so that low- or very low-income households can purchase or rent units.

The U.S. Department of Housing and Urban Development (HUD) defines a **low-income household** as a household whose income is between 50 percent and 80 percent of the median household income in the area where they live adjusted for family size. HUD defines a **very low-income household** as a household whose income is less than 50 percent of the median household income in the area where they live adjusted for family size. Often the only way that very low-income and often low-income households can afford to live in high-priced communities is in subsidized housing. Many different federal housing subsidy programs exist and these may be supplemented by state and local housing subsidy programs. Federal low-rent public housing, tax credits, below-market interest rate projects, and **Section 8 certificates** can bring the cost of decent, safe, and sanitary housing down so that low- and very low-income households can afford it. A Section 8 certificate entitles the holder to pay only 30 percent of his or her income toward rent, with the federal government paying the difference between that amount and a federally determined fair market rent for the area. Unfortunately, there are too few of these deep housing subsidies to go around. In addition, jurisdictions where affordable housing is most needed often choose not to compete to get what housing subsidies do exist.

Fair-share housing

Even communities of good will are reluctant to be the only ones to welcome subsidized housing for low- and very low-income households, or to accept more than their fair share of such housing.

A **fair-share housing plan** is a plan by cities and counties in a metropolitan region to assure that each jurisdiction accepts its fair share of affordable housing. The council of governments (COG) for the region often brokers the fair-share plan. A COG may set the number of housing units for low- and very low-income households that constitutes the jurisdiction's fair share based on factors such as the jurisdiction's total population and the amount of affordable housing already in the community. Spatial analysis of the income distribution of households, the location of existing subsidized housing, and the location and cost of other types of housing in communities within a region is very helpful in fair-share planning.

Environmental justice

While most environmentalists focus their concerns on the issues raised in part II of this book, such as preservation of open space, prime farmland, wetlands, and endangered plant and animal species, there is increasing recognition of the impact that degraded physical environments have on human beings and recognition that low-income and minority households are disproportionately impacted by negative environmental conditions.

A vigorous national **environmental justice movement** is working to improve the physical environment in low-income and minority neighborhoods. The environmental justice movement focuses on understanding disparities in the physical environment where low-income and minority people live compared to the environment in moderate- and upper-income predominately white areas. People interested in environmental justice focus on many different dimensions of inequality, such as the presence or absences of park and open space land and air and water quality. A particular focus of the environmental justice movement is on toxics and dangerous forms of pollution that pose potential health risks. The environmental justice movement is led by activists who have more than an academic interest in environmental justice. They use research findings to try to make positive change like cleaning up dangerous, contaminated areas and getting more neighborhood parks into underserved poor and minority areas.

Understanding and dealing with toxic contamination is a three-step process: (a) defining precise standards of what contamination is, (b) measuring samples from the field to determine whether a site qualifies as contaminated given the standards, and then (c) developing a remediation program to clean up the contamination. Mapping sites with GIS and creating an attribute table with details on the type and amount of contamination at each site is an important tool in dealing with toxics.

Step b is a process that geographers refer to as **ground truthing**—making sure that something that is mapped is actually true by going to the location and carefully checking (Pickles 1994). Ground truthing is an essential step in mapmaking. It is absolutely essential for sensitive mapping work such as describing the location of contaminated sites, the precise legal boundaries of parcels, the location of underground electrical power lines, and the presence of endangered species. In these highly charged situations, accidentally adding an extra foot to a lot line, showing toxics where they do not exist, mapping an endangered species as present where it is not, or failing to indicate an underground power line can create big problems. Imagine the consequences if a landowner builds her house onto a foot of a neighbor's land, a contractor digs through an electrical power line, or an angry landowner proves that an incorrectly mapped endangered animal species has prevented development worth millions of dollars without saving a single animal.

Earlier maps in this section have documented the much greater concentration of low-income and minority households in Camden. Further analysis of specific contaminated sites in relation to the demographics of the surrounding community might show that racial minorities have a greater risk of being exposed to dangerous toxic substances that whites.

At the heart of any environmental justice study is analysis of two data layers—data on environmental hazards and data on the demographics of the area. If a spatial overlay shows spatial coincidence between the hazards and poor minority communities, this suggests a problem. Of course, establishing the nature and extent of environmental injustice and laying the foundation for change requires careful analysis of the nature of the hazard and precise analysis of the spatial dimensions of the problem.

Different federal, state, and local agencies have different ways of defining contaminated sites. Map 9.7 shows the location of known contaminated sites in Camden that are on the New Jersey Site Remediation Program (SRP) Comprehensive Site List where groundwater contamination had been identified as of 2001 (NJDEP 2001). The sites were selected using the *select by location* operation you learned in exercise 2. This list does not include sites that are known to contain contaminated soils and may not show other contaminated sites in the area.

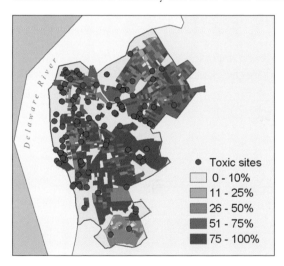

Map 9.7 Known contaminated sites in Camden (city) with groundwater contamination (2001) and the percentage of the population non-white by census tract (2000).
Source: New Jersey Department of Environmental Protection

Map 9.7 also displays the percentage of the population of Camden census tracts that were non-white in 2000. Just because a site is classified as contaminated does not necessarily mean that it poses any health or safety risk to people. But the presence of groundwater contamination in an area raises health and safety concerns. Drilling or digging in the area, for example, might bring toxic substances to the surface where some could harm people. These particular contaminated sites are concentrated in the older industrial core city of Camden. Camden had a lot of polluting industries long before the dumping of toxic waste was regulated. There are many fewer toxic waste sites in Mount Laurel than in Camden. You will explore the relationship between toxic sites and race further in exercise 5.

Municipal fiscal and service equality

Space has an important impact on how much property owners have to pay in local property taxes, and how much local (own-source) revenue is available to local governments to pay for services for their residents. **Own-source revenue** refers to the revenue cities and counties can raise themselves from the local property tax or other revenue sources in contrast to money they receive from their state government or the federal government in the form of intergovernmental transfers. The amount of revenue a community has available will largely determine the quality of police, fire, library, park, and other public services citizens get, including public school education for their children.

Fiscal capacity

Some jurisdictions have much greater **fiscal capacity** than others—that is they are able to generate larger amounts of own-source revenue more easily. The largest local revenue source in New Jersey and most other states is the local **property tax**: an annual tax on individual homes, apartment buildings, stores, factories, and other real property. Typically county assessors determine the **assessed value** of every individual house, store, factory, and other real property each year based on what comparable properties have sold for. A tax rate is then applied to the assessed value to specify exactly how much property tax the property owner must pay that year. Cities with a lot of valuable real property like new office parks, auto malls, and corporate headquarters buildings can raise more property tax revenue than cities with only old housing and small businesses. Depending on the state, local governments have more or less discretion to decide their tax rate or must follow specific uniform state standards.

Map 9.8 is a choropleth map that shows per capita tax capacity for municipalities in Camden and Burlington counties classified into five classes. Missing data is in gray. The amount is expressed in per capita terms (the total tax capacity divided by the total population), to make it easier to compare small and large municipalities.

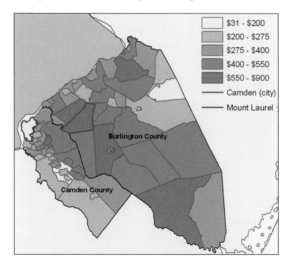

Map 9.8 Per capita tax capacity: Camden and Burlington counties cities, 2000

Source: 2000 U.S. Census of Population and Housing

Camden (city) falls in the lowest category in terms of per capita tax capacity. It has a total combined per capita property and income tax capacity of $77. Mount Laurel falls in the top category with per capita tax capacity of $571. In other words, if Mount Laurel set its property tax rate the same as Camden's, it would have over six times as much property tax revenue per capita to spend on schools, police and fire services, libraries, parks, and other services. A municipality's **tax base** is very important. Cities that have a lot of tax base can raise a lot of local property tax revenue to spend on public services. Cities that do not have strong tax bases are not able to raise as much without a higher tax rate. As you will see in exercise 6, the per capita tax capacity of municipalities is quite varied, and Camden has a low per capita tax capacity compared to Mount Laurel.

There are many other sources of local revenue besides property taxes, such as transient occupancy taxes charged to people who stay in hotels, revenue from ticket sales at the city zoo, rental income from city-owned facilities, and fines from parking meter violations.

Cities also get **intergovernmental transfers**—money from federal and state government. State school equalization aid to help equalize the amount of money available per pupil across jurisdictions helps level the playing field in education in New Jersey and other states. Federal community development block grants help cities with physical community development projects like repairing old curbs and gutters, acquiring sites for affordable housing, and rehabilitating deteriorated buildings.

Some individuals require more public services than others. People who are attending public primary or high school require more local funding to cover education costs than employed adults who are not in school. People who are unemployed, sick, elderly, or drug dependent may require money to meet living and medical expenses. People who are incarcerated require funding to cover prison costs. The dependent poor need money for food, medical care, and shelter, rather than amenities like pleasant parks and well-stocked libraries. Generally municipalities with the greatest needs have the least financial resources.

There is a vicious cycle in which the capacity of a locality to pay for services from its own revenue declines as needs increase. As a jurisdiction has more and more poor and dependent people, the property in the community is usually worth less and less. The jurisdiction generates less and less property tax revenue even if it increases property tax rates. At the same time, the jurisdiction's needs grow because their poor residents require more welfare, health care, job training, housing subsidy, and other social service assistance. Cities in this situation have only two choices: raise taxes or cut services. Neither ends the downward spiral. Whichever they choose will make them less attractive to people who have the option of moving out of the jurisdiction (often the wealthiest, best educated, most employable people) and less desirable to people who have choices of moving into the jurisdiction or somewhere else.

The cities of Camden and Mount Laurel illustrate the dilemma described above. The relatively affluent growing suburb of Mount Laurel, with modest social service needs, has a property tax rate of 2.63 percent (Orfield and Luce 2003). The old core city of Camden, with high poverty rates and many social service needs, has a property tax rate of 4.49 percent—almost double Mount Laurel's rate (Orfield and Luce 2003). In other words, Camden is taxing its poor property owners at a much high rate than Mount Laurel is taxing its much better off property owners. Since you have already seen that Camden has a much lower per capita tax capacity than Mount Laurel, even Camden's much higher property tax rate doesn't generate as much per capita revenue as Mount Laurel generates. This is surely one contributing factor to businesses moving out of Camden and new businesses choosing to locate in Mount Laurel.

While inequality can take many forms, it often has a spatial dimension. Segregation is, by definition, spatial. Now that this chapter has explored different dimensions of metropolitan inequality and some promising approaches to improving spatial equality and regional integration, it is time to return to spatial analysis and data visualization concepts.

Armed with knowledge of the vector and raster models and essential GIS operations, you are ready to focus in greater depth on GIS output. Chapter 10 focuses on how to symbolize map features and create map layouts. The first part of chapter 10 systematically reviews how attention to symbol shapes and sizes, fill and outline colors, transparency, and related symbology can produce superior maps that communicate information clearly.

The final chapter in part III, chapter 11, returns to data graphics. Using spatial inequality as an example, it describes some of the theory behind visual communication. Chapter 11 also describes how visual communication can fit into a broader strategy to communicate research findings in written and oral reports, PowerPoint presentations, and in other ways.

Terms

advocacy planning. An approach to city planning proposed by planner and lawyer Paul Davidoff. Davidoff criticized city planning departments for creating single, unitary plans that often represented establishment consensus views about the future of cities rather than incorporating minority views. He suggested an alternative system in which city planning commissions would function more like courts and planners more like lawyers. In his view, advocates for poor people, environmentalists, developers, and small business owners arguing vigorously in favor of plans their respective constituencies favored would provide planning commissioners with a wider range of views and options and lead to fairer and more democratic planning. Some planners today style themselves advocacy planners.

assessed value. The value of real property for local property tax purposes. The assessed value of every single-family home, apartment building, store, factory, vacant lot, and every other type of real property is determined each year by local (usually county) tax assessors. The property tax that owners of real property must pay is determined by multiplying the local tax rate times the assessed value of the property.

contemporary racism. Harvard sociologist William Julius Wilson's term for prejudice and discrimination based on race. Contemporary racism is more subtle than legally sanctioned racism that existed before legal reforms growing out of the civil rights movement of the 1960s.

environmental justice movement. A political movement intended to have low-income and minority communities treated more fairly in relation to the natural environment. A major thrust of the environmental justice movement is to clean up toxic waste sites and other contaminated sites near low-income and minority communities. The environmental justice movement also seeks to assure that low-income and minority communities will have access to parks and other environmental amenities.

equalization aid. Financial aid that state government provides to local school districts to equalize the amount of revenue available to poor school districts that cannot raise as much own-source revenue as rich school districts. The purpose of state education equalization aid is to minimize disparities in revenue per student among school districts.

equity planning. An approach to city and regional planning developed by Cleveland State University professor and former Cleveland city planning director Norman Krumholz and practiced by some urban planners. Equity planning tests each urban planning policy against the standard of assuring equity for everyone—including the poor and disenfranchised.

exclusionary land-use practice. A local government zoning or other land-use practice that has the effect of excluding some households from the community because of their income, family composition, or—indirectly—race.

fair-share housing plan. A regional plan in which cities and counties in a region agree upon each jurisdiction's fair share of affordable housing. Because affordable housing will cost the jurisdiction more in expenditures than it will bring in through property tax, local governments are reluctant to approve affordable housing developments. Each jurisdiction wants to avoid being known as the place in a region where affordable housing is located and low-income people live. Participating in an agreement with other jurisdictions in which each pledges to accept their fair share of affordable housing may make approving affordable housing more palatable to them.

fiscal capacity. The ability of a jurisdiction to pay for services it needs from own-source revenues, such as the local property tax.

greenlining. A policy of extending mortgage and other credit in marginal communities in order to encourage property maintenance and reinvestment. Greenlining is the opposite of redlining.

ground truthing. The process of checking to make sure that information which appears on maps is actually true by going to the location and checking it. Ground truthing is an important step in mapping.

historical racism. Sociologist William Julius Wilson uses this term. Wilson, an African-American, distinguishes between historical racism—state-sanctioned racism in which members of minority race(s) were discriminated against by law—from contemporary racism in which discrimination does not have the backing of the state.

inclusionary land-use policy. A policy intended to encourage low- and moderate-income households to live in a community rather than to exclude them. Inclusionary land-use policies are the opposite of exclusionary land-use policies. Requiring that 15 percent of the units in a new condominium project be sold at prices that moderate-income households can afford is an example of an inclusionary housing policy.

intergovernmental transfer. A transfer of funding from a higher level of government, such as the federal government, to a lower level of government, such as a city. Many local governments receive intergovernmental transfers from the federal government (such as community development block grants) and from their states (such as education equalization aid).

locally unwanted land use (LULU). Locally unwanted land uses—referred to as LULUs—are kinds of land uses that local governments usually do not want located within their borders. Local governments may agree in principle that the region needs landfills, toxic waste disposal sites, prisons, and housing for very low-income households, but they often prefer that these LULUs are located in some other jurisdiction.

low-income household. The U.S. Department of Housing and Urban Development (HUD) defines a low-income household as a household earning between 50 percent and 80 percent of the median household income of the Standard Metropolitan Statistical Area (SMSA) where the household lives adjusted for household size. Being classified as a low-income household may qualify a household for subsidized housing.

own-source revenue. Revenue that local governments (cities and counties) derive from the property tax, user fees, and other local sources as opposed to intergovernmental transfers from the state or federal government.

PITI payment. Payment of principal, interest, (property) taxes, and (hazard) insurance by a homeowner. These four recurring payments are the main components of the cost of owning a home in the United States.

property tax. An annual tax on the value of real property such as single-family homes, apartment buildings, stores, factories, and vacant lots. A tax rate is applied to the assessed value of real property to determine the amount of property tax due. In the United States, the property tax is the most important source of local government revenue.

redlining. A practice by some banks of excluding entire neighborhoods from credit such as mortgage loans, based on a belief that the neighborhoods are too risky. Without access to credit, homeowners in redlined neighborhoods are not able to maintain their homes and the housing stock will physically deteriorate. New home buyers, unable to get mortgages, won't buy houses in the redlined area or will pay much less for them. Redlining thus becomes a self-fulfilling prophecy. Redlined neighborhoods decline.

Section 8 certificate. A certificate funded by the federal government but administered by a local housing authority to a very low-income household that has applied for housing assistance. A Section 8 certificate entitles the household to receive the difference between 30 percent of their household income and an amount deemed sufficient to permit them to rent a decent, safe, and sanitary housing unit in the area where they live.

social stratification. A term used by sociologists and others to describe the class structure of a society with members of some groups at a higher level than members of other groups.

tax base. The value of property subject to the property tax in a community.

tax rate. A percentage applied to the assessed value of real property to determine the amount of property tax landowners pay.

underclass. The social class at the very lowest rung of the economic ladder.

upzoning. Rezoning a parcel of land to permit more intensive development. For example, if a parcel of land zoned to permit only construction of single-family detached houses is rezoned to permit building of apartment houses, the land has been upzoned.

very low-income household. The U.S. Department of Housing and Urban Development (HUD) defines a very low-income household as a household earning less than 50 percent of the median household income of the Standard Metropolitan Statistical Area (SMSA) where the household lives. This definition is important for purposes of determining eligibility for subsidized housing.

Questions for further study

1. According to William Julius Wilson, what is the difference between historical racism and contemporary racism? What does Wilson believe best explains the continued existence of black ghettos and a black underclass in American cities today?

2. Where do local governments get their revenue? Why are there large differences between the fiscal capacity, own-source revenue, and per capita expenditures among different jurisdictions in the same metropolitan region?

3. What policy options do local governments have when they begin to decline economically? What is the vicious cycle that is likely to follow?

4. What does Myron Orfield mean by metropolicy? Why is he optimistic that core cities and at-risk suburbs can achieve a more equitable distribution of tax revenue than they have today?

5. What can be done to make more affordable housing available through metropolitan regions? How can spatial analysis help?

Annotated bibliography

A recent overview of social inequality is Martin Marger's *Social Inequality: Patterns and Processes* (Marger 2001).

David Kirp's *Our Town: Race, Housing, and the Soul of Suburbia* (Kirp 1995) describes the decades-long battles over Mount Laurel, New Jersey's exclusionary land-use policies. It is the most complete account of the struggle over exclusionary land-use practices and the attempt to increase equality in New Jersey. Kirp is a professor of public policy at the University of California, Berkeley.

Myron Orfield's books *American Metropolitics: The New Suburban Reality* (Orfield 2002) and *Metropolitics: A Regional Agenda for Community and Stability* (Orfield 1999), present the results of Orfield's pioneering GIS analyses of tax and service inequality in metropolitan American regions.

Geographer David Harvey's *Social Justice and the City* (Harvey 1973; reissue edition 1992) is a classic theory of social justice for urban planning using a neo-Marxist approach.

Paul Davidoff's important article "Advocacy and Pluralism in Planning," (Davidoff 1965) describes Davidoff's vision of planners acting as advocates before city planning commissions on behalf of disenfranchised neighborhoods.

Former Cleveland, Ohio planning director Norman Krumholz describes his experience practicing equity planning in *Making Equity Planning Work* (Krumholz and Forester 1990), coauthored with John Forester, and the experience of other equity planners in *Reinventing Cities: Equity Planners Tell Their Stories*, coedited with Pierre Clavel (Krumholz and Clavel 1994).

Chester Hartman's *City for Sale: The Transformation of San Francisco* (Hartman 2002) describes how low-income communities in San Francisco organized and opposed insensitive redevelopment plans for their neighborhoods.

Peter Medoff and Holly Sklar's *Streets of Hope: The Fall and Rise of an Urban Neighborhood* (Medoff and Sklar 1994) describes the successful efforts of the poor, minority, inner-city Dudley Street Triangle area to make plans and carry out a successful grassroots program of neighborhood revitalization.

Jonathan Kozol's *Savage Inequalities: Children in America's Schools* (Kozol 1992) is a devastating first-hand account of what poor, segregated primary and high schools are like. Kozol is a former teacher who taught in both affluent suburban schools and very poor inner city schools. It includes a chapter on schools in Camden, New Jersey, that illustrates material in this chapter and exercise 5.

Chapter 10

Symbolizing map features and creating map layouts

"Not only is it easy to lie with maps, it's essential. There's no escape from the cartographic paradox: to present a useful and truthful picture, an accurate map must tell white lies."

Mark Monmonier (1996)

Introduction

In addition to being an attention grabber, the above quote from Mark Monmonier (Monmonier 1996) embodies a central truth about displaying the results of spatial analysis. All maps are models of the real world that simplify and distort reality. It is never possible to depict physical space perfectly on a paper map or computer screen. Good distortions aid understanding even if they don't accurately represent physical space.

Harry Beck's 1933 London tube map described in the chapter 3 gallery of great maps and displayed below as map 10.1 is a brilliant piece of map distortion. Subway line lengths and directions are skillfully distorted so that the subway rider can clearly see which line goes where. Colors (a different color for each separate line), symbols (circles for transfer points), and labels (station names) convey all the essential information a subway rider really needs. The map legend at the lower left explaining the map symbols is very clear. The London tube map is, however, filled with white lies. Lines have been shortened, bent, and moved in space to create a functional map-rider's map. If the London tube map shown here were laid over an accurate map of the London subway system, where all the lines were proportional to their real length and all directions were correct, the two would not match very well, if at all.

White lies and wasted ink

In *How to Lie with Maps*, Monmonier distinguishes what he calls "white lies" from other forms of cartographic deception (Monmonier 1996). Monmonier argues that white lies are good; indeed, paradoxically, they are necessary. They aid understanding. Drawing the London tube to scale

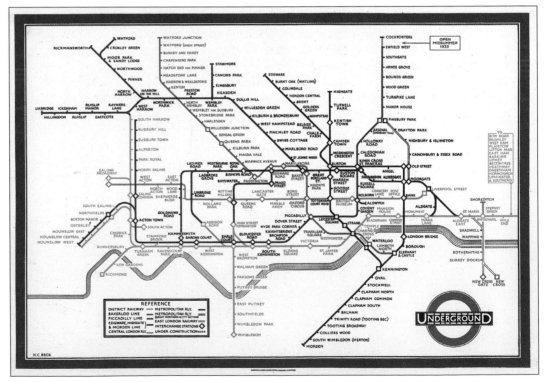

Map 10.1   Harry Beck's 1933 map of the London tube tells the truth by distorting reality.

Source: London's Transport Museum

would produce a map with long stretches of tube line that are there, but knowing that they are there does not help the riders visualize how to get from one place to another. By shortening and bending the lines, Beck made the tube lines fit clearly on the map. Colors and labels make the London tube map easy to understand. The map tells the truth about what is important to tube riders without unnecessary detail.

In contrast to the helpful white lies of the London tube map, lying with maps through ignorance or malice can be deceptive, politically reprehensible, costly, or even deadly. What Monmonier calls map blunders include the American Automobile Association accidentally leaving Seattle off its U.S. road map in the early 1960s (Monmonier 1996)!

The brilliant sixteenth century mapmaker Gerardus Mercator invented a map projection for navigators that distorts area—particularly near the North and South Poles—in such a way that navigators can easily sail in straight lines—what are referred to as great circles on the globe. In the map of the world in map 10.2a, which is in a Mercator projection, Greenland, near the North Pole, appears larger than the huge continent of South America.

Map 10.2a The world in a Mercator projection.
Source: ESRI Data and Maps 2003

Generations of American school children grew up with maps of the world in a Mercator projection on their classroom walls. Their mental map of the relative size of countries is wrong. A significant amount of the land area of Canada, Russia, and China is located in the far north of the northern hemisphere close to the North Pole. The Mercator projection significantly exaggerates the size of these areas. People who grew up with Mercator maps as their reference point have an ingrained image of these countries as much larger than they actually are. Harmless? Perhaps. But it is no accident that during the Cold War the virulently anticommunist John Birch Society used maps with a Mercator projection to dramatize the communist threat (Monmonier 1996). Communist Russia and China with their large land areas near the poles appear as big threats, compared to the proportionally smaller noncommunist Western European countries and the United States located nearer the equator.

The Mercator projection of map 10.2a makes Africa look smaller than North America. In fact, it is about 20 percent larger. That made U.N. organizations, the National Geographic Society, and evangelical Christian missionary groups odd bedfellows in a successful campaign during the

1980s to substitute a map projection that more faithfully represents the actual area of continents and countries. Map 10.2b shows the resulting Robinson projection. The Robinson projection is an equal area projection that more accurately represents the relative size of different continents and countries. The Robinson projection depicts the size of Africa and its countries more accurately than a Mercator projection.

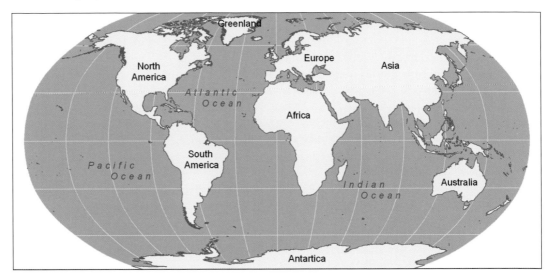

Map 10.2b   The world in a Robinson projection.
Source: ESRI Data and Maps 2003

Few social scientists and public policy researchers are rogues and rascals, but many maps that social scientists produce with the best of intentions fall short of Monmonier's principles of cartographic excellence or practice recommended by standard cartography textbooks (Robinson et al. 1995; Dent 1999; Slocum et al. 2003).

Symbolizing map features

Creating maps during the process of social science and public policy research serves two functions. First, maps work as research tools to help visualize reality more clearly. Often rough maps will work for this purpose, without a lot of attention to getting the colors, labeling, and all the map elements just right. A second purpose of making maps is to communicate the results of a finished analysis clearly to a wider audience. For that purpose, careful attention to symbology is very important. However brilliant the insight represented in a map, if others cannot understand it, the map is a failure. Good analysis that is poorly presented undermines the credibility of a researcher. GIS symbology concepts and operations are succinctly presented in one introductory text (Ormsby et al. 2004). Following is a discussion of symbolizing map features.

Cartographic generalization

All maps are simplifications of reality. Cartographers distinguish a number of different simplification techniques.

Selection is one approach to cartographic generalization. Some features can be deliberately left out of a map. A good example involves depicting the boundaries of coastal cities whose area includes underwater land or islands. The city and county of San Francisco consists of a densely populated fifty-square-mile peninsula surrounded by the Pacific Ocean on the west, San Francisco Bay on the north and east, and San Mateo County on the south. A populated man-made island (Treasure Island) is also part of San Francisco. For representing what San Francisco physically consists of, the peninsula and Treasure Island *(map 10.3a)* show all of the populated land area of the city. When the San Francisco *Chronicle* recently asked people most knowledgeable about the city, namely the mayor, the city planning director, and other experts, how big San Francisco was, they all came up with different answers. San Francisco owns various odd bits of real estate, including the rocky, uninhabited Farallone Islands about ten miles into the Pacific Ocean, and the ocean floor extending into the Pacific Ocean, under San Francisco Bay and surrounding the Farallones. An accurate representation of all of San Francisco's land produces one blob consisting of the peninsula and underwater land and another blob ten miles into the Pacific Ocean consisting of the Farallone Islands and underwater land surrounding them. This is an endless source of annoyance to analysts working with San Francisco data. It is a problem for cartographers working with areas like the coast of Maine, the Florida Keys, Greece, Indonesia, and other geographical areas with islands and underwater land legally part of the area.

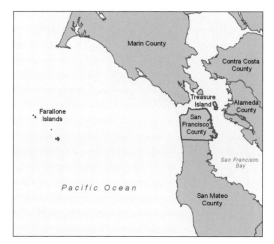

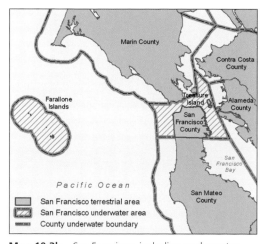

Map 10.3a San Francisco, showing land on the peninsula, Treasure Island, and the Farallone Islands.
Source: 2000 U.S. Census of Population and Housing

Map 10.3b San Francisco, including underwater land owned by the city.
Source: 2000 U.S. Census of Population and Housing

For the purpose of a legal survey, a map showing all of the odd bits of San Francisco land would be necessary. But for thematic maps analyzing census data, a map showing all the land area is confusing and deceptive. San Francisco's borders (if underwater land belonging to the city is included, as in map 10.3b) are not the shape San Franciscans recognize. "Wait a minute," map viewers looking at an accurate representation of San Francisco's area might say, "San Francisco isn't shaped like that." Calculating population per square mile for the city produces absurd results if the underwater and barren island land is included. This is a good case for selection—simply omitting the underwater land and Farallone Islands. A footnote can reference the fact that these features are omitted. In describing research results there could be a description in the text, a footnote, or a methodological appendix, explaining what was done.

Simplification is another common approach to map generalization. Complex shapes are simplified for purposes of clarity or for depiction at coarser scales. An example might be agricultural land in Contra Costa County. Vector GIS polygons have vertices (connecting points) at each location where a line changes direction. The shape of a parcel of agricultural land could be precisely represented as a polygon with connected lines going from one vertex to another. There would be a lot of small changes of direction. For some purposes—such as a U.S. Department of Agriculture survey of farmlands—this precise detail might be necessary.

For a thematic map illustrating the location of a parcel to inform citizens, detailed information on the precise shape of the agricultural land may not be necessary. The essential facts can be illustrated with a simple polygon approximating the shape of the parcel. Removing some of the vertices produces a less accurate map, but helps keep a map reader from being distracted by zigs and zags that really add nothing to the essential story of the thematic map.

Figure 10.1a is a vector GIS polygon showing a parcel of agricultural land in Contra Costa County with precise borders that have many vertices. Figure 10.1b shows the same polygon with the borders simplified for a general audience by removing some of the vertices.

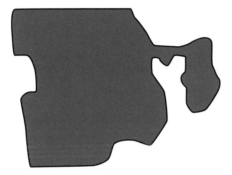

Figure 10.1a Vector GIS polygon representing precise borders of Contra Costa County farmland.

Source: Adapted from California Department of Conservation Farmland Mapping and Monitoring Project data

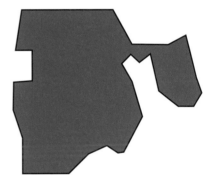

Figure 10.1b Vector GIS polygon representing simplified borders of Contra Costa County farmland.

Source: Adapted from California Department of Conservation Farmland Mapping and Monitoring Project data

Most small-scale maps exaggerate features for clarity. For example, points representing cities on world maps are almost always exaggerated. If you look carefully at map 1.2 showing world cities, you will notice that the point representing Madrid, Spain, covers much of central Spain!

Displacement may help with map clarity even if it produces technical inaccuracy. For example, if a road and railroad run parallel very close together through a narrow mountain gorge, producing them to scale and in their correct location may cause overlap and make the map hard for readers to understand. If a cartographer slightly displaces the railroad line twenty feet from the road, map readers may easily see that both the road and rail line exist at the expense of misinformation about the exact physical location of the railroad line that may not be important given the map purpose.

Throughout this book, you have been using symbols to construct models of reality. From the time when Neolithic artists began symbolically representing woolly mammoths on cave walls, humans have used tools to create symbols. Cavemen used drawing sticks and natural paints as their tools. They were selective about what aspects of the world they chose to depict and had a set of aesthetic conventions to communicate information effectively to other members of their clan. These early humans used symbology to depict aspects of their world in relation to their religious beliefs and mythology to make the world more comprehensible. You have been using different tools—computers and GIS software—to create symbols depicting selected aspects of reality in order to make the world more comprehensible to social science researchers and public policy professionals. The tools are different and the elements of the world depicted are different—census tracts and highways rather than woolly mammoths and cave bears. So too are the conventions for symbolizing the world. You have already encountered many conventions for symbolizing spatial and aspatial information in the preceding chapters. Now it is time to start to learn the art and science of symbolizing information yourself.

Map elements and symbols

You have already seen map symbols in maps throughout this book and have been working with symbols in the step-by-step exercises. Left to their own devices, beginners usually make reasonable choices regarding how to symbolize maps so that the end product is understandable to a map viewer. But without a theoretical foundation about how people perceive images or cartographic training in how to symbolize information on maps, their maps are almost never as sophisticated as maps produced by trained cartographers. While this book cannot substitute for a cartography course or specialized education in the psychology of perception, color theory, and all of the other knowledge that can produce excellent visual communication, the following material introduces nonexperts to some important theory that will help guide good mapmaking and describes good practice in map symbology that will help produce better maps.

In the discussion of data graphics, you learned that a variable is something that can have different values. A visual variable is a variable related to human perception. According to Jacques Bertin, four primary visual variables have the greatest impact on how map readers perceive maps (Bertin 1967). They are shape, size, orientation, and color (hue and value). Good map design involves using these variables intelligently to create legible maps. One notch down from the primary visual variables are secondary visual variables. These are all aspects of pattern, including arrangement, texture, and orientation.

Map symbols represent physical features on maps. A key aspect of graphical excellence in map design involves the choice of appropriate map symbols.

Circles are the most common symbol to identify the location of point features on a map. The measure cartographers and typographers use to define point symbol size is a **point**. There are seventy-two points to an inch, so ten points equal about one-eighth of an inch. Points can also be symbolized by color and shape. Triangles, squares, and other shapes may also be used to represent point features. Some maps use combinations of circles, triangles, squares, hexagons, and other shapes to differentiate features according to their attributes. You will learn to create different point symbols yourself in exercise 5.

In vector GIS, lines may be symbolized by size, color, width, or other symbology. For example, major highways on a map might be symbolized by two parallel dark black 8-point lines with an 8-point white dashed line in the middle; major roads as two parallel black 6-point lines; and small roads as single gray lines 4 points wide. You will symbolize road and street line symbols in the Camden, New Jersey, area in exercise 5.

Color

Color can be used to differentiate points, lines, or polygons. For example, capital cities of countries represented as points might be identified by red circles, and all other cities by blue circles. Interstate highways on most road maps are red and secondary roads blue. American Indian author William

Least Heat-Moon chose only blue highways for a long meandering voyage of self-discovery across America in his delightful book *Blue Highways* (Heat-Moon 1982).

Color conventions on maps vary, but some are used so frequently that it is prudent to use them. Water is universally represented in cyan (light blue), vegetation almost always in green, land frequently in brown, and deserts in yellow.

Color progression is commonly used (and abused) to represent quantitative data at the ordinal, interval, or ratio level, as you learned in chapter 2. Hue is the dimension of color associated with different dominant wavelengths. Colors can also be ranked in terms of their value (how light or dark they are) and the perceived amount of white relative to hue (chroma). Colors are created by mixing hue, value, and chroma.

In a single hue color progression (also called a monochromatic color ramp), the value in a color decreases and the chroma increases systematically as colors change from white to a pure hue. Both value and chroma have a spontaneous visual association with magnitude increasing as the hue becomes more pure.

Map 10.4 is a monochromatic color ramp showing the number of crimes committed per one hundred thousand residents in Camden and Burlington counties during 2000. Light colors represent smaller numbers of crimes per one hundred thousand population; darker ones represent larger numbers of crime per one hundred thousand population. The city of Camden, which has more than 8,159 crimes per one hundred thousand, is a high-crime area with four times as many crimes as Mount Laurel, which has 2,056 crimes per one hundred thousand population.

Bi-polar color progressions, also called dichromatic color ramps, use two hues. They are used if there is a natural break point in data such as a zero with values above and below zero. A dichromatic color ramp would be a good way to show the progressions from below zero to zero to temperatures above zero. It would also be a good way to symbolize New Jersey municipalities with crimes per one hundred thousand population below or above the average number of crimes per one hundred thousand population in all New Jersey municipalities.

Reproducing black-and-white monochromatic maps with values progressing from very light to very dark gray is an inexpensive way to achieve nearly the same effect as color progression. Map 10.5 shows the percentage of the population in Camden census tracts that were African-American in 2000 classified into five categories symbolized in a light-to-dark gray. Blocks where African-Americans constituted less than 20 percent of the population are classified a very light gray; ones where African-Americans constituted more than 80 percent of the population are classified with a very dark gray.

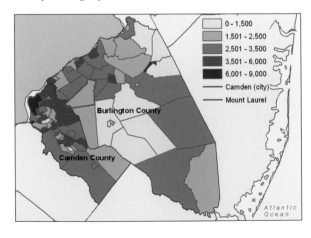

Map 10.4   Crimes per 100,000 people, Camden and Burlington counties, 2000.

Source: Ameregis

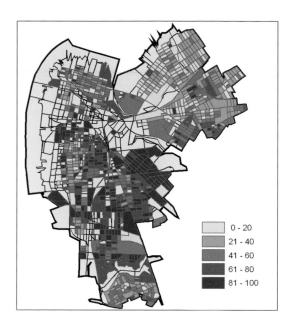

Map 10.5 Monochromatic five-class grayscale color ramp showing the percentage of African-Americans in Camden census tracts.

Source: 2000 U.S. Census of Population and Housing

If you intend to use grayscale maps like map 10.5 in a photocopied report, it is important to make sure the quality of the photocopy reproduction is good enough to accurately show the progression.

Studies have shown that most human beings can differentiate thousands of different color hues if they appear side by side on a color chart. But it is much harder for humans to clearly see which color on a map matches the color in a map legend. Most humans can link only about seven colors to a map legend in a single glance. The human eye can easily differentiate up to seven shades of gray. Based on these findings, it is a good idea to limit color ramps to seven or fewer colors.

ColorBrewer is an online diagnostic tool to help people select appropriate color schemes for maps and data graphics. It was created by Pennsylvania State University geography professor Cynthia Brewer. ColorBrewer is easy to use and provides precise guidance on how to combine different combinations of colors to produce effective maps and data graphics. Brewer has written additional theoretical and applied material about effective use of colors in mapping (Brewer 1994a, 1994b, and 2005). ColorBrewer is described in box 10.1.

GIS systems usually include specialized color ramps. For example, elevation may be artistically represented using light green (suggesting vegetation) for lower elevations to white (suggesting snow) for the highest elevations. This symbology is easy for map readers to understand but may be misleading. The color scheme suggests that lower elevations have vegetation and the highest ones have snow. The viewer can imagine green grassy fields rising up to a snowy mountaintop. But this may not be the case. Perhaps there is desert at lower elevations and it never snows on the mountaintop.

Map viewers may misunderstand color ramps by interpreting a color intended to be low for high. Text can help them avoid this mistake.

In symbolizing data in a color ramp, it is important to distinguish areas with missing data from areas in which the data value is zero. Black, white, and gray are good colors to represent missing data (referred to as NoData). The information that no data is available for these areas should appear in the map legend.

Box 10.1   ColorBrewer

ColorBrewer is an online diagnostic tool available for use on the Web without cost *(ColorBrewer.org)*. The purpose of ColorBrewer is to help people select good color schemes for maps and other graphics. ColorBrewer helps people see what color schemes work well. The colors chosen can then be used in a GIS. This tool is particularly helpful in selecting good color schemes for choropleth maps.

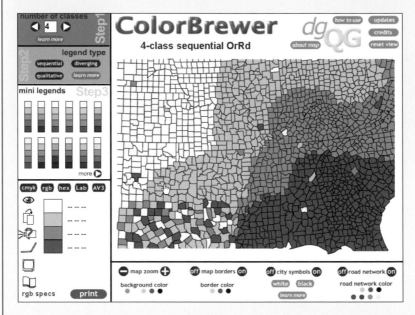

The ColorBrewer interface (shown above) consists of a map of counties in the southeastern United States. Using ColorBrewer involves simple steps: (1) setting the number of map classes you would like to use, (2) choosing a sequential, diverging, or qualitative color scheme, (3) selecting a color scheme from one that appears in response to steps 1 and 2, and (4) selecting the type of color specifications you would like to see to describe each of the colors in the color scheme so it can be replicated in a map of your own.

The figure shows how ColorBrewer looks after a user has specified four classes, chosen a sequential color ramp, selected a pale yellow to dark brown color scheme, and asked for a display of rgb (red, green, blue) specifications.

Icons on the bottom left of the ColorBrewer interface show a user how well the color scheme will work in different situations: for people with color blindness; as a photocopy; projected; displayed on a laptop screen; displayed on a computer monitor; and printed in hard copy. The icons for the color scheme above—a four-class sequential color ramp from light yellow to dark brown—show that this particular color scheme will work in all of the above cases except possibly when projected. The red question mark (?) on the third icon from the top that looks like a projector alerts a potential user that this particular color scheme may not work well if projected.

ColorBrewer was developed by Cynthia Brewer, associate professor of geography at Pennsylvania State University, with interface design and programming by Mark Harrower, an assistant professor of geography at the University of Wisconsin, Madison.

Map labeling and annotation

A map feature can be assigned a **label**: a word or words describing what the feature represents. In a GIS, any value that appears in any field in an attribute table can be used to automatically label features. Usually a text field in the attribute table with the name of the feature is used. It may be useful to label features with data from other fields. For example, if the attribute table accompanying a map of prime farmland had both the name of the farm owner and the soil classification represented by codes such as P-1, P-2, etc., a map labeled with the soil classification field would show a map reader where different types of soil are located. For understanding the location of different kinds of soil that labeling choice would be preferable to labeling parcels with the farm owner's name.

Sometimes two or more fields are combined to make a label. For example, the largest cities in Europe in map 1.4 are labeled with both the city name from the attribute table's CITYNAME field and their population from the attribute table's POPULATION field.

In addition to deciding which attribute table field to use to label a feature, labeling involves map generalization decisions. Often the most important features are labeled, but less important features are not.

Digital maps may be set so that labels are not visible at small scales where they would not be readable, but only appear when users zoom in to a specified map scale. Map labels can also be set to disappear at large scales if they would clutter the map.

Labeling involves lots of fussy, detailed work. Labels need to be close enough to the feature that the map reader knows what feature the label is labeling. Consistent placement of labels always at the same location, such as top left, increases clarity and reduces the burden on the map reader of interpreting which label belongs with which feature. Overlapping labels should be avoided. Labels need to be big enough, but not too big, and in an appropriate font. Fancy labeling options in GIS software include splines, where the letters of a label can twist along the curvature of a river, and halo effects, where a label will be surrounded by a light color to distinguish it from the map background.

Modern GIS software partially automates labeling. Since GIS software is reading values from an attribute table to create the labels, it is possible to automatically label every feature with a few mouse clicks. GIS software can also reduce the tedium of labeling by automatically making decisions about labeling. For example, the software may automatically determine the best location to place a label to avoid overlapping other labels. Depending on the software, users may be able to set label preferences. They can usually override defaults in the software and manually adjust labels for best effect. Learning to label features involves mastering details of how the labeling part of GIS software works and then using the software labeling features skillfully and artistically.

Labels are transitory additions to a map layer that can be toggled on and off. A map **annotation** looks similar to a label, but it is embedded in a map layer. Rather than being a transitory map feature that can be toggled on and off, an annotation has been made part of a map layer itself.

Symbolizing data frames

You learned in exercise 1 that GIS features are located in data frames as map layers. A data frame may have a background frame color. Users can determine the frame color. Map 10.6 shows cities in the British Isles in 1850 symbolized with points of a uniform size. Here the choice of frame color is obvious. Since the United Kingdom is surrounded by water, cyan (light blue) is appropriate. For features that are not surrounded by water on one or more sides, a neutral frame color such as beige or gray may be appropriate.

Map 10.6   Cities in the British Isles in 1850 with a cyan (light blue) data frame and uniform point symbols.
Source: Tertius Chandler and Gerald Fox, *3000 Years of Urban Growth*

Symbolizing vector GIS features

You learned in chapter 2 that in vector GIS all geographical features are symbolized with points, lines, or polygons. Vector features can be symbolized using combinations of size, shape, and color and in more subtle ways using transparency, texture, and other symbology. Symbolizing points and lines is straightforward but requires attention to detail and an aesthetic sense. Symbolizing polygons is a bit more complicated.

Symbolizing points

GIS point features represent a location but do not have any area. In vector GIS, points are represented by small symbols—usually circles. In raster GIS, they are represented as a single (square) grid cell. Three main attributes of points can be varied—size, color, and shape.

Point symbols can be differentiated by size based on classes that attribute values fall within. In that case they are referred to as **graduated point symbols**. For example, point symbols representing cities in the British Isles in map 10.6 are all the same shape (circles) and color (red with black borders). But in map 10.7 cities are symbolized using five different graduated point sizes ranging from 1 to 11 points. All cities within each of the five classes are symbolized by circles that are the same size. The smallest cities (1 point in size) show cities with populations between 60,000 and 100,000 in 1850; the largest show cities with populations over 450,000 in 1850. Map 10.7 has five classes, one of which shows cities with populations ranging from 150,001 to 300,000. A city like Leeds, which had 184,000 people in 1850, will be represented with the same point size as Birmingham, which had a population of 294,000 at that time.

Determining how many classes to have and how to divide them is a classification issue. You learned in chapter 3 that in GIS users can either create different classes of features using standard classification methods or classify features manually. You can refer back to chapter 3 to review the discussion of classification and to exercise 2 where you used the natural breaks (Jenks) classification method. In exercises 4 and 5 you will extend your understanding of classification by using the equal interval and quantile classification methods as well as the natural breaks (Jenks) method.

There is an important distinction in symbolizing points by size between graduated and proportional point symbols. The area of a **proportional point symbol** is proportional to the value of

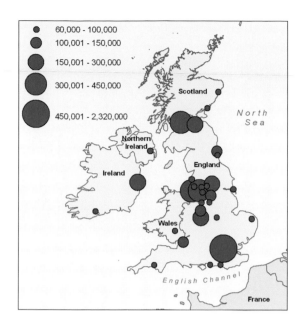

Map 10.7 Population of cities in the British Isles in 1850 symbolized as graduated point symbols.

Source: Tertius Chandler and Gerald Fox, *3000 Years of Urban Growth*

the point's attribute. A city with a population of 1,000,000 would have an area ten times the area of a city with 100,000 people if the cities were symbolized with proportional point symbols. You may recall from primary school that the area of a circle is calculated using the formula $\pi \times r^2$. You do not need to know this to create proportional point symbols because GIS software automatically calculates the area of proportional symbols once the user clicks on the appropriate command on a graphical user interface.

Why would anyone symbolize point features using graduated symbols, which depict values less accurately than proportional symbols? There are two reasons. The first is that, for analytic purposes, knowing what range of values a feature falls into may be all that is needed, and a small number of categories are easier for viewers to grasp visually than symbols of many different sizes. The second is to avoid having large values overwhelm maps or create overlaps as illustrated in map 10.8.

Map 10.8 is a map of world cities in 1850 represented by proportional symbols. At that time, several cities—London, Moscow, Milan—were much larger than other cities. Depicted proportionally, these cities overlap with each other and overwhelm other cities in Europe and even the Middle East. The edge of the circle representing Moscow in map 10.8 stretches almost to Paris. Map 10.8 is a horrible map, deliberately drawn for effect and to make a point. It obscures information and confuses the map viewer rather than conveying information about historical city size in 1850.

Point symbols can also be differentiated by color. A map showing important cities in the United States could represent state capitals with red points and all other major cities with black points.

A third way of differentiating point symbols is by shape. While circles are overwhelmingly the shape of choice to represent point features, points may be symbolized by triangles, squares, or other shapes. Used in moderation, variation in shape is an important way to differentiate GIS point data. At most scales, variations in shape are harder for the human eye to distinguish clearly than variations in color. Combinations of shape and color are often most effective for differentiating point features. Too many different shapes make it hard for viewers to understand the map.

Map 10.9 shows urban agglomerations with more than five million people in 2000 represented as 4-point red circles. Twenty-one of these cities that some scholars consider to be global cities

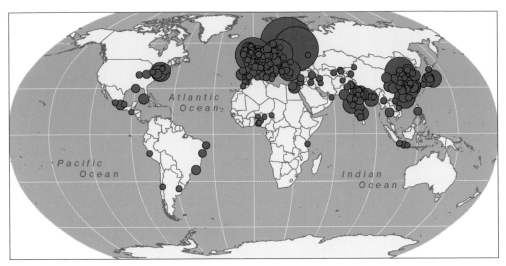

Map 10.8 World cities in 1850 symbolized using proportional symbols.
Source: Tertius Chandler and Gerald Fox, *3000 Years of Urban Growth*

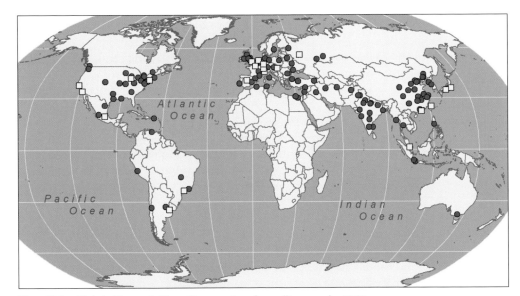

Map 10.9 Global cities and cities with more than five million people, 2000.
Source: United Nations (cities with more than five million people); Globalization and World Cities Study Group and Network (global cities)

because of their important positions in the world economy (Taylor 1999) are symbolized by 4-point yellow squares.

Mimetic symbols

In the public space of New York, London, Paris, and other large cities, mimes are a common sight. Along a short stretch of Barcelona's Ramblas on most sunny days, strollers will see mimes dressed as Christopher Columbus, Mick Jagger, George Bush, Don Quixote, Jesus Christ, and other well-known people and characters. Christopher Columbus's distinctive hat and fifteenth century mariner's clothing cue passersby to his identity. Similarly, a **mimetic symbol** mimes the feature it represents by providing the map viewer with visual cues. A toxic site might be depicted by a symbol of a small barrel with a skull-and-crossbones, an airport by a small symbol of an airplane, and the location of a red-legged frog habitat conservation area by a symbol that looks like a frog.

GIS software contains libraries of mimetic symbols that users can substitute for more conventional point symbols like circles and triangles. The symbols may be organized by category such as transportation, the environment, and education. Operationally, symbolizing point features using mimetic symbols only requires GIS users to select an appropriate symbol and point and click to make it the symbol for the points.

Figure 10.2 contains five mimetic symbols that might be used to symbolize locations of features in an urban area. Rather than use abstract symbols like circles or squares and differentiate features by shape, size, or color, a map might show the locations of hospitals, fire hydrants, industrial complexes, and other features using mimetic symbols.

Mimetic symbols should be used sparingly and with care. The human eye has trouble sorting out more than a few different mimetic symbols at a single glance.

Figure 10.2 Mimetic point symbols.

Symbolizing lines

Line features may be symbolized by width, color, and mimetic symbology. A combination of width and color is often more effective than either alone. Since length is a basic feature of the line, length is not used for symbolizing lines. A mimetic symbol for a two-lane highway might use lines on either side of a center dividing line. Two parallel lines with little lines at right angles could be used to mimic a railroad track. Map 10.10 shows roads, streets, and major arterials in Camden, New Jersey. Roads are symbolized as thin gray lines, streets as thicker gray lines, and major arterials with a gray line that is both thicker and darker. Map 10.10 would be very useful for congestion management or capital improvement planning. A transportation planner could use combinations of locational and attribute queries to select just certain types of roads or streets in certain areas perhaps based on additional data on their need for repair.

Symbolizing polygons

Symbolizing polygons correctly is more complicated than symbolizing points and lines. A major source of GIS error among first-time GIS users is in symbolizing polygons in thematic maps in ways that are inappropriate or wrong. Learning to symbolize vector polygons appropriately is important because many vector GIS maps in urban analysis use polygons to represent countries, cities, census tracts, or other features that are legally defined with precise borders for governmental purposes.

Multiple polygons of the same type in one map layer can be symbolized using a single color. This is called single-symbol classification. Single-symbol classification is often appropriate where the polygons are included to provide context.

Map 10.11 shows the size of Italian cities in 1850. Cities—the real geographical feature of interest in map 10.11—are represented as bright red graduated circles with thin black borders.

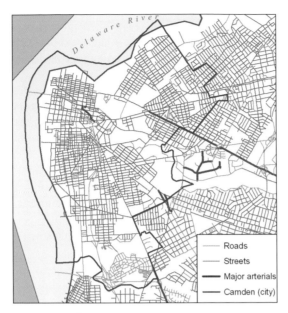

	Roads
	Streets
	Major arterials
	Camden (city)

Map 10.10   Camden roads, streets, and major arterials.
Source: Ameregis

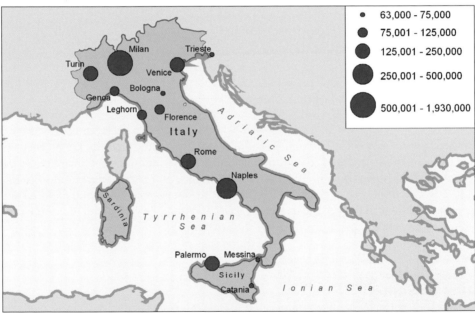

•	63,000 – 75,000
●	75,001 – 125,000
●	125,001 – 250,000
●	250,001 – 500,000
●	500,001 – 1,930,000

Map 10.11   Populations of Italian cities in 1850.
Source: Source: Tertius Chandler and Gerald Fox, *3000 Years of Urban Growth*

The data frame color is blue. The fill color of Italy is olive, strong enough to focus the map viewer's attention there. The line color of Italy is one point wide and charcoal colored, further emphasizing Italy and differentiating it from surrounding countries. The land area comprising other countries is included on the map to provide context, so that Italy is not suspended in space; but since the other countries are not really important to the substance of the map, they are all classified the same way with a light gray fill. Notice that the borders of countries other than Italy have been dissolved and the countries are not labeled. The map viewer correctly perceives that there are other countries around Italy, but is not distracted by detail on their borders or names. GIS software graphical user interfaces make it easy to change the color of features by pointing and clicking on a color palette or color picker. You will learn how to classify polygons by color in exercise 5.

Different polygon layers in a map can be symbolized by two different kinds of color: fill color within the polygon itself and outline color around the edge of the polygon. Users may also vary the width of the outline line or—an important point—have no polygon outline at all. One of Bertin's secondary visual variables—texture—may be used sparingly in symbolizing polygons.

Polygons may each be assigned a unique symbology to make individual polygons readily distinguishable from each other. This is called unique value symbology. For example, a map of the United States might symbolize each state using a different unique color to make the states readily distinguishable from each other. Some GIS software organizes colors into styles such as muted or bright colors or pastels that look good together. The choice of a color scheme is largely a question of aesthetic judgment by the map creator—sensitive always to conveying information clearly.

Often the message of a map involves focusing on just one feature, two features, or a few features from among many. Features other than the feature(s) of primary interest may be included to provide context. You have frequently seen examples in this book like map 10.11 where important features appear in color against a light gray background that provides context. Making key features stand out is an important consideration. For polygon features, symbolizing the key features in a brighter color, outlining them, or (perhaps) applying a texture will make them stand out.

An analysis of regional spatial inequality might focus on the contrast between the cities of Camden and Mount Laurel, New Jersey. In order to orient a map viewer to where these two cities are located, municipalities other than Camden and Mount Laurel might be symbolized using muted pastel colors and Camden and Mount Laurel symbolized using bright colors. Map 10.12 symbolizes municipalities in southern New Jersey this way. Camden is a bright red color; Mount Laurel is bright amethyst. Box 10.2 (next page) describes how to use color to symbolize polygons.

You learned in chapter 2 that GIS maps are organized in layers. Often analysts want to depict features from two or more layers at once in order to show relationships among features on different layers. GIS layers may be made more or less transparent. In fact, the level of transparency can be set from a very low percentage, like 1 percent, to nearly totally transparent, like 99 percent. Map viewers can see layers underneath a transparent layer more or less distinctly depending on the percentage of transparency of the top layer(s).

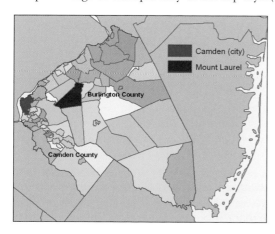

Map 10.12 Municipalities in Camden and Burlington counties symbolized to call attention to Camden (city) and Mount Laurel.

Source: Ameregis

> ### Box 10.2   Symbolizing polygons with color
>
> - Background elements should be in unobtrusive colors like gray, beige, or light green.
> - Features classified as unique values should usually be represented in muted or pastel colors in a consistent style.
> - Emphasized features should be in bright colors like mars red or amethyst.
> - Mimetic colors (colors that suggest the feature) should be used where appropriate: cyan (a shade of blue) for water, green for agricultural land, yellow for desert.
> - Outlines should usually be black and thick enough to be visible, but not obtrusive.
> - Thick or colored outlines may be used to emphasize features.

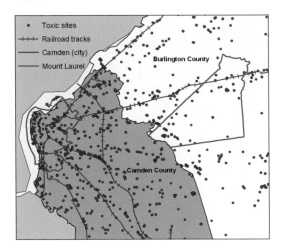

Map 10.13   Toxic sites in Camden and Burlington counties.

Source: New Jersey Department of Environmental Protection

When a layer of point features or a layer of line features is superimposed over a layer of polygon features, it is important that the map viewer be able to interpret the relationship between features in both layers. Map 10.13 contains a layer of point features representing the location of contaminated sites superimposed over polygon layers showing Camden and Burlington counties (solid colors) and the cities of Camden and Mount Laurel (outlined in red and amethyst, respectively). The map viewer can see how many contaminated sites there are in each municipality and where within the municipality the contaminated sites are located.

Map viewers can usually understand additional point or line layers superimposed over polygon layers. Just looking at the distribution of features in a map often provides insights. It is not surprising that map 10.13 shows many known contaminated sites clustered within the borders of the old industrial city of Camden. A careful look at the spatial distribution of known contaminated sites outside the border of Camden city in map 10.13 shows that many are arrayed in linear patterns. Ah-ha! our team thought when we were exploring this data—known contaminated sites outside Camden are probably found along roads and highways where factories are (or were) located. Adding a layer of highways to map 10.13 did show that many of the known contaminated sites outside Camden were along highways, but we were surprised to find many fewer than we anticipated. There were clear linear patterns of known contaminated sites where there were no roads or highways. Adding a layer of railroad lines did the trick; we found many contaminated sites along these rail lines. Historically, many factories were located on railroad lines so they could get raw materials and ship finished goods by rail.

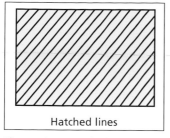
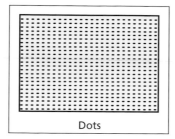
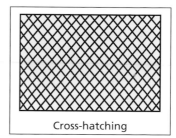

Figure 10.3   Hatched lines, dots, and cross-hatched lines.

Showing relationships between two different polygon layers at the same time is more of a challenge than showing relationships between a polygon layer and one or more point or line layers. If a top polygon layer is opaque, it will be impossible to see part or all of the layer below it wherever there is overlap.

Depicting both layers in separate maps can always solve the problem of one polygon layer hiding another. A disadvantage of this approach is that the map viewer must look first at one map and then the other map(s) to compare them.

A more elegant solution to the problem of how to depict two polygon layers at the same time is to make one of the layers partially transparent. GIS software permits users to set the percentage of transparency for any map layer. For example, a GIS user might make a map layer showing attributes of cities 50 percent transparent so that a layer below it showing attributes of counties would also be clearly visible. You will learn how to make layers transparent in exercise 5.

A third solution to showing two polygon layers at the same time involves using fills consisting of horizontal, vertical, or slanted lines, small dots, or hatch marks (lines slanted at 45-degree angles or crossing each other) for the top layer instead of a solid color. Because the space between the slanted lines, dots, or hatching is transparent, map viewers can see the layer underneath. Figure 10.3 illustrates these kinds of layers.

Choropleth maps are a common type of thematic map used to depict differences among areas represented as polygons. Choropleth maps are usually created in vector GIS, but may also be created in raster GIS. Choropleth maps are usually symbolized using color ramps. A color ramp uses variations in chroma to represent change along an ordinal scale from low to high. Light colors usually represent lower values, dark colors higher values.

A **monochromatic color ramp** consists of color ranging from light to dark created using only one chroma. Most choropleth maps use monochromatic symbology.

A **dichromatic color ramp** consists of color ranging from light to dark using two different chromas. One part of a dichromatic color ramp is created by increasing the amount of one chroma, the other part by increasing the amount of a different chroma. Dichromatic color ramps are used less commonly that monochromatic color ramps. They are appropriate when there is a zero point in the data. A dichromatic color ramp would be a good choice for mapping percentage population change in New Jersey cities between 1990 and 2000. Some New Jersey cities lost population, so their population change was less than 0 percent; most cities gained population, so their population change was greater than 0 percent.

The value mapped on a choropleth map may be an absolute number—like the total population in a census block—a ratio, proportion, or percent, such as the percent of the households in a census tract that own their homes.

Perhaps the most common map blunder beginning GIS users make is to create choropleth maps using absolute values symbolizing polygons of different areas when they are trying to illustrate different percents of a value that occurs in that location. This creates the wrong impression for viewers that values are greater where polygons are bigger. Imagine a choropleth map in which census tracts with more than fifty homeowners are symbolized with dark purple and census tracts with fewer than fifty homeowners with light purple. In a map like that, a physically tiny census tract with only ninety-eight households—forty-nine of whom were homeowner households—would be colored light purple. A huge census tract, covering a large geographic area and with 1,020 households (only fifty-one of whom were homeowners) would be colored dark purple. Many map readers would get the wrong impression that there is more homeownership in the large census tract than the small one. While the *absolute* number of homeowners in the huge census tract (fifty-one) is higher than the absolute number of homeowners in the tiny census tract (forty-nine), in fact the rate of homeownership is much higher in the tiny tract.

The conventional way to deal with this recurring choropleth map issue is to **normalize** the data—that is, divide the value of interest (number of homeowners in the above example) by the total number of cases (households in the above example). For example, in the situation described above, if the forty-nine homeowners in the little census tract are divided by the total number of households (98), the normalized data value would be 0.50 (50 percent) homeowners. If the fifty-one homeowners in the large census tract are divided by 1,020 (the number of homeowners in the census tract) the normalized value would be 0.05 percent. When the values of 0.50 and 0.05 are mapped, the resulting map would convey the accurate information that the small census tract has a much higher percentage of homeowners than the large census tract.

Dot density maps

Dot density maps are similar to choropleth maps but use randomly distributed dots instead of a color ramp to represent density. More dots indicate larger values and hence greater density.

Dots on a dot density map do not symbolize one occurrence at the specific location where the dot appears. Rather, the dots are randomly distributed by a computer algorithm to symbolize density. If you create a dot density map a second time using the same values, the location of the dots will be different, because the computer algorithm distributes them in a different random pattern. While the number of occurrences in a dot density map can be set to equal one, ordinarily one dot represents some larger number; for example, one dot might indicate fifteen people. Creating a dot density map involves choosing the value the dot represents, a dot size, a dot color, and how many occurrences of the value one dot represents. This can be done by pointing and clicking in a GIS graphical user interface. You created a dot density map in exercise 2 and will learn how to create another in exercise 5.

How accurately a dot density map depicts density depends on the area within which the dots are being distributed. An extreme example may help clarify this. If you were creating a dot density map of the home address of living popes with each dot symbolizing "1" and using the world as your area, GIS software would faithfully execute the appropriate commands and randomly assign one dot somewhere in the world; the location might be in China or San Francisco or Des Moines, Iowa. This would be technically correct (just one living pope on the globe), but very misleading, since the pope actually lives in Rome. The next time you mapped living popes, the dot density computer algorithm would faithfully assign the pope to another location on the globe. The pope would be equally likely to end up in Rome or Mecca or Honolulu. More likely, the computer algorithm would assign the poor pope to the middle of one of the oceans that cover most of the globe. The above example, based on a dot density map, is one instance of a general problem in symbolizing spatial quantities on a map. More broadly, this general problem is known as the modifiable area unit problem.

The modifiable area unit problem (MAUP)

The **modifiable area unit problem** (MAUP) in geography is caused by the fact that areas of different sizes and scales can be selected for analysis. The results of an analysis will be different depending on the size of the area chosen. For example, the smaller the area within which the computer is instructed to randomly assign dots in a dot density map, the more accurate the dot density map's symbolization of density will be. If the area within which a living pope could be located were limited to Vatican City you would get a more accurate dot density map than if the area were Italy, which would in turn be more accurate than if the area were the entire world. You can never overcome the modifiable area unit problem, but the smaller the area within which attributes are mapped the more accurate your representation will be.

By combining small area analysis with a map symbology trick you can produce superior dot density maps. An illustration will help make this clear. The U.S. Census enumerated 2,467 African-Americans in Mount Laurel, New Jersey, in 2000. If you map the density of Mount Laurel's African-American population using the entire area of the municipality for a dot density map (a large area) and instruct the computer to generate one dot for each African-American resident of Mount Laurel, this will produce the pattern shown in map 10.14a. The 2,467 dots are randomly distributed over the entire area of Mount Laurel. One dot in a dot density map can symbolize any number of occurrences of a feature. In Map 10.14a, each dot represents one African-American. This makes it appear that Mount Laurel's African-American population is about equally dense everywhere, which is not the case. School integration or affordable housing location policy based on that erroneous assumption would be misguided. Mount Laurel's African-American population is concentrated in the Springvale neighborhood in the northern part of the city.

Using smaller geographical areas to create a dot density map showing the location of Mount Laurel's African-American population produces a more accurate map. The smallest geographical unit for which the U.S. Census provides information on the race of the population is a census block. Map 10.14b shows Mount Laurel's 520 census blocks. It is possible to create a dot density map mapping African-Americans within all these small areas rather than the entire area of Mount Laurel. Map 10.14c does that. Map 10.14c is strikingly different from map 10.14a. Both maps have 2,467 dots, and the dots are randomly distributed in both maps. You saw in exercise 2 that there are many census blocks in each census tract. The population of Mount Laurel's 520 census blocks range from 0 to more than 1,000 residents with an average of 77 residents per census block. In map 10.14c, the dots are randomly distributed within census blocks based on the number of African-Americans in the block rather than distributed randomly throughout the entire township as in map 10.14a. Map 10.14c is still a model—a symbolic representation of reality. But it is a much more accurate representation of reality than map 10.14a that mapped Mount Laurel's African-American population using the entire municipality as the mapping area. Map 10.14c correctly shows that Mount Laurel's 2000 African-American population was unevenly distributed throughout the township.

One small symbology issue with map 10.14c is that the census block lines clutter the map and detract somewhat from the map's message. Map 10.14d removes that small symbolgy problem by giving the census block boundaries zero width so that they do not show at all. Map 10.14d is a good symbolic representation of the density of Mount Laurel's African-American population. It would be very useful in determining school district boundaries, sites for affordable housing, or other policies to reduce racial segregation in Mount Laurel.

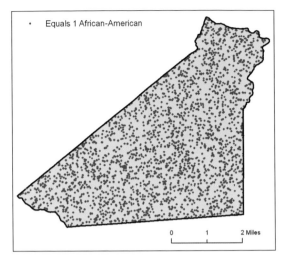

Map 10.14a Dot density map of Mount Laurel's African-American population, using entire city as the area, 2000.

Source: 2000 U.S. Census of Population and Housing

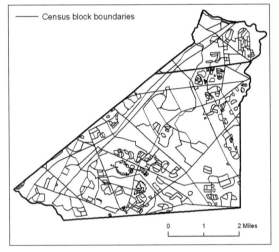

Map 10.14b Mount Laurel census blocks.

Source: 2000 U.S. Census of Population and Housing

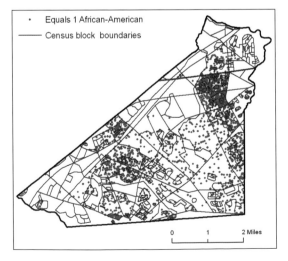

Map 10.14c Dot density map of Mount Laurel's African-American population, using census blocks as the area, 2000.

Source: 2000 U.S. Census of Population and Housing

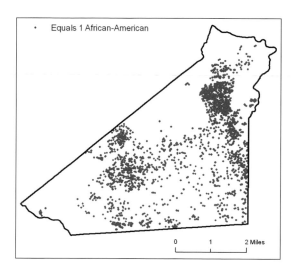

Map 10.14d Dot density map of Mount Laurel's African-American population, with census block boundaries dissolved, 2000.

Source: 2000 U.S. Census of Population and Housing

Map resolution, accuracy, precision, and scale

The same geographical features can be depicted in a map as if the viewer is very close to the features or far away. This requires consideration of the appropriate scale for a map.

Map **scale** refers to the ratio between map features and the objects they represent on the ground. A fundamental decision in creating a map is at what scale to create it.

Scale issues create a greater possibility of abuse with digital than with analog paper maps. A cartographer producing one paper map has to decide on an appropriate scale to represent the map data: perhaps a large-scale detailed neighborhood map or a very small-scale generalized world map. The decision about scale involves balancing the map purpose, how detailed available data is, the need for as much detail as possible, and avoiding cluttering the map. In contrast, digital databases are scaleless; it is possible to represent the data in the same database in a GIS at different scales.

Three common ways of indicating map scale are in words like "one inch represents one mile," a ratio like 1:24,000, or with a scale bar. Scale bars look like a ruler with distance indicated. You have seen many scale bars in the maps in this book and will insert a scale bar yourself in exercise 6. Scale ratios relate one distance unit on the map to the same distance unit on the ground. The part of the ratio to the left of the colon is always one. Thus, if the map unit is inches, a ratio of 1:24,000 means that one inch on the map represents 24,000 inches on the ground. The smaller the denominator is, the larger the scale. Scales with progressively smaller denominators are larger. A scale of 1:24,000 is larger than a scale of 1:240,000. An easy way to remember that a small denominator means a large scale is that a denominator of 1 in a scale ratio would mean that the map is life size. Since a scale ratio is a ratio, as long as they are the same, the units don't matter.

In GIS systems, the map scale becomes larger as the viewer zooms in. Features that are too small to be meaningfully represented at a small scale may be set to appear at a certain ratio. For example, a map of world cities at a scale small enough to represent the whole world on a computer screen might be at 1:225,000,000. At that scale, just showing country boundaries and cities might make sense. Zooming in to a large scale like 1:10,000, features like roads and rivers might be set to become visible. Table 10.1 provides examples of map scales and their equivalents as measured on the surface of the earth.

Map scale is closely related to issues of map generalization, discussed previously. A small-scale map—such as a map showing all of New Jersey—must be more generalized than a larger scale

Table 10.1 Map scale and equivalents measured on the earth's surface				
Map scale	**1 inch on map equals**	**1 mile on map equals**	**1 centimeter on map equals**	**1 kilometer on map equals**
1:1000	83.45 feet	63.36 inches	10 meters	100 centimeters
1:2400	200	26.40	24	41.66
1:12,000	1000	5.28	120	8.33
1:24,000	2000	2.64	240	4.17
1:50,000	0.789 mile	1.127	500	2
1:100,000	1.58	0.634	1000	1
1:500,000	7.89	0.127	5000	0.20
1:1,000,000	15.78	0.063	10 kilometers	0.10
1:10,000,000	157.82	0.006	100	0.01
1:25,000,000	394.57	0.002	250	0.004

map showing just Mount Laurel, or an even larger scale map showing just the Springvale neighborhood in Mount Laurel.

Map resolution refers to the smallest feature or distance that can be recorded true to scale on a map. A mark representing the location of New York City on a map of the world on a standard 8 1/2" x 11" piece of typing paper could not achieve very high map resolution because the extent of the map is so large and the piece of paper is so small.

Map accuracy refers to a measure of how close a recorded location comes to its true value. Depending on a map's purpose, map accuracy may be more or less important. Street locations on a thematic map showing where affordable housing projects in Camden, New Jersey, are located in relation to streets do not need to be very accurate if the map reader is only interested in the relationship between the housing and the general location of the streets. A map of street centerlines to guide the Camden Department of Public Works where to dig for buried electrical cable might need to be very accurate, as digging in the wrong place by even a few inches could result in accidentally severing an electrical line with serious risk to workers and huge inconvenience to customers.

Map precision is a measure of how exactly a location is specified—indicated by the number of significant digits. A map with precision measured to five decimal places contains much more precise data than one measured to one decimal place.

Map projections

Fortunately for Columbus, but unfortunately for mapmakers, the world is in fact round (or more precisely an oblate spheroid). Columbus did not fall off the edge of the world as some predicted. But cartographers ever since have had to expend a great deal of mathematical ingenuity figuring out ways to represent locations from the spherical earth on two-dimensional flat paper maps and, more recently, computer screens.

Map projections transform the curved, three-dimensional surface of the earth into a flat two-dimensional plane. To do this, they must distort some combination of shape, area, distance, and direction. Some projection systems are faithful to one or two of these attributes of physical space, but all maps other than three-dimensional globes distort the real shape of physical features.

This creates a host of interesting issues for the mathematically inclined and booby traps for the inexperienced mapmaker or map reader. Fortunately for the mathematically challenged, GIS systems automate map projections. Canned libraries of hundreds of standard map projections make it unnecessary to do the math to make the map projections. All of the exercises in this book use projected data with coordinate systems defined and all layers in a satisfactory projection and consistent with each other. So long as you work with this data or other properly projected data, you do not have to do map projections yourself. You do need to be sensitive to the strengths and limitations of the map projection you are working in and be careful not to make cartographic blunders by doing analyses the projection cannot support. Calculating areas using a projection system that does not have equal areas is an example of such a cartographic blunder. As you venture out on your own to create your own data or combine data from different sources, or if you proceed to more advanced spatial analysis, you will need to dig into the conceptual issues associated with coordinate systems and map projections. You will need to master some intricacies of getting data from different sources to match. This will require reprojecting maps when necessary. Fortunately, computer technology has made this much easier than it once was.

Creating map layouts

Cartography texts (Robinson et al. 1995; Dent 1999; Slocum et al. 2003) contain detailed descriptions of mapmaking principles and operations. Cartographers use standard **map elements** to enhance and clarify maps. A map **layout** may include one or more maps and other map elements. In addition to a map, common map elements include a legend north arrow, neatline, and scalebar. A map title may be included as part of the map itself or created independently and included with the map as described in box 10.3. Box 10.3 is a summary of what map elements can be included in layouts.

A common cartographic blunder for beginning mapmakers is to overemphasize map elements. GIS encourages this practice. Since it is easy to insert north arrows, scale bars, neatlines, and other map elements, beginning mapmakers tend to use lots of these elements. They often make them too big or place them prominently on the map in places that are inappropriate. While the resulting maps will not be wrong, they are likely to be cluttered and to distract the map viewer from the essential message of the maps. Viewers should focus on map content. Their eyes should be drawn to features such as ozone pollution levels and municipalities with particularly high or low tax rates rather than obtrusive north arrows.

In the recent past, cartographers physically glued templates of map elements onto their maps or drew them in by hand in pen and ink. Today, GIS software has automated the layout process. Users can select scale bars and north arrows from libraries of different north arrow and scale bar styles, add a neatline by pointing and clicking, and add a customizable legend or text box from a pull-down menu or wizard that automates the process. The map title and other text are as easy to insert and edit as with a word processor. GIS software even simulates the look of a layout board with orienting lines so GIS users can move elements of the final map into the right positions and snap them into place. The process of map design in GIS now involves inserting map elements into a layout and then arranging and modifying them to produce well-designed, elegant, and information-rich maps. You will learn how to create a map layout and insert common map elements in exercise 6.

Box 10.3   What to include in map layouts

The map **title** should describe what the map is in such a way that if a person received the map with no other information, he or she could tell what the map is about. In written reports and books, map titles may be placed below the maps and written with a word processor. The map titles in this book were created this way. On large stand-alone or poster-size maps, titles are usually placed at the top with a large enough font size to catch the map reader's attention. Some map templates have different arrangements of maps titles and other map elements that work well together.

One or more **maps** may be included in a layout. Sometimes a small orientation map is included to show the general location of a main map. Inset maps within the rectangle around a main map may be effective to show an area of detail. Some map layouts include two, three, four, or more maps of different sizes.

Supportive material may include images, charts, tables, and explanatory text that can be inserted into the map layout itself.

A **north arrow** tells the viewer which direction is north. In most maps, north arrows are not necessary because the map viewer already knows what direction is north, or that information is not important in the context of the map. You will notice that only a few of the maps in this book have north arrows. Ordinarily north is assumed to be at the top of the map. When used, north arrows should be large enough to be clearly seen, but not obtrusive. They may be placed anywhere on the map that makes aesthetic sense. It may be necessary to rotate a north arrow after inserting it so that it does in fact point north.

A **neatline** is a line that encloses all the map elements or a subset of them in order to create clarity and aesthetic unity. Ordinarily, a single black neatline around all the map elements will make the map more attractive. Neatlines in different colors, double lines, or different line thicknesses may be effective. Too many neatlines or too much complexity of thickness and color are distracting.

A **scale bar** shows the viewer the scale of the map in units such as miles or kilometers so that the viewer can understand how the map is representing distance. Sometimes scalebars are not necessary. In layouts with one main and multiple smaller maps showing details of the main map, one scalebar in the main map is usually sufficient.

Scale text describes the map scale—usually as a ratio such as 1:24,000.

The map **legend** explains the meaning of feature symbology by showing a small part of a feature and describing it in words. You may not need a legend entry for every map feature. Blue river lines, for example, may be obviously recognizable as rivers to the viewer and require no label.

A **label** specifies the name of a feature such as a city, river, or road. Labeling requires mapmakers to consciously decide how much labeling to do and what to omit. Not every feature should or can be labeled.

Box 10.3 What to include in map layouts (cont.)

The map **source** identifies where map data originated. In written reports, the map source can be written with a word processor and placed below the map. That is the convention used in this book. If a map source is created as text in a GIS and inserted on the map, it should be legible but unobtrusive—usually in a relatively small font near the bottom of the map.

This chapter described theory on how humans perceive information and how this perception affects mapmaking. It described choices mapmakers face in creating maps and provided suggestions on how to make good maps.

The next chapter continues the discussion about perception in the context of data graphics. Like this chapter, it links theory to practice—showing how theory can lead to graphical excellence. Unlike two prior chapters (4 and 8) that describe standard data graphics, chapter 11 does not describe additional commonly used data graphics. Rather, it urges readers to think about how to create original data graphics to effectively communicate information. To that end it provides an example of an excellent New York *Times* data graphic that communicates information well. Finally, chapter 11 describes the strengths and limitations of maps and data graphics in comparison to writing, oral briefings, and PowerPoint presentations.

Terms

annotation. A map annotation is similar to a map label except that it has been made a part of a map layer.

dichromatic color ramp. A color ramp using two chromas. For example, states that had a budget deficit might be symbolized in the bottom part of a dichromatic color ramp in different shades of red where darker red indicated a larger budget deficit. States that had a budget surplus could be symbolized in grays and black in the top part of the same color ramp, with darker shades of gray indicating a larger surplus.

graduated point symbol. A symbol in a vector GIS assigned a size category to symbolize one range of values. If an attribute that is being mapped at a location has a small value, a small circle may be used to symbolize the value. If the value is large enough that it falls into a larger class, a larger sized circle is used. Unlike proportional symbols, a graduated symbol's area does not precisely represent the quantity—only the class into which it falls.

label. In GIS, a label is text that describes a geographic feature. For example, point features representing cities could be labeled with the city name. Labels help map viewers interpret the features on a map.

layout. An arrangement of different components that make up and complement a map. A cartographer working by hand may lay out one or more maps and then a title, legend, neatlines, north arrow, scale bar, and other elements. In GIS, layouts can be produced on a computer screen and then printed out in hard copy.

map element. A component of a map layout such as a title, legend, north arrow, scale bar, or neatline that complements the map or maps in the layout.

mimetic symbol. A map symbol that looks like the thing it represents. A simplified sketch of a church as a rectangle with a little triangle representing a steeple is an example of a mimetic symbol.

modifiable area unit problem (MAUP). The modifiable area unit problem refers to the fact that calculations and map displays will be different depending on the geographical area selected. For example, a map calculating population density using the entire United States as an area unit will produce a low average density because so much of the Great Plains and western desert areas have little or no population. Maps using an individual state as an area unit will provide more accurate density estimates and maps based on them will more accurately depict true population densities. Analysis using a metropolitan region or city as the area unit will be even more accurate.

monochromatic color ramp. A color ramp using a single chroma. For example, a purple color ramp might use very light purple to symbolize census tracts with very few foreign-born residents moving to very dark purple for census tracts with large numbers of foreign-born residents.

normalize. To remove an effect biasing a statistic such as sample size. In choropleth maps, data normalized by the area of features provides a more accurate representation of density than unnormalized absolute values.

point. A unit of measurement used by cartographers and typographers to describe the size of a font. There are seventy-two points in one inch.

proportional point symbol. A map symbol whose size is mathematically in proportion to a quantity depicted.

scale. The ratio between map features and the objects they represent on the ground.

Questions for further study

1. Explain the apparent conflict between Edward Tufte's assertion that above all else a data graphic must tell the truth and Mark Monmonier's assertion that all maps must tell lies.

2. What frame color would you use for a map of the United States? For Hawaii? Why?

3. What is the difference between a graduated and a proportional point symbol? Why don't you always use proportional point symbols?

4. What is a mimetic symbol? Why should mimetic symbols be used sparingly and with care?

5. Why is it more difficult to depict two or more polygon layers than one polygon layer and two or more point and line layers? What are ways to overcome this problem?

6. There are nine U.S. Supreme Court justices, all of whom live in the Washington, D.C., area. Recall the example of how a dot density map of the world would locate one living pope, and retell the story using the nine justices as the people to be located on a map. Make clear what this story illustrates about dot density maps and the modifiable area unit problem.

Annotated bibliography

Mark Monmonier's *How to Lie with Maps*, second edition (Monmonier 1996) is a readable and provocative introduction to the way in which maps always require some departure from the truth. It contains excellent examples of common and amusing map errors and a lucid description of principles of good map design. Monmonier's *Mapping It Out: Expository Cartography for the Humanities and Social Sciences* (Monmonier 1993) is another readable guide to spatial representation for the nonspecialist by the same author.

Leading college cartography texts include Arthur H. Robinson et al., *Elements of Cartography*, sixth edition (Robinson et al. 1995); Borden D. Dent's *Cartography: Thematic Map Design*, fifth edition (Dent 1999); and Terry A. Slocum, Bruce B. McMaster, Fritz C. Kessler, and Hugh H. Howard's *Thematic Cartography and Geographic Visualization*, second edition (Slocum et al. 2003).

Tim Ormsby, Eileen Napoleon, Robert Burke, Carolyn Groessl, and Laura Feaster's *Getting to Know ArcGIS Desktop*, second edition (Ormsby et al. 2004) chapter 5 "Symbolizing features and rasters" contains a lucid description of GIS map symbology and step-by-step instructions on how to symbolize data using ArcGIS.

Chapter 11

Multiple media and the theory and practice of graphic communication

"Graphical excellence is that which gives to the viewer the greatest number of ideas in the shortest time with the least ink in the smallest space."

Edward Tufte (2001)

Introduction

Communicating information effectively is essential. Unless the intended audience understands the findings, research fails. Consumers of research are usually busy and often less expert than the researchers. They don't have the kind of hands-on familiarity with the data that the author of a report acquires in the course of his research. It is essential to reduce the burden of interpreting results for them. One way to communicate information clearly is to use an appropriate mix of media. Another is to understand the theoretical basis for visual communication and practical principles for creating good data graphics. The first part of this chapter discusses how to communicate information in multiple media. The second part discusses theories of how to visually represent information and practical details of how to construct good data graphics.

Communicating in multiple media

This book has a heavy emphasis on maps and data graphics as vehicles for spatial analysis and communication. But maps and data graphics are only parts of a continuum of ways to communicate information. Written text, output from statistical packages and spreadsheets, and oral briefings are other standard media used to communicate the results of social science and public policy research. PowerPoint presentations are now a nearly universal medium accompanying research reports. Because they are so widely used (and abused), PowerPoint presentations merit special attention. This chapter begins with a discussion of how to communicate research results in different media. It places data graphics and maps in context with written reports, oral briefings, and presentation of statistical output. It describes the proper role for PowerPoint and how not to abuse it.

Maps, written reports, and oral briefings

Maps are the vehicles of choice for communicating spatial information. Creating a map, like creating a written report, requires thought about the subject matter, careful selection of what to include and exclude, attention to truthful and understandable communication, and attention to detail in crafting an effective final product. Jacques Bertin emphasizes the nonlinear quality of maps (Bertin 1967). Bertin points out that in a map, two, three, or more dimensions of information can be seen at once. This is quite different from the linear flow of words in a written report.

Written reports can explain complex ideas in words. Like a paper analog map, a written report is a one-time final summary of information. Unlike GIS, a written report is not a vehicle for further analysis and can't be electronically tailored by changing scale, panning, or zooming. Reports are linear. The reader can't grasp the totality of what the writer is conveying at once, but must proceed word by word from beginning to end. A lovely little expository book on effective writing is *The Elements of Style* by William Strunk Jr. and Elwyn Brook White (Strunk and White 2000), who express the Shaker ideal in expository prose writing.

Oral briefings can convey meaning through the speaker's tone and emphasis. They offer the opportunity for questions and answers. Unlike a map, the audience hears, but does not see, what the speaker is talking about. This makes it difficult to communicate dense information that may be readily apparent in a map, table, or data graphic. At about 100 to 160 words spoken a minute, oral briefings are a slow way to communicate information compared to written reports, maps, or data graphics.

Output from spreadsheets, statistical packages, and database programs

Data that is stored in a GIS attribute table is in a file format that can be manipulated by other kinds of software: spreadsheets, statistical packages, and database programs. The output from spreadsheets and statistical packages is frequently used in written reports and PowerPoint briefings about social science and public policy issues. Database programs perform a somewhat different role: they facilitate storage and organization of data.

A **spreadsheet** program allows users to manipulate financial and other quantitative data. Microsoft Excel is a commonly used spreadsheet. Because Microsoft Excel is usually bundled with Microsoft Word, it is very widely available. Spreadsheets work well for calculations of data in rows and columns such as a GIS attribute table. While it is possible to do some statistical analysis with spreadsheets, and skilled users can get spreadsheets to do quite sophisticated kinds of analysis, spreadsheets are not as well suited for statistical analysis as statistical packages.

A **statistical package** is a type of software program designed specifically to perform statistical analysis on data. Statistical packages commonly used in social science and public policy research include the Statistical Package for the Social Sciences (SPSS), SAS, and STATA. MINITAB is a statistical package that is widely used in introductory college data analysis courses. Most students in social science and public policy disciplines are exposed to statistical packages in data analysis courses. Ayse Pamuk's *Mapping Global Cities: GIS Methods in Urban Analysis* (to be published by ESRI Press in 2006) will explain more about the relationship between data analysis and GIS. The *ESRI Guide to GIS Analysis, Volume 2: Spatial Measurements and Statistics*, by Andy Mitchell (Mitchell 2005), describes spatial statistics.

A computer **database program** allows users to create the digital equivalent of digital filing cabinets, enter data into them, retrieve data, and produce summaries of information in the database. Computerized indexes make it possible to retrieve subsets of data from a computer database easily and virtually instantaneously. Microsoft Access and FileMaker™ Pro are examples of microcomputer database programs. While it is possible to use database software to perform some of the same

Data from GIS attribute tables can be used in spreadsheet, database, and statistical package programs.
Source: Richard LeGates

operations as a spreadsheet and even to do some statistical analysis, the most useful role for a database program is to organize and store data, not to analyze it.

GIS programs themselves typically have limited capacity to perform the kind of operations that database programs, spreadsheets, and statistical packages perform. Therefore, advanced GIS analysis often involves passing data back and forth between the GIS software (which is best for mapping) and database programs and statistical packages that are specifically designed to manage data and perform statistical analysis.

Box 11.1 illustrates the way in which data from a GIS attribute table can be analyzed in a spreadsheet program and a statistical package. The screenshot in the top left of the box shows six fields from an ArcMap GIS attribute table of San Francisco 2000 census block data. You already know how GIS can classify and display data like this as maps. The screenshot in the top right of box 11.1 shows the same data imported into a spreadsheet (Microsoft Excel). A new column (labeled F) shows a calculation in process—calculating the number of households by dividing the population of each block by the average household size. The screenshot in the bottom left of box 11.1 shows the same data imported into a statistical package (SPSS). On the bottom right is a correlation matrix produced by SPSS that shows the correlation between four of the variables. This book does not assume that you have had a statistics course. If you have had a statistics course, you can tell from the correlation matrix in box 11.1 that there is a strong, positive relationship between two of the variables (median age of people within a census tract and the number of people age 65 and older within the census tract). The correlation matrix shows that this relationship is statistically significant: there is less than a 1 percent probability that it occurred by chance. Relationships among the other variables vary in strength and direction, but none of them are statistically significant. If you have not had a statistics course, you may not be able to interpret the meaning of the correlation matrix. But the idea is clear—the same data can be passed between different software programs and each can be used to do what it does best. Hopefully, you will be motivated to learn more about what the resulting output means and how to do statistical analysis yourself.

PowerPoint presentations

PowerPoint presentations are computerized slide shows that speakers use to support oral reports. PowerPoint slides can contain text, images, charts, and other material. PowerPoint has simplified what were once the cumbersome, time-consuming, and costly processes of creating photographic slides and using a slide carousel projector or making Mylar transparent overlays and using an overhead projector to enhance an oral presentation.

The purpose of PowerPoint presentations is to provide an outline of the speaker's points and to illustrate spoken words with visual images, including photographs, maps, and data graphics. Printed handouts of PowerPoint slides can orient listeners to an oral briefing while it is in progress and serve as a written record to remind viewers of the presentation content at a later date. Compared to written reports, maps, and data graphics, PowerPoint slides contain very little information. PowerPoint is not a good medium for communicating substantive content in depth.

Unfortunately, PowerPoint comes with complex and visually distracting slide templates. Libraries of banal clip art are routinely used to enhance presentations. It is fun and easy to use PowerPoint to create slide transitions such as slides zipping in from the left or right and even sound effects like the sound of a typewriter, screeching tires, and breaking glass.

Nothing provokes a graphic minimalist more than a bad PowerPoint slide. Edward Tufte, the Yale professor emeritus introduced in chapter 4, has spent his lifetime developing a graphical style that emphasizes content and condemns what he calls **chartjunk**: material included on charts that conveys no information. The hundred billion to one trillion bad PowerPoint slides created each

Box 11.1 Using GIS data in spreadsheets and statistical packages

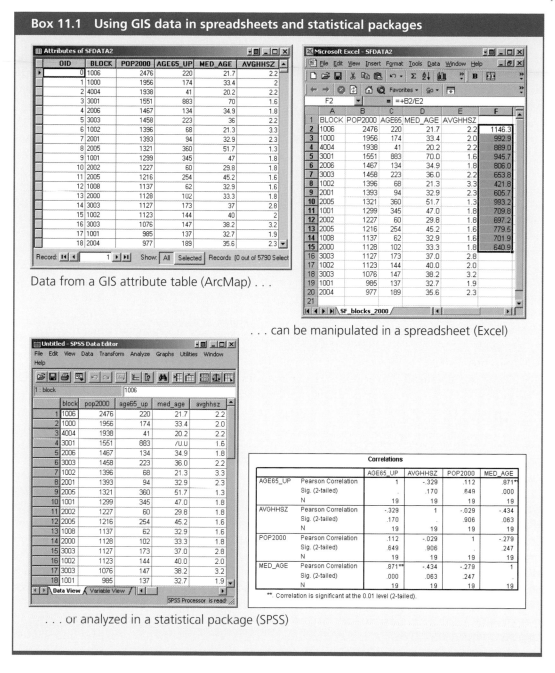

Data from a GIS attribute table (ArcMap) . . .

. . . can be manipulated in a spreadsheet (Excel)

. . . or analyzed in a statistical package (SPSS)

year provoked Tufte to write an essay titled "The Cognitive Style of PowerPoint" (Tufte 2003) documenting PowerPoint's extremely low information content.

A mainstay of every PowerPoint presentation is bulleted lists of points. Tufte argues that bulleted lists of points are typically too generic to convey much real information, leave critical relationships unspecified, and omit critical assumptions.

He concedes that by insisting that points be placed in an orderly structure, bulleted lists may help extremely disorganized speakers get themselves organized and for the naive may create the appearance of hard-headed, organized thought. But Tufte sees the cognitive style of PowerPoint as mostly "faux-analytic phluff."

Tufte concedes that PowerPoint is a competent slide manager and projector, but that is the only use he sees for it. "If your numbers are boring, then you've got the wrong numbers," Tufte writes. "If your words or images are not on point, making them dance in color won't make them relevant" (Tufte 2003).

As an example of PowerPoint banality, Tufte reproduces portions of Abraham Lincoln's Gettysburg Address, reduced to PowerPoint slides produced by Peter Norvig, a software engineer at Google. One of the slides is in figure 11.1.

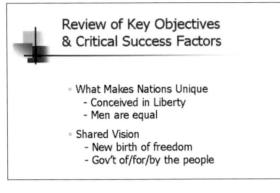

Figure 11.1 "Gettysburg Address" PowerPoint slide.
Source: Peter Norvig

Tufte is too harsh on PowerPoint. His critique is based on the incorrect assumption that PowerPoint is used as the primary vehicle to convey content—which is rarely the case. Used as an aid to oral communication and a device to orient audiences, PowerPoint serves a purpose. But Tufte is right to condemn distracting clip art, artistic chartjunk, and distracting sound that accompany many PowerPoint presentations. Indeed, colorful flimflam is less than useless because it distracts viewers from content, which is what the presentation is really about. Tufte is right that bulleted lists are usually superficial and that hierarchical organization of bulleted lists beyond three layers deep is confusing. Most important of all, Tufte is correct that there is no substitute for good content to any communication.

PowerPoint should be used to enhance oral briefings by providing an outline of the speaker's points. Despite Tufte's ridicule, studies have shown that audiences will better understand and remember more of what was said if there are clear, written, bulleted points accompanying the talk. PowerPoint presentations can contribute visual images to an oral talk and these can enhance understanding. Any visual image can be scanned and put into a PowerPoint presentation—including excellent maps that Tufte has reproduced in his books. Snow's map of cholera deaths and Minard's map of Napoleon's invasion of Russia that are reproduced in the gallery of great maps in chapter 3 could be inserted into a PowerPoint presentation with good effect. The audience can see information in such a map or data graphic that a speaker cannot communicate as effectively orally.

In summary, PowerPoint is a useful but limited medium for communicating information. The fact that it is much misused does not mean that it cannot be used well. PowerPoint can enhance oral communication and increase audience understanding. PowerPoint handouts can be a useful summary of a talk. It creates exciting possibilities for combining data graphics and maps with oral communication.

Posters and combinations of media

Combining text, maps, data graphics, photos, tables, and statistical output can provide extremely rich information content. If each of these media is used to best advantage, the combination can be very effective.

Posters are often used to display combinations of material like this. You probably created a poster for a high school science or history project by gluing text, photographs, and perhaps pie or bar charts to poster board. Poster sessions are common at academic conferences. Experts stand next to a poster summarizing their work so that people strolling through the poster session can quickly focus on material of interest to them and then chat with the person who created the poster.

Computers have changed the way in which posters are created in two ways. Higher-quality posters can be created digitally. The scale of the poster can be changed—and often part or all of the poster can be reprinted on standard 8 1/2" x 11" paper to insert into written reports. Alternatively, combinations of media created for a report can be expanded to become a poster.

The *New York Times* is particularly skillful at creating combinations of text, images, maps, and graphics. Figure 11.2 accompanied a 2003 *New York Times* story about the decline of the Great Plains region of the United States. Newspaper staffers with writing, cartographic, graphic design, and analytical skills worked under the direction of Matthew Ericson to create this extremely interesting and information-rich combination of words, maps, and data graphics. The *New York Times* staff used GIS to create a dichromatic color ramp showing population change in U.S. counties between 1990 and 2000. Alaska and Hawaii are included in the map as insets. Counties that lost population are symbolized in orange and counties that gained population in purple. The dark orange counties lost the most population; the dark purple counties gained the most population. The bar charts on the lower left show the cumulative percent change in population each decade since 1950 for the United States and the rural Great Plains. They tell a striking story. While the population of the United States grew each decennial census between 1950 and 2000, and overall grew 86 percent during this fifty-year period, the population of the rural Great Plains decreased during three of these decades (between 1950 and 1960, 1960 and 1970, and 1980 and 1990) and decreased overall 21 percent during these fifty years.

The three columns on the right in figure 11.2 include small maps illustrating the location of the rural Great Plains and of the rest of the United States and then a series of percentages and small charts illustrating differences between the rural Great Plains and the rest of the United States in terms of population, median household income, people employed in agriculture, self-employed people, race and ethnicity, age, education, and median home values. A note explains the precise definition of the area in question. Figure 11.2 is an excellent, data-rich graphic. The **data-ink ratio**—Tufte's term for the amount of ink that conveys information compared to the total ink in the graphic—is very high. There is no chartjunk.

Lacking the *New York Times* graphics technology, you could still create a data graphic like figure 11.2 by creating text in a word-processing program, GIS maps using skills from this book, and bar charts using ArcGIS, Microsoft Excel, or a statistical package. Each of the elements could be assembled by pasting them to a poster board or assembled in an appropriate computer program. PowerPoint is a reasonably good software vehicle for creating complex graphics like this. It is ubiquitous and easy to use. While PowerPoint lacks some of the bells and whistles of more sophisticated dedicated illustration software programs like MacroMedia Freehand and Adobe Illustrator, it allows users to create text and insert, move, crop, and resize visual images such as photographs, maps, and data graphics in .jpg, .gif, .tiff and other standard image formats. Any visual image can be scanned into a computer image file and inserted into PowerPoint. Even a graphic as complex as the *New York Times* graphic in figure 11.2 can be assembled in PowerPoint using scanned images or .jpg files from a digital camera or the Web. Once it has been created, a

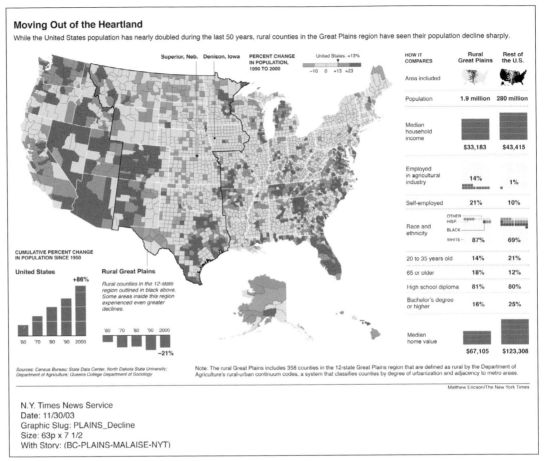

Figure 11.2 *New York Times* graphic on people moving out of the U.S. Heartland.
Source: © The New York *Times* Graphics

graphic like this can be printed out at sizes larger than a standard page—including 36" x 48" poster format.

The theory and practice of graphic communication

Now that you have seen an exemplary data graphic, it is time to dig deeper into the theory and practice of graphic communication.

Tufte's theory of data graphics

One part of Tufte's classic book *The Visual Display of Quantitative Information* (2001) is titled "Theory of Data Graphics." It is only one hundred pages long and consists mostly of images. Tufte is a graphical minimalist, and his approach is similar to Mozart's approach to musical composition. Mozart was convinced that he used exactly as many notes as his music demanded and no more. "Above all else show the data" is Tufte's first principle of excellence in visually representing data (Tufte 2001). Other of Tufte's concepts and principles are summarized in box 11.2.

Box 11.2   Selected concepts and principles in Tufte's "theory of data graphics"

Data ink is the ink on a graphic that presents information. The **data-ink ratio** is the ratio of data ink to total ink. Data graphic designers should strive for high data-ink ratios.

Chartjunk consists of design elements in a data graphic that don't convey information. Data graphic designers should eliminate chartjunk.

Data density refers to the number of entries in a data matrix divided by the area of a data graphic. Data graphic designers should maximize data density within reason.

Small multiples resemble the frames of a movie: a series of graphics, showing the same combination of variables, indexed by changes in another variable. Well-designed small multiples can efficiently convey a large amount of information. Data graphic designers should use small multiples where appropriate.

Source: Edward Tufte, *The Visual Display of Quantitative Information, 2nd ed.* (2001)

Jacques Bertin's semiology

In 1967, French semiologist Jacques Bertin published a book—*Semiology of Graphics: Diagrams, Networks, Maps*—that didn't fit into any existing librarian's classification scheme (Bertin 1967). Bertin's niche lies somewhere between semiology (the science of visual signs), cartography (map-making), and graphic design. His theory blends psychology, art, and statistics. Bertin's book is dense reading, filled with conceptual material that requires careful study, but even nonexperts can understand Bertin's profoundly useful semiotic principles.

Bertin distinguished what he calls *retinal variables* (things perceived by the eye) and *locational variables* (things that symbolize where objects are in space). Bertin identified two locational variables (location along an x-axis and location along a y-axis), and five retinal variables (size, shape, orientation, texture, and color). Figure 11.3 illustrates Bertin's five retinal variables. Bertin developed ways to represent reality clearly using the seven variables (two locational and five retinal). Of course, mapmakers have used these variables for centuries, but often unconsciously or with less rigorous theoretical understanding of how to use them effectively than Bertin provides. Software illustration programs and GIS software makes it possible to work with all of Bertin's variables to create data graphics and map symbology.

You have seen examples of ways in which retinal variables can be skillfully designed in the maps and data graphics throughout this book. While you may not have been conscious that you were doing this at the time, you have worked with visual variables in all of the exercises and explicitly practiced how to select appropriate visual variables and combine them to produce high-quality maps in exercise 5. Armed with Bertin's theoretical framework and these operational skills, you are well on your way to creating effective map symbology and data graphics.

Creating data graphics

Communicating the results of analysis need not stop with the basic univariate and multivariate data graphics discussed in chapters 4 and 8. Theory about data visualization and principles for graphing data have evolved rapidly over the last two centuries. Creative thinkers from eighteenth

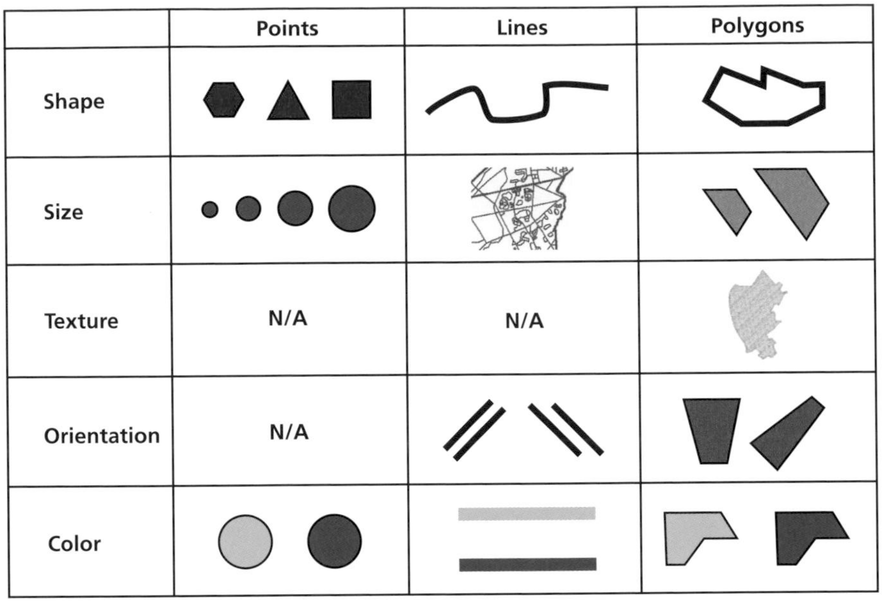

	Points	Lines	Polygons
Shape			
Size			
Texture	N/A	N/A	
Orientation	N/A		
Color			

Figure 11.3 Jacques Bertin's retinal variables.

Source: Based on Jacques Bertin, *Semiology of Graphics: Diagrams, Networks, Maps*

century polymath William Playfair (Playfair 1786) to Tufte (Tufte 2001) have invented ways of communicating quantitative information in visual form. Tufte's writings on visualizing data (1990, 1997, 2001, 2003) are filled with useful concepts, principles, and examples. William S. Cleveland's *The Elements of Graphing Data* (Cleveland 1994) is an excellent synthesis of principles for good data graphic design. Robert T. Harris's book *Information Graphics: A Comprehensive Illustrated Reference* (Harris 1996) is an encyclopedia of data graphics filled with details about how to construct them properly. The *New York Times* and many other newspapers and news magazines use high-quality data graphics. Scientific journals and the better social science scholarly journals now insist on high-quality data graphics. Statistical packages, spreadsheets, and GIS software are incorporating ever-better data graphing capability into their software.

A good data graphic should tell a story. Figure 11.4 is a multiple line chart showing the percentage of the population that was urban for three countries: Botswana, Saudi Arabia, and the United States at five-year intervals from 1960–2000. It was created from World Bank data used to create maps 1.3a and 1.3b. Figure 11.4 conveys a lot of information in a small space very clearly. It tells a powerful story about how rates of urbanization have varied for different countries during the last forty years. Some developed countries were already heavily urbanized by 1960 and have had very slow urbanization rates since then. They are little more urbanized today than they were forty years ago. The United States—represented by the nearly level red line at the top of figure 11.4—was already 70 percent urban by 1960 and has been urbanizing only gradually during the last forty years. In stark contrast, some developing countries, like the impoverished African country of Botswana—represented by the green line that begins near 0 on the x-axis—are urbanizing very fast. Only 2 percent of Botswana's population was urban in 1960. However, during the forty years between 1960 and 2000, Botswana urbanized at a rate more than ten times as fast as the United States. By 2000, almost half of Botswana's population was urban. Less than one third of the people in the oil-rich country of Saudi Arabia, represented by the blue line, were urban in 1960; but today almost nine out of every ten Saudis live in cities.

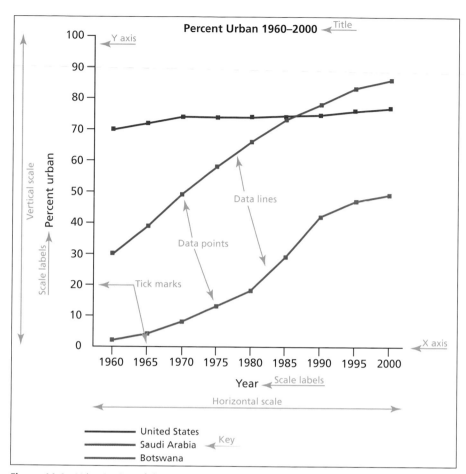

Figure 11.4   Urbanization of three countries, with graphical elements identified.

Source: World Bank

Creating data graphics is an iterative process like writing an essay. It requires thinking about what the data means, preparing a draft of the data graphic, thinking about flaws in the graphic and ways to improve it, and then preparing a second and subsequent drafts until the graphic is as polished as the final draft of a report that has been carefully revised.

Figure 11.4 contains many common elements included in data graphics. The x- and y-axes, tick marks, horizontal and vertical scales, scale labels, data points, data lines, and the key are indicated on the figure. Every data graphic should have a title that succinctly describes what it is about. It may also include a caption with a longer explanation of the data graphic. Most data graphics contain most or all of the elements illustrated and labeled in figure 11.4. It is not necessary to include all of these elements in every data graphic, and more advanced graphics may contain additional elements. Command of this starter set of data graphic elements will permit beginners to create good, clear data graphics.

It is important to focus on what you want to accomplish with a data graphic and not get lost in the mechanical details. The information on a graphic is the reason for its existence. Above all else, information must be made clear. Other elements should not obscure them. Four ways to achieve these goals with data graphics are to make the data stand out, eliminate superfluity, proofread the work, and try the graphics out on someone to see if they do in fact tell the intended story clearly.

In creating effective data graphics the devil is in the details. Little things matter. William Cleveland provides advice on how to handle these details (Cleveland 1994). Some of his principles are summarized in box 11.3.

What a graph shows can be summarized in text as part of the graphic caption or in the body of a report. It is important to describe everything significant that is graphed and summarize conclusions based on the data. Cleveland has concluded from his study of hundreds of data graphics that including too little information in graphic captions is more common than including too much. He favors somewhat longer and more detailed captions than common, but within limits. If captions become too long, the substantive material they contain should be moved to the body of a report or an appendix.

The quality of graphics created by a computer change depending on the quality of the printer on which they are printed. If the graphics are photocopied, they may be less clear than the originals. It is important to design data graphics so that visual clarity will be preserved when the images are reduced or reproduced. An essential step before finalizing a report is to print out drafts of the graphics and examine them to make sure the images are clear. If a report is going to be photocopied or the images will be reduced, the best way to make sure they will remain clear is to photocopy or reduce one test copy first. If the test copy is clear, the data graphic will work when it is reproduced. If it is not, it must be changed. A brilliant analysis with a clear caption accompanying a photocopied data graphic fails if the gray scales all blend together and the graphic is incomprehensible.

Box 11.3   William Cleveland's elements of graphing data (selections)

- Make the data stand out. Avoid superfluity.
- Use visually prominent graphic elements to show the data.
- Do not overdo the number of tick marks.
- Use a reference line when there is an important value that must be seen across the entire graph, but do not let the line interfere with the data.
- Overlapping plotting symbols must be visually distinguishable.
- Visual clarity must be preserved under reduction and reproduction.
- Put major conclusions into graphical form. Make captions comprehensive and informative.
- Describe everything that is graphed.
- Draw attention to the important features of the data.
- Describe the conclusions drawn from the data on the graphic.

Source: William S. Cleveland, *The Elements of Graphing Data* (1994)

Since information can be communicated in many different media—text, maps, data graphics, oral briefings, statistical output, PowerPoint slideshows, and other media—it is important to have a comprehensive strategy about what media to use and how to use them to most effectively convey information.

With the conclusion of this final chapter in section III you are ready to put all the pieces of this book together. Chapter 12 describes the way in which Metro in the Portland, Oregon, region combines GIS and regional planning.

Terms

chartjunk. Edward Tufte's term for design elements in a data graphic that do not convey information. Tufte urges that all chartjunk should be eliminated from data graphics.

database program. A type of software program that allows users to create a structure to hold data, enter data into it, retrieve data, produce summaries of the data, and perform calculations and data transformations.

data-ink ratio. Tufte's term for the ratio of ink in a data graphic that presents information, compared to the total ink. Tufte argues that designers of data graphics should strive for high data-ink ratios within reason.

PowerPoint presentation. A computerized slideshow. Speakers can use Powerpoint presentations to support oral reports. PowerPoint slides can contain text, images, charts, and other material.

statistical package. A type of software that allows the user to perform statistical analysis on data—primarily quantitative data. Statistical packages commonly used in social science and public policy research include the Statistical Package for the Social Sciences (SPSS), SAS, and STATA.

spreadsheet. A type of software that allows a user to manipulate quantitative data. Microsoft Excel is a commonly used spreadsheet.

Questions for further study

1. What are the particular strengths and weaknesses of each of the following ways of communicating information: written reports, maps, statistical output, oral briefings, and PowerPoint presentations?

2. What are Edward Tufte's main criticisms of PowerPoint? Do you agree with him? What is the purpose of a PowerPoint presentation?

3. According to Tufte, what is chartjunk? What is a data-ink ratio? How are these theoretical constructs useful in creating better maps and better data graphics?

4. What are Bertin's five retinal variables? Why are they important in designing good visual images?

5. What do database programs, spreadsheets, and statistical packages do? Why might you want to use these programs to supplement data in a GIS?

Annotated bibliography

Edward Tufte's pioneering book *The Visual Display of Quantitative Information*, second edition (Tufte 2001) contains brilliant epigrammatic principles for properly displaying quantitative information visually as well as fascinating examples—past and present—of good practice and spectacular abuse of his principles. Other books by Tufte developing his theories about the visual display of quantitative information include *Envisioning Information* (Tufte 1990) and *Visual Explanations: Images and Quantities, Evidence and Narrative* (Tufte 1997).

William Cleveland's *The Elements of Graphing Data*, revised edition (Cleveland 1994) is an excellent guide to the theory and practice of visual representation of quantitative data.

Jacques Bertin's theories about how human beings perceive visual representations of reality are contained in *Semiology of Graphics: Diagrams, Networks, Maps*, translated by William J. Berg (Bertin 1983) originally published as *Semiologie Graphique* in 1967.

A classic book on expository prose writing is William Strunk Jr. and E. B. White's *The Elements of Style* (Strunk and White 2000).

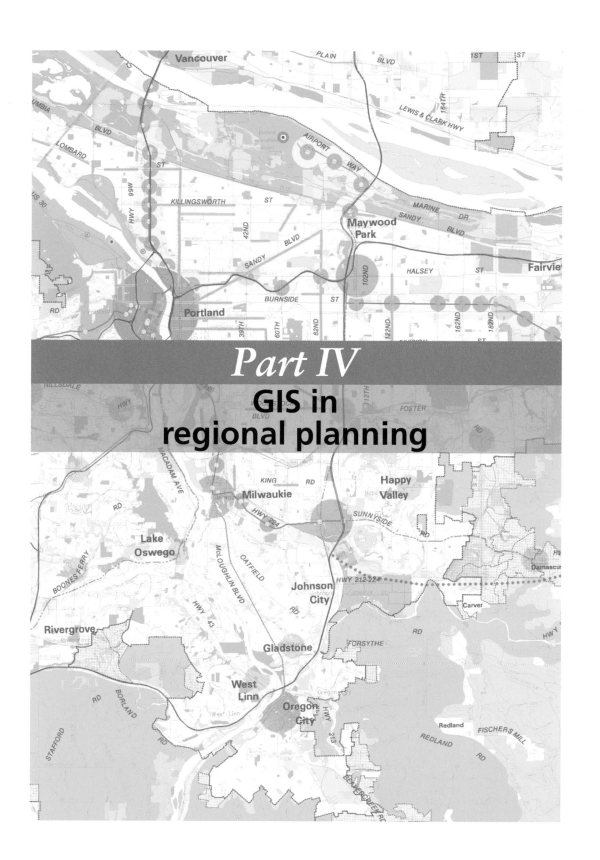

Part IV
GIS in
regional planning

Chapter 12

Bringing it all together
in the Portland, Oregon, region

> *"Clean air and clean water do not stop at city limits or county lines.*
> *Neither does the need for jobs, a thriving economy, and good*
> *transportation choices for people and businesses . . .. A regional*
> *approach simply makes sense when it comes to protecting open*
> *space, caring for parks, planning for the best use of land, manag-*
> *ing garbage disposal, and increasing recycling."*

Metro (2004)

Introduction

Metro, in the Portland, Oregon, metropolitan region, is the only elected regional commission in the United States with regionwide planning responsibilities and some service delivery powers (Abbott 2001; Knaap, Bolen, and Seltzer 2004). Metro has used GIS to develop a fifty-year vision of its future as a compact, city-centered region that brings together many of the concepts for good regional planning described in this book. The vision is summarized in a 2040 Growth Concept map produced by GIS. Metro has devised a regional framework plan to reach this vision (Metro 1997) and functional plans dealing with matters of regional significance for transportation (Metro 2000), habitat conservation (Metro 2004b), and other areas. Each of the three counties and twenty-four cities in the Metro region has land-use, transportation, open space, and other plans consistent with Metro's regional framework plan.

Long-range, progressive, visionary plans are being implemented in the Portland region to implement the vision. Programs to translate the 2040 Growth Concept into action include phased construction of additions to the regional light-rail system, transit villages, urban growth boundaries (UGBs) around cities within the region and the entire region, acquisition of a regional system of open space and parkland, and a regional framework for habitat conservation.

Change is always controversial, and serious urban planning is a fiercely political enterprise (Forester 1987). Metro has critics and is under continuous political attack. As this book goes to press, the impact of **Measure 37**—an important statewide initiative passed in 2004 intended to protect private property rights against Oregon's planning system—is being hotly contested. But friends and foes agree that since its inception in 1978, Metro has made a big difference in the region. Visitors to Portland today can ride a convenient light-rail system, visit thousands of acres of newly acquired open space and parkland, and tour attractive new transit villages planned by Metro. The discerning visitor will find many examples of infill development where formerly vacant lots have been put to use in ways that are both consistent with the fabric of the neighborhood and exemplary of good planning. Apartments above retail stores on public transit lines and buildings with living units and offices stacked on alternate floors are examples of good infill development in Portland.

Less visible, but even more important, the density of development in Portland is already changing. Density is being increased at places where it is appropriate, such as transit nodes and is being held constant in most residential neighborhoods. A look at aerial photographs or a short ride to the edge of the Metro regional urban growth boundary reveals a clean separation between urban development and undeveloped land that contrasts with the sprawl found in other metropolitan areas. Equally important changes Metro has made in the Metro region take the form of inventories and maps that are guiding development. Riparian habitats along streams and riverbanks and habitats classified as upland regions are particularly important to preserving biodiversity in the Metro region. These two important types of land have been inventoried and mapped. Work on a comprehensive regional habitat conservation system is well underway.

Urban planners increasingly use computerized "decision support systems" to inform their planning decisions (Brail and Klosterman 2001). Portland has created what is arguably the best regional planning GIS decision support system in the world (Knaap, Bolen, and Seltzer 2004). Metro maintains consistent, seamless, regularly updated digital data about the Metro region helpful for regional planning. Using GIS map layers, planners and policy makers throughout the Metro region can see the exact status of development in the whole region or zoom in and look at development in particular locations in great detail. They can make informed planning decisions in a way that is impossible elsewhere. The next section describes the Portland region, and the chapter goes on to describe Metro's most important plans: the 2040 Growth Concept, the regional framework plan, the regional urban growth boundary, and functional plans for transportation and habitat protection. Then it explains the way in which collaborative planning between Metro, city and county governments, other partners, and citizens produced these plans. The final sections describe Metro's regional land information system (RLIS) and the role it has played in regional planning and policymaking.

The following discussion offers Metro as a model of how to integrate digital information technology with regional planning, it also discusses critiques of Metro from property rights advocates who say that Metro, as a key player in implementing Oregon's statewide planning goals, has infringed unfairly on property rights, and planners who contend that Metro has not done enough in some areas. The ongoing conflict between planners and property rights advocates is particularly important now as Measure 37 may require dramatic changes in urban growth boundaries or hundreds of millions of dollars in compensation to landowners.

This chapter's title uses the phrase "bringing it all together" in the present tense. Metro's work is not perfect and its job is far from done. But Metro and its RLIS are works in progress that anyone interested in thinking globally and acting regionally should examine carefully.

Welcome to the Portland, Oregon, metropolitan region

Metro's region covers 462 square miles. It contains the urban areas of three counties—Multnomah, Clackamas, and Washington counties—and twenty-four cities, including Portland. About 1.3 million people live in the Metro area today. Metro's population is projected to increase to 1.8 million people by 2040 (Metro 1997).

Metro does not replace the three county and twenty-four city governments in the region or substitute its plans for their local land-use plans. Rather, Metro has worked with local government partners and citizens to define the following: (a) a 50-year vision for the region, (b) a **regional framework plan** with broad principles to guide local plans, (c) the regional urban growth boundary, and (d) functional plans in substantive areas such as transportation. This collaborative process has created much more proactive and coordinated local government decision making than elsewhere in the United States. Urban planning and policy in Portland and the Metro region are discussed in a recent anthology titled *The Portland Edge* (Ozawa 2004).

Metro works hard to achieve consensus rather than imposing its decisions top-down. In the long run, Metro needs the good will of local governments and other partners. But Metro is legally empowered to require local governments to conform their local plans to its functional plans—"an incredible power found nowhere else in America" (Knaap, Bolen, and Seltzer 2004).

The main map in map 12.1 shows the Metro region (symbolized in an orange color) and the regional urban growth boundary (symbolized as a dashed red line). Portland (yellow) is within both the Metro region and the urban growth boundary. Notice that the urban growth boundary—the area within which development can occur over the next twenty years—includes much, but not all, of the Metro region. The urban growth boundary was not intended to be static. As the region grows, it must periodically be revised to assure that a twenty-year supply of developable land remains within the urban growth boundary. Since the late 1970s, the boundary has been moved about three dozen times. Most of those moves were small—twenty acres or less. Four large additions to the urban growth boundary have occurred since 1998. You will notice that there is a substantial amount of orange-colored land in the south and east that is within the Metro area but beyond the urban growth boundary. It is possible that this land will one day be within the urban growth boundary if that boundary is expanded. However, right now property owners in this area face the prospect of not being able to develop their land for more than twenty years.

The small map on the lower left of map 12.1 shows Metro area watersheds. The Rock Creek watershed is highlighted in red. Later in this chapter you will see a map of floodplains and locations

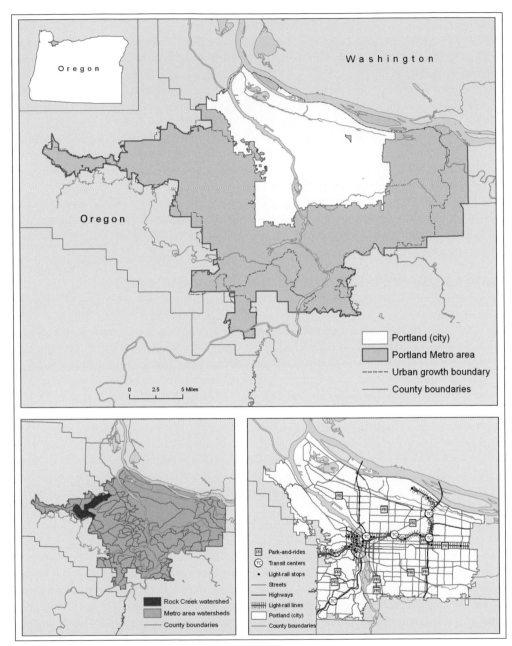

Map 12.1   Metro region, Portland, Oregon.
Source: © Metro, Portland, Oregon 2005

where building permits have been granted within the Rock Creek watershed, a digital orthophoto of part of the floodplain, and the location of recent building permits. In exercise 7, you will have an opportunity to explore flood risk and environmental education opportunities the Rock Creek watershed offers.

The small map on the lower right of map 12.1 shows key transportation features within the city of Portland. The portion of **Metropolitan Area Express (MAX)**—the region's light-rail system—that runs through Portland is symbolized in red. Transit stops are symbolized as black points. (There have been recent extensions of the system not shown on the map.) Transit centers and park-and-ride locations are identified by symbols with the letters TC and PR, respectively. The map also shows highways and streets in Portland.

The evolution of Metro

In 1978, Portland area residents voted to create Metro to replace the Columbia Region Association of Governments (CRAG). CRAG was a council of governments (COG) that suffered from the same weaknesses that plague COGs in other metropolitan areas of the United States as described in chapter 1: it lacked a clear vision for the region, did little regional planning, and did not have the authority to have its decisions accepted by local governments. Metro also took over the responsibilities of an existing regional metropolitan service district (MSD)—an institution that Portland State University historian Carl Abbott terms "a governmental box that could hold as many service responsibilities as voters or the legislature were willing to assign to it" (Abbott 2001). At the time Metro was created, the only significant regional service function in its governmental box was solid waste disposal.

 In 1992, residents of the region voted to allow Metro to function under a home-rule charter (Metro 1992), and in 2000 they amended the charter to provide for six councilors elected by districts, a council president elected at large, and an appointed administrator (Abbott 2001).

Metro still provides a few services on a regional basis. It continues to handle solid waste disposal for the entire region. In 1995, voters gave Metro authority to issue $135 million in bonds to acquire open space, parks, and land to protect streams. Metro has acquired more than eight thousand acres of open space land with this bond money (Metro 2004b). Metro does some other minor service delivery functions, but most services in the Metro region are still provided by county and city governments, a regional transit district (TriMet), and special districts such as the Port of Portland.

Metro has been designated the metropolitan planning organization (MPO) for allocating federal transportation funds within the region. This gives Metro great power to shape the region's public transportation infrastructure. Metro's regional transportation plan (RTP) establishes the framework for regional transportation planning and consistent goals and objectives for the region.

Metro's vision and regional plans

Metro limits its concerns to what urban and regional planners term **matters of regional significance** as opposed to matters of local significance. Matters of regional significance include airports, harbors, and mass and light-rail transit systems. Examples of matters of local significance are local street repairs, parking lots, and city parks. Thus, for example, Metro inventoried and mapped habitat throughout the region. It is using $135 million of its own bond funds to acquire what it considers to be habitat of regional significance. It has established goals and standards for habitat conservation throughout the region. However, the task of developing a habitat conservation plan within a city to preserve habitat deemed only of local significance would fall on the city. Similarly, Metro has defined a long term multimodal vision for the region's transportation system that emphasizes light rail, bicycle, pedestrian, and other alternatives to private automobile use; a framework within which transportation is to be developed; and a regional transportation plan. But Metro leaves construction and operation of transit infrastructure of regional significance (such as extension of the light-rail system) to the independent regional transit agency, TriMet, and transportation issues of local significance such as providing for sufficient local parking to city and county governments.

The 2040 Growth Concept

The 1992 Metro charter made regional growth management Metro's primary mission. The charter required Metro to adopt a future vision—a long-range statement of the region's future. In response to the charter mandate, beginning in 1992, residents of the Portland region went through an extensive planning process to develop a vision for the region fifty years into the future, using 1990 as a starting date (Knaap, Bolen, and Seltzer 2004). The result of this exercise is Metro's **2040 Growth Concept**.

GIS was important in creating the 2040 Growth Concept. GIS professionals at Metro analyzed the long-term impacts of continuing development. They mapped how much land would be consumed if current development trends continued and how this pattern of development would affect air quality. They prepared maps illustrating current levels of congestion, transit ridership, and vehicle miles traveled along highways within the urban growth boundary. Then they used GIS to model impacts that each of four alternative growth concepts would have in each of these areas. The results of their modeling were surprising. Metro concluded that continuing along the current path of development or any one of the alternatives they had identified would not be optimal. Citizens and government representatives reviewed and debated the alternatives. Finally, a preferred alternative concept incorporating features of several of the different growth concepts was adopted.

Metro did not do its 2040 Growth Concept planning in a vacuum. A questionnaire was sent to every home in the region—over five hundred thousand homes. Metro conducted dozens of public workshops, forums, and open houses to solicit input on the proposed plan. Videos on the region's future were distributed free to everyone who rented a Blockbuster video. There was what Robert Putnam and Lewis M. Feldstein termed "a positive epidemic of civic engagement" (Putnam and Feldstein 2003).

GIS can be an important tool to encourage community participation in planning (Craig, Harris, and Weiner 2002). In the 2040 Growth Concept planning process, drafts of the 2040 Growth Concept GIS map were the focus of much debate. Because people could visually see the consequences of different growth scenarios, GIS focused the debate and helped contribute to agreement on a preferred alternative.

Metro also worked with the governments of the region's three counties and twenty-four cities as they developed the 2040 Growth Concept plan. Independent special districts providing park, water, open space, and other services also participated in the regional planning process.

The Metro commissioners adopted the 2040 Growth Concept in December 1995 with all commissioners voting for approval and with the unanimous endorsement of local government partners. Using 1990 as the base year, the Portland 2040 Growth Concept established a fifty-year framework for managing the region's growth. A single map summarizes the concept visually. The completed Metro 2040 Growth Concept plan map is reproduced as map 3.15 in the gallery of great maps. Map 12.2 shows a portion of the concept plan. It is an excellent example of how GIS symbology can be used to convey complex information clearly. Box 12.1 describes the central components of the 2040 Growth Concept plan.

The Metro 2040 Growth Concept is intended to manage growth, protect natural resources and make improvements to facilities and infrastructure while maintaining the region's quality of life. It is designed to accommodate approximately 720,000 additional residents and 350,000 additional jobs in the region by 2040.

The vision calls for compact, city-centered development. Downtown Portland would remain the hub of the region. Eight regional, mixed-use urban centers within the urban growth boundary

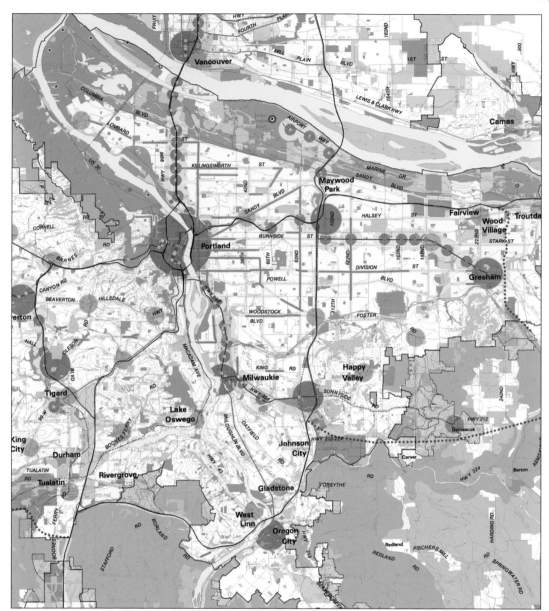

Map 12.2 Part of the Metro 2040 Growth Concept plan.
Source: © Metro, Portland, Oregon 2005

are intended to be centers of employment and housing. Each would be well served by transit. They would form compact areas of retail, cultural, and recreational activities in a pedestrian-friendly environment. Town centers would provide localized services. The regional and small-town centers do not exactly follow Ebenezer Howard's prescription for garden cities (Howard 1898) as described in chapter 1, but they are strongly influenced by his ideas of manageable, human-scale cities separated from each other by greenbelts as an alternative to huge, sprawling, formless conurbations.

Box 12.1   Understanding the 2040 Growth Concept map

Following is an explanation of the most important symbols used in constructing the Metro 2040 Growth Concept plan map:

Central city
Downtown Portland serves as the hub of business and cultural activity in the region. It has the most intensive form of development for both housing and employment, with high-rise development common in the central business district. Downtown Portland will continue to serve as the finance and commerce, government, retail, tourism, arts, and entertainment center for the region.

Regional centers
Eight regional centers have concentrations of commerce and local government services serving hundreds of thousands of people each. They are characterized by two- to four-story compact employment and housing developments served by high-quality transit.

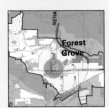

Town centers
Town centers provide localized services to tens of thousands of people within a two- to three-mile radius. Town centers have a strong sense of community identity and are well served by transit. They are characterized by one- to three-story buildings for employment and housing.

Main streets
Main streets are similar to town centers. They have a traditional commercial identity but are on a smaller scale with a strong sense of the immediate neighborhood. Main streets feature good access to transit.

Corridors
Corridors are major streets that serve as transportation routes for people and goods.

Neighborhoods
Most existing neighborhoods will remain largely the same. Some vacant or underused buildings will be redeveloped. New neighborhoods are likely to have an emphasis on smaller single-family lots, mixed uses, and a mix of housing types, including row houses and accessory dwelling units.

Box 12.1   Understanding the 2040 Growth Concept map (cont.)

Neighboring cities and green corridors
Neighboring cities with a significant number of residents who work or shop in the metropolitan area are connected to the metro area by green corridor transportation routes.

Rural reserves and open space
Rural reserves are lands outside the urban growth boundary that provide a visual and physical separation between urban areas and forests and farmlands. Open spaces include parks, stream and trail corridors, wetlands, and floodplains.

Industrial areas and freight terminals
Industrial areas serve as hubs for regional commerce. Freight terminals facilitate the movement of goods in and out of the region.

Station communities
Station communities are areas of development centered around a light rail or high-capacity transit station that feature a variety of shops and services. They are accessible to bicyclists, pedestrians, and transit users as well as cars.

Source: The Nature of 2040 (Metro 2000)

A string of station communities along the light-rail system would reduce auto dependency. The 2040 Growth Concept map identifies and maps corridors that serve as transportation routes for people and goods, main streets lined with commercial uses, and green corridors connecting neighboring cities to the metropolitan region.

In response to overwhelming input from neighborhoods that did not want to see too much change and particularly no significant increases in density, the 2040 plan leaves the density of existing neighborhoods largely unchanged.

The growth concept recognizes and protects open space, both inside and outside the urban growth boundary. Green areas on the 2040 Growth Concept map may be designated as regional open space. That removes these lands from the inventory of urban land available for development. Rural reserves—already designated for farms, forestry, natural areas, or rural-residential use—would remain and be further protected from development pressures.

Metro's functional plans

Metro has developed a series of functional plans dealing with specific topics. They are consistent with the 2040 Growth Concept plan and the regional framework plan, but provide greater detail.

The regional transportation plan (RTP)

Many urban planners encourage strategies to reduce automobile dependence and broaden transportation options. They favor multimodal transportation that includes light-rail systems, pedestrian ways, and bicycle paths as well as improvements to highways and streets. The Oregon Land Conservation and Development Commission has adopted a statewide rule encouraging governments to reduce the total number of automobile miles driven by 10 percent by 2020 and 15 percent by 2040. Planners like Peter Calthorpe and Robert Cervero advocate light-rail lines with transit villages around light-rail stops (Bernick and Cervero 1997; Ditmar and Ohland 2003).

Portland Metro adopted a regional transportation plan in 2000 (Metro 2000) that follows this approach. In addition to long-range planning for conventional transportation such as highways and streets, the Portland regional transportation plan relies heavily on a light-rail system and many park-and-ride centers. The plan also emphasizes both walking and bicycling as important transit alternatives. Portland's long-term transportation plan will encourage use of these modes of transportation wherever possible. Map 12.3 shows highways, streets, the MAX light rail, and transit centers in the Portland area. In exercise 7, you will have an opportunity to work with these and other layers of transportation-related information.

MAX, the region's light-rail system, was begun with a westside line in 1986. An eighteen-mile eastside line opened in 1998. A north-south line has proven more problematic. Three Oregon counties approved the line, but Clark County rejected the ballot measure. Statewide, voters

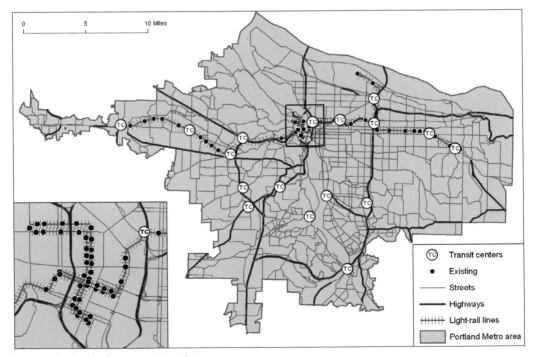

Map 12.3   Portland area transportation.
Source: © Metro, Portland, Oregon 2005

Figure 12.1 Metropolitan Area Express (MAX) light-rail train, Portland, Oregon.
Source: Bruce Forster

rejected a statewide contribution to the proposed north-south line in 1996 (Abbott 2001). Since that time, the eastside line was extended to serve the Portland airport, and a six-mile line from downtown through northside neighborhoods was opened in 2004. Plans are in process for the next expansion southward into Clackamas County.

Regional habitat protection planning

Metro seeks to balance the natural and human environments in three main ways: (a) by protecting undeveloped agricultural, forest, and other land outside of the urban growth boundary from development, (b) by acquiring open space, parks, and streams of regional significance, and (c) by creating a regional framework for protecting fish and wildlife habitat that would guide local habitat protection efforts.

Metro is in the middle of a multiyear process to protect fish and wildlife habitat (Metro 2004b). In 2000, Metro and local partners collaborated to prepare a vision statement that called for habitat protection and restoration for fish and wildlife in the region. The following year, Metro began a three-step process to reach an agreement on a regional fish and wildlife habitat protection program. By 2004, they had inventoried and used GIS to map regionally significant fish and wildlife habitat using an approach similar to habitat conservation planning discussed in chapter 5 and planning for a red-legged frog habitat conservation area in exercise 4. The Metro Council anticipates selecting a preferred habitat protection concept and providing guidance for local governments to protect fish and wildlife habitat in 2005. If this plan is implemented, cities will have two years to adopt local programs to implement Metro's fish and wildlife protection plan. Metro's habitat conservation planning has been controversial. There has been criticism that Metro's mapping was too broad-brush and tended to include too much nonsensitive land. At the time of this writing, some members of the Metro Council are in favor of taking a less-aggressive posture toward habitat conservation and encouraging voluntary efforts.

The habitat inventory focused on two kinds of habitat that are particularly important in the region: waterside (riparian) habitat and drier upland habitats. Metro used GIS to map specific landscape features associated with these habitats such as the location of trees, shrubs, wetlands, flood areas, and steep slopes and ranked habitat areas based on their suitability for benefiting fish and wildlife (Metro 2004b). Once the inventory was complete and field-tested, the riparian and upland wildlife habitat inventories were classified and habitat areas were categorized according to their quality. Riparian areas were classified as class I, II, or III and wildlife areas as class A, B, or C. Class I riparian and class A wildlife habitat provide most of the primary habitat in the region. Approximately one-third of the riparian habitat and one-quarter of the upland habitat are classified as the highest-quality habitat.

Metro conducted a two-stage analysis of the economic, social, environmental, and energy (ESEE) impacts of protecting—or not protecting—fish and wildlife habitat. They sought to balance economic, social, and environmental tradeoffs to achieve a politically and economically acceptable regional habitat conservation plan.

Managing water resources in the Portland region

The Metro area has two major rivers (the Columbia and Willamette rivers) and many smaller rivers, streams, and ponds. There are wetlands and floodplains throughout the region. As part of its regional planning, Metro has developed plans and policies to minimize risks from flooding in floodplains, to capitalize on the recreational potential of the rivers, streams, and ponds, and to preserve environmentally valuable wetlands.

By overlaying watersheds and floodplains over a digital orthophoto of the Metro region, it is easy to see development in relation to important water-related areas. Since Metro tracks and geocodes building permits, it is possible to see where developments have been built near or in floodplains. This can help planners regulate risky new construction and prepare programs to protect older development in floodplains. In exercise 7, you will have an opportunity to use GIS

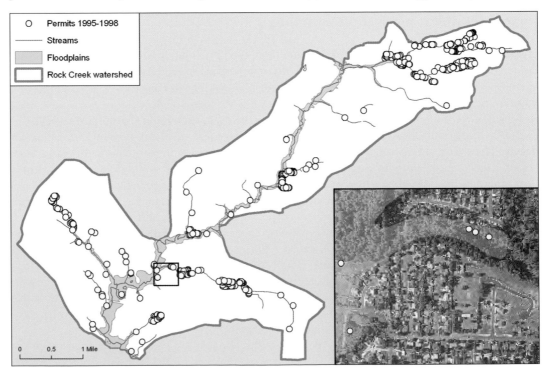

Map 12.4 Rock Creek watershed.
Source: © Metro, Portland, Oregon 2005

to do water-related risk assessment and planning to both guard against harm and take advantage of recreational opportunities that water resources in the Portland region afford.

Map 12.4 is a map of the Rock Creek watershed that includes streams, floodplains, and locations where building permits were issued between 1995 and 1998. One area of detail where building permits appear to have been granted for construction very near or even within part of the floodplain is indicated by a black box at the lower center of the map. The inset in the lower right corner of map 12.4 consists of a digital orthophoto underneath a transparent layer showing the floodplain for the area of detail. The locations where building permits were issued are symbolized on the inset as yellow points. At this larger scale you can see that five of the building permits are within the floodplain. The inset illustrates the way in which aerial photography and GIS mapping can converge. It was created in a GIS, but because the dominant layer is an orthophoto it appears more like a photo inset than an inset map. In exercise 7, you will have an opportunity to use layers of RLIS data on floodplains, streams, and building permits to analyze flood risk in the region. Using additional layers on the location of schools and bicycle paths, you will explore how an environmental education program might be developed to educate school children about the importance of wetlands and risks that floodplains present.

The regional urban growth boundary

Oregon state law requires local governments to establish **urban growth boundaries (UGBs)**. Urban growth boundaries are intended to distinguish land that is intended for development within twenty years from land that is being protected from development for at least twenty years. As a local governmental entity, Metro is required to establish an urban growth boundary. Since its jurisdiction is regionwide it must, by law, establish a **regional urban growth boundary**. Metro's regional urban growth boundary contains 369 square miles of land. Rural reserves are intended to assure that Metro and neighboring cities remain separate. The result is intended to be a compact urban form for the region to retain the region's sense of place. Metro adopted the regional UBG in 1979 after five years of staff work and hearings.

Oregon discourages piecemeal extensions of urban growth boundaries, but from time to time major changes in the boundaries are necessary to respond to population growth. In 2002, twenty-three years after the Metro regional urban growth boundary was established, it was expanded by 7 percent to include almost eighteen thousand additional acres (Metro 2002). GIS analysis was used extensively to determine how much additional land needed to be added to the UGB to accommodate anticipated population growth and the best places to extend the boundary.

Metro's regional land information system (RLIS)

Underlying Metro's planning is a remarkable GIS called the **regional land information system (RLIS)**. RLIS is a decision support system—a computerized information system designed to make information available to urban planners and policy makers to help them make decisions (Brail and Klosterman 2001). RLIS was designed for regional planning. It incorporates layers of digital information essential for land-use planning, urban growth management, environmental planning, transportation planning, open space acquisition, habitat conservation, and other planning and policy information (Knaap, Bolen, and Seltzer 2004).

Metro began developing its RLIS in 1988. Before that time almost no local government information in the Portland area was digital. Individual jurisdictions maintained spotty information in inconsistent formats. It was not possible to fit data from one city together with similar data from another city because of inconsistent definitions and data formats. Data that could be displayed regionally as a single map layer was not compatible with other map layers.

Before the RLIS, planners at Metro's predecessor agency, CRAG, prepared a few maps of the region based on Ian McHarg's approach (McHarg 1969). They created layers of information on separate transparent acetate sheets. They drew in the urban growth boundary by hand. Corrections were made using whiteout and a kind of press-on tape called zipline. CRAG had only one set of maps. A fire at CRAG could have destroyed the entire system (Knaap, Bolen, and Seltzer 2004).

Today the RLIS has over one hundred different compatible digital layers of information. The maps in this chapter showing the boundaries of Metro, the urban growth boundary, transportation infrastructure, watersheds, and a digital orthophoto of the Portland region introduce some of the many RLIS data layers. In exercise 7, you will have an opportunity to work with these and many additional RLIS data layers.

Each year Metro commissions updated high-resolution color aerial photographs of the entire region. These are digitized and used as an essential base layer. The digital orthophoto in map 12.4 shows how useful aerial photography can be. Much more detailed aerial photographs from Metro can provide clearer detail on areas of interest.

RLIS includes the boundaries of each city and county, information on local plans, zoning, land use, and the locations of hospitals, schools, and police stations.

Every tax lot in the Metro region is in the RLIS database and local jurisdictions update information on attributes of each lot on a quarterly basis in a consistent format. Each tax lot is classified annually as vacant, partially vacant, underdeveloped, or developed (Knaap, Bolen, and Seltzer 2004). This makes it possible to identify all of the vacant land in the region. This information and regional records of building permits make it possible to see exactly what has been built and what is being built at any given time.

U.S. Census data from 2000, 1990, and 1980 has been integrated into the RLIS so that it is possible to analyze the most recent census information and compare it to the two prior censuses and to other data layers.

The RLIS system contains environmental information on rivers, streams, watersheds, wetlands, floodplains, earthquake hazards, and soils.

RLIS has been used to develop all of Metro's plans. GIS maps have been a fundamental tool in Metro's extensive public outreach program. Maps of conditions and alternatives are hotly debated as plans are formulated.

Metro: a work in progress

Like all institutions, Metro is far from perfect. Because it is proactive and visionary, it is a target of criticism as well as a source of inspiration. In the region, most people are supportive of Metro, though suburban jurisdictions are sometimes critical of the agency as overly serving the interests of the city of Portland. Carl Abbott, an astute observer of regional planning in the Portland region, estimates that about 65 percent of the residents of the city of Portland support Metro and its goals (Abbott 2005). Abbott feels that in Clackamas and Washington counties the level of support among residents is about 50 percent, but that a majority of political leaders support Metro.

The main opposition to Metro has come from property owners who feel that urban growth boundaries have unfairly taken development value away from them. Measure 37 is a response to this concern. It will have a major impact on urban planning throughout Oregon, particularly related to urban growth boundaries. Exactly what the impact of Measure 37 will be depends on what happens in the state legislature and courts in the next few years. Fair treatment of property

Figure 12.2 Portland skyline with Mount Hood.
Source: Bruce Forster

owners is a serious issue that needs to be resolved for regional planning in Oregon or elsewhere to succeed.

Metro's main strengths lie in its remarkable regional land information system, its bold vision, and the framework and functional plans it has developed to rationalize planning on a regional basis. As a service-delivery entity, Metro is still in its infancy. Transportation planning and service delivery remain divided between Metro and TriMet (a separate regional transit agency). A third regional entity, the Port of Portland, operates airports, marine terminals, and some very substantial industrial parks. The Oregon governor appoints the boards of TriMet and the Port of Portland. Of the many kinds of services that might be delivered on a regional basis, solid waste disposal and open space acquisition represent a modest start.

Bringing it all together in exercise 7

For each part of this book, you completed step-by-step exercises to learn how the GIS concepts you read about are actually carried out. In addition to building operational GIS skills, you learned more about material in the policy-related chapters in each section by working with real data on exactly the kinds of urban problems and opportunities discussed. "Your Turn" exercises pushed you to gain a higher comfort level with GIS operations by replicating the step-by-step exercises with different data and less hand-holding.

Exercise 7 is different from the six step-by-step exercises. It groups data from Metro's RLIS into four topic areas dealing with urban growth management, the natural environment, transportation, and water resources. Exercise 7 provides suggestions concerning kinds of spatial analysis to do with the four data sets. But it doesn't provide either step-by-step instructions on what to do or as much structured guidance as the Your Turn exercises.

For exercise 7, you should pick one of the four topic areas that most interests you and complete a culminating experience project using the data related to the topic. You will have to think through the concepts and all the operations you have learned in this book and apply them to an important real-world regional planning problem of your choosing.

You will probably have to reread some of the chapters and go back over some of the operations you learned by looking at the step-by-step exercises again to refresh your memory about how to do steps you want to apply to the Metro data.

Exercise 7 is intended to be a challenge. You will run up against some barriers. But you can complete exercise 7. And when you do, you will know that you have mastered basic skills to do useful spatial analysis for your own research papers and in the job market. You will need to get more advanced GIS and statistical training if you want to pursue spatial analysis further. Completing exercise 7 will give you a solid foundation for more advanced work.

Today many aspects of urban planning and governance in metropolitan America should be organized regionally. Problems such as air and water pollution, congestion, loss of biodiversity, disappearing farmland, and a host of other issues are regional in nature. They cannot be adequately addressed at the level of individual cities. Metropolitan regions also have regional assets—some land within a region is more appropriate for regional parks, harbors, airports or transportation hubs than other land. Only regional planning can adequately manage these regional assets to the best advantage.

Metro stands out as the leading example of a region that has consistently pursued regional planning and governance. It has succeeded in building a formidable regional land information system. Metro has integrated use of GIS into planning—not only its own regional planning, but by governments throughout the region.

The final exercise will help bring together the material in this book on substantive regional problems, spatial analysis and data visualization concepts, and GIS operations. When you have completed exercise 7, you will know how to think globally and act regionally.

Enjoy!

Terms

matter of regional significance. In urban and regional planning, a matter of regional significance is one that affects an entire region. The decision where to locate an airport, for example, is a matter of regional significance.

Measure 37. A statewide initiative approved by Oregon voters in fall 2004. Measure 37 was placed on the ballot by critics of Oregon's urban planning system. It requires government to pay landowners for decreased value of their land if an urban growth boundary makes it difficult or impossible to develop the land for a long time.

Metropolitan Area Express (MAX). The Portland, Oregon, region's light-rail system. MAX consists of thirty-eight miles of light rail. It is operated by TriMet—the Portland area's regional transportation agency.

regional framework plan (Metro). Metro's plan broadly defining how the 2040 Growth Concept plan will be implemented. It is consistent with the 2040 Growth Concept plan, but provides more current and detailed direction. It guides functional plans such as the regional transportation plan. Local governments look to the regional framework plan for guidance in preparing general plans for physical development within their city.

regional land information system (RLIS). The planning and policy decision support system created by Metro. RLIS contains more than one hundred GIS layers with related attribute information for the entire Metro region. It includes a base layer of aerial photos. Metro oversees the entire system and creates and maintains some of the data itself. Most data in the RLIS is produced by the entities that have the largest stake in the data. For example, data on individual city land parcels is maintained by the cities where the parcels are located.

regional urban growth boundary. The boundary around the region within which all urban growth in the Metro area for twenty years is expected to occur. Metro's urban growth boundary was created in 1979. Little land was added to the area within the UGB until 2000 when the urban growth boundary was expanded by about 7 percent and eighteen thousand acres were added to the area within the boundary. The regional UGB is intended to assure development at appropriate densities, reduce sprawl, and protect agricultural land, forests, and open space on the urban fringe. Oregon's Measure 37, passed in fall 2004, threatens the regional UGB (and UGBs around other urbanized areas in Oregon). It gives owners of land outside the UGB the right to seek compensation for the loss of development value the UGB has caused or permission to develop their land.

TriMet. The Portland, Oregon, regional transportation agency. TriMet operates MAX (the region's light-rail system), most of the region's bus system, and paratransit such as a dial-a-ride service.

2040 Growth Concept. Metro's long-term vision for how the Portland region will develop over fifty years (starting in 1990). The 2040 Growth Concept is represented by a GIS map. It was adopted in 1995 to implement Metro's 1992 charter requirement that Metro adopt a long-term future vision.

urban growth boundary (UGB). A boundary around a city or region within which all growth is contained for a specified time into the future. Oregon pioneered the concept of urban growth boundaries. Oregon requires communities to designate boundaries that can accommodate twenty years of growth. Once the boundaries are designated, all development, with very limited exceptions, occurs within the boundary. The idea is to assure development at appropriate densities, reduce sprawl, and protect agricultural land, forests, and open space on the urban fringe.

Questions for further study

1. Why are many urban problems best addressed regionally rather than on a city-by-city basis?

2. Describe the Portland 2040 Growth Concept. What is your opinion of it?

3. What is an urban growth boundary? A regional urban growth boundary? What is the intended purpose of growth boundaries? How could spatial analysis help establish urban growth boundaries?

4. What is transit-oriented development?

5. What is multimodal transportation? How can multimodal transportation planning reduce auto dependency?

6. How can environmental planners use GIS to manage watersheds? To protect wetlands? To identify and regulate floodplains?

Annotated bibliography

Connie P. Ozawa's *The Portland Edge: Challenges and Successes in Growing Communities* (Ozawa 2004) is an anthology on urban issues and urban planning in Portland, Oregon, and the Portland region. Thirteen chapters—mostly written by faculty members at Portland State University—describe planning, housing, redevelopment, transportation, open space and parks, and other planning issues. Ethan Seltzer's chapter titled "It's not an experiment: Regional planning at Metro, 1990 to the present" summarizes Metro's evolution and current work.

Carl Abbott's *Greater Portland: Urban Life and Landscape in the Pacific Northwest* (Abbott 2001) describes the cultural history that gave rise to Portland area planning. Abbott's earlier book *Portland: Planning, Politics, and Growth in a Twentieth Century City* (Abbott 1983) and his book chapter titled "The capital of good planning: Metropolitan Portland since 1970" in Robert Fishman's *The American Planning Tradition: Culture and Policy* (Abbott 2000) are important sources of information on urban planning in the Portland region. Abbott is the coeditor of *Planning the Oregon Way: A Twenty-Year Evaluation* (Abbott, Howe, and Adler 1994), along with Deborah Howe and Sy Adler.

Gerrit Knaap, Richard Bolen, and Ethan Seltzer describe Metro's Regional Land Information System (RLIS) in "Metro's Regional Land Information System: The Virtual Key to Portland's Growth Management Success" (Knaap, Bolen, and Seltzer 2004).

An orientation to the exercises

This section of the book contains exercises designed both to reinforce the concepts you are learning and to introduce you to GIS operations using ArcMap and related ArcGIS software components to create the kinds of maps discussed throughout the book. Before beginning the exercises, it is important to pause for a moment to think about how to get the most out of them. A brief introduction to ArcMap will help you get oriented as you begin.

Thinking about GIS operations step-by-step

One good way to begin learning computer software operations is to first follow step-by-step instructions to see how the software works. But doing step-by-step exercises is useful only if you think about what you are doing at each step and internalize the operations so that you can use them yourself. Just proceeding mechanically through step-by-step operations without reflecting on what you are doing is a waste of time.

Three ways to get the most out of step-by-step operations are to do the following:

- Constantly ask yourself "what did I just do, and why?"
- Replicate the operations you just learned with different data and without detailed instructions.
- Use the operations to solve a problem that requires spatial analysis.

Following are six step-by-step exercises that closely track material in the first three parts of this book and a final project exercise that requires you to apply the step-by-step material.

Some questions are sprinkled throughout the exercises. Answers to the questions are at the end of each exercise. You should stop and answer each of these questions and then check the answers.

In addition to answering the questions posed, you should be asking yourself similar questions at each step of the exercises.

Even if you pay attention to what you are doing in an exercise, it is unlikely that you will remember how to do everything you just learned—even after you have just completed the exercise. There are too many details. At the end of each exercise there is a supplemental exercise named "Your Turn." To help make sure you understand the concepts and operations you have completed, the Your Turn exercises ask you to replicate what you have just done, but using different data and without step-by-step instructions.

If time permits, you should do the Your Turn exercise associated with an exercise immediately after you complete the main exercise. If that is not possible, then complete the Your Turn exercise at your earliest convenience before going on to the next step-by-step exercise. If you hit a snag, go back and redo the step in the main exercise that is giving you trouble. The Your Turn exercises are organized in the same order as the main exercises. You should be able to easily find the step in the main exercise that matches any step in a Your Turn exercise that you can't remember how to do.

Active learning during the step-by-step exercises, working out the answers to questions posed in the exercises and that you yourself pose, and doing the Your Turn exercises will equip you to do a final project. That's the role of exercise 7. Exercise 7 provides a very rich dataset with many layers of information on the Metro region in Portland, Oregon. This data is drawn from Metro's regional land information system (RLIS) that you read about in chapter 12. You can choose from four topics that require you to work with this data to produce maps. The four topics in exercise 7 require you to answer important questions of the kind that social scientists, urban planners, and public policy professionals pose and answer.

The text and illustrations in the exercises will introduce you to ArcMap—the mapping component of ArcGIS. Exercises 3 and 4 also introduce the Spatial Analyst extension and ArcToolbox—two important components of ArcGIS that supplement ArcMap. Before embarking on the exercises, however, an orientation to the ArcMap interface is in order.

An orientation to ArcMap

The opening screen for ArcMap offers users a choice of starting to use ArcMap with a new, empty map, a template, or an existing map by clicking one of three *radio buttons*. Each radio button appears as an empty round circle when it is not selected. When you click a radio button to select it, a black circle appears inside it. Only one radio button can be selected at one time.

If you click the *An existing map* radio button, you can navigate to an existing map and open it. In the first and second steps of exercise 1, for example, you will click the *An existing map* radio button, browse to the folder where the relevant ArcMap files are stored, and open a map that looks like this:

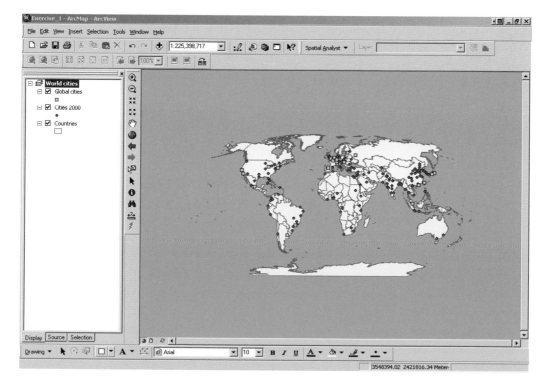

Along the top of the *application window* are *pull-down menus* named *File, Edit, View, Insert, Tools, Window,* and *Help.* These menus make available common generic file functions such as opening, saving, and printing files; inserting material; navigating among windows; and providing help. For example, if you want to save a file you have created using ArcMap, you would click the **File** pull-down menu, and navigate to a folder named **MyWork** in the folder named **TGAR** that holds all of the exercise data. You may be familiar with pull-down menus from word-processing and other programs you have used. You will learn to use other features of the ArcMap pull-down menus in this and the following exercises.

Just below the pull-down menus is the *Standard toolbar* with a row of *buttons* and *tools.* Buttons and tools are very similar. When you click a **tool** nothing happens immediately, but the appearance of the cursor changes, signaling you to click somewhere else. When you click a **button** there is an immediate change to the map. The way in which the map changes in response to clicking a button is different for each button. For example, when you click the **Zoom In** button, the map zooms in. You will learn how to use these and other ArcMap buttons and tools in the exercises.

Another *toolbar* is docked at the left of the map. You use ArcMap's tools to perform operations such as *zooming* in and out to a feature, *panning* around the screen, and *identifying* map features.

In exercise 1, you will learn how to dock the *Tools* toolbar (connect it to the side of the map window) and to use the tools it contains.

The computer screen on the previous page shows a map with information about the population of world cities in 2000 and global cities as the screen looks when the ArcMap *application window* is opened. The application window has two *panes:*

- The pane on the left is the *table of contents.* The table of contents contains one *data frame* named *World cities.* In other ArcMap projects you may see two or more data frames.

Only one data frame is active (in use) at a time. In this map there is only one data frame—*World cities*—so it is the *active* data frame. You can tell which data frame is active because the title of the data frame is bolded.

You will learn how to create data frames, add layers to them, and change which data frame is active in the following exercises.

A data frame can be expanded by clicking the small expand sign ⊞ next to it and collapsed by clicking on the collapse sign ⊟ that appears when the data frame has been expanded. The expand and collapse signs act as a toggle, so when you click on a minus sign, the data frame collapses and the sign in front of it turns into a plus sign and vice versa. When a data frame is expanded, you can see the *map layers* within it, and when a layer is expanded you can see symbols of map layers they contain. The *World cities* data frame is expanded, and the *Global cities, Cities 2000,* and the *Countries* layers are also expanded so you can see the symbols of map *features* they contain. Each layer contains different map features: cities classified as global cities in the *Global cities* layer and cities with more than five million people in 2000 in the *Cities 2000* layer. The *check box* next to a layer indicates whether it is turned on (visible) or not. In the map, all three layers are checked (turned on).

• The pane on the right is a map. It shows features in the map layers turned on in the active data frame. Since the *Global cities*, *Cities 2000*, and *Countries* layers are turned on, the map that appears shows features in all three layers.

You learned in chapter 2 that attribute tables with information on attributes of map features may be linked to map layers. Part of the attribute table for the *Cities 2000* layer looks like this:

FID	Shape*	CITY_NAME	COUNTRY	2000_POP
0	Point	Saint Petersbur	Russian Federation	5214000
1	Point	Moscow	Russian Federation	10103000
2	Point	Hamburg	Germany	2668000
3	Point	Manchester	United Kingdom	2223000
4	Point	Berlin	Germany	3325000
5	Point	Birmingham	United Kingdom	2243000
6	Point	Warsaw	Poland	2194000
7	Point	London	United Kingdom	7628000
8	Point	Essen	Germany	6542000
9	Point	Kiev	Ukraine	2606000
10	Point	Katowice	Poland	3069000
11	Point	Paris	France	9693000
12	Point	Stuttgart	Germany	2677000
13	Point	Munich	Germany	2295000
14	Point	Seattle	United States of America	2727000
15	Point	Harbin	China	2928000
16	Point	Montreal	Canada	3409000
17	Point	Milan	Italy	4183000
18	Point	Minneapolis	United States of America	2397000

Record: 1   Show: All Selected   Records (0 out of 151 Selected.)   Options ▾

To open this attribute table you would right-click on the *Cities 2000* layer and select *Open Attribute Table*. You can perform many useful operations on the data in the attribute table: sorting values of a field, rearranging the order of fields, creating new fields, correcting data errors, entering new data, and calculating summary statistics such as the count, sum, and mean for values of any field. You will learn to work with attribute tables in exercise 1.

The map on page 291 has properties such as the units of measurement (miles, kilometers, etc.), the map *symbology*, and whether features are labeled. Right-clicking a *layer* in the table of contents pane and selecting *Properties* takes you to a menu of tabs that allows you to see the existing properties of the map and change them. A particularly important set of map properties relates to symbology. You will begin to work with map symbology in exercise 1 and return to symbology in greater depth in exercises 5 and 6.

Maps contain features. In the map on page 291, the features of interest are cities and global cities. You might add other layers of features to the map—such as rivers symbolized as lines or lakes as polygons. Each feature may have attributes associated with it such as the attributes of cities in the attribute table above.

With this introduction you are ready to start with the step-by-step exercises. The exercises illustrate both the conceptual material described in chapters 2 and 3 and the operations necessary to use them in ArcMap. You will use the ArcMap procedures and commands to get familiar with how ArcMap works and to produce your first analyses and maps. Exercises 1 and 2 draw on material in part I of the book.

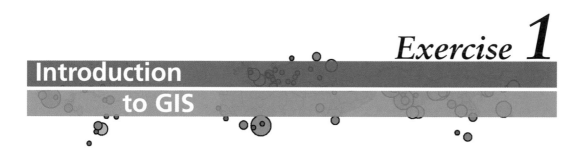

Introduction to GIS

Exercise 1

Learning objectives

In exercise 1, you will learn to use ArcMap to analyze data on estimates of the population of cities in 1800 by authors Tertius Chandler and Gerald Fox and of urban agglomerations in 2000 assembled by the United Nations. The exercise should take about one hour to complete. You will learn how to do the following:

- *open* ArcMap
- open an existing ArcMap *document* (.mxd) file
- change the *order* of map layers
- work with *toolbars*
- turn map *layers* on and off so that they are visible or invisible
- *find* geographical features on a map
- *zoom* in and out to geographical features of interest
- *identify* features in a map layer
- use a *bookmark* to find a geographical area
- *pan* around a map
- create your own *bookmarks*
- open an *attribute table* associated with a layer
- *sort* a field in an attribute table
- add a *layer* to an existing *data frame*
- make a data frame *active*
- *select* features by *location*

- *select* features by *attribute*
- *create* a new *map layer*
- *export* a map as a JPEG image file

Step 1   Open ArcMap

Click the *Start* button on the Windows taskbar on the lower left of your computer screen.

Click *Programs*.

Click *ArcGIS*.

Click *ArcMap*.

You will see a window that asks if you want to start using ArcMap with *A new empty map*, *A template*, or *An existing map*. (There is a remote chance that default settings in the software you are using have turned off this window. If this is the case, click *File*, then click *Open* and proceed with step 2.)

Click the *An existing map* radio button to select it.

By default, a choice called *Browse for maps* is highlighted.

Click *OK*.

Step 2   Open an existing ArcMap document (.mxd) file

Navigate to the **TGAR\Part_1\Exercise_1** folder and open the folder. The **TGAR\Part_1\Exercise_1** folder is installed to the C: drive by default.

Notice the folder in the **TGAR** folder named **MyWork**. You will save work you produce in step 18 of this exercise and your subsequent work in the **MyWork** folder.

Click *Exercise_1.mxd*.

Click *Open*.

The ArcMap application window opens. The map display is open to a map of the world showing the locations of countries.

If necessary, maximize the ArcMap window by clicking the *maximize* button ☐ at the top right of your ArcMap application window.

The table of contents contains one *data frame* named *Historical city populations*. The *Historical city populations* data frame is *active*. Its title is bold.

The *Historical city populations* data frame contains three *map layers*: *Countries*, *Cities 2000*, and *Global cities*. The layers are stacked on top of each other, like layers in a cake.

Only the countries are visible on the map; all of the global cities and all but a few of the cities on the *Cities 2000* layer are hidden underneath the *Countries* layer.

In the next step, you will change the order of the map layers to make the cities visible. Now you will rename the data frame.

Right-click the words *Historical city populations*.

Click *Properties*.

Click the *General* tab.

In the *Name* box, change the data frame name to *World cities*.

Click **OK**.

Your computer screen should look like this:

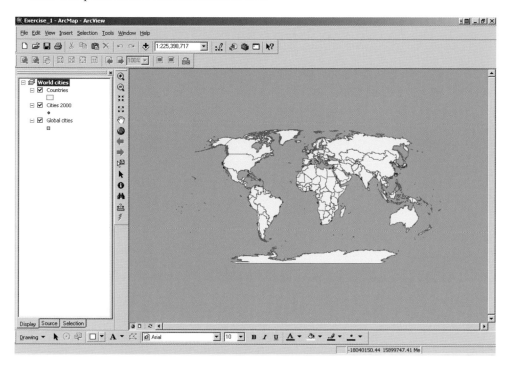

Notice the *Tools* toolbar docked on the left side of the map application window. The *Tools* toolbar contains the fourteen *tools* depicted below. The toolbar is represented horizontally below but contains the same tools in the same order as they appear in the application window above.

On your computer screen, the *Tools* toolbar may be located somewhere else. The tools may be arranged in one or two rows. The rows may be vertical or horizontal.

If your *Tools* toolbar is not docked on the left side of the map, click the **toolbar**, drag the toolbar to the top left of the map window as illustrated, and dock it (attach it) to the edge of the map window. When the *Tools* toolbar touches the edge, it will dock itself.

If you need to make the *Tools* toolbar into a single column, click the right side of the **Tools** toolbar and drag it left until the *Tools* toolbar is a single, vertical column docked to the side of the map window.

What if the toolbars are somewhere else or not there?

Toolbars can be toggled on and off so they are visible or hidden. They also may be dragged to different locations on the computer screen.

If you do not see one of the toolbars, click *View* | *Toolbars* | and click the desired ***toolbar***. A check mark will indicate that the toolbar is turned on.

If one of the toolbars is somewhere other than the top of the page, just use it in that location or ask your instructor or a lab tech to drag the toolbar into the proper place. Dragging it yourself should work fine, but moving toolbars can sometimes be tricky for beginners.

Find the *Standard* toolbar and take a moment to examine the tools it contains. By default the *Standard* toolbar is turned on and docked at the top of the application window. It looks like this:

If the *Standard* toolbar is not visible, click ***View***, click ***Toolbars***, and click the ***Standard*** toolbar to enable it.

Step 3   Examine different layers within a data frame

A data frame contains one or more layers of data. The layers in a data frame are usually related to a single theme, such as features in a county—streets, census tracts, and bus stops. Think of a data frame as its own map. In this exercise, the data frame is named *World cities* and contains the outlines of countries and points indicating the location of world cities.

Click the ***Cities 2000*** layer, hold down the left mouse button, and drag the *Cities 2000* layer up above the *Countries* layer.

A horizontal black line indicates whether the *Cities 2000* layer is above or below the *Countries* layer.

Release the mouse button.

Now the cities are visible. Your computer screen should look like the one on the following page:

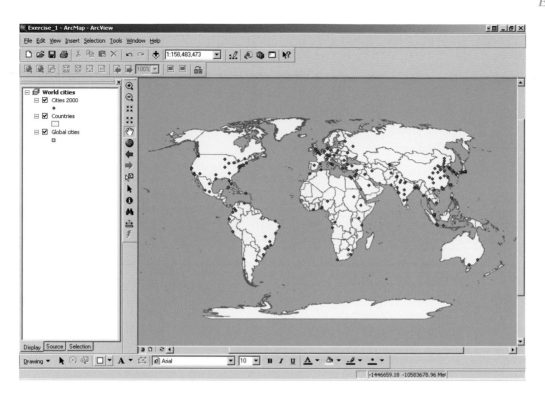

Notice that *Cities 2000*, *Countries*, and *Global cities* have a check mark next to them in the table of contents. A check mark indicates a layer is turned on and therefore visible in the map. However, top layers can obscure or hide layers below them in the map even when they are turned on. The *Global cities* layer is beneath the *Countries* layer in the table of contents and in the map.

Turn off the *Countries* layer by clicking the **check mark** next to *Countries*.

The green countries disappear and you see the cities and global cities.

Click the **Countries** check box again.

The *Countries* layer is turned back on, and the countries reappear.

Click the **check mark** to the left of the *Cities 2000* layer to make the cities disappear.

Check the **Cities 2000 check box** to turn the cities back on.

Step 4   Find a geographical feature

Click the **Find** button 🔍 —the button on the *Tools* toolbar that looks like a pair of binoculars.

Make sure the *Features* tab is selected and enter the word *India* in the *Find* field.

Select the *Countries* layer in the *In* box by clicking the **pull-down menu** and clicking **Countries**.

Click the **Find** button.

ArcMap shows the country of India as well as a listing for British Indian Ocean Territory. Your computer screen should look like the one on the following page:

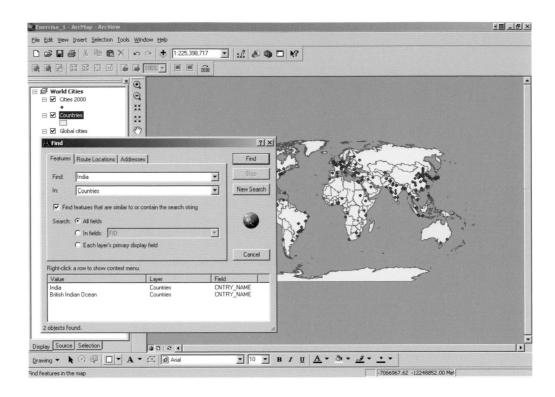

Right-click the row stating *India* in the box at the bottom of the page below the instruction to right-click a row to show context menu.

A *context menu* opens.

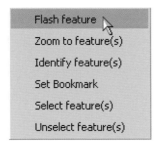

Click the words *Flash feature* on the context menu.

India *flashes* on the map so you can see where it is.

Right-click the row that contains *India* again.

Click *Zoom to feature(s)* on the context menu.

ArcMap zooms in to India on the map display.

Do searches to find Cameroon, Belarus, and Guyana. Zoom to each feature.

Question 1: Which of these three countries touches an ocean?

Close the *Find* window by clicking the *Close* button ☒ in the top right corner of the *Find* window.

Step 5   Zoom in and out to features

The six buttons circled below on the ArcMap *Tools* toolbar help you *zoom in*, *zoom out*, and *pan* to features around the map. Zooming is fun. Next you will experiment with these buttons to learn how to zoom.

Click the *Full Extent* button ◉ .

The view zooms to the full extent of the data frame. Whenever you get lost in a digital map, you can use the *Full Extent* tool to reorient yourself.

Click the *Fixed Zoom In* button ⵣⵣ .

The view zooms in so that the countries appear larger.

Click *Fixed Zoom In* three more times.

The view continues to zoom in, and the countries appear still larger.

Click four times on the *Fixed Zoom Out* button ⵣⵣ .

The view zooms back out and most of the world should be visible.

Click the *Zoom In* tool ⊕ and place the cursor over the map.

The cursor changes into an icon of a magnifying glass with a plus sign as soon as the cursor moves over the map.

Click just to the top left of India and hold the left mouse button down.

Still holding down the left mouse button, draw a rectangular box around India.

Release the mouse button.

India fills the map.

Experiment with the other ArcMap zooming buttons.

Click the *Full Extent* button ◉ to return to the map extent of the entire world.

Step 6   Identify features in a layer

Click the **check box** next to *Cities 2000* to turn off the *Cities 2000* layer.

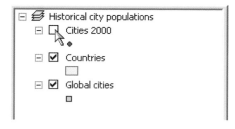

Zoom to Africa using the *Zoom In* tool 🔍 .

Click the *Identify* tool ⓘ .

Click the little country entirely surrounded by South Africa.

Question 2: What is the name of this country?

Note the information about attributes of the country, such as the country's population and area in square miles, in the *Identify Results* box.

Close the *Identify Results* box.

Zoom in to the southern tip of Africa. The names of the countries—including Lesotho—appear. This is because a scale range has been set for the country labels so that labels appear when the scale is 22,000,000 meters or larger.

Step 7   Use an existing bookmark

Click the *View* pull-down menu.

Click *Bookmarks* and click *Italy*.

> The map zooms to Italy. ArcMap allows users to create *bookmarks*. A bookmark for Italy was created for exercise 1. In step 9, you will learn how to create your own *bookmark*.

Step 8   Pan around the map

Click the *Pan* tool ✋ .

Click anywhere on Italy. Don't release the left mouse button.

Still holding down the left mouse button, drag the map to the left until Greece appears.

Click the *Full Extent* button 🌐 to zoom to full extent.

Step 9   Create your own bookmark

Click the check box next to *Cities 2000* to turn on the *Cities 2000* layer.

Use the *Find* button to find the city of Bogota. Remember to select the *Cities 2000* layer as the *In* layer.

Use the *Zoom to feature(s)* option to locate Bogota.

> Three cities in Colombia appear. Bogota is near the center of the country.

Close the *Find* box.

Use the *Identify* tool to confirm which city is Bogota.

Close the *Identify Results* box.

From the *View* menu, select *Bookmarks* and then click *Create*.

Enter *Bogota* for the bookmark name.

Click *OK*.

Click the *Full Extent* button ⚫ to zoom to the full extent.

Click the *View* menu.

Click *Bookmarks*.

Select *Bogota*—the new bookmark you just created.

The bookmark returns to the location showing Colombia at the same scale.

Zoom to the full extent.

Step 10 Open the attribute table associated with a layer

Right-click *Cities 2000*.

Click *Open Attribute Table*.

	FID	Shape*	CITY_NAME	COUNTRY	2000_POP
▶	0	Point	Saint Petersbur	Russian Federation	5214000
	1	Point	Moscow	Russian Federation	10103000
	2	Point	Hamburg	Germany	2668000
	3	Point	Manchester	United Kingdom	2223000
	4	Point	Berlin	Germany	3325000
	5	Point	Birmingham	United Kingdom	2243000
	6	Point	Warsaw	Poland	2194000
	7	Point	London	United Kingdom	7628000
	8	Point	Essen	Germany	6542000
	9	Point	Kiev	Ukraine	2606000
	10	Point	Katowice	Poland	3069000
	11	Point	Paris	France	9693000
	12	Point	Stuttgart	Germany	2677000
	13	Point	Munich	Germany	2295000
	14	Point	Seattle	United States of America	2727000
	15	Point	Harbin	China	2928000
	16	Point	Montreal	Canada	3409000
	17	Point	Milan	Italy	4183000
	18	Point	Minneapolis	United States of America	2397000

Attributes of Cities 2000

Record: 1 Show: All Selected Records (0 out of 151 Selected.) Options ▾

An *attribute table* containing data on *Cities 2000* opens. Each row contains information on a city and each column contains attribute values for the cities. At the bottom of the dialog box there are buttons named *All* and *Selected*. The *All* button is depressed. This indicates that all the records for *Cities 2000* are visible. The *Selected* button would be used when one or more features (in this case one or more cities) have been selected.

Step 11 Sort a column in an attribute table

Right-click the gray area in the *CITY_NAME* column.

Click *Sort Ascending*.

The 151 cities are sorted from Abidjan to Zhengzhou.

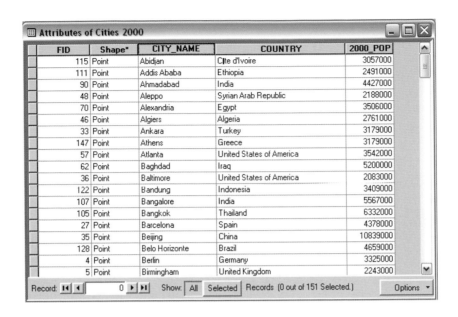

Question 3: What was the population of Brasília, Brazil, in 2000? Of Harbin, China?

Question 4: What field would you use to sort the attribute table so it is easy to find cities with a specific population? What city had a population in 2000 of 2,194,000 people?

Click the **Close** button ⊠ in the top right of the *Attributes of Cities 2000* window to close the table.

Click and drag the **Global cities** layer above the *Cities 2000* layer.

You can see twenty-two cities that one group of scholars considers to be global cities.

Open the *Global cities* attribute table and see if you recognize any of the cities listed.

Close the attribute table.

Step 12   Insert a new data frame

As you learned earlier, a data frame shows one area. An ArcMap document can contain more than one data frame. Next, you will insert a new data frame, copy layers from the *World cities* data frame, and add data to view the population of cities in 1800.

Click the **Insert** menu.

Click **Data Frame**.

A new data frame called *New Data Frame* is inserted into the table of contents. The map of countries and city populations is replaced with an empty map.

Step 13   Add layers to a map

In this step, you will first copy and paste a layer from the *World cities* data frame and then use the *Add Data* button to add a layer of city populations in 1800.

Right-click **Countries** in the *World cities* data frame.

Click **Copy**.

Right-click the name of the new data frame.

Click **Paste Layer(s)**.

The *Countries* layer is added to the new data frame and appears in the data view.

Click the **Add Data** button ✚ located on the *Standard* toolbar.

Navigate to the **Historical_cities** folder within the **Exercise_1** folder.

If this is the first time data has been added, ArcMap defaults by displaying only the local hard drives. If the exercise data is located in **C:\TGAR\Part_1\Exercise_1**, double-click **C:** and navigate to the **Historical_cities** folder. Highlight the **Historical_cities** folder and click **OK**.

If you installed the exercise data in a different location, a connection may need to be established. Click the **Connect To Folder** button ⬚ . Use the *Connect to Folder* dialog box for navigation to the **Historical_cities** folder using the plus signs next to each element. Highlight the **Historical_cities** folder and click **OK**.

The *Add Data* dialog box should display the contents of the **Historical_cities** folder.

Click the **Cities_1800_pop.shp** file to select it.

Click the **Add** button.

The *Cities_1800_pop* layer is added to your map.

Finally, copy and paste the *Cities 2000* layer into the new data frame.

Uncheck the *Cities 2000* layer to turn it off.

Your computer screen should look like the one on the following page (the symbol color for countries may be different on your computer screen):

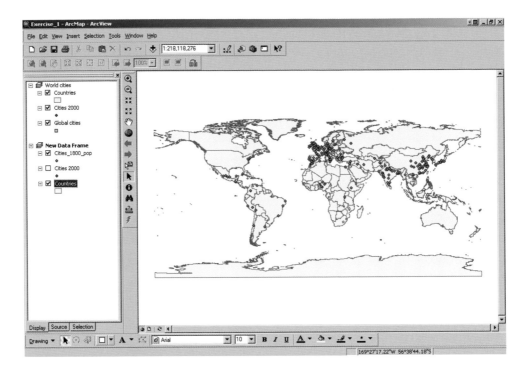

Step 14   Edit the data frame name and background

Right-click *New Data Frame*.

Click *Properties* located at the bottom of the context menu.

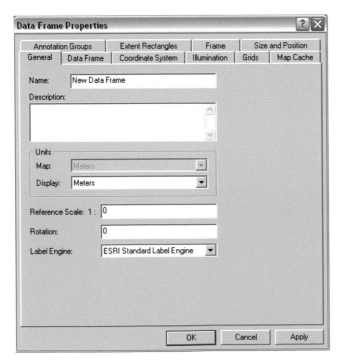

The *Data Frame Properties* dialog box appears displaying several tabs.

If necessary, click the *General* tab and rename the data frame to **City population in 1800.**

Click the *Frame* tab.

Changes can be made to the border, background, and drop shadow of the data frame.

Click the *down arrow* in the *Background* box and select *Lt Cyan.*

The color appears in both the box next to the pull-down menu and the color palette to the far right.

Click *OK.*

Step 15   Select world cities by attribute

Click the *Selection* pull-down menu from the main toolbar.

Click *Select By Attributes.*

Make sure the *Layer* box shows *Cities_1800_pop.*

Make sure the *Method* box shows "Create a new selection."

In the *Fields* list, double-click "*1800_POP*".

"1800_POP" is added to the **SELECT FROM Cities_1800_pop WHERE:** box (the empty white box at the bottom of the page).

Click the *greater than* sign (>).

Enter **200000.**

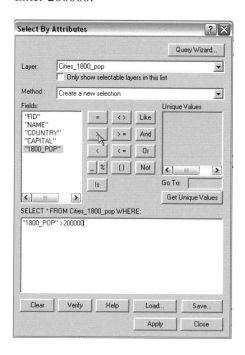

Click *Apply.*

Close the *Select By Attributes* box.

The selected cities are highlighted in cyan. Your computer screen should look like this:

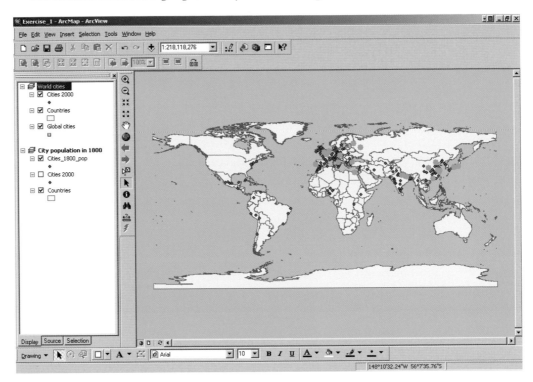

Almost all of the largest cities in the world in 1800 were in Europe or Asia.

Step 16   Create a new layer of world cities

With the cities with populations more than 200,000 in 1800 still selected, right-click the *Cities_1800_pop* layer in the table of contents.

Click *Selection*.

Select *Create Layer From Selected Features*. Your computer screen should look like the one on the following page:

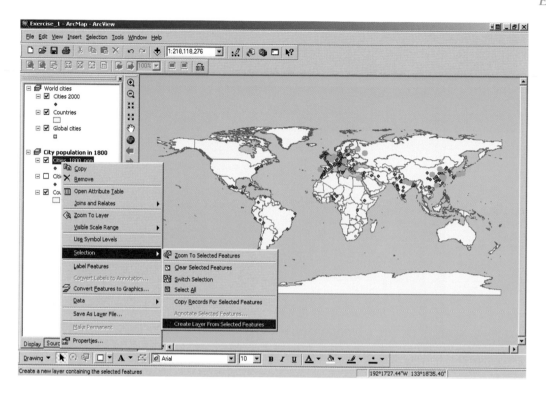

Click *Create Layer From Selected Features.*

A new layer with a default name of *Cities_1800_pop selection* appears at the top of the table of contents in the *City population in 1800* data frame. It is hard to tell where the cities with populations over 200,000 in 1800 were because the *Cities_1800_pop* layer is still on and the point symbol is not very distinct.

Turn off the *Cities_1800_pop* data layer.

In the table of contents, click the ***point symbol*** under the *Cities_1800_pop* layer name. Change its size to 7 points and its color to Mars Red.

Now you see just the cities with populations above 200,000 in 1800. Your computer screen should look like the one on the following page:

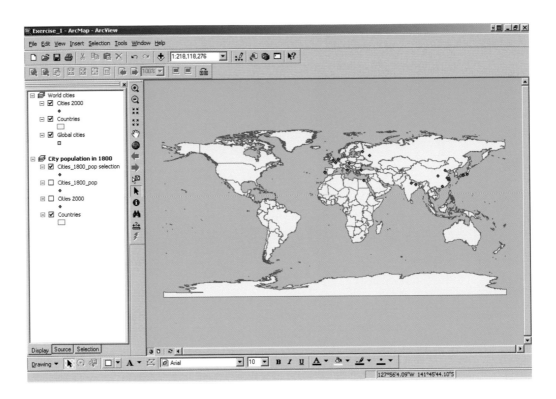

The title created by default—*Cities_1800_pop selection*—could be clearer.

Right-click the **Cities_1800_pop selection** layer.

Click **Properties**.

Click the **General** tab.

In the *Layer Name box*, rename the layer **Large cities in 1800**.

Click **OK**.

Step 17   Analyze population growth

Open the attribute table called *Attributes of large cities in 1800*.

Notice there were only twenty-one cities in 1800 with populations over 200,000. You can tell this because the attribute table indicates that there are twenty-one records at the bottom of the table.

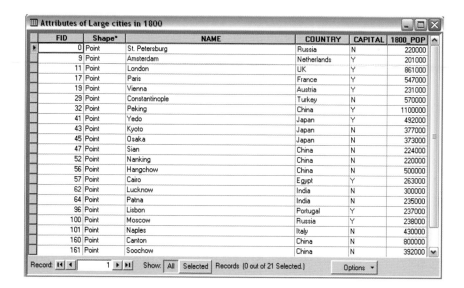

Close the attribute table.

Turn on the *Cities 2000* layer.

Many more cities with population over 200,000 as of 2000 appear—151 in all.

Step 18   Export a map as a JPEG file

Turn off all the layers except *Cities_1800_pop* and *Countries*.

If you were doing a report on large cities at the beginning of the Industrial Revolution, you might want to use this map in the report.

Question 5: How many cities had populations of 40,000 or more in 1800?

Click the *File* pull-down menu.

Click *Export Map*.

The *Export Map* dialog box opens.

In the *File name* field enter: **Cities_1800**.

In the *Save as type* pull-down menu, set the file type to JPEG (*.jpg).

Click the *down arrow* in the *Save in* box at the top of the dialog box and navigate to the **TGAR\ MyWork** folder.

Click the *Save* button.

A JPEG image of the map is exported. You can insert this map into a Microsoft Word document, PowerPoint presentation, or in any other file that supports JPEGs.

Step 19   Continue or exit ArcMap

This completes exercise 1. You may close ArcMap. Alternatively, you may proceed directly to the Your Turn exercise that follows or to exercise 2.

If you chose to close ArcMap, do the following:

Click the *File* pull-down menu.

Click *Exit*.

Click the *No* button in response to the question "Save changes to Exercise_1?"

Answers to exercise 1 questions

Question 1 (step 4)

Cameroon and Guyana touch oceans; Belarus does not.

Question 2 (step 6)

The little country entirely surrounded by South Africa is Lesotho.

Question 3 (step 11)

The population of Brasília, Brazil, in 2000 was 2,746,000.
The population of Harbin, China at that time was 2,928,000.

Question 4 (step 11)

You would sort the 2000_POP field. The country with a 2000 population of 2,194,000 was Warsaw, Poland.

Question 5 (step 18)

According to this source, 160 cities had populations of 40,000 or more in 1800.

Your Turn

1. If you are continuing from Exercise_1, navigate to the **TGAR\Part_1\Exercise_1\YourTurn** folder, open it and open the **YourTurn_1.mxd** file. Don't save changes to **Exercise_1**.

    Otherwise open ArcMap, navigate to the **TGAR\Part_1\Exercise_1\YourTurn** folder, open the folder and open the **YourTurn_1.mxd** file.

2. A map with one data frame of North American cities opens. The map shows the population of North American cities in 2000.

3. Turn off the *Cities 2000* layer and turn on the *Cities 1900* layer.

4. Open the *Cities 1900* attribute table. Examine attributes associated with the map.

    Question 1: How many fields are there in the *Cities 1900* attribute table? What are the fields named?

5. Close the attribute table.

6. Find Los Angeles on the map, searching in the *Cities 1900* layer.

7. Flash Los Angeles.

8. Zoom in to Los Angeles.

9. Use the *Identify* tool to learn about attributes of Los Angeles in 1900.

    Question 2: What was the population of Los Angeles in 1900?

10. Identify another U.S. city of your choice.

11. Zoom in and out to features of interest.

12. Turn off *Cities 1900* and turn on *Cities 1850*.

13. Use an existing bookmark to find Boston.

    Question 3: Was Boston the capital of Massachusetts in 1850?

14. Find New Orleans.

15. Create a bookmark for New Orleans.

16. Open the *Cities 1800* attribute table.

17. Sort the population in the *Cities 1800* attribute table in descending order.

    Question 4: What was the largest city in the world in 1800?
    Question 5: How many of the ten largest cities in the world in 1800 were located in China?

18. Exit the ArcMap program. Do not save changes to **YourTurn_1**.

Answers to exercise 1 Your Turn questions

Question 1: There are six fields in the *Cities 1900* attribute table: FID, Shape, NAME, COUNTRY, CAPITAL, and 1900_POP. (The FID and Shape fields are automatically created and maintained by ArcGIS; the remaining four fields are user defined.)

Question 2: The population of Los Angeles in 1900 was 107,000.

Question 3: No, Boston was not the capital of Massachusetts in 1850.

Question 4: According to this source, the largest city in the world in 1800 was Peking, China. Its population in 1800 was 1,100,000.

Question 5: According to this source, four of the ten largest cities in the world in 1800 were located in China: Peking, Canton, Hangchow, and Soochow.

Exercise 2

Taming urbanization with vector GIS

Learning objectives

In exercise 2, you will learn to use ArcMap to analyze San Francisco Bay Area demographic data from the 2000 U.S. Census and data on affordable housing projects in San Francisco from the San Francisco Redevelopment Agency. The exercise should take one hour to complete. You will learn how to do the following:

- *select* features
- *promote* and examine *attributes* of selected features
- calculate *summary statistics* about features
- make *fields* in a file *visible* or *invisible*
- add a *table* to an ArcMap document
- *join fields* from a data file to a shapefile
- *select* features by *attribute*
- *classify features* using standard classification methods
- *symbolize* features using a *color ramp*
- *symbolize* features as a *dot density* map
- examine U.S. Census *tracts*, *block groups*, and *blocks*
- *query* a GIS
- *measure* the distance between two points
- *identify* features near other features with a *location query*
- *identify* features within another feature with a *spatial query*

Step 1   Open a new map document (.mxd)

If ArcMap is already open, do the following:

Click *File*.

Click *Open*, navigate to the **TGAR\Part_1\Exercise_2** folder, then open the folder.

Open **Exercise_2a.mxd**.

Click *No*, if prompted to save changes.

Otherwise

Start ArcMap and choose to open an existing map.

Navigate to the **TGAR\Part_1\Exercise_2** folder, then open the folder.

Open **Exercise_2a.mxd**.

Step 2   Zoom in to census tracts in one part of the San Francisco Bay Area

Click the *check mark* next to the *Bay Area cities 2000* layer to turn it off so that just the census tracts are visible.

Click the *View* pull-down menu.

Click *Bookmarks*.

Click *Southern Santa Clara County*.

The view zooms in to census tracts in southern Santa Clara County. Your computer screen should look like this:

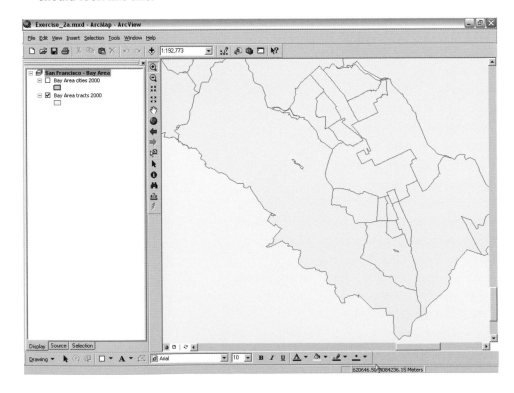

Step 3   Select a subset of census tracts

Click the *Selection* pull-down menu.

Click *Set Selectable Layers*.

Make sure only the *Bay Area tracts 2000* layer is checked. If *Bay Area cities 2000* is checked, click the **check mark** to unselect it.

Click the **Close** button in the *Set Selectable Layers* dialog box.

Click the *Select Features* tool ⬚ .

Use the *Select Features* tool to draw a box around the twelve census tracts of interest at the extreme southwest of the Bay Area. Hold down the left mouse button and click and drag to the right to draw a box around them.

Release the left mouse button.

Each census tract is outlined in cyan to indicate it has been selected.

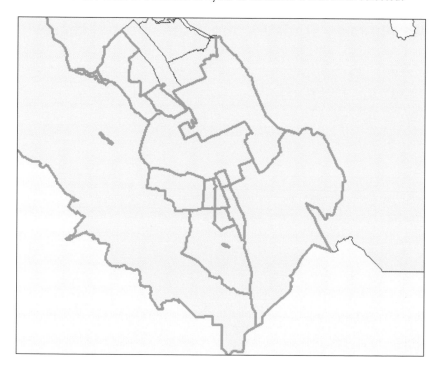

If the tracts are not exactly the ones you intended to select, hold down the shift key and click a tract to add or delete it from the selection of tracts.

Step 4   Promote and examine attributes of selected census tracts

Right-click the *Bay Area tracts 2000* layer in the table of contents.

Click *Open Attribute Table*.

The attribute table opens showing attributes of all 1,405 Bay Area census tracts.

Skim down through the table by pulling down on the slider bar on the right.

The census tracts you selected are highlighted in cyan. They are too far from each other to easily examine.

Click the *Selected* button at the bottom of the attribute table screen.

Now only the selected census tracts are visible. You can now easily look at information about just these census tracts of interest, such as population, race, modes of transportation, and housing.

Skim across the census tract attribute table to fields related to commuting behavior in the census tracts.

Two fields you read about in chapter 2 are in the attribute table: the number of workers age 16 and older who drive to work alone (field name **DRVALONE**) and the number of workers age 16 and older who carpool to work (field name **CARPOOL**).

Step 5   Calculate summary statistics about the selected census tracts

Right-click the *column header* (the gray area at the top with the column name) of the field named **CARPOOL**. The following context menu opens:

Click *Statistics.* . . on the context menu.

A box opens with statistics about the **CARPOOL** field. Among the statistics generated is a *count* of the number of census tracts and the sum showing how many people age 16 and older in the census tracts at the extreme southern end of the Bay Area carpool to work.

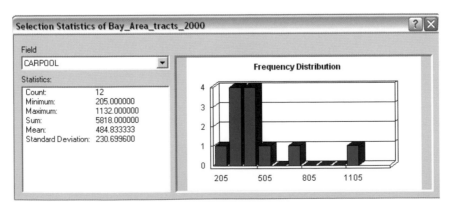

Question 1: Looking at the *Statistics* box, how many people in the tracts you selected carpool? The answer to this question and other questions are at the end of the exercise before the Your Turn exercise.

Close the *Statistics* box by clicking the *Close* button ⊠ .

Right-click the *column header* in the **DRVALONE** field.

Click *Statistics. . .* from the context menu.

 You see the same count and how many people in the census tracts age 16 and older drive to work alone.

Close the *Selection Statistics of Bay_area_tracts_2000* box.

Close the *Attribute Table*.

Click the *Selection* pull-down menu.

Click *Clear Selected Features* to clear the selected census tracts.

Step 6   Make fields in an attribute table visible or invisible

 Often researchers work only with data in a few fields of an attribute table. Making fields in an attribute table invisible makes it easier to see just the fields of interest. The fields made invisible are not deleted. They can be turned back on.

Right-click the *Bay Area tracts 2000* layer.

Click *Properties*.

Click the *Fields* tab.

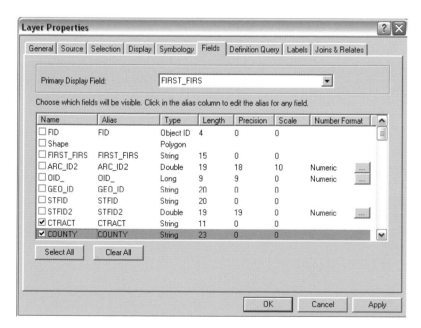

A list of each field associated with the *Bay Area tracts 2000* layer appears along with information about them. There is a check box next to each field. A check mark indicates the field is visible in the attribute table. All the fields appear as fields in the data table, but only ones marked as visible appear when a user opens the attribute table.

Scroll down to the **CARPOOL** field.

The box is checked, indicating that the carpool field is visible. The check boxes next to **PTRANSIT, BUS,** and **BIKE** are not checked. These fields are not visible when you look at the attribute table.

Uncheck **CARPOOL** and **DRVALONE** to make them invisible.

Check **PTRANSIT, BUS,** and **BIKE** to make them visible in the attribute table.

Click *OK.*

When you look at the attribute table now, you won't see the **CARPOOL** and **DRVALONE** fields, but you will see the **PTRANSIT, BUS,** and **BIKE** fields.

Step 7   Add a table

Sometimes researchers want to add additional data to an existing dataset. Data already in shapefiles can be added to an ArcMap project as new layers. Data in a table can be added and then joined to a shapefile. In this step, you will learn how to add a table. In the next step, you will learn how to join a table to a shapefile.

Click the *Add Data* button ✛.

Navigate to the **Exercise_2** folder.

Open the **More_trans** folder.

You will see a file named **More_trans.dbf.** The **.dbf** extension indicates that this is a database file. **More_trans.dbf** contains data about the number of people over the age of 16 who worked at home or walked to work in Bay Area census tracts in 2000.

Click *More_trans.dbf.*

Click *Add.*

The *More_trans.dbf* file is added to the **Exercise_2a** map document.

Notice that the table of contents has changed to the *Source* tab instead of the *Display* tab. The *Source* tab displays and organizes data by the path in which it is located.

The table is not connected to the map of the census tracts. Now you will join the table to the shapefile of Bay Area census tracts.

Step 8   Join fields from a table (.dbf file) to a shapefile

Right-click *Bay Area tracts 2000.*

Point to *Joins and Relates.*

Click *Join.*

Click the *What do you want to join in this layer?* pull-down menu.

Click *Join attributes from a table.* (This is already selected.)

Click the *Choose the field in this layer that the join will be based on* pull-down menu.

Click *FIRST_FIRS* (a field that contains a unique code for each census tract).

Click the *Choose the table to join to this layer, or load the table from disk* pull-down menu.

Click *More_trans.*

Click the *Choose the field in the table to base the join on* pull-down menu.

Click *FIRST_FIRS.*

Click *OK.*

> Note: The *Create Index* dialog box may open. If so, click *Yes* to create an index of the attribute table. Indexing a field will make subsequent operations faster.

Open the *Bay Area tracts 2000* attribute table and scroll to the right of the table.

> The *More_trans* table is joined with the *Bay Area tracts 2000* layer. It contains information on people who work at home (AT_HOME) and people who walk to work (WALK). ArcMap displays the table name followed by a period in the column header for each field. For example, the field FIRST_FIRS from the **More_trans.dbf** file is shown as **Bay_Area_tracts_2000.FIRST_FIRS**. Scroll to the last two fields. They are named **More_trans.WALK** and **More_trans.AT_HOME**.

Close the attribute table.

Right-click *Bay Area tracts 2000.*

Click *Joins and Relates.*

Point to *Remove Join(s).*

Click *Remove All Joins.*

Click the *Display* tab underneath the table of contents.

Step 9   Select features by attribute

Use the *SF—Bay Area* bookmark to view the entire Bay Area.

Click the *Selection* pull-down menu.

Click *Set Selectable Layers.*

Make sure only *Bay Area tracts 2000* is checked.

Close the *Set Selectable Layers* box.

Click the *Selection* pull-down menu.

Click *Select By Attributes.*

> The *Select By Attributes* box opens.

In the *Layer* pull-down menu, make sure the *Bay Area tracts 2000* layer is selected.

In the *Method* pull-down menu, make sure *Create a new selection* is selected.

Scroll down the *Fields* list on the left-hand side to the field "*HR_400*" (the number of units in a census tract renting for $400 or less a month in 2000).

Carefully double-click "***HR_400***".

HR_400 appears in the box below the field list to indicate that it has been selected as the first part of an expression.

Click the ***greater than*** sign (>) in the calculator buttons to the right of the field list. The *greater than* sign moves into the expression box after HR_400.

On the right-hand side of the dialog box is a *Unique Values* column. Click the ***Get Unique Values*** button located below the column.

This will populate the column with each unique value of the *HR_400* field.

Scroll down the box of *Unique Values* and double-click the value ***100***.

Your completed expression appears as the following:

"HR_400" > 100

Which means

"Show all the census tracts in the San Francisco Bay Area where more than 100 units rented for $400 a month or less in 2000."

Click the ***Apply*** button.

The census tracts with more than 100 units renting for $400 or less in 2000 are displayed. Your computer screen should look like this:

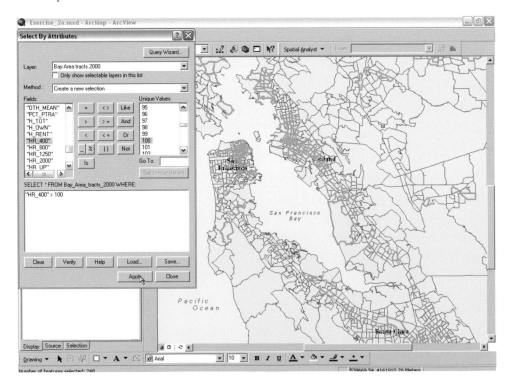

Click *Close* to close the *Select by Attributes* box.

All the tracts with more than 100 units renting for $400 or less a month in 2000 are outlined in cyan.

Question 2: How many census tracts in the Bay Area had more than 100 housing units renting for less than $400 in 2000?

Zoom in to San Francisco to see where the most low-rent units were located in 2000. (Remember: San Francisco is the tip of the southern peninsula at the mouth of San Francisco Bay.)

The census tracts with more than 100 units renting for less than $400 a month are mostly located in low-income and minority neighborhoods like the South Bayshore area (where many African-Americans live), the Mission District (where many Hispanic residents live), and the Downtown area, which includes both San Francisco's Chinatown (where many Chinese residents live) and the Tenderloin (where many Vietnamese residents live).

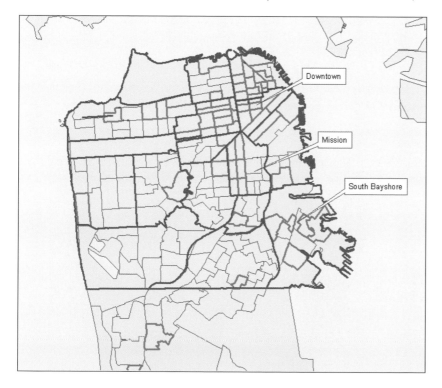

Click the *Selection* pull-down menu.
Click *Clear Selected Features* to unselect the census tracts with low-rent housing.
Click the *Go Back To Previous Extent* button ⬅ to return to the previous extent.

Step 10   Classify features and symbolize them using a color ramp

Classifying features and symbolizing the classes with a color ramp helps researchers see patterns in the data.

Make sure only the *Bay Area tracts 2000* layer is turned on and *Bay Area cities 2000* layer is turned off.

Right-click the *Bay Area tracts 2000* data layer.

Click *Properties* located at the bottom of the menu.

Click the *Symbology* tab.

Click *Quantities* in the *Show* window on the left.

Click *Graduated colors* from the list that appears below *Quantities*.

Click the *Value* pull-down menu under the *Fields* section.

Click *PCT_FBOR* (the percentage of the population in the census tract in 2000 that was foreign born).

In the *Classification* section to the right, accept the default value, 5, in the *Classes* pull-down menu.

Right-click on the *color ramp* and uncheck *Graphic View*.

Click the *Color Ramp* pull-down menu.

Click the *Purple-Blue Light to Dark* color ramp.

Click *OK*.

All of the Bay Area's 1,405 census tracts are classified according to the percentage of foreign-born residents living in them in 2000. Your computer screen should look like this:

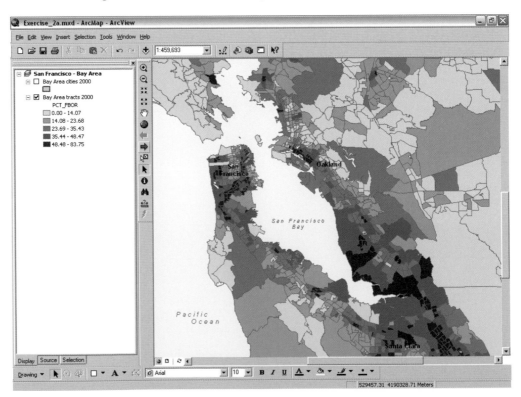

Step 11   Examine foreign-born residents in Silicon Valley

Click the *View* pull-down menu.

Point to *Bookmarks.*

Click *Silicon Valley.*

You can see that there were many foreign-born residents in Silicon Valley in 2000.

Step 12   Symbolize features in a dot density map

Turn on the *Bay Area cities 2000* layer.

Go to *Bookmarks* and click the *SF/Oakland/Berkeley* bookmark.

Right-click *Bay Area tracts 2000* layer in the table of contents.

Click *Properties* from the context menu.

Make sure the *Symbology* tab in the layer properties box is selected. If not, select it.

If necessary, click *Quantities* in the *Show* window on the left.

Click *Dot density* from the list that appears below *Quantities.*

In the *Field Selection* section, scroll down the field list and select **HHLDPOOR** (poor households), the second field from the bottom.

Click the *right pointing arrow* (>) to move **HHLDPOOR** into the *Symbol and Field* window.

HHLDPOOR moves into the *Symbol and Field* window. Your *Symbol and Field* window should look like this (the Dot Color and default Dot Size and Dot Value may differ):

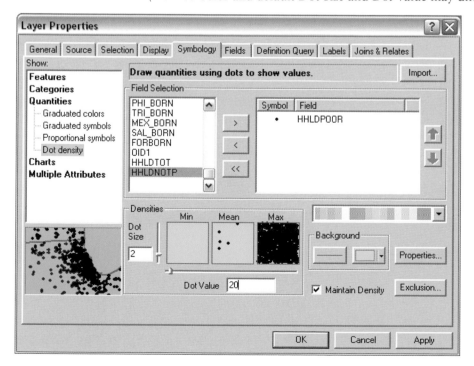

Double-click the *small dot* below the word *Symbol* in the window.

In the *Symbol Selector* dialog box, click the ***Color patch*** in the *Options* box.

Click the color ***Black***. (As you hover over a color with your pointer, you will see the color name.)

Click ***OK*** to close the *Symbol Selector* dialog box.

In the *Background* section, click the ***color patch*** and click ***Tzavorite Green*** located in the middle of the first row.

Enter **20** in the *Dot Value* field near the bottom of the *Layer Properties* box to indicate that each dot should represent 20 poor households.

The *Dot Size* field should already have 2 entered. If not, enter 2 in the *Dot Size* field.

Click ***OK*** again to close the *Layer Properties* dialog box.

Turn off the *Bay Area cities 2000* layer.

You see a dot density map. Each dot represents 20 poor households. Your computer screen should look like this:

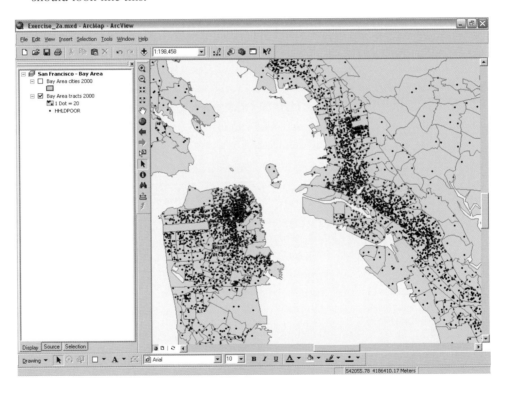

Zoom around the map to explore areas where the greatest densities of poor households are located.

Many of the areas are in the large cities of San Francisco, San Jose, and Oakland where minorities and recent immigrants are most heavily concentrated, but there are pockets of poverty and some poor households widely dispersed in other parts of the Bay Area.

Step 13   Examine U.S. Census geographical units

The U.S. Census provides demographic and other data organized into many different geographic areas. Census data for the entire United States is available at the census tract, block group, and block level. This exercise shows what these census units are like in San Francisco. Similar data is available for these and other census units in the area where you live.

Click *File*.

Click *Open*.

Navigate to the **Exercise_2** folder.

Click *Exercise_2b.mxd*.

Click the *No* button when asked if you want to save changes to **Exercise_2a.mxd**.

A map opens with a view of San Francisco. The table of contents contains only one data frame, *San Francisco*, which contains seven layers: S.F.R.A. housing, S.F. streets, S.F. planning districts, S.F. tracts 2000, S.F. block groups 2000, S.F. blocks 2000, and Bay Area counties.

The S.F.R.A. (San Francisco Redevelopment Agency) housing and S.F. planning districts layers are turned off. All the other layers are turned on.

Turn off the *S.F. streets* layer.

The San Francisco census tracts appear in yellow. There are 181 census tracts in San Francisco.

Turn off *S.F. tracts 2000*.

The census tracts layer disappears, and the block groups layer becomes visible.

Question 3a: How many census block groups are there in San Francisco?

Turn off *S.F. block groups 2000*.

The San Francisco block groups layer disappears, and the smaller blocks layer becomes visible.

Question 3b: How many census blocks are there in San Francisco?

Turn off *S.F. blocks 2000*.

Step 14   Query the S.F. streets layer by attributes

Turn on the *S.F.R.A. housing* and *S.F. streets* layers.

Line data showing San Francisco's streets and point data showing the location of affordable housing units built by the S.F.R.A. appear in the map window.

Click the *Selection* pull-down menu.

Click *Select By Attributes*.

Click the *Layer* pull-down menu.

Click *S.F. streets*.

Make sure the *Method* box reads *Create a new selection*.

In the *Fields* box, double-click *STREETNAME*.

The field should appear in the *SELECT * FROM S.F. streets WHERE* box. It is enclosed in quotation marks.

Click the *equals* sign (=).

The next step is to identify a feature using the STREETNAME field. In this case, the feature will be Mission Street. Use the *Unique Values* box to select the feature.

Click the *Get Unique Values* button.

The *Unique Values* box populates with each unique value found for STREETNAME. These unique values are the name of each street in San Francisco.

Scroll down the *Unique Values* box.

Double-click *Mission.*

Mission is added to the equation and your query should now look like this:

"STREETNAME" = 'Mission'

Click *Apply.*

Mission Street is highlighted in cyan on the map.

Click the *Close* button of the *Select By Attributes* box.

Step 15   Measure the distance between two points

Click the *View* pull-down menu.

Click *Bookmarks.*

Click the *Sixth Street area* bookmark.

The map zooms in to an area of San Francisco with a heavy concentration of S.F.R.A. affordable housing projects. Sixth Street is an inner city area close to downtown with a mix of residential hotels and businesses. Your screen should look like this:

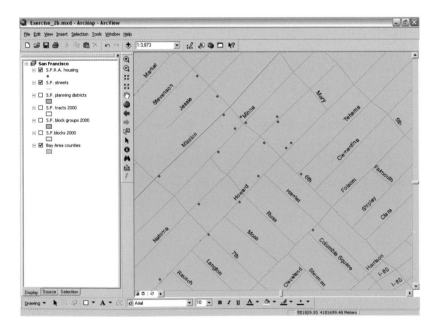

If you don't see the labels, set the map scale on the *Standard* toolbar to 1:4,000.

> (A scale range was set for the streets instructing ArcMap not to show labels when zoomed out beyond 4,000 feet. This keeps the map from being cluttered with many small, unreadable street names at larger scales. You can set a scale range for labels in the label properties.)

Use the *Find* button 🔍 to locate a street named Columbia Square.

In the *Find* field, enter **Columbia Square**.

Click the *In* pull-down menu.

Click *S.F. streets*.

In the *Search* section, click the *In fields* radio button.

Click *STREETNAME* from the pull-down menu.

Click *Find*.

Flash Columbia Square.

Close the *Find* dialog box.

Click the *Identify* tool ⓘ .

Click the S.F.R.A. affordable housing project near the corner of Columbia Square and Folsom Street.

Question 4: Who is the housing near the corner of Columbia Square and Folsom Street for? How many units does it have?

Close the *Identify Results* box.

Click the *Measure* tool 📏 .

Click the S.F.R.A. affordable housing project near the corner of Columbia Square and Folsom Street and hold down the left mouse button while you drag the mouse to the intersection of Folsom and Sixth streets.

Click the mouse once, and still holding down the left mouse button, drag the mouse to the intersection of Sixth and Mission streets (highlighted in cyan).

Click again once at the intersection of Sixth and Mission streets.

Note the distance in the lower left-hand corner of your screen.

> A general rule of thumb in transportation planning is that transit is accessible within walking distance if the passenger needs to walk no more than a quarter mile to the stop (1,320 feet is one-quarter of a mile). Is the affordable housing project at Folsom and Columbia Square within walking distance of Mission Street?

Double-click to dismiss the representation of the measured distance.

Try an alternate walking route to Mission Street from the same S.F.R.A. housing project.

Zoom out using the *San Francisco* bookmark.

Step 16   Create a new layer consisting just of Mission Street

Make sure Mission Street is highlighted in cyan. If it is not, go back to step 14 and select it.

Right-click the *S.F. streets* layer.

Point to *Selection* from the context menu.

Click *Create Layer From Selected Features*.

> A new layer is added to the map. By default it is named *S.F. streets selection*. This name is clear enough that you can tell what the new feature is, but it is not a very good name. Mission Street would be better.

Turn off the *S.F. streets* layer.

Step 17   Rename the S.F. streets selection layer and change symbology

Right-click the *S.F. streets selection* layer.

Click *Properties* at the bottom of the context menu.

Click the *General* tab.

Change the layer name to **Mission Street**.

Click the *Symbology* tab.

In the *Symbol* section, click the *Symbol* button.

In the *Symbol Selector* dialog box, change the line width to **2**.

Click the *Color* patch and click *Autunite Yellow* in the second row of the color palette.

Click *OK* to close the *Symbol Selector* dialog box.

Click *OK* to close the *Layer Properties* dialog box.

Step 18   Select features by location

Click the *Selection* pull-down menu.

Click *Select By Location*.

In the *I want to* box, make sure *select features from* is selected.

In the *the following layer(s)* box, scroll down and check the *S.F.R.A. housing* layer.

Click the *that* pull-down menu.

Click *are within a distance of*.

Click the *the features in this layer* pull-down menu.

Click *Mission Street*.

Make sure the *Apply a buffer to the features in Mission Street* box is checked.

Enter **500** for a distance.

Click the pull-down menu next to the distance box.

Click *Feet*.

> The *Select By Location* dialog box should look like the dialog box on the following page:

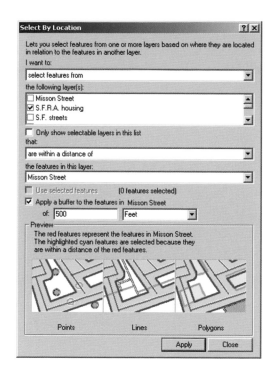

Click *Apply*.

Close the *Select By Location* dialog box.

All S.F.R.A. affordable housing units within 500 feet of Mission Street are selected and high-lighted in cyan.

Click *Selection*.

Click *Clear Selected Features*.

Step 19   Identify features within another feature with a spatial query

Turn off all the layers except *S.F.R.A. housing*, *S.F. planning districts*, and *Bay Area counties*.

Planning districts that the San Francisco City Planning Department uses for neighborhood planning appear, including the Mission District and the South Bayshore area. Many Hispanics live in the Mission and many African-Americans live in the South Bayshore area. You also see the *S.F.R.A. housing* layer that you are already familiar with.

Click the *Selection* pull-down menu.

Click *Set Selectable Layers*.

Click the *Clear All* button to clear all layers.

Check the check box next to *S.F. planning districts*.

Click *Close* to close the *Set Selectable Layers* box.

Click the *Select Features* button 🔲 .

Select both Mission and South Bayshore planning districts by holding down the shift key and clicking on each.

Click the *Selection* pull-down menu.

Click *Select By Location*.

> *Select features from* should already be selected. If it is not, click the *I want to* pull-down menu and select it.

In the *the following layers* box, the *S.F.R.A. housing* layer should already be checked. If it is not, check it.

Click the *that* pull-down menu.

Click *are completely within*.

Click the *the features in this layer* pull-down menu.

Click *S.F. planning districts*.

Make sure the *Use selected features* box is checked.

Make sure the *Apply a buffer to the features in S.F. planning districts* is unchecked.

Click *Apply*.

Click the *Close* button to close the *Select By Location* dialog box.

> All S.F.R.A.-assisted affordable housing units within the South Bayshore area and Mission District are selected and highlighted in cyan. Your screen should look like this:

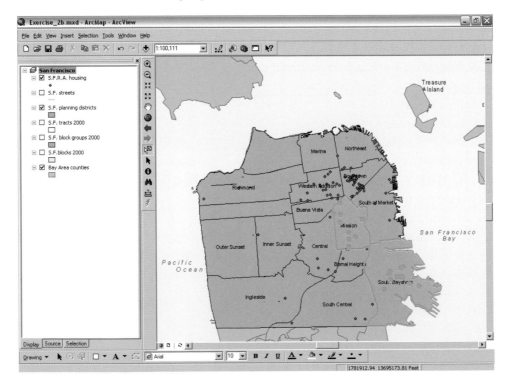

Click some of the projects in the Mission District and South Bayshore areas with the *Identify* tool. See who built the projects and how many units there are.

Question 5: How many units are there in the affordable housing project in the Ingelside district? What type of project is it? Who was the contractor?

Close the *Identify Results* window.

Clear the selected features.

Step 20   Explore relationships among layers

Turn off the *S.F. planning districts* layer.

Turn on the *S.F. blocks 2000* layer.

Click the *Selection* pull-down menu.

Click *Set Selectable Layers*.

Click the *Clear All* button to clear all layers.

Check the *S.F. blocks 2000* check box.

Close the *Set Selectable Layers* box.

Click the *Zoom In* button 🔍 and zoom in to some of the S.F.R.A. housing projects.

Question 6: Use the *Identify* tool ⓘ to click some of the census blocks where S.F.R.A. housing is located and examine selected demographic characteristics of blocks where the S.F.R.A. housing is located: age, household size, tenure status (owner or renter), race, and number of female-headed households with children (FHHCHILD). Compare the demographics of the blocks where the three scattered housing sites are located in the western part of San Francisco to blocks in the southeastern part of the city. What patterns do you discover?

If you are continuing with the Your Turn exercise or exercise 3, leave ArcMap open. Otherwise, click the *File* menu and click *Exit*. Click *No* if prompted to save your changes.

Answers to exercise 2 questions

Question 1 (step 5)

In the *Statistics* box shown in step 5, 5,818 people age 16 and older carpool to work. The number in the *Statistics* box on your computer screen will be different if you selected different census tracts.

Question 2 (step 9)

Two hundred forty-eight (248) census tracts in the Bay Area had more than 100 housing units renting for $400 or less in 2000.

Question 3 (step 13)

(a) There are 579 census block groups in San Francisco.
(b) There are 5,791 census blocks in San Francisco.

Question 4 (step 15)

The affordable housing project near the corner of Columbia Square and Folsom Street is for low-income families. It has fifty units.

The distance from the affordable housing project located near the corner of Columbia Square and Folsom Street is about 1,320 feet.

Question 5 (step 19)

There are sixteen units in the housing project in the Ingelside district. It is an acquisition/rehabilitation project. The contractor was Swords to Ploughshares.

Question 6 (step 20)

There are many more African-Americans in the census tracts in the southeastern part of San Francisco than in the census tracts where the three scattered housing sites are located in the western part of San Francisco. Many of the people living in the census tracts where the scattered site housing is located are Asians. You may have identified other differences between these tracts.

Your Turn

1. If you are continuing from **Exercise_2b**, navigate to the **TGAR\Part_1 Exercise_2\YourTurn** folder, open it, and open the **YourTurn_2.mxd** file. Don't save changes to **Exercise_2b**.

   Otherwise open ArcMap, navigate to the **TGAR\Part_1\Exercise_2\YourTurn** folder, open the folder, and open the **YourTurn_2.mxd** file.

2. A map of the San Francisco Bay Area opens.
3. Select cities with populations under 20,000 in 2000 by attribute.
4. Open the attribute table for *Bay Area cities 2000*.

   Question 1: How many Bay Area cities had fewer than 20,000 people in 2000?

5. Create a new map layer of Bay Area cities under 20,000.
6. Rename the new map layer: **Bay Area cities under 20,000 pop.**
7. Open the *Bay Area cities 2000* attribute table. Calculate statistics on the POP2000 field.

   Question 2: How many people did the U.S. Census enumerate living in the San Francisco Bay Area in 2000?

8. Calculate summary statistics on each of the following fields: **WHITE, BLACK, ASIAN,** and **HISPANIC.**

   Question 3: How many members of each ethnic group were there in the Bay Area in 2000?

9. Use the *Oakland* bookmark to zoom in to Oakland.
10. Use the **HHLDPOOR** field to symbolize the *Bay Area tracts 2000* layer as a *graduated color*. Select the *Purple-Blue Light to Dark* color ramp.
11. Turn off all layers except *City of Oakland* and *Bay Area tracts 2000*.
12. Use the *SF – Bay Area* bookmark to zoom back to the full extent of the Bay Area.
13. Use the **MEX_BORN** field to create a dot density map. Symbolize the dots with a size of 2, value of 100, and the color *Rhodolite Rose* (first row, last color of the color palette).

    Question 4: Are Mexican-born individuals widely dispersed or clustered within the Bay Area?

14. Change the *dot density* field to **HHLDTOT.**
15. Continue using the dot density map to examine the **DRVALONE** and **BUS** fields. Use the same dot size and value as above.
16. Activate the *San Francisco* data frame.
17. Navigate to the **TGAR\Part_1\Exercise_2\YourTurn** folder and add the **Rent_overpay.dbf** table from the **Data** folder. Remember a data table just contains attribute data.

18. Join *Rent_overpay* to *S.F. tracts 2000*.

Question 5: What is the appropriate field on which to join *S.F. tracts 2000* and *Rent_overpay*? Do the names of the two fields for the join have to be the same? Do the data types of the two fields for the join have to be the same?

19. Open the *Select By Attributes* dialog box. Query the census tracks where greater than 1,000 people are paying rent of 30% or more (**RENT30UP**).
20. Open the *Select By Location* dialog box. Select S.F.R.A. housing projects that are completely within the selected census tracks.
21. Open the *S.F.R.A. housing* attribute table. Click the **Selected** button and look at how many projects fall within the selected census tracts.
22. Use the *Northeast S.F.* bookmark or zoom in to the northeast corner of the city. Turn on the *S.F. planning districts* layer.

Question 6: What planning district contains the most selected housing projects?

23. Explore the demography of the block groups around the projects using the *Identify* button.
24. Exit ArcMap. Do not save changes to **YourTurn_2**.

Answers to exercise 2 Your Turn questions

Question 1: Thirty-seven Bay Area cities had fewer than 20,000 people in 2000.

Question 2: The U.S. Census enumerated 6,128,547 people living in the San Francisco Bay Area in 2000.

Question 3: In 2000, the Census enumerated the following numbers of people living in the Bay Area:

White:	3,460,404
Black:	479,704
Asian:	1,245,484
Hispanic:	1,183,900

Question 4: There were few Mexican-born people living near the coast to the northwest of San Francisco in 2000.

Question 5: The appropriate field to join *S.F. tracts 2000* and *Rent_overpay* is GEO_ID. This field exists in both files. The name of the field does not have to be the same, but the field's data type (such as text or short integer) does.

Question 6: The Downtown planning district contains the most S.F.R.A. housing units.

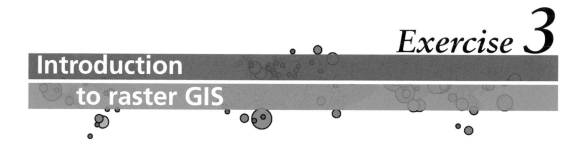

Exercise 3

Introduction to raster GIS

Learning objectives

In exercise 3, you will use the ArcMap Spatial Analyst extension to examine data related to environmental problems in Contra Costa County involving ozone pollution, sites where used automobile engine oil might be disposed, and changes in the amount of prime farmland in the county. You also will perform distance calculations involving the locations of libraries. You will learn how to do the following:

- prepare ArcMap to analyze raster data by enabling the ArcMap *Spatial Analyst extension* and adding the *Spatial Analyst toolbar*
- establish a *working environment* for a raster analysis by defining an analysis *extent*, specifying a *cell size*, specifying where *raster output* you create will be stored, and specifying an *analysis mask*
- examine the difference between the vector and raster GIS models
- create *raster representation models*
- measure *straight line distance*
- create *Thiessen polygons*
- *convert* a vector GIS data layer of land use to raster format
- *convert* a raster GIS data layer to vector format
- create a *statistical surface*

Step 1   Start ArcMap

If ArcMap is already open, do the following:

Click *File*.

Click *Open*, navigate to the **TGAR\Part_2\Exercise_3** folder, then open the folder.

Open **Exercise_3a.mxd**.

Click *No*, if prompted to save changes.

Otherwise

Start ArcMap and choose to open an existing map.

Navigate to the **TGAR\Part_2\Exercise_3** folder, then open the folder.

Open **Exercise_3a.mxd**.

Before you start doing raster GIS analysis with ArcMap, you need to enable the Spatial Analyst extension, make the Spatial Analyst toolbar visible, and set up a working environment.

Step 2   Turn on the Spatial Analyst extension

Click the *Tools* pull-down menu.

Click *Extensions*.

Click the *Spatial Analyst* check box to turn on the Spatial Analyst extension. (If it is already checked, you can skip this instruction.)

Click the *Close* button to close the *Extensions* dialog box.

Step 3   Make the Spatial Analyst toolbar visible

Click the *View* pull-down menu.

Click *Toolbars*.

Scroll to *Spatial Analyst*. If it is already checked, the Spatial Analyst toolbar will be visible on the computer screen. If it is not checked, check *Spatial Analyst*. The Spatial Analyst toolbar appears.

Dock the Spatial Analyst toolbar at the top of your screen.

Step 4   Define a working environment.

Click the *Spatial Analyst* pull-down menu.

Click *Options*.

Three tabs let you define a Spatial Analyst working environment. You will use a raster named *County_grid* to establish an analysis extent that includes Contra Costa County. You will also use *County_grid* to set an analysis mask and the cell size. The cell size of the *County_grid* is

100 x 100 feet. By setting cell size the *Same as County_grid*, the rasters you produce will have 100 x 100 foot cells.

Click the *Extent* tab.

Click the *Analysis extent* pull-down menu.

Click *Same as Layer "County_grid"*.

The analysis extent is set to a rectangular area that includes Contra Costa County and surrounding areas. The *Options* dialog box should look like this:

Click the *Cell size* tab.

Click the *Analysis cell size* pull-down menu.

Click *Same as Layer "County_grid"*.

Now you will define a working directory where output from your analysis will be stored.

Click the *General* tab.

Enter the path to the location where you will store new rasters you create (the **TGAR\MyWork** folder or another location where you chose to store your work).

Note: Spatial Analyst does not allow the path name to contain a space.

Click the *Analysis mask* pull-down menu.

Click *County_grid*.

An *analysis mask* is set so that only cells within Contra Costa County are included in the analysis. After you have set the *working directory* and *analysis mask*, the *General* tab will look like the graphic on the following page (the working directory may be different if you select a different location):

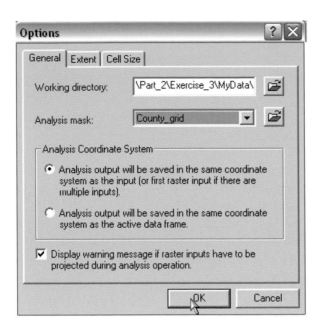

Click **OK**.

Step 5   Examine Exercise_3

Your initial map has two data frames: *Bay Area ozone pollution* and *Contra Costa County*. The *Contra Costa County* data frame is active. The *Contra Costa County* data frame has eight layers:

- Libraries
- Cities
- Highways
- Farms2000
- Farm84_grid
- Farms1984
- County_grid
- Bay Area counties.

The *Farm84_grid* legend should already be expanded. If it is not, click the **plus sign** ⊞ next to the *Farm84_grid* layer to expand it.

Look at the labels for the eight different kinds of farmland:

Question 1: Where is most of the prime farmland in Contra Costa County located?

The *Farms1984* legend should already be expanded. If not, click the **plus sign** ⊞ next to *Farms1984* to expand the legend.

Notice the *Farms1984* labels are identical to the *Farm84_grid* labels.

Click ⊟ next to the *Farms1984* legend to collapse the legend.

Click ⊟ next to the *Farm84_grid* legend to collapse the legend.

Step 6   Compare vector and raster representation of the world

Turn off all layers except *Cities*, *Farms1984*, and *Bay Area counties*.

Farms1984 is a vector GIS polygon layer showing attributes of farms (and also urban land, water, and other land uses) in Contra Costa County in 1984.

Click the **View** pull-down menu.

Point to *Bookmarks*.

Click the **Walnut Creek** bookmark.

You are zoomed in to a part of Contra Costa County near the city of Walnut Creek, California. Notice that the edges of the vector urban land polygons are smooth. This is characteristic of vector polygons.

Turn on *Farm84_grid* (a raster layer with the same information as *Farms1984*).

Notice that the edges of the different kinds of land use are jagged. Values in this raster grid are stored in square cells. At this level of detail, you can see the jagged outer edges of cells (pixelation).

Click the **Go Back To Previous Extent** button ◄ .

Turn the *Farm84_grid* layer off and on several times.

First you see raster and then you see vector representations of farmland in Contra Costa County. At this scale, the representations look the same. The pixelation (cell boundaries) in raster representation become increasingly visible close up. At a distance, the jagged edges of the raster grids (sometimes called *jaggies*) appear smooth.

Step 7   Measure straight line distance

Turn off all the layers except for *Libraries*, *County_grid*, and *Bay Area counties*.

Click the *Spatial Analyst* pull-down menu.

Point to *Distance*.

Click *Straight Line*.

> In the *Distance to* box, *Libraries* should already be selected. If not, click the *pull-down menu* and select it.

Accept defaults for the other information in the *Straight Line* dialog box. The straight line distance dialog box should look like this:

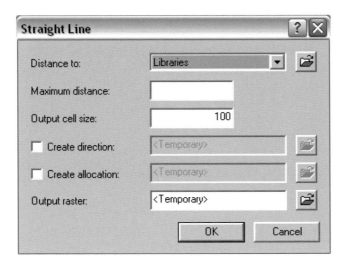

Click *OK*.

> A raster named *Distance to Libraries* is created and added to your map. It shows the *straight line distance* from every raster cell to the nearest library. The colors symbolically show distance from light yellow closest to libraries to dark blue farthest away. The distance is in feet (the *map unit*). The map showing distance to libraries is an example of a representation model—a simplified map representing distance.

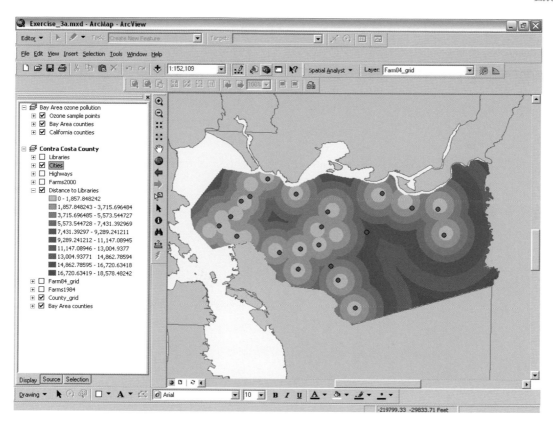

Click the **minus sign** ⊟ next to Distance to Libraries.

Click the **Selection** pull-down menu.

Click **Set Selectable Layers**.

Click **Clear All**.

Check the *Libraries* check box.

Click the **Close** button.

Using the *Identify* button **ⓘ** , click an area close to a library.

  The *Identify Results* pop-up box tells you the distance.

Question 2: Using the map on the following page as a reference, about how many feet is it from the tip of the small white arrow icon next to the *Identify* button **ⓘ** to the nearest library?

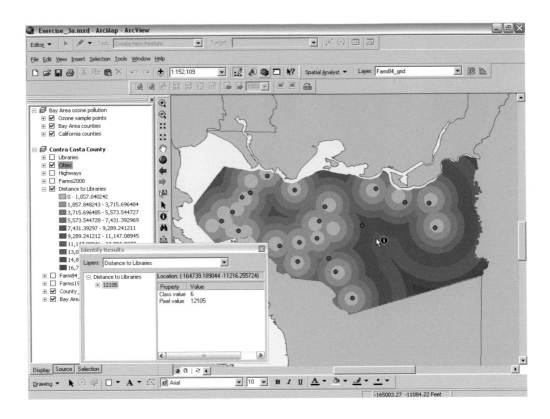

Click the small blue area at the far southeast of Contra Costa County. How far is it from this location to the nearest library?

Turn off the *Libraries* and *Distance to Libraries* layers.

Close the *Identify Results* box.

Step 8   Create a Thiessen polygon

Now you will use the Spatial Analyst distance allocation function to create Thiessen polygons around hypothetical used-oil disposal sites for each city in Contra Costa County. This exercise assumes that there is a used-oil disposal site at the location of each city as represented by a point.

Turn on the *Cities* layer.

Click the **Spatial Analyst** pull-down menu.

Point to *Distance*.

Click **Allocation**.

Click the **Assign to** pull-down menu.

Click **Cities**.

Accept defaults for the other information in the distance allocation dialog box.

Click **OK**.

Thiessen polygons appear around each city's used-oil disposal site. A new raster layer named *Allocation to Cities* is added to your map. This map is another example of a representation model—in this case, representing the shortest distance from any point to a used-oil disposal site.

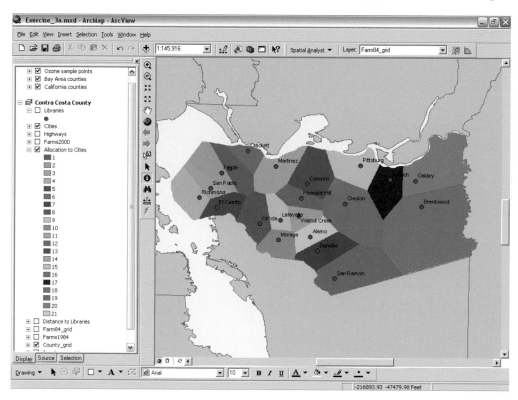

Question 3: What is the closest city to a resident living in the polygon at the very southernmost part of Contra Costa County?

Click the **minus sign** ⊟ to close the *Allocation to Cities* legend.
Turn off the *Allocation to Cities* layer.

Step 9   Convert a vector feature to a raster

Turn off all the layers except *Farms2000*, *County_grid*, and *Bay Area counties*.
  Farms2000 is a vector GIS feature showing land-use data. Currently, it is not symbolized to reflect the land-use categories.
Click the **Spatial Analyst** pull-down menu.
Point to *Convert*.
Click **Features to Raster**.

In the *Features to Raster* dialog box do the following:

Click the **Input features** pull-down menu.

Click **Farms2000**.

Click the **Field** pull-down menu.

Click **landcover**.

The *Output cell size* box should already be set to "100". If it is not, enter "100".

In the *Output raster* box, click the **Browse folder** button ![folder icon] and navigate to the folder where you want to save new rasters (the **MyWork** folder in the **TGAR** folder or another location you specified).

Name the file **Farms00_grid**.

Click *Save*.

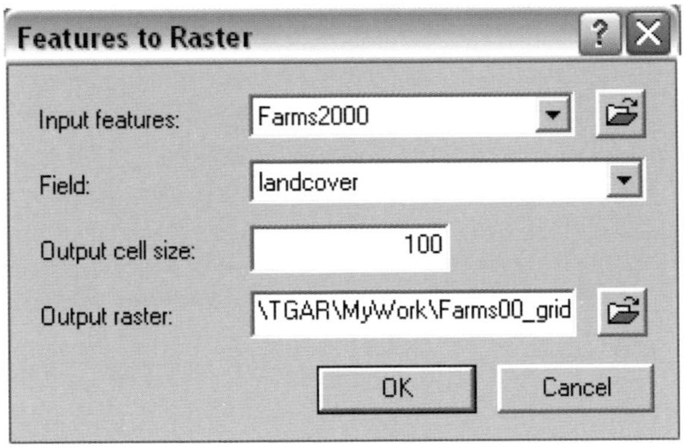

Features to Raster

Input features:	Farms2000
Field:	landcover
Output cell size:	100
Output raster:	\TGAR\MyWork\Farms00_grid

OK   Cancel

Click **OK**.

ArcMap Spatial Analyst converts the vector layer to a raster and adds the raster to the table of contents.

When ArcMap converts vector to raster data, it applies a new random symbology, so the color scheme no longer matches that of the properly symbolized F*arms2000* and *Farm84_grid* legends. To analyze *Farms00_grid*, the symbology needs to match *Farms1984*.

Step 10   Change the symbology of a raster

Expand the *Farms1984* layer.

Notice that in *Farms1984* there are eight values, prime farmland is appropriately symbolized with a dark green (Leaf Green), and the values are labeled *Prime Farmland, Farmland of statewide significance*, etc.

Now you will resymbolize the colors of the *Farms00_grid* to match the colors in the *Farms1984* layer, and add the same informative labels as *Farms1984*.

Right-click **Farms00_grid**.

Click **Properties**.

Click the **Symbology** tab.

In the *Show* box, *Unique Values* should already be selected. If it is not, select it.

The eight land-use values appear in the center of the *Properties* dialog box. Right-click each color in turn, then click **Properties for selected Colors** and enter the appropriate color, then enter the corresponding label as follows:

Value	Color		Color palette location	Label
1	Mango		Line 2, Column 4	Other
2	Sodalite Blue		Line 1, Column 9	Water
3	Gray (10%)		Line 2, Column 1	Urban
4	Olivine Yellow		Line 1, Column 6	Unique farmland
5	Yucca Yellow		Line 1, Column 5	Grazing
6	Tzavorite Green		Line 1, Column 7	Farmland of local importance
7	Leaf Green		Line 5, Column 7	Prime farmland
8	Peridot Green		Line 3, Column 6	Farmland of statewide significance

Click **OK** to close the *Layer Properties* dialog box.

Turn off *Farms2000*.

Your *Farms00_grid* raster layer is now properly symbolized and named.

Step 11   Covert a raster GIS feature to a vector polygon

Click the *Spatial Analyst* pull-down menu.

Point to *Convert*.

Click **Raster to Features**.

Click the **Input raster** pull-down menu.

Click **Farm84_grid**.

Accept the default for *Field* and *Output geometry type*.

In the *Output features* box, click the **Browse folder** button 📂 and navigate to the **TGAR\ MyWork** folder or another location you have specified to save your work.

The *Raster to Features* dialog box should look like the graphic on the following page:

Click **OK**.

> ArcMap Spatial Analyst converts the raster grid to a vector polygon and adds it to the table of contents.
>
> You could resymbolize the values using the same method as you did in step 8. Since you already know how to resymbolize layers, you'll move on to other Spatial Analyst operations using additional Contra Costa County data.

Step 12   Prepare the environment to interpolate an ozone pollution surface

Right-click the *Bay Area ozone pollution* data frame.

Click **Activate**.

> A map of Northern California opens with three layers. The first layer is named *Ozone sample points*. It contains forty-three locations in northern California from which ozone samples are collected. The second layer—*Bay Area counties*—contains sixteen northern California counties. Contra Costa County is symbolized in red.

Click the **Spatial Analyst** pull-down menu.

Click **Options**.

Click the **Extent** tab.

Set the Analysis extent to *Same as Layer "Bay Area counties"*.

Click the **Cell size** tab.

Set the Analysis cell size to *Maximum of Inputs*.

Click the **General** tab.

> Set the working directory to **TGAR\MyWork** or another location you have specified to save your work.

Set the Analysis mask to *Bay Area counties*.

Click **OK**.

Step 13   Interpolate an ozone pollution statistical surface

Click the *Spatial Analyst* pull-down menu.

Point to *Interpolate to Raster*.

Click **Inverse Distance Weighted**.

    The ArcMap *Inverse Distance Weighted interpolation* dialog box opens. "Ozone sample points" is already in the *Input points* box.

Click the **Z value field** pull-down menu.

Click **OZONE**.

Make sure *Search radius type* is set to **Variable**.

Make sure *Number of Points* is set to **12**.

No value is necessary for *Maximum distance*.

Make sure the *Output cell size* box value is greater than **1000**.

Accept the default in the *Output raster* box.

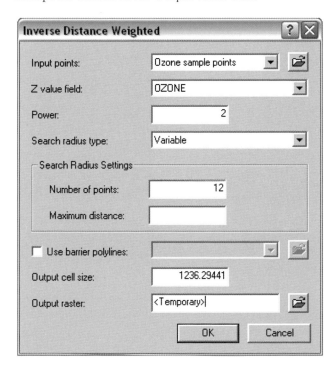

Click **OK**.

    A new temporary raster grid named *IDW of Ozone sample points* is added to your map, showing a statistical surface of ozone pollution.

    Note: You may need to turn off the *Bay Area counties* layer to view the *IDW of Ozone sample points* layer.

    Every cell in the grid has been assigned a value based on analysis of the values in nearby cells weighted (Power of 2) so that close cells have more influence than cells that are farther away.

Collapse the *IDW of Ozone sample points* legend.

Question 4: Is the concentration of ozone relatively high or relatively low near San Francisco Bay? What might explain this finding? What would be good research practice in a study like this.

Step 14   Rename the new raster

Right-click *IDW of Ozone sample points*.

Click *Properties*.

Click the *General* tab.

Rename the layer **Ozone surface**.

Click *OK*.

Step 15   Open a new map document on Contra Costa County farmland and set the environment

Navigate to the **TGAR\Part_2\Exercise_3** folder and open **Exercise_3b.mxd**. Click *No* when prompted "Save changes to Exercise_3a?"

There are two raster layers in the table of contents: *Farm84_grid* and *Farm00_grid* as well as the outline of Bay Area counties and vector point data showing the location of Contra Costa County cities.

Make sure the Spatial Analyst extension is turned on and the Spatial Analyst toolbar is visible. If they are not, return to steps 2 and 3 and follow the instructions to perform these tasks.

Now you will set the *analysis environment* for Contra Costa County.

Click the *Spatial Analyst* pull-down menu.

Click *Options*.

Click the *Extent* tab and set the Analysis extent to *Same as Layer "Farm00_grid"*.

Click the *Cell size* tab and set the Analysis cell size to *Same as Layer "Farm00_grid"*.

Notice that the *cell size* is set to 100. This means cells in this raster are 100 x 100 map units. As you will see in the next step, the map units are meters, so each cell in this raster is 10,000 square meters (100 x 100 meters) or one hectare—a common unit of measurement.

Click the *General* tab and set the working directory to the location where you will save new rasters you create.

Set the Analysis mask to *Farm00_grid*.

Click *OK* to close the *Options* dialog box.

Step 16   Check the map units

Right-click on the data frame label (*Farmland*).

Click *Properties*.

Click the *General* tab to select it.

Notice that the map units are meters. This will be useful information in step 17.

Click *OK* to close the dialog box.

Step 17   View a histogram of a variable

Expand the *Farm84_grid* legend. Notice that prime farmland is dark green.

Click the layer drop-down list to the right of the Spatial Analyst pull-down menu and make sure the layer is set to *Farm84_grid*.

Click the *Histogram* button 🏛 on the Spatial Analyst toolbar.

A histogram of *Farm84_grid* opens. The dark green column on the left shows there were about sixteen thousand cells of prime farmland in 1984.

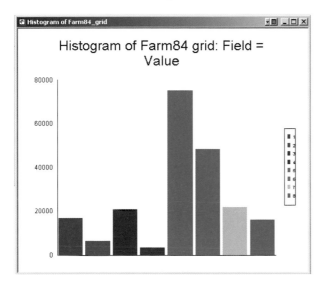

Click the dark green column representing prime farmland.

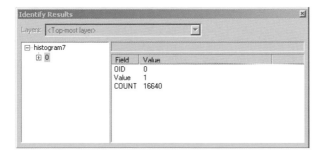

The COUNT in the *Identify Results* dialog box shows that 16,640 in the *Farm84_grid* had the value "1" (prime farmland) in 1984. You know from your examination of the map units and cell size that each cell in this raster has been set to be 100 meters on each side, or 10,000 square meters in all. Ten thousand square meters equals one hectare. This means that there were 16,640 hectares of prime farmland in Contra Costa County in 1984.

Close the *Identify Results* box.

Close the *Histogram of Farm84_grid*.

Step 18   Group values of a variable

Turn off *Farm84_grid*.

You can see that there is less prime farmland (dark green) in 2000 than there was in 1984.

If necessary, expand the *Farm00_grid* legend.

Notice there are eight values of land-use in Contra Costa County. Grouping classifications can make it easier to see land-use patterns in the county.

Right-click *Farm00_grid*.

Select *Properties*.

Click on the *Symbology* tab.

Click value **2** labeled *Farmland of statewide significance*.

Hold down the Shift key and click value **5** labeled *Grazing*.

Release the Shift key.

This selects all of the values that are not prime farmland up until value 6 (*Urban*).

Hold down the control key and click value **8** labeled *Other*. (You may need to scroll to do this).

This adds the value *Other* to the already selected values.

Right-click any of the selected values.

Click *Group Values*.

The values are grouped into just four categories—prime farmland (green), urban (gray), water (blue), and all other values (grouped 2;3;4;5;8).

Double-click the color symbol for the values **2;3;4;5;8** and select the lightest green (Tzavorite Green) from the color palette (first row, seventh column).

In the *Label* column, click **2;3;4;5;8** and type "Other land".

Click *OK*.

Close the *Layer Properties* box.

All the values representing farmland except for 1 (prime farmland) are grouped together. The two uses that are not farmland—urban (6) and water (7) are not grouped.

The legend for *Farm00_grid* now displays four categories of land use: *Prime farmland*, *Other land*, *Urban*, and *Water*. This simplification brings clarity and meaning to the map.

Step 19   Ungroup a variable

Right-click *Farm00_grid*.

Click *Properties*.

The *Symbology* tab should already be selected. If it is not, select it.

Right-click the grouped values *2;3;4;5;8*.

Click *Ungroup Values*.

   The values are ungrouped. Unfortunately, you have lost their symbology.

Click *OK* to close the *layer properties* box.

Collapse the *Farm00_grid* legend.

Turn off *Farm00_grid*.

Step 20   Use raster layer (.lyr) files to examine loss of prime farmland

Make sure that all of the layers except *Bay Area counties* and *Cities* are turned off.

Click the *Add Data* button ✚ .

Navigate to the **Exercise_3** folder and open the *Farms* folder.

Click the *Prime84_grid.lyr* file.

Hold the Control key down and select the *Prime00_grid.lyr* file.

   Both files should be selected.

   Note: Make sure you click *Prime84_grid.lyr*, not *Prime84_grid*. *Prime84_grid.lyr* is a layer file that saves symbology; *Prime84_grid* is a raster grid file.

Click *Add*.

If necessary, click *OK* to dismiss the spatial reference message.

   Both *Prime84_grid.lyr* and *Prime00_grid.lyr* files are added to the data frame and map.

Make sure the *Prime84_grid.lyr* layer is above the *Prime00_grid.lyr*.

If it is not, click it, hold down the left mouse button and drag it above *Prime00_grid.lyr*.

Expand the *Prime84_grid* legend.

   The symbology in these files does not need to be recoded. Layer (.lyr) files store layer symbology. The *Prime00_grid* file was symbolized to show prime farmland in a dark green (Leaf Green) and all other land in gray.

   Most of the prime farmland in Contra Costa County in 1984 (symbolized in dark green) was located in eastern Contra Costa County. There was just a small amount of urbanization (symbolized in gray) mixed in with the prime farmland in eastern Contra Costa County at that time.

Turn off *Prime84_grid*.

   You can see that there was quite a lot less prime farmland in eastern Contra Costa County in 2000.

Click the *View* menu on the *Main Menu*.

Select *Bookmarks*.

Click the *Prime Farmland* bookmark.

   The map zooms in to the area around Brentwood in eastern Contra Costa County.

Turn on the *Prime84_grid* layer. Your screen should look like this:

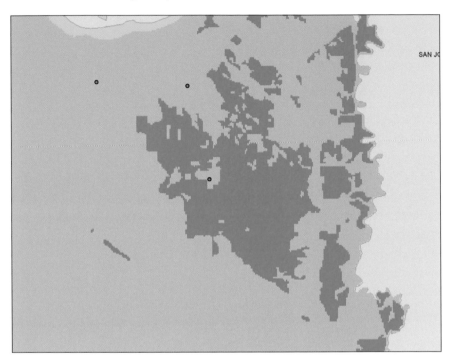

Turn off the *Prime84_grid* layer. Your screen should look like this:

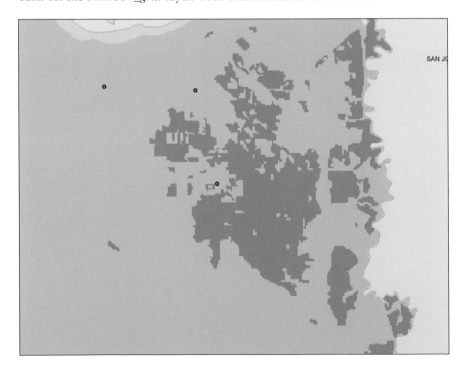

You can see that quite a lot of prime farmland in eastern Contra Costa County was lost between 1984 and 2000.

Collapse the *Prime84_grid* legend.

Turn off both *Prime84_grid* and *Prime00_grid*.

Use the *Contra Costa County* bookmark to zoom out.

Step 21   Use the Spatial Analyst Raster Calculator to analyze loss of prime farmland

Click the *Spatial Analyst* pull-down menu.

Select *Raster Calculator*.

The *Raster Calculator* opens. You will enter the following expression as it appears in the *Raster Calculator* below. The expression is space sensitive and will not work unless you enter the proper spacing. Note: Do not type the periods at the ends of the next eight lines of instructions; they are punctuation and not something to be entered.

Type Primeloss= .

Double-click *Farm84_grid*.

Click = .

Click *1*.

Click *And*.

Double-click *Farm00_grid*.

Click <> .

Click *1*.

The completed expression in the Raster Calculator should look like this:

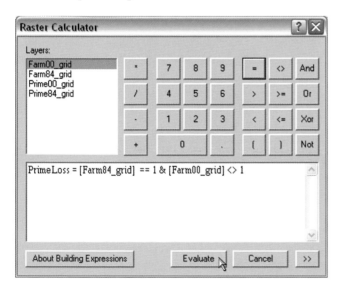

Click *Evaluate*.

A new raster grid named *PrimeLoss* is added to the map. It shows land that was prime farmland in 1984 ([*Farm84_grid*] = = 1) and which was not prime farmland in 2000 ([*Farm00_grid*] <> 1). The new grid colors are assigned at random. You can change the farmland to Leaf Green and the other land to 10% Gray to match the colors in the map on page 358.

Look at the map. You can see where prime farmland was lost.

Open the *PrimeLos*s attribute table.

Question 5: How many hectares of prime farmland were lost in Contra Costa County between 1984 and 2000?

Close the *Attribute table*.

If you are continuing with the next exercise, leave ArcMap open. Otherwise, turn off the Spatial Analyst toolbar and extension. Click the **File** menu and click **Exit**. Click **No** if prompted to save your changes.

Answers to exercise 3 questions
Question 1 (step 5)
Most of the prime farmland in Contra Costa County is located in eastern Contra Costa County.

Question 2 (step 7)
The *Identify Results* box shows that it is about 12,100 feet from the tip of the small white arrow icon next to the *Identify* button to the nearest library. This is an approximation. Your answer may differ, depending on exactly where you clicked.

Question 3 (step 8)
The closest city to a resident living in the southernmost part of Contra Costa County is San Ramon.

Question 4 (step 13)
The concentration of ozone is relatively low near San Francisco Bay. This might be explained by the cleansing effects of air from the bay. It would be important to ground truth this hypothesis. Other factors—such as fewer automobiles or the absence of other sources of ozone—might help explain the low concentrations of ozone in this area.

Question 5 (step 21)
There were 2,386 hectares (cells) of prime farmland lost in Contra Costa County between 1984 and 2000. Each cell is 100 meters x 100 meters (one hectare).

Your Turn

1. If you are continuing from Exercise_3b, navigate to the **TGAR\Part_2\Exercise_3\YourTurn** folder, double-click the folder to open it and open the **YourTurn_3.mxd.** file. Click *No* when prompted "Save changes to Exercise_3b?"

   Otherwise open ArcMap and navigate to the **TGAR\Part_2\Exercise_3\YourTurn** folder, double-click the folder to open it and open the **YourTurn_3.mxd.** file.

2. A map opens showing the locations of redwood, hardwood, and wetland areas in Contra Costa County (outlined in purple).

   Almost all of the forestland in Contra Costa County consists of hardwoods in green. There is only a small area of redwoods in the southwest corner of Contra Costa County. You may have to look hard to see it.

3. Before you begin working with the Exercise_3 YourTurn data, prepare ArcMap to analyze raster data by doing the following:
   • enabling the ArcMap Spatial Analyst extension
   • making sure the Spatial Analyst toolbar is visible and docked

4. Establish a working environment for raster analysis by doing the following:
   • specifying a folder as the working directory (remember no spaces in the path name)
   • specifying *Ownership* as the Analysis mask
   • defining *Ownership* as the Analysis extent
   • specifying *Redwood forests* as the Cell size

5. Use the Redwoods bookmark to zoom in to the area where the redwoods are located.

   Question 1: What type of layer is Redwood forest, raster or vector? How can you tell?

6. Calculate a straight line distance to the *Urban centers*.
7. Collapse the legend of the new *Distance to Urban centers* layer and move it below wetlands.
8. Look at the distance from the city of Moraga to the redwoods and hardwoods.
9. Use the *Contra Costa County* bookmark to zoom out.
10. Use the *Identify* tool to find approximate distances from the surrounding urban centers to critical habitat. (You may need to set the identifying layer to *Distance to Urban centers*.)

    Question 2: Are there areas where there are still remaining redwood forests near urban centers in Contra Costa County? Hardwood forests? Wetland areas?

11. Turn off the Redwood forests, Hardwood forests, and Wetland areas.
12. Use the *Distance Allocation* function to create Thiessen polygons around the urban centers. Collapse the *Allocation to the Urban centers* legend.

    Question 3: Which city has the largest Thiessen polygon around it? What is the implication for locating a city service in the center of the polygon?

13. Turn off the *urban centers* and *distance allocation* layers.
14. Turn on the *Ownership* layer and expand its legend. Notice the thirteen categories of ownership. They can be consolidated into groups such as State, Federal, Local, and Other. Use the list below to group the values into the above mentioned groups. Give each group a new color and label them correctly.
    Bureau of Land Management—Federal
    Central Coast Water District—State
    City and County Park—Local
    Dept. of Parks and Recreation—State
    DOD-Army—Federal
    DOD-Navy—Federal
    East Bay Municipal Utility District—Local
    East Bay Regional Park—Local
    Muir Heritage Land Trust—Other
    NPS–Historical Site—Federal
    Save Mount Diablo—Other
    State Lands Commission—State
    Unclassified—Other

    Now it is easier to understand the land types in the county.
    Ungroup these values.
15. Turn off *Ownership*.
16. Turn on *Vegetation type* and expand its legend.
17. Convert the *Vegetation type* to a raster grid using the field **GRIDCODE**.
18. Open the new raster grid layer properties, change the symbology to match that of the vector layer, and rename it **Vegetation_grid**.
19. Display the histogram of the *Vegetation* layer and find the approximate amount of grassland.

    Question 4: Approximately how many hectares of grassland are there in Contra Costa County?

20. Activate the *Ozone in Contra Costa* data frame.
21. Set the mask and extent to Contra Costa County.
22. Perform an IDW interpolation for ozone sample points based on **OZONE**. Leave the *Output cell size* at **100**.

    Question 5: Does the statistical surface created by interpolating just sample points located in Contra Costa County approximate the surface created by interpolating samples from many more sample points as you did in the main exercise? Since you limited your analysis just to Contra Costa County data, is this a more accurate representation of ozone pollution in Contra Costa County?

23. Turn off the Spatial Analyst toolbar and the Spatial Analyst extension.

24. Exit ArcMap. Do not save changes to **YourTurn_3**.

Answers to exercise 3 Your Turn questions

Question 1: Redwoods is raster data. You can tell by the jagged boundaries showing cell boundaries.

Question 2: Yes, all three types of areas—redwoods, hardwoods, and wetlands—exist near urban areas in Contra Costa County.

Question 3: Brentwood has the largest Thiessen polygon around it. If service centers were located in cities, some people in the Brentwood area would have to travel farther to reach a service center than anyone else in Contra Costa County.

Question 4: There are approximately 79,464 hectares of grassland in Contra Costa County.

Question 5: Yes, the statistical surface of ozone pollution based on IDW interpolation from a small number of sample points in Contra Costa County is similar to the statistical surface created by interpolating data from many more points collected both within Contra Costa County and beyond. Ozone concentration is higher in urban areas near the interior of the county and lower near San Francisco Bay. This statistical surface is not as accurate a representation of ozone pollution in Contra Costa County as the model created from more sample points, even though they are all from within the county. More sample points permit more accurate interpolation. Air pollution is not affected by political boundaries.

Balancing nature
with raster GIS

Learning objectives

In exercise 4, you will use the ArcMap Spatial Analyst extension to examine endangered red-legged frogs and prime farmland in Contra Costa County. You will learn to use ArcToolbox and ModelBuilder to create a raster showing suitability of land for a habitat conservation area (HCA) to preserve endangered red-legged frogs.

You will learn how to use ArcToolbox to do the following:

- set a toolbox *environment*
- *clip* a feature
- *dissolve* features
- *convert* vector features to rasters
- *reclassify* a raster
- *create a new toolbox* to store a model

You will learn how to use ModelBuilder to do the following:

- *create a suitability model*
- *assign properties* to a model
- *add components* to a model
- *run* a model
- add model *output* to a map
- *create a weighted overlay*

Step 1   Open Exercise_4

If ArcMap is already open, do the following:

Click *File*.

Click *Open*, navigate to the **TGAR\Part_2\Exercise_4** folder, then open the folder.

Open **Exercise_4.mxd**.

Click *No* if prompted to save changes.

Otherwise

Start ArcMap and choose to open an existing map.

Navigate to the **TGAR\Part_2\Exercise_4** folder, then open the folder.

Open **Exercise_4.mxd**.

A map of Contra Costa County opens with layers related to endangered red-legged frogs.

Step 2   Examine Exercise_4

There is some data that you are already familiar with from chapter 6: Contra Costa County, Bay Area counties, highways, rivers, red-legged frog habitat, and toxic release sites. There is also a layer of (hypothetical) frog sightings. Three additional raster layers show distance from rivers, toxic sites, and highways. There is also a raster layer for land cost.

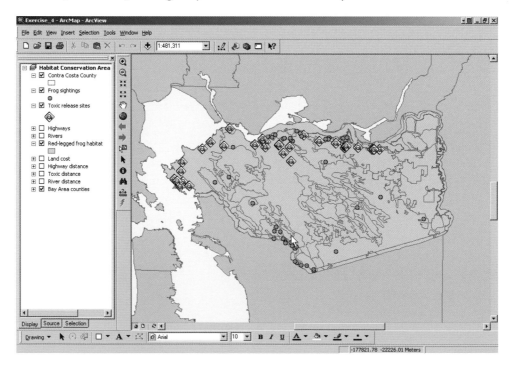

Step 3   Set an ArcToolbox toolbox environment

Click the *ArcToolbox* button 🎲 on the *Standard* toolbar.

The ArcToolbox window opens. Your screen should look something like this:

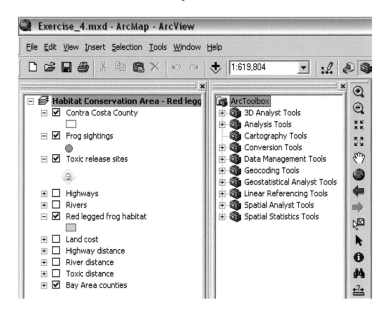

The location and size of the ArcToolbox window may be different on your computer screen. The number of toolboxes may differ depending on the version of ArcGIS you are using and what extensions are installed. Each *toolbox* 🎲 contains *toolsets* 🗂, and each toolset contains *tools* 🔨 that perform geoprocessing tasks. In this exercise, you will use tools from the *Analysis Tools, Conversion Tools, Data Management Tools,* and *Spatial Analysis Tools* toolboxes.

Remember from exercise 3 that before doing raster GIS analysis with ArcMap you need to set up a working environment. In exercise 3, this was accomplished through the Spatial Analyst toolbar. In this exercise, you will set the working environment from ArcToolbox. The *Environment Settings* in ArcToolbox are the same as when set from the Spatial Analyst toolbar.

Right-click the *ArcToolbox root folder* 🎲 .

Click *Environments.*

The *Environment Settings* dialog box opens.

Click *General Settings* from the *Environment Settings* list.

The *General Settings* window opens:

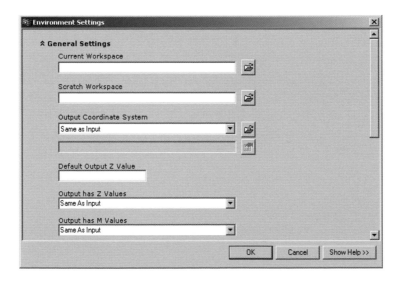

In the *Current Workspace*, click the **Browse folder** button .

Navigate to the **TGAR\MyWork** folder or another location you specified to save your work.

Make sure the folder name appears in the *Name* window in the dialog box.

Click **Add**.

Output you create will be saved in the folder you have specified.

Now you will set the output extent, cell size, and mask to be the same as the *Land cost* layer. (The *Land cost* layer is the same size and shape as Contra Costa County, so it is a good layer to set other layers to.)

In the *Environment Settings* dialog box, scroll down to the *Output Extent* box.

Click the **pull-down menu** and select *Same as Layer "Land cost"*.

Scroll to the top of the *Environment Settings* dialog box.

Click **General Settings** again to close the section. (*General Settings* appears at the top of the environment settings window.)

Click **Raster Analysis Settings** from the *Environment Settings* list.

Another *Environment Settings* dialog box opens. This time it is set to raster analysis settings.

In the *Cell Size* box, click the **pull-down menu** and select *Same as Layer "Land cost"*.

In the *Mask* box, click the **pull-down menu** and select *Land cost*.

Click **OK** to apply the settings and close the *Environment Settings* dialog box.

The environment is now set. It will be applied to any tool that you use.

You will begin by clipping the *Red-legged frog habitat* layer to match the *Contra Costa County* layer. Before clipping, the habitat layer covers an extent nearly one-half mile wider than the official political boundary of Contra Costa County.

Step 4   Clip a feature

Expand the *Analysis Tools* toolbox.

Each toolbox contains one or more toolsets. Within each toolset you'll find tools. The *Analysis Tools* toolbox offers three toolsets to choose from: *Extract*, *Overlay*, and *Proximity*.

Expand the *Extract* toolset.

The *Extract* toolset has a tool named *Clip*. Your toolbox may include a slightly different set of toolsets.

Double-click the **Clip** tool.

The *Clip* dialog box opens.

In the *Input Features* box, click the **pull-down menu** and select *Red-legged frog habitat*.

In the *Clip Features* box, click the **pull-down menu** and select *Contra Costa County*.

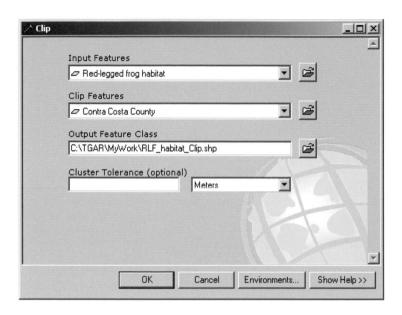

Notice the *Output Feature Class* box creates the name of the output feature class in the workspace you assigned in the *Environment Settings*. ArcMap assigns the new clipped feature class the default name *RLF_habitat_Clip.shp*. (If you can't see the file name, left-click and hold, then move your mouse to the right.)

Click *OK* to run the *Clip* process.

A dialog box opens to show the progress of the *Clip* process.

Click *Close* when the process is completed.

Collapse the *Extract* toolset.

Collapse the *Analysis Tools* toolbox.

A new layer appears in the data frame called *RLF habitat_Clip*.

You should see a new, smaller layer with some of the original purple *Red-legged frog habitat* layer remaining extending beyond it.

The *RLF_habitat_Clip* layer is confusing. It contains many polygons all symbolized in the same color. The polygons are based on several different classifications of the habitat layer. For this analysis, you will use an attribute named **rating,** which classifies habitat in Contra Costa County into three types based on the land's suitability for frogs: (1) Prime habitat, (2) Acceptable habitat, and (3) Unacceptable habitat.

Question 1: If you add a layer of all California state parks to the map and want to clip it to show only state parks within Contra Costa County, which layer would be the *Input Features* layer? The *Clip Features* layer? Using the analogy of cookie dough and a cookie cutter, which layer is the dough and which is the cookie cutter?

Step 5 Dissolve features

Turn off *Red-legged frog habitat*.

> The (clipped) boundaries of Contra Costa County are visible. Some frog sightings occurred just beyond the country borders.

Expand the *Data Management Tools* toolbox.

Expand the *Generalization* toolset.

Double-click **Dissolve**.

> The *Dissolve* dialog box opens.

In the *Input Features* box, click the **pull-down menu** and select *RLF_habitat_Clip*.

> The *Output Feature Class* box automatically names the shapefile in the workspace you selected.

In the *Dissolve_Field(s)* (optional) box, click the **rating** check box.

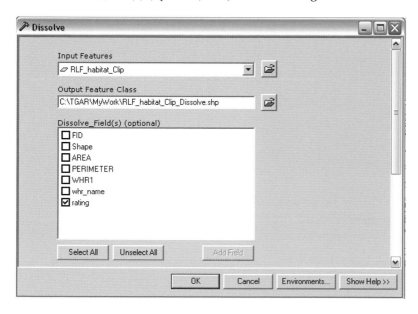

Click **OK**.

Close the *Dissolve* progress box when the process is complete.

> A new layer appears in the data frame called *RLF_habitat_Clip_Dissolve*. The layer contains only three features. They are based on the rating values in the table.

Question 2: If you wanted to dissolve all of the nine Bay Area Counties, what characteristics of a field would you need to do this? What would the resulting layer be like? Why might this be useful?

Collapse the *Generalization* toolset.

Collapse the *Data Management Tools* toolbox.

Turn off *RLF_habitat_Clip*.

Turn off *RLF_habitat_Clip_Dissolve*.

Step 6 Convert vector features to rasters

Expand the *Conversion Tools* toolbox.

Expand the *To Raster* toolset.

Double-click the **Feature to Raster** tool.

> The *Feature to Raster* dialog box opens.

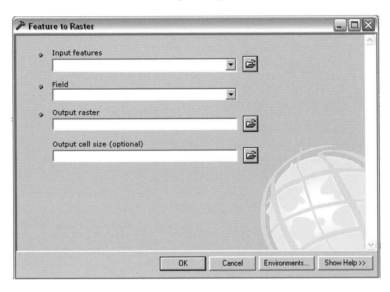

In the *Input features* box, click the **pull-down menu** and select *RLF_habitat_Clip_Dissolve*.

> The *Field*, *Output raster*, and *Output cell size* (optional) boxes automatically populate from the environment settings.

Change the cell size to **100**.

Click **OK**.

> A new layer appears in the data frame called *feature_rlf_1*. A random symbology has been applied.

Close the *Feature to Raster* progress box when the process is completed.

Open the *Properties for feature_rlf_1*.

Make sure the *General* tab is selected.

Rename the *feature_rlf_1* layer **Frog_habitat_grid**.

Click **OK** to rename the grid and close the *Layer Properties* dialog box.

Right-click **Frog_habitat_grid**.

Click **Open Attribute Table**.

> Notice the three values of 1, 2, and 3 and each corresponding count. In the value field, 1 represents prime frog habitat. The cell count shows that only a small amount of land in Contra Costa County is prime habitat for red-legged frogs (value 1); the balance of the county is about equally divided between acceptable habitat (value 2) and unacceptable habitat (value 3).

Close the *attribute table*.

Collapse the *To Raster* toolset.

Collapse the *Conversion Tools* toolbox.

Step 7   Reclassify a raster

In order to use the ArcToolbox *Reclassify* tool, you'll need to make sure the Spatial Analyst extension is turned on. If Spatial Analyst is not turned on, click **Tools** from the *Tools* menu. Click **Extensions**. Click the check box for Spatial Analyst to turn it on. Click the **Close** button. If the Spatial Analyst toolbar is not visible, click **View**, select *Toolbars*, click the **Spatial Analyst** toolbar, and drag it to the top right of your map application window.

Expand the Spatial Analyst *Tools* toolbox.

Expand the *Reclass* toolset.

Double-click the **Reclassify** tool.

In the *Input raster* box, click the **pull-down menu** and select *Frog_habitat_grid*.

The *Reclass field* and *Reclassification* boxes automatically populate.

In the *Reclassification* box under the *New values* column, replace the value of **2** with **5**. Then replace the value of **3** with **10**. When you reclassify the frog habitat, this will assign values that are more distinct from each other than sequential values like 1, 2, and 3. With numbers that are quite distinct when the layer is combined with other layers to complete a frog habitat conservation area model, the values will serve to differentiate cells in the resulting model. For example, when a high value like 10 (very bad for frogs) is added to other layers, the resulting layer will have quite a high value. This will make it very unlikely that that area would be chosen for a red legged frog habitat area.

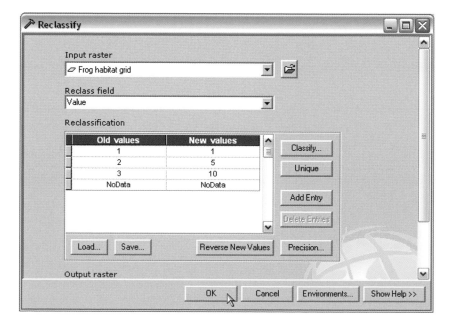

Click *OK* to begin the *reclassify* process.

Close the *progress* box when the process is completed.

> A new layer called *Reclass_Feat1* appears in the data frame. A random symbology has been applied to the new layer.

Question 3: If you made a mistake and classified land near highways with a low value like 1 and land far away from highways with a high value like 10, what would the impact of this mistake be on a model using this information to identify possible red-legged frog habitat conservation areas?

Right-click *Reclass_Feat1*.

Click *Open Attribute Table*.

> The old values of 1, 2, and 3 have been replaced by the new values of 1, 5, and 10.

Close the table.

Collapse the *Reclass* toolset.

Collapse the Spatial Analyst *Tools* toolbox.

Step 8   Import symbology

Right-click *Reclass_feat1*.

Click *Properties*.

Click the *Symbology* tab.

Click *Import*.

> In the *Look in* box, click the **pull-down menu** and navigate to the *Frog_analysis* folder in Exercise_4.

Click *Frog_habitat_raster_legend.lyr*.

> This is a layer (.lyr) file with symbology appropriate to symbolizing the frog habitat.

Click *Add*.

> New symbology appears, classifying the three categories of habitat. The prime habitat is bright red, acceptable habitat green, and unacceptable habitat beige.

Click the *General* tab and rename the layer **Reclass of frog habitat**.

Click *OK*.

> You will use the *Reclass of frog habitat* raster as one part of a model that will help you select land appropriate for a red-legged frog habitat conservation area (HCA).
>
> You will use ModelBuilder to build the model.
>
> First, you will create a new toolbox to store your model.

If you get confused as you build the model

You can open a file in the **TGAR\Exercise_2** folder named **Start_model**. **Start_model** begins with the files you have just created with the clip, dissolve, conversion from vector to raster, and resymbolization complete. That way you will not have to go back to the beginning of the exercise to build the model.

Step 9   Create a new toolbox to store a model

Right-click the *ArcToolbox root folder.*

Click *New Toolbox.*

A new toolbox appears named *Toolbox.*

Rename the new toolbox **HCA**. (HCA stands for habitat conservation area.)

Step 10   Create a model using ModelBuilder

The ArcGIS ModelBuilder allows users to create and store models. Once a model has been created, it can be run to produce a final output. A convenient use of models is if parameters of your project change or you want to run a model to make a prediction. You can simply change the inputs and rerun the model as many different times as you want.

The final output you want to create in this exercise is a map of potential frog habitat conservation areas to purchase. You will create a model that reclassifies highways, rivers, and toxic release sites. Then you will ask the model to combine these three layers plus the *Reclass of frog habitat* and *Land cost* layers with appropriate weights to create the HCA grid.

ModelBuilder can be used to build representation models like the straight line distance to libraries and distance allocation around used-oil disposal sites representation models you created in exercise 3. In this exercise, you will build a suitability model—a very useful type of model representing the suitability of geographical locations for some use. In this exercise, the model will represent the suitability of land in Contra Costa County for red-legged frogs.

Right-click the *HCA* toolbox.

Select *New.*

Click *Model.*

An icon showing that a model is present is added to the *HCA* toolbox:

The ModelBuilder dialog box opens.

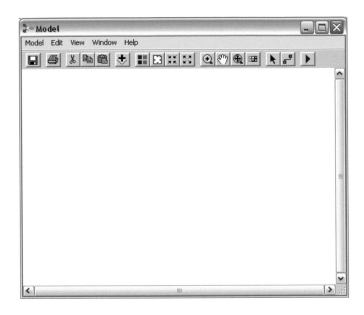

Step 11   Assign properties to a model

In the ModelBuilder window, click **Model** from the ModelBuilder Main menu.

Click **Model Properties**.

   The *Model Properties* dialog box opens.

Click the *General* tab.

In the *Name* field, enter **Frog habitat**.

In the *Label* field, enter **Frog habitat**.

In the *Description* box, enter "**Potential HCA areas for red-legged frogs.**" Your *Model Properties* dialog box should look like this:

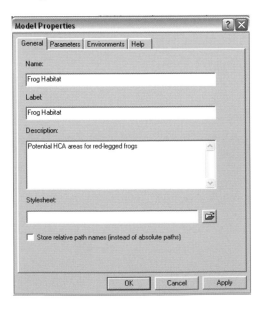

Click the *Environments* tab.

Expand the *General Settings*.

Click the check box for *Current Workspace*, *Output Coordinate System*, and *Output Extent*.

Click the *Raster Analysis Settings* check box to activate the *Cell size* and *Mask*.

Expand the *Raster Analysis Settings* to confirm your changes.

  The *Cell Size* and *Mask* check boxes are checked.

Click *OK* to apply the settings and close the *Model Properties* box.

Click the *Save* button 🖫 on the ModelBuilder toolbar.

Step 12   Add components to a model using ModelBuilder

Expand the Spatial Analyst *Tools* toolbox in ArcToolbox.

Expand the *Reclass* toolset.

Click the *Reclassify* tool, hold down the left mouse button, and drag the *Reclassify* tool into the ModelBuilder window.

Release the left mouse button to drop the tool into the center of the ModelBuilder window. Your screen should look like this:

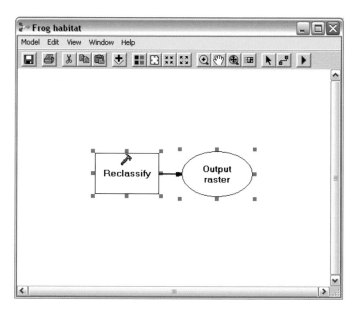

Two elements appear—the *tool* (a rectangle with the word *Reclassify* in it) and *Output raster* (an oval). Both have a clear fill color indicating the model is incomplete and blue squares indicating the elements are currently selected. Now you will add an input data element to complete a model.

Click the *Highway distance* layer on the data frame, hold down the left mouse button, and drag it directly on top of the *Reclassify* tool (the rectangle).

Release the left mouse button.

The *Highway distance* appears as a blue oval connected to the *Reclassify* tool, which changes to a yellow rectangle connected to an *Output raster* (green oval).

Click in the white space to remove the blue bounding boxes.

The ModelBuilder window should look like this:

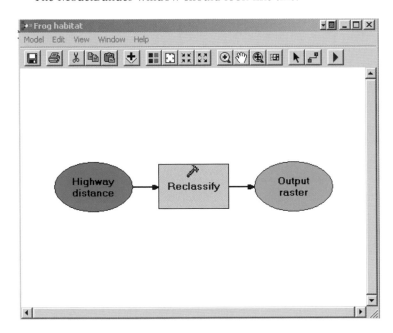

The colors indicate the model is ready to run. Default settings to the reclassify tool will be applied if you run the model. You need to change these defaults.

Step 13   Reclassify the data

You would like to classify distance from highways into just two classes: 1 (good) for distance more than one mile from highways; 5 (bad) for distances closer to highways.

Double-click the **Reclassify** tool (yellow rectangle).

The *Reclassify* dialog box opens and is populated with information already. If you scroll down, you can see the file has ten classes in addition to *NoData*—too many classes for our analysis.

The classification will need to be edited so that the output has only two classes.

Click the **Classify** button.

In the *Classification* section, change the *Method* from *Manual* to *Natural Breaks (Jenks)* and set the number of *Classes* to **2**.

In the *Break Values* box, enter **1688** (meters) for the first break value. One thousand, six-hundred-eighty-eight meters is approximately one mile.

Click **OK**.

In the *New values* column, change the value of **1** to **5** and the value of **2** to **1**.

The values are reclassified into just two classes. Your screen should look like this:

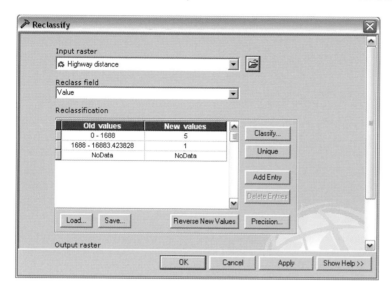

This assigns a low (good) value of 1 for areas that are more than a mile from the highway. This models the fact that from one mile and beyond the red-legged frogs are safe from the danger that highways pose. The value of 5 (bad) indicates that the land within one mile of the highway is not very good for frogs. The value of 5 is higher (significantly worse) than a value of 2, so that when this layer is added to other values in a model, areas near highways will get a quite high value and will not be chosen for a habitat conservation area.

Click **OK** to close the *Reclassify* dialog box.

Right-click the ***Reclass_high1*** oval.

Click **Open** and change the file name to **rc_hwy**.

Click **OK**.

The output file will be processed and saved in the folder you specified in the *General Settings*. Note: The output file name cannot have more than thirteen characters and no embedded blanks.

Step 14   Run a model

Click the ***Run*** button ▶ at the top right of ModelBuilder.

The model will run as a process. A *progress* box will appear, and the model will highlight the active process in red. In this case, there is just one process (reclassify), so the *Reclassify* rectangle turns red as the reclassification is taking place. The model may take several minutes to complete.

Close the *progress* box when the process is complete.

The shadows underneath the *Reclassify* rectangle and the *rc_hwy* oval indicate that the model has been run.

Minimize ModelBuilder so you can see the entire ArcMap application window.

ModelBuilder did not add the new layer to your map. You can right-click *rc_hwy* and click **Add** to add the layer, or add it using the *Add* button. In the next step, you will add it using the *Add* button.

Step 15   Add model output to a map

In ArcMap, click the **Add Data** button and navigate to the current workspace—**TGAR\MyWork** or another location you specified.

Add the *rc_hwy* raster.

Notice the layer is reclassified into the two categories you assigned. All the land in Contra Costa County is classified into two types: land within a mile of a highway (bad for frogs) and all other land.

Now you will reclassify the other layers: *Toxic_distance* and *River_distance*.

Step 16   Create additional model elements

Repeat step 12 to create an output raster for *Toxic distance*.

Rename the resulting output raster *rc_tox*.

The model should look like this:

Notice that there are no shadows in this model. This shows that the model has not yet been run.

Click the **Save** button 💾 to save your work.

When you have created the new model, double-click the **Reclassify** rectangle for *Toxic distance*.

Click the **Classify** button and change the classification to *Equal Interval* with 5 classes.

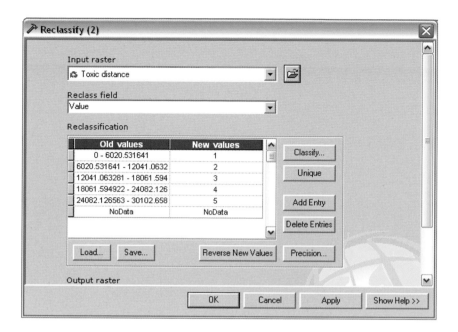

Click **OK** and return to the *Reclassification* dialog box.

Click the **Reverse New Values** button.

    Now the lowest (best) score corresponds to areas farthest away from toxic release sites.

Click **OK** to apply the new values and to close the *Reclassification* dialog box.

Repeat step 12 again to create an output raster for *River distance*.

Rename the resulting output raster *rc_riv*. The model should look like this:

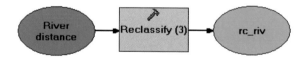

Click the **Save** button to save your work.

Double-click the **Reclassify** rectangle for *River distance*.

Click the **Classify** button and change the classification to *Equal Interval* with 3 classes.

In the *Break Values* field, enter **540** and **3700** for the first two values.

Click **OK** to return to the *Reclassification* dialog box.

In the *New values* column, change the value of **2** to **3** and the value **3** to **5**.

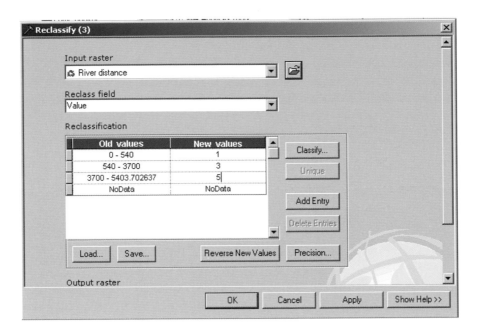

Click **OK** to apply the new values and to close the *Reclassification* dialog box.

Now all of the layers are ready to be used in the model.

Click and drag the *Reclass of frog habitat* and *Land_cost* layers into the ModelBuilder window. Use the following graphic as a guide:

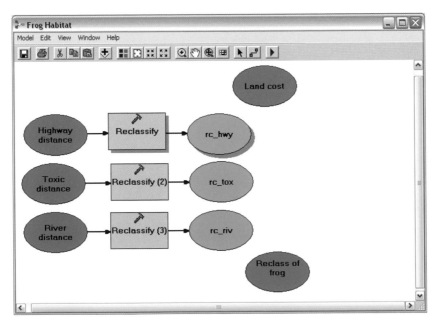

Click *Save* on the ModelBuilder toolbar.

Question 4: If you thought that actual sightings of red-legged frogs were a positive indicator that nearby land (say land within one thousand feet of a sighting) was appropriate for a red-legged frog habitat conservation area, how might you include this element in a habitat conservation area model?

Step 17   Find the Weighted Overlay tool

You will complete the model by adding the last element, a *Weighted Overlay*. This will allow layers containing different units to be added using a common scale. You can also apply an influence on how much each layer is scaled.

There is a tool to create a *Weighted Overlay*. If you don't know where any tool is located, you can search for it.

At the bottom of the ArcToolbox window, click the *Search* tab.

Type *Weighted Overlay*.

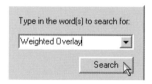

Click the *Search* button.

In the *Tool* column, highlight *Weighted Overlay*.

Click *Locate*.

You can see the *Weighted Overlay* tool is located in the Spatial Analyst *Tools* toolbox in the *Overlay* toolset.

Step 18   Create a Weighted Overlay

Click and drag the **Weighted Overlay** tool from the ArcToolbox into the ModelBuilder window to the right of the *rc_tox* oval. You may need to resize the window to see the tool entirely.

Double-click the **Weighted Overlay** tool.

Scroll down until you see the *Evaluation scale* section on the left side.

Notice the three text boxes to the right of the *Evaluation scale*.

Enter **1** for *From*, **10** for *To*, and **1** for *By*.

Click **OK**.

Click the **Connect Elements** tool.

The mouse pointer changes to a wand when you move it over the ModelBuilder window.

Click inside the blue oval of *Land cost*, hold down the mouse button, and drag the wand toward the *Weighted Overlay* tool.

A blue arrow appears.

Keep dragging until the blue arrow is inside the *Weighted Overlay* tool rectangle and release the mouse button.

The *Weighted Overlay* should now have a color fill indicating it is ready to run.

Connect each of the remaining four elements (*rc_hwy, rc_riv, rc_tox*, and *Reclass of frog habitat*) to the *Weighted Overlay* tool.

Click the **Save** button 💾 to save your work.

Double-click **Weighted Overlay** once more.

Click the **Collapse Arrow** ⦙ in the Raster column for each row.

Assign an influence of 30% to *Reclass of frog habitat* and *Land cost*, 20% to *rc_hwy*, and 10% to *rc_riv* and *rc_tox*.

If necessary, click anywhere in the gray margin to clear the red and white error indicator.

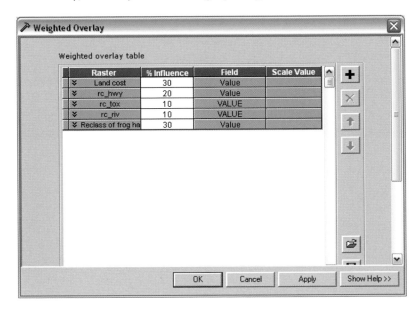

Click **OK** to close the *Weighted Overlay* dialog box.

Double-click the element for the *Weighted Overlay* output (the green oval named *Weighte_land1*).

Click the **Browse folder** button 📂 .

Navigate to the **TGAR\MyWork** folder or another location you specified to save your work and save the output file as *HCA_grid*.

Click **OK** to close the *Weighte_Land1* dialog box.

The output element name changes to *HCA_grid*.

Now you finally have a complete model to run.

Your final model should resemble the diagram below:

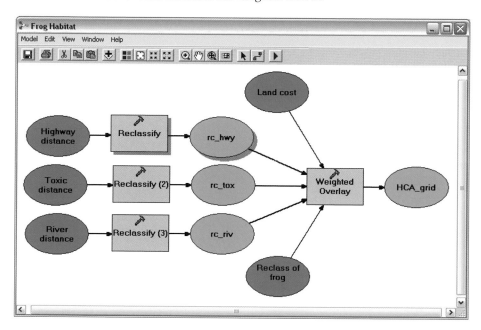

Question 5: Imagine that you have just finished describing your model at a conference of the Endangered Frog Society of America (EFSA). Your professional colleagues are enthusiastic about your research, but in the discussion that follows a consensus develops that your model understates the importance of distance from rivers and overstates the importance of land costs. What could you do?

Step 19   Run the model

Click the **Run** button ▶ .

> The process may take several minutes to complete as it will run three processes. The model shows four processes (represented by yellow rectangles), but the reclassified *Highway distance* has already been created, as you can tell from the shading.

Close the *progress* box when the process is complete.

Close the ModelBuilder dialog box.

Click **Yes** if you are prompted to save the model.

Step 20   Add the HCA_grid and change symbology

Click the **Add Data** button in ArcMap, navigate to the folder where you specified output rasters, and add the new *hca_grid*.

A map of Contra Costa County opens with land classified based on your weighted overlay. However, the symbology is poor. You would like the land to be symbolized so that you clearly see how appropriate different land is for the HCA. Ideally, your symbology should make prime habitat stand out, with the balance of the county symbolized with just two values for acceptable and unacceptable habitat.

Right-click the *hca_grid* layer.

Click *Properties*.

Click the *Symbology* tab.

Use the drop-down color ramp to apply an appropriate monochromatic color.

Make sure the lightest shade represents the value of 1. You may need to flip the ramp colors.

Click *OK* to close the *Layer Properties* dialog box.

Now it is easier to see where the best areas are to establish a habitat conservation area, at least based on the assumptions and input from this model.

Next you will import symbology similar to that of the original habitat layer. This will group values into three classes: Prime HCA property, Acceptable HCA property, and Unacceptable HCA property.

Open the *hca_grid* layer properties again.

If necessary, click the *Symbology* tab.

Click the *Import* button and navigate to the **Exercise _4 Frog analysis** folder.

Add the *hca_grid_raster_legend.lyr*.

Click *Add*.

The HCA classification symbology is applied.

Click *OK* to close the *Layer Properties* dialog box.

Try applying your own ideas of model parameters in the weighted overlay tool, running the model, and analyzing the results. Remember all of the processes are already done and saved in your model.

If you are continuing with the next exercise, leave ArcMap open. Otherwise, click the *File* menu and click *Exit*. Click *No* if prompted to save your changes.

Congratulations—you have created your first model using ModelBuilder.

Answers to exercise 4 questions

Question 1 (step 4)

The *Input Features* layer would be *state parks* (the layer that acts like cookie dough). The *Clip Features* layer would be *Contra Costa County* (the layer that is like a cookie cutter). The resulting layer would contain just state parks within Contra Costa County.

Question 2 (step 5)

If you dissolved all of the nine Bay Area counties, you would need to have a field that was common to all of them such as the name California (indicating they are all in California). The resulting layer would be shaped like the outer outline of the nine counties, but would not contain county boundaries. A dissolve like this might be useful in a small-scale map of the western United States to show where the San Francisco Bay Area is located.

Question 3 (step 7)

If you made a mistake and assigned areas close to highways a low number like 1 (indicating excellent land for a red-legged frog habitat) and land farther away a value of 10 (indicating very poor for red-legged frog habitat), the resulting model would be much more likely to include land near highways in recommended red-legged frog habitat.

Question 4 (step 16)

If you wanted to include frog sightings in your model, you might create one-thousand-foot buffers around each frog sighting and create a layer with dichotomous values: 1 if the area was within a buffer, and 0 if it was not in a buffer. You could assign land that had a value of 1 (within a thousand feet of a frog sighting) a positive value in the model.

Question 5 (step 18)

You could change the weights assigned to distance from rivers and land cost in your model. For example, you might reduce the weight of land cost in the model from 30 percent to 20 percent and increase the weight of distance from rivers from 10 percent to 30 percent. You would not have to create a new model from scratch—simply tweak the values in the existing model and rerun it. Sophisticated models are constantly extended and calibrated based on better measurements or new theory. Operationally, you could just open the properties of the weighted overlay and type in different percentage figures.

Your Turn

1. If you are continuing from Exercise_4, navigate to the **TGAR\Part_2\ Exercise_4\YourTurn** folder, double-click the folder to open it, and open the *YourTurn_4.mxd file*. Click **No** when prompted to "Save changes to Exercise_4?"

   Otherwise open ArcMap and navigate to the **TGAR\Part_2\ Exercise_4\YourTurn** folder, double click the folder to open it, and open the *YourTurn_4.mxd* file.

2. A map opens showing habitat for the California vole. You will create a potential vole habitat conservation area (HCA) using tools from ArcToolbox.

   Question 1: If you were going to just analyze land within the city of Brentwood, which covers only a small part of the total land area within Contra Costa County, would you set your cell size to be larger or smaller than if you were going to analyze land in the entire county?

3. Make sure the Spatial Analyst extension is turned on, then set up the ArcToolbox environment. Use the same environment setting as in exercise 4.

   Question 2: Why is 100 meters an appropriate cell size for this analysis?

4. Clip the *vole habitat* layer to match the *Contra Costa County* layer.

   Question 3: In this clip, which is the *Input features* layer and which is the *Clip features* layer?

5. Dissolve the new clipped layer (*Vole_habitat_Clip*) by **LANDTYP**.
6. Convert the new dissolved vector layer to a raster grid with a cell size of 100.
7. Reclassify the new raster habitat grid to have four classes—unacceptable for water and woodland where voles cannot live, poor for barren and urban land, good for woodlands and croplands, and excellent for the grasslands that voles prefer. Rename the new raster **Vole_habitat_reclass**. Use the following values for the reclassification:

Old value	Meaning	New value	Suitability for voles
1	Barren	7	Poor
2	Croplands	3	Good
3	Grasslands	1	Excellent
4	Urban	7	Poor
5	Water	10	Unacceptable
6	Wetlands	10	Unacceptable
7	Woodlands	3	Good

8. Reclassify river distance using the *Value* field to have three classes using the natural breaks method. Name the reclassified layer *river_reclass*.

9. Reclassify highway distance using the *Value* field to have five classes using the equal interval method. Name the reclassified layer *hwy_reclass*.

10. In ArcToolbox, create a new toolbox. Name it *vole_toolbox*. Add a new model to the toolbox. Name it *vole_suitability_model*.

11. Using the Model Properties tab, name the model *Vole habitat*, label it "Contra Costa County vole habitat," and write the following description: "Suitability analysis of Contra Costa County vole habitat."

12. Add the *Vole_habitat_reclass*, *River_reclass*, *Hwy_reclass*, and *Land_cost* layers to ModelBuilder.

13. Add the *Weighted Overlay* tool to ModelBuilder.

14. Connect the four layers to the *Weighted Overlay* tool.

15. In the Evaluation scale section of the *Weighted Overlay* dialog box, enter 1 to 10 by 1. Assign 25% to the percentage influence of each of the four variables.

16. Run the model.

17. Add the raster created by the model showing suitability of land in Contra Costa County for voles to your map.

Answers to exercise 4 Your Turn questions

Question 1: If you were going to analyze only land in a small area, such as Brentwood, you could set your cell size to be smaller than if you were analyzing the entire county. A smaller cell size would not increase the accuracy of your results.

Question 2: A cell size of 100 meters is appropriate because the cell size—about 900 square feet—is large enough to populate a geographical area as large as a county with an appropriate number of grid cells. Grid cells an inch on a side would be much too small; grid cells a mile on a side would be too big. Since cells 100 x 100 meters are one hectare in size and hectares are common units of measurement, this is a good choice.

Question 3: The *Input features* layer would be vole habitat. The *Clip features* layer would be Contra Costa County.

Exercise **5**

Creating map symbology

Learning objectives

In exercise 5, you will continue to work with data (a) at the world scale that you examined in exercise 1—historical city population data from authors Tertius Chandler and Gerald Fox and United Nations data on current world city populations, (b) at the regional level on Burlington and Camden counties in southern New Jersey with data that University of Minnesota law professor Myron Orfield assembled, and (c) at the local level on a subset of Orfield's data within the older core city of Camden and the nearby growing suburb of Mount Laurel. You will learn how to do the following:

- set the *color* of a *data frame* background
- set the *fill color* of a *polygon*
- set the *width* of a *polygon outline*
- *symbolize* points by *size*, *shape*, and *color*
- *symbolize* points using *graduated symbols*
- *symbolize* points using *proportional symbols*
- *autolabel* features
- change label *symbology*
- change label *placement*
- *symbolize* features with *unique colors*
- create a *monochromatic color ramp* showing absolute values
- *symbolize* features with *unique values*
- *normalize* data

- *symbolize* a line feature with *mimetic symbols*
- create a *dot density* map
- change symbology using the *classification dialog box*
- do *advanced editing* of symbol properties
- create a *buffer*
- make a layer *transparent*

Step 1   Open and examine Exercise_5a

If ArcMap is already open, do the following:

Click *File*.

Click *Open*, navigate to the **TGAR\Part_3\Exercise_5** folder, then open the folder.

Open **Exercise_5a.mxd.**

Click *No* if prompted to save changes.

Otherwise

Start ArcMap and choose to open an existing map.

Navigate to the **TGAR\Part_3\Exercise_5** folder, then open the folder.

Open **Exercise_5a.mxd.**

A map opens with one data frame named *Cities of the past*. The *Countries* and *Cities 1600* layers are turned on. Your screen should look like this:

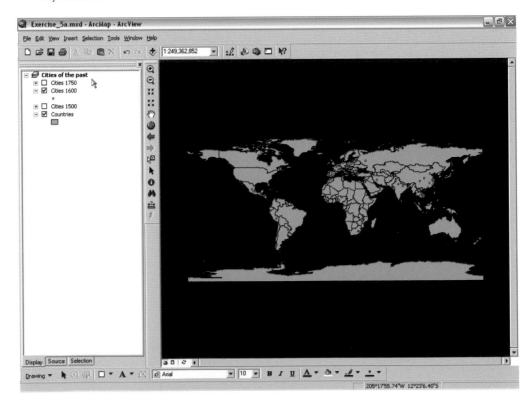

The map has terrible symbology. The data frame background is black, the vector country polygons are cantaloupe colored, and the cities (vector GIS point data) are tiny green circles. Drawing on material in chapter 10, you will change the map symbology to make the map more aesthetically pleasing and easier to interpret.

Question 1: Would you change the symbology of each of the following features? If so, how would you change them?
  (a) the color of the data frame (ocean)
  (b) the fill color of the cities
  (c) the fill color of the countries
  (d) the size of the cities

Step 2   Set the color of a data frame background

Right-click the data frame name *Cities of the past*.
Click *Properties*.
Click the *Frame* tab if necessary.
Click the *Background* pull-down menu.
Click *Lt Cyan*.
Click *OK*.

  The background of the map changes to a light cyan color to symbolize the ocean.

Step 3   Set the fill color of a polygon

Click the symbol for the *Countries* layer in the table of contents.

  The *Symbol Selector* dialog box opens. On the right side of the dialog box, three properties can be edited: *Fill Color*, *Outline Width*, and *Outline Color*.

Click the *Fill Color* pull-down menu.
Click the *Sahara Sand* color patch (top row, third column).

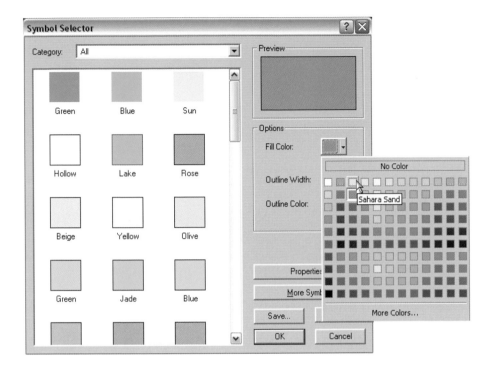

Click **OK**.

> The color of the countries changes to a neutral yellow color. There is a problem. The country borders are from 2000, but the cities are from 1600. Many of the country borders were different in 1600 than they were in 2000.

Step 4   Set the width of a polygon outline

Click the **Countries** symbol again.

Change the *Outline Width* to 0.

Click **OK**.

> The country borders disappear and just the shapes of the continents remain. There are no outlines.

Step 5   Symbolize points by size, shape, and color

Click the small green point symbol for **Cities 1600**.

> The *Symbol Selector* window opens.

Click the **Triangle 1** symbol in the *Symbol Selector* window.

In the *Options* box, change the *Color* to a bright red and the *Size* value to 6.

Click **OK**.

> The *Cities 1600* symbol size changes to 6 points and becomes a triangular shape and red color.
>
> Your screen should look like the one on the following page:

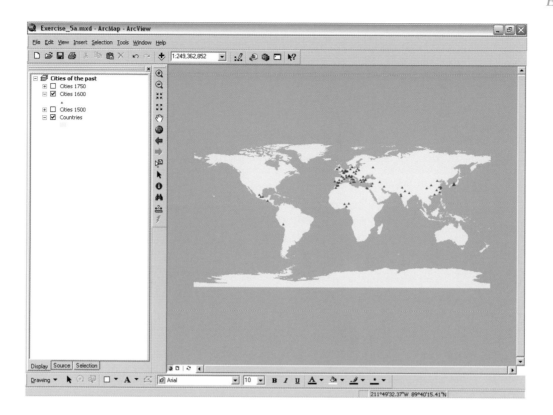

Step 6   Symbolize points using graduated symbols

Click the *View* pull down menu.

Click *Bookmarks*.

Click the *Europe* bookmark.

> The map zooms to Europe.

Turn off *Cities 1600*.

Turn on *Cities 1500*.

Right-click the *Cities 1500* layer.

Click *Properties*.

> The *Symbology* tab should be open. If not, click it.

Click *Quantities* in the *Show* box on the left.

Click *Graduated symbols*.

In the *Fields* section, click the *Value* box *pull-down menu*.

Click **1500_POP**.

> The size of the city point symbols changes so that there are five different sizes of point symbols.
>
> Larger point symbols indicate larger cities.

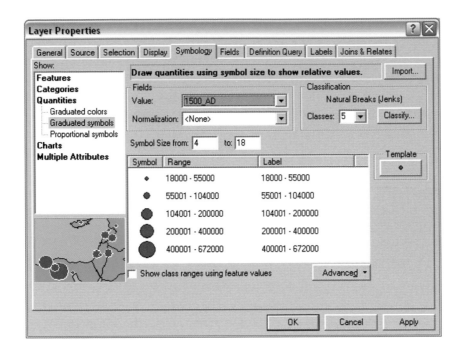

Question 2: Is the default value of five classes appropriate? Would you increase or decrease the number of classes? Why?

Click *OK*.

The cities are symbolized with graduated symbols.

Step 7   Symbolize points using proportional symbols

Make sure the map is zoomed in to Europe. Use the *Europe* bookmark if it is not.

Right-click the **Cities 1500** layer.

Click *Properties*.

The *Layer Properties* box opens. The *Symbology* tab should already be open and *Graduated Symbols* under quantities selected in the *Show* window. If not, click the *Symbology* tab and click *Quantities* in the *Show* window.

Click *Proportional symbols*.

In the *Fields* section, click the **Value** box pull-down menu and click **1500_POP**.

A new box opens below the *Fields* box named *Symbol*. In this box you can change the symbol sizes.

Click the **Min Value** button and change the size to **4**.

Click *OK*.

Click the *Number of Symbols to display in the Legend* **pull-down arrow** and click **5**.

Click **OK**.

> The size of the city point symbols changes. There are five different sizes of circles with population labels in the table of contents. The circles are proportional to the population size of the cities. Your screen should look like this:

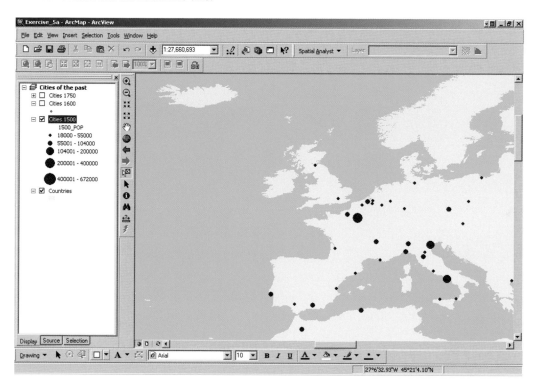

Click the **View** pull-down menu.

Click **Bookmarks**.

Click the **Asia** bookmark. Your screen should look like the screen on the following page:

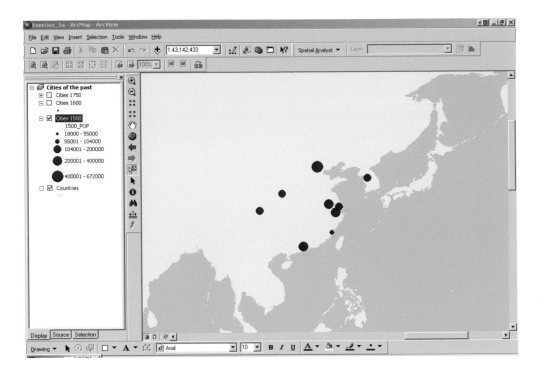

Question 3: How does the population of Paris in 1500 (the largest city in Europe at that time) compare to the population of large cities in China: Peking (Beijing), Hangchow, Nanking, and Canton? Refer to the attribute table to find the populations of these cities.

Step 8   Autolabel the cities

Click the *View* pull-down menu.

Click *Bookmarks*.

Click the *England* bookmark.

> The map zooms in to England. Only London, England, and Edinburgh, Scotland, had populations of 18,000 or greater in 1500.

Turn off *Cities 1500* and collapse its legend.

Turn on *Cities 1750*.

Right-click *Cities 1750*.

Click *Label Features*.

> The names of the cities appear. In autolabeling, the city reads the text from a field in the attribute table. One of the fields is the city's name. ArcMap assigns the name to the point.

Right-click the **Cities 1750** layer and uncheck *Label Features*.

> The labels disappear. *Label Features* is a toggle.

Turn the labels back on.

> These labels are helpful, but the font is a little small and there are some placement problems.

Step 9 Change label symbology

Right-click the *Cities 1750* layer.

Click *Properties*.

Click the *Labels* tab (the second tab from the right). The *Labels* tab opens up. Notice three options for labeling features: *Text String*, *Text Symbol*, and *Other Options*.

In the *Text Symbol* box click the *Symbol* button.

The *Symbol Selector* dialog box appears. This time it provides choices for editing text rather than features.

Click the *Color* patch in the *Options* box and click *Black*.

Click the *Size* pull-down menu and click *12* for the font size.

Click the *font style* pull-down menu and change the font style to Arial.

Click the *Italics* button to remove the italics.

Click the *Bold* button below the font option to make the font bold.

Click *OK*.

Click *OK* again.

The label color, size, and font have been changed to more appropriate settings.

Step 10 Change label placement

Right-click the *Cities 1750* layer.

Click *Properties*.

If the *Labels* tab is not already selected, click the *Labels* tab. Click the *Placement Properties* button in the *Other Options* box at the bottom of the screen.

If necessary, click the *Placement* tab.

Click the *Change Location* button.

Use the slider on the right to scroll down to see different label placement options. Click the *Prefer Top Left, all allowed* icon.

Click *OK*.

Click *OK* to close the *Placement Properties* dialog box.

Click *OK* to close the *Layer Properties* dialog box.

The label placement changes so that labels appear at the top left of the cities. Your screen should look like the screen on the following page:

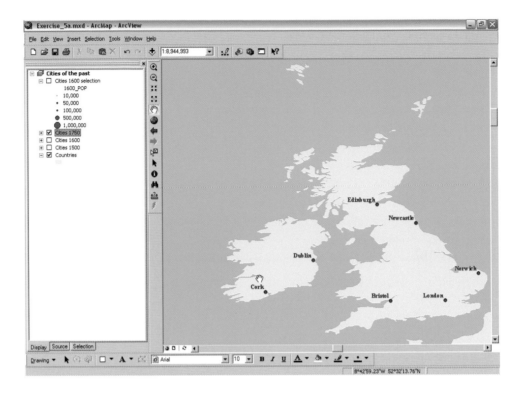

Step 11   Open and examine Exercise_5b

Click the *File* pull-down menu.

Click *Open*.

Navigate to the **Exercise_5** folder.

Open **Exercise_5b.mxd**.

> Click *No* when asked if you want to "Save changes to Exercise_5a?"

> A map opens with one data frame showing the boundaries of Camden (red) and Burlington (purple) counties in southwest New Jersey.

Step 12   Symbolize features with unique colors

Right-click the *Municipalities* layer.

Click *Properties*.

Click the *Symbology* tab.

Click *Categories* from the *Show* window on the left.

Click *Unique Values*.

Click the *Value Field* pull-down menu and select **NAME** as the value by which to classify the cities.

Click the *Add All Values* button.

> Each municipality is added. The colors are assigned at random.

Your *Color Scheme* box should contain colors in a style. (This box acts as a toggle. If a word describing a color scheme is in the box, right-click and uncheck *Graphic View* to toggle the color scheme on.)

Right-click the **colors** in the *Color Scheme* box.

Uncheck *Graphic View*.

Select *Pastels* from the pull-down menu.

The colors change to pastels.

Right-click **Pastels** in the *Color Scheme* box.

Uncheck *Graphic View* to toggle from the word *Pastels* to the pastel color scheme represented by the colors themselves.

Your screen should look like this:

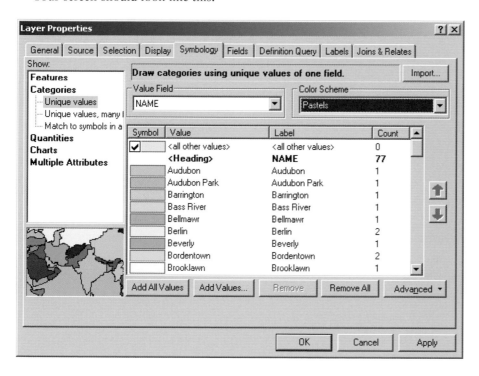

Click **OK** to close the *Layer Properties* dialog box.

The municipality polygons are filled with their new unique symbology.

Step 13   Create a monochromatic color ramp showing absolute values

Right-click the **Municipalities** layer.

Click **Properties**.

The *Symbology* tab should already be selected. If not, click it.

Click **Quantities**.

Click *Graduated colors.*

In the *Fields* section, click the *Value* pull-down menu.

Click **TOTPOP**.

In the *Color Ramp* pull-down menu, select the *Blue Light to Dark* color ramp.

Accept the default in the *Classification* box of five classes classified using the *Natural Breaks* (*Jenks*) method.

Click *OK.*

> The map shows each municipality's population using a graduated range of values.

Step 14   Symbolize features with unique values

Click the *View* pull-down menu.

Click *Bookmarks.*

Click the *Cities of Camden and Mount Laurel* bookmark.

Right-click the *Municipalities* layer.

Click *Properties.*

The *Symbology* tab should already be selected. If not, click it.

Click *Categories* from the *Show* window on the left

Unique Values should already be selected. If not, click it.

Click the *Value Field* pull-down menu and select **NAME** as the value by which to classify the municipalities.

Click the *Add Values* button.

In the *Add Values* dialog box, scroll down the list and click *Camden.*

Hold down the Control key on the keyboard.

In the *Add Values* dialog box, scroll down the list farther and click *Mount Laurel.*

Click *OK.*

> Both Camden and Mount Laurel appear with a random color in the dialog box.

Double-click the symbol for *<all other values>* .

> The *Symbol Selector* dialog box opens.

Click the *Fill Color* patch.

Click *No Color.*

Click *OK* to close the *Symbol Selector* dialog box.

Double-click the *symbol* for Camden.

Click the *Fill Color* patch.

Click *No Color.*

Click the *Outline Color* patch.

Click *Mars Red* (third row, second column).

Change the *Outline Width* value to **2**.

Click *OK* to close the *Symbol Selector* dialog box.

Repeat this process for *Mount Laurel*, except make the outline color *Amethyst.*

> Amethyst is in the third row, eleventh column (the second column from the right).

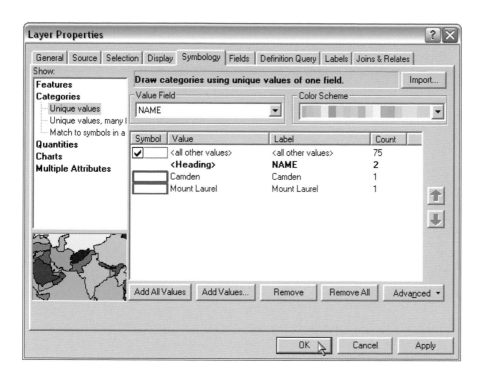

Click **OK** to close the *Layer Properties* dialog box.

Step 15   Normalize data

Turn on the *Census blocks* layer.

Right-click the **Census blocks** layer.

Click **Properties**.

The *Symbology* tab should already be selected. If not, click it.

Click **Quantities**.

Graduated colors should already be selected. If not, click it.

In the *Fields* section, click the **Value** pull-down menu.

Click the value **BLACK**.

The sample size warning appears.

Click **OK** twice to dismiss the warning.

Question 4: Based on chapter 10, what does normalizing data do? Why is normalizing the African-American population of Camden and Burlington counties helpful in understanding spatial segregation?

Select **POP2000** from the *Fields Normalization* pull-down menu.

The sample size warning appears.

Click **OK** twice to dismiss the warning.

In the *Color Ramp* pull-down menu, select a *Yellow to Red* color ramp.

Right-click any of the ***range symbols.***

Click ***Properties for All Symbols.***

In the *Symbol Selector* dialog box; change the *Outline Width* to 0.

Click **OK** to close the *Symbol Selector* dialog box.

Click the ***Label*** column header.

Select ***Format Labels.***

 The *Number Format* dialog box opens.

Click ***Number of decimal places*** (in the rounding section) and change the number of decimal places from 4 to 2.

Click **OK** to close the *Number Format* dialog box.

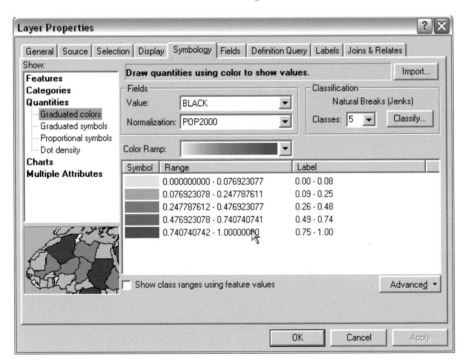

Click **OK**.

 A map showing the percentage of African-Americans in census blocks in Camden and Burlington counties in 2000 appears. Since the census blocks have different sizes and different total populations, this map makes it much easier to see where African-Americans are concentrated. Census blocks where African-Americans have a value of zero do not appear because a division by zero results in no value.

Turn on the ***Census blocks background*** layer.

A background layer appears where there was no data, improving the appearance of the map. African-Americans are quite concentrated in some areas and not in others. Camden is one area of heavy concentration, but not the only one. Mount Laurel has a much lower percentage of African-Americans than Camden, but higher percentages than some other areas.

Step 16   Look at the location of African-Americans in Mount Laurel and Camden

Use the *Mount Laurel* bookmark to zoom in to the Mount Laurel area.

The block colors are quite light with many yellow blocks indicating low percentages of African-Americans living in these blocks in 2000.

Zoom to Camden using the *Camden* bookmark.

The block colors are much darker, indicating high percentages of African-Americans living in these blocks in 2000.

Turn off the *Census blocks* and *Census blocks background* layers.

Step 17   Symbolize a line feature with mimetic symbols

Turn on the *Camden streets* layer.

Expand *Camden streets*.

Click the gray line symbolizing major arterials.

Among the symbols that appear, some look like different types of streets and roads. For example, a symbol with two solid lines and a broken line in the middle looks like a divided highway. You could use one of these mimetic symbols to symbolize major arterials.

Click the **More Symbols** pull-down menu.

Click *Transportation*.

Additional transportation-related symbols are added to the symbol selector window. These symbols have been placed below the default symbols, so you need to scroll down to see them.

Scroll down through the list of symbols until you find symbol **A08**.

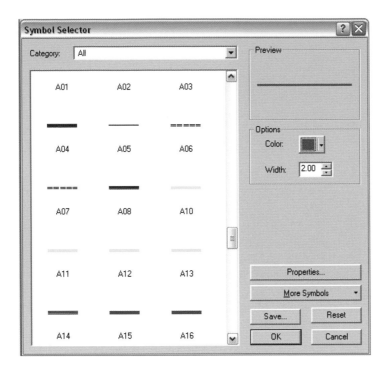

Click symbol *A08*.

Enter **4** as the Width in the *Options* field to the right.

Click *OK*.

The symbology of the major arterial changes to a thick red line with a black line divider.

Click the line symbolizing the *Streets*.

Click the *Residential Street* symbol.

Click *OK*.

The *Roads* layer has already been symbolized. If you wish, change the symbology of the roads to an appropriate transportation symbol and size of your choosing.

Close **Exercise_5b**. Do not save changes.

Step 18   Create a dot density map

Navigate to the **Exercise_5c folder** and open Exercise_5c.mxd.

A map opens with two data frames: one of Mount Laurel, New Jersey, and the other of Camden, New Jersey. Make sure the Mount Laurel data frame is active.

The Mount Laurel map has three layers: (a) the outline of the township itself in black, (b) census blocks in a single symbol (Sahara Sand), and (c) elementary schools symbolized as 8-point Mars Red circles.

The 2000 Census reported 2,367 African-Americans living in Mount Laurel. You are interested in where the township's African-American population is located in relation to the elementary schools.

Right-click the *Census blocks* layer.

Click *Properties*.

The *Symbology* tab should already be selected. If not, click it.

Click *Quantities*.

Click *Dot density*.

Click **BLACK** from the *Field Selection* list.

Click the right arrow   [>]   to move **BLACK** into the *Symbol Field* column.

If necessary, enter **2** for *Dot Size*.

Enter **1** for *Dot Value* (one dot represents the approximate location of one African-American within a census block).

Double-click the *dot* in the *Symbol* column. (You may have to look hard to see the dot. It is small and may be in a light color.)

Click the *Color* pull-down menu and change the color to Yogo Blue. Yogo Blue is in the second row, tenth column.

Click *OK*.

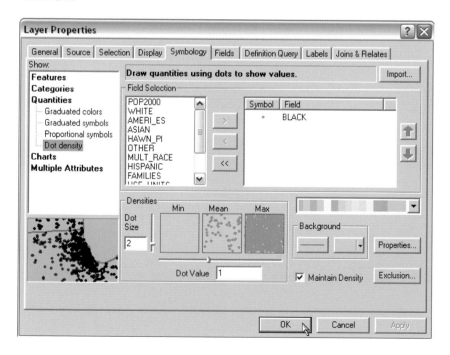

Click *OK* to close the *Layer Properties* dialog box.

A dot density map appears. The dots are distributed randomly within each census block. The larger the number of dots within a block, the higher the density of African-Americans in that area. As you learned in chapter 10, dots in a dot density map symbolize density; they do not indicate the precise location of individual features. Because the dot value in this map has been set to "1" and the area within which to randomly assign dots has been defined as one census block (a small area), one dot in this map represents the approximate location of one African-American.

Right-click the *Elementary schools* layer.

Click *Label Features*.

The schools are labeled with the school name.

Question 5: Near which schools were African-Americans clustered in 2000? Were there African-Americans near other Mount Laurel schools?

Step 19   Change symbology using the classification dialog box

Open the layer properties for the *Census blocks* layer.

The *Symbology* tab should already be selected. If not, click it.

Click **Quantities**.

Click *Graduated colors*.

Right-click the *color bar* and uncheck *Graphic View*.

Click the *Color Ramp* pull-down menu.

Click the *Blue Light to Dark* color ramp.

In the *Fields* section, click the *Value* pull-down menu.

Click the value *BLACK*.

Click the *Classify* button.

The *Classification* dialog box opens. The dialog box displays a default classification method—natural breaks (Jenks). It also shows classification statistics, break values, a default number of classes (5), and a histogram.

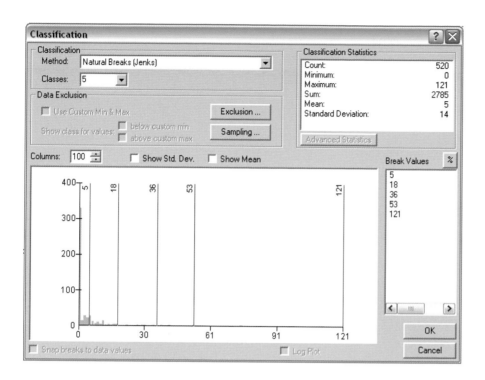

In the classification statistics box, you can see that there are 520 census blocks in Mount Laurel. There were no African-Americans in some census blocks in 2000, and one block had 121 African-Americans. While the average (mean) number of African-Americans per census tract was 5, Mount Laurel's 2,776 African-Americans were not equally distributed.

You will use the natural breaks (Jenks) method to classify this data shortly, but first you will classify it using an inappropriate classification method.

By looking at the intercept of the x- and y-axes in the histogram, you can see that most Mount Laurel census blocks had few African-Americans; but at this scale it is hard to interpret the histogram. Focusing on the left side of the histogram helps make things clearer.

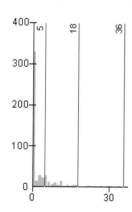

Now you can see that no African-Americans were living in more than three hundred of Mount Laurel's census blocks and most of the others had five or fewer African-Americans.

In the *Classification* section, click the **Method** pull-down menu.

Click **Equal Interval**.

Click **OK** to close the Classification dialog box.

Click **Apply**.

Your screen should look like this:

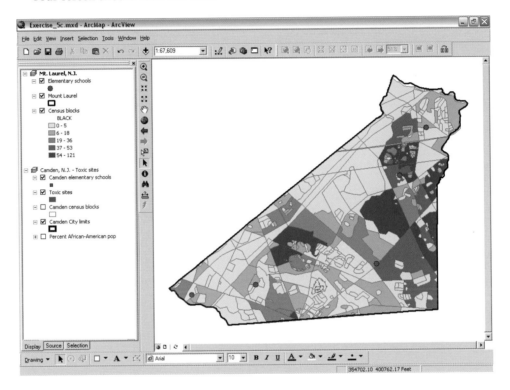

Darker areas represent areas in Mount Laurel where more African-Americans are concentrated.

Question 6a: Based on this equal-interval map, how would you describe the way in which Mount Laurel's African-American population is distributed?

Click the **Classify** button.

In the *Classification* section, click the **Method** pull-down menu.

Click **Quantile**.

Click **OK** to close the *Classification* dialog box.

Click **Apply** to apply the classification and leave the *Layer Properties* box open.

Your screen should look like the screen on the following page:

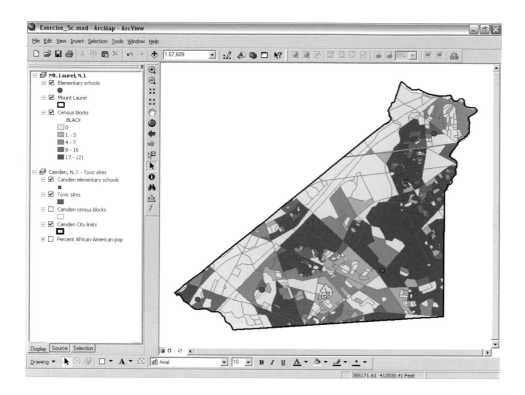

Again, dark blue areas indicate higher concentrations of African-Americans.

Question 6b: Based on this quantile map, how would you describe the way in which Mount Laurel's African-American population is distributed?

Finally, change the classification to *Natural Breaks (Jenks)*.

Click **OK** to close the *Layer Properties* dialog box and to apply the classification.

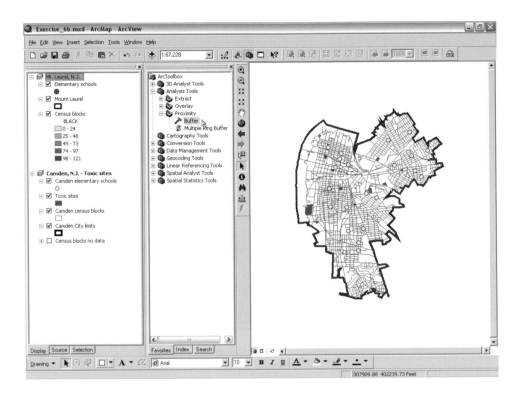

The ArcToolbox dockable window opens. (ArcToolbox may open in a different location on your computer screen from the image above.)

Expand the *Analysis Tools* toolbox.

Expand the *Proximity* toolset.

Double-click the **Buffer** tool.

Click the **Input Features** pull-down menu.

Click *Camden elementary school*s.

Click the **Browse folder** button ☞ next to *Output Feature Class* and navigate to the **TGAR\ MyWork** folder where you have permission to save files.

Name the file **buffer_schools.**

Select *Linear unit* for distance. Enter **.25** (one-quarter mile).

Select *Miles* in the pull-down menu to the right.

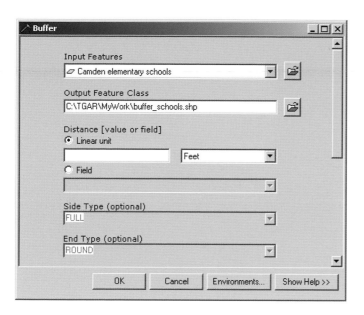

Click **OK**.

A *Process* box appears showing that ArcMap is executing the *buffer* process.

Close the *Process* box when it reads **Completed**.

ArcMap creates a circular buffer around each of the elementary schools and adds a new layer named *buffer_schools* to the map.

Because the new buffers are opaque, you cannot see the toxic sites or schools underneath them. You could drag the toxic sites layer above the buffers, but instead you will make the buffers transparent.

Close the *ArcToolbox* dockable window.

Step 22   Make a layer transparent

Right-click the *buffer_schools* layer.

Click **Properties**.

Click the *General* tab and change the name of the layer to **Buffer of elementary schools 1/4 mile**.

Click the *Display* tab.

In the *Transparent* box, enter **60%**.

Click **OK** to close the *Properties Layer* dialog box.

The buffers become 60 percent transparent and the layers below become visible. If it is still difficult to make out schools or toxic sites, increase the percentage of transparency or lighten the fill color of the buffer.

Your screen should look like the screen on the following page:

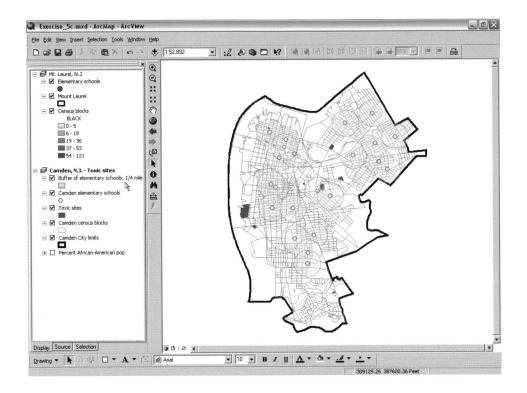

Step 23   Examine the location of toxic sites in relation to schools minority students attend

Click on the *Buffer of elementary schools 1/4 mile* symbol.

Change the *Fill Color* to *No Color* and the *Outline Width* to **2**.

Click **OK**.

Turn on the *Percent African-American pop* layer.

Use the *Schools near contaminated sites* bookmark to zoom in to the large toxic site near two schools in the area in the center right of the map.

Click **Selection**.

Click **Set Selectable Layers**.

Click **Clear All**.

Check the *Camden elementary schools* and *Contaminated sites* layers.

Click the **Close** button.

Click the **Identify** tool.

Click the **Layers** pull-down menu in the *Identify Results* box and select *Camden elementary schools*.

Click one of the schools near the toxic site.

Look at the variable **PCT_NAM00** (percentage of the students who were non-Asian minorities in 2000).

Click on the other school and look at the same variable.

Click the **Layers** pull-down menu in the *Identify Results* box.

Click *Contaminated sites.*

Click the large red toxic site near the two schools.

Note its size and what substances were present in 2001.

Question 7: What have you found out about this site and the demographics of people living near the site? What would be good practice to better understand the nature of contamination at the site and community features such as schools, parks, homes, and people of different races near the site? Based on this analysis, have you proven that minority children are at risk from toxic sites or that environmental racism exists in Camden?

Answers to exercise 5 questions

Question 1 (step 1)

(a) The color of the data frame representing the oceans should be changed to cyan or a similar shade of blue.

(b) The fill color of the cities should be changed. One good choice would be Mars Red. Any distinct, aesthetically pleasing color will work.

(c) The fill color of the countries should be changed. An unobtrusive light color would be best. Sahara Sand or a light green are good choices.

(d) The size of the city point symbols should be increased.

Question 2 (step 6)

The default value of five classes is appropriate. You do not want to have so few classes that the map does not show differences among cities or so many that it is hard to interpret.

Question 3 (step 7)

According to this source, the populations of Paris, Peking (Beijing), Hangchow, Nanking, and Canton in 1500 were

Paris:	225,000
Peking (Beijing):	672,000
Hangchow:	375,000
Nanking:	285,000
Canton:	250,000

Question 4 (step 15)

Normalizing the African-American population of census blocks by the total population of the census blocks will divide the African-American population of each census block by the total population of that block—producing the percentage of the block's population that is African-American. If the data was not normalized, a choropleth map would classify census blocks by the absolute number of African-Americans. Since the population of census blocks varies, a choropleth map that is not normalized would make it appear that African-Americans are more concentrated in census blocks that have more total population. Normalizing the data differentiates census blocks by the percentage of their population that is African-American.

Question 5 (step 18)

African-Americans in Mount Laurel were somewhat clustered near Larchmont Elementary school in 2000. Yes, there were African-Americans living near other Mount Laurel schools in 2000.

Question 6 (step 19)

(a) The map produced by the equal-interval classification method makes it appear that African-Americans in Mount Laurel are quite concentrated in the north central part of the township.

(b) The map produced by the quantile classification method makes it appear that African-Americans in Mount Laurel are quite dispersed throughout the township.

(c) The map produced by the natural-breaks classification method suggests that African-Americans are somewhat concentrated in the north central area and that there are some parts of the township where few African-Americans live. It also suggests that some African-Americans live in a number of different areas within the township.

Question 7 (step 23)

Spatial analysis reveals suggestive information about the location of features. Data in the attribute table associated with a map provides factual information.

This map shows that there was a site on New Jersey's toxic site list in 2001 where groundwater contamination had been identified, and the site was close to two schools. Attribute table data shows that a number of contaminants were present at that time. Before forming conclusions from this preliminary analysis, it would be important to check on the current status of this area, do field research to ground truth the facts, and carefully research the details and implications of the data. Exploratory research at this level of detail does not prove that children are at risk or that this situation is the result of environmental racism. It can help activists, policymakers, and landowners focus on potential problems and devise solutions.

Your Turn

1. If you are continuing from Exercise_5, navigate to the **TGAR\Part_3\Exercise_5\YourTurn** folder, open it, and open the **YourTurn_5.mxd** file. Click *No* when prompted "Save changes to Exercise_5c?"

    Otherwise open ArcMap and navigate to the **TGAR\Part_3\Exercise_5\YourTurn** folder, open it, and open the **YourTurn_5.mxd** file.

2. A map opens showing Burlington and Camden counties with poor symbology and background. You will improve the map symbology.

3. Change the data frame background to white.

4. Click the **Camden County symbol** and change the symbol *Outline Width* to .40, and *Outline Color* to Gray 60%.

5. Open the *Burlington County* layer properties. Change the symbology to *Features* with a *Single symbol*. Then make the *Fill Color* Sugilite Sky (top row).

6. Turn on the *Schools* layer.

7. Change the point symbol color to **Mars Red** and size to **4** points.

8. Change the *Schools* layer to *Graduated symbol* using the **NAM00** (number of non-Asian minority students in 2000) field. Use the *Identify* tool to identify the community in Burlington County with the highest concentration of non-Asian minority students in schools.

    Question 1: Are non-Asian American students clustered in certain areas of Burlington County? What community in Burlington County had many non-Asian minority students in its schools in 2000?

9. Use the *Camden City* bookmark to zoom in to that area.

10. Turn on the labels for *Schools*.

11. Change the labels for *Schools* so the font size is 7 points. Remove the *bold* font weight. Change the label placement to *Prefer Bottom Left, all allowed*. Click the **Conflict Detection** tab and change the *Feature Weight* to *High* and add a *Buffer* of .50.

12. Use the *Burlington/Camden County* bookmark to zoom to the extent of the two counties. Create a *dot density* map based on crimes per ten thousand people (crimeper10) using the *Burlington County* layer and the field **CRIMEPER10**. Make the *Dot Size* 2 and *Dot Value* 100.

13. Repeat the process for *Camden County*.

    Question 2: Are crimes per ten thousand people more densely concentrated in some areas than others?

14. Open the Burlington County attribute table and sort the crimes per 10,000 column in descending order. Click on the city with the most crimes per ten thousand and, holding down the shift key, drag down through the first seven cities. Then open the Camden County attribute table and do the same for crimes per 10,000 in Camden County.

> **Question 3:** Are the seven high-crime cities in Burlington County clustered together? How about the high-crime cities in Camden County—are they clustered in any way?

15. Collapse the *Burlington/Camden county - Crime* data frame.
16. Expand and activate the *Camden-contaminated site analysis* data frame.
17. Create a *Blue Light to Dark* monochromatic map of **FAMILIES** using the *Census blocks* layer with an *Equal Interval* classification.
18. Toggle the *Contaminated points* layer on and off to examine the location of contaminated sites.
19. Change the classification of census blocks to *Quantile* and turn on the *Contaminated points* layer again.
20. Change the classification to *Natural Breaks (Jenks)*.

> **Question 4:** How do the different classifications affect the map symbology?

21. Turn off the *Census blocks* layer.
22. Create a .25 mile buffer of the *Contaminated points* layer. Rename the layer **Buffer of contaminated sites - 1/4 mile** and make it 60 percent transparent.
23. Turn on the *Schools* layer. Zoom in to the Camden and Mount Laurel areas.

> **Question 5:** Are all of the schools in Camden within contaminated site buffers? What about the schools in Mount Laurel?

24. Turn off the *Contaminated points* layer.
25. Zoom back out using the *Burlington/Camden County* bookmark.
26. Turn off *Schools* and turn on the *Railroads* layer.
27. Use the *Symbol Property Editor* to change the railroad to a *Simple Line Symbol*.
28. Turn on the *Contaminated points* layer;
29. Create a .5 mile buffer of the railroads, rename the layer **Buffer of railroads - 1/2 mile**, change the color to Sodalite Blue, and remove the outline.

> **Question 6:** Are contaminated sites located near railroad lines?

30. Exit ArcMap. Do not save changes to **YourTurn_5**.

Answers to exercise 5 Your Turn questions

Question 1: Yes, non-Asian minority students are clustered in some areas of Burlington County. Willingboro schools have substantial numbers of non-Asian minority students.

Question 2: Yes, crimes per ten thousand people are more densely concentrated in the city of Camden and some other areas.

Question 3: In Burlington County the high-crime cities are all in the northwest, but they are not all close together. In Camden County there are two clusters of high-crime cities: in the northwestern and central parts of the county.

Question 4: The maps produced by both the equal interval and quantile methods make it appear that families are quite concentrated in these two counties. The map produced by the natural-breaks classification method suggests that they are somewhat more widely dispersed.

Question 5: No, some schools in both communities are not within the contaminated sites buffers.

Question 6: Many, but not all, contaminated sites are located close to railroad lines.

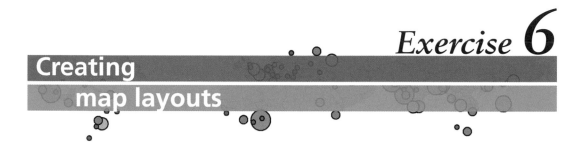

Learning objectives

In exercise 6, you will continue to work with Professor Orfield's data (a) at the state level, (b) at the regional level for Burlington and Camden counties in southern New Jersey, and (c) at the local level for the cities of Camden and Mount Laurel. You will learn how to do the following:

- switch from *data view* to *layout view*
- add a *map title* to a map layout
- *format* a *map title*
- add a *north arrow* to the map layout
- add a *scale bar* to a map layout
- add a map *legend* and format it
- add a *neatline* to a map layout
- work with *layout elements*
- use *page guides* to align *map elements*
- add a *picture* to a layout
- use the layout *zoom tools*
- *align* the title and subtitle
- add *text* and *leader lines* to a map layout
- export a map as a *PDF file*

Step 1   Open and examine Exercise_6a

If ArcMap is already open, do the following:

Click *File*.

Click *Open*, navigate to the **TGAR\Part_3\Exercise_6** folder, then open the folder.

Open **Exercise_6a.mxd**.

Click *No* if prompted to save changes.

Otherwise

Start ArcMap and choose to open an existing map.

Navigate to the **TGAR\Part_3\Exercise_6** folder, then open the folder.

Open **Exercise_6a.mxd**.

Step 2   Switch from data view to layout view

Now you will create a map layout with a title, legend, north arrow, scale bar, and neatline. Up until this point you have done all of your ArcMap work in *Data View*. Now you will change to *Layout View*.

Click the *View* pull-down menu.

Click *Layout View*. Your screen should look like this:

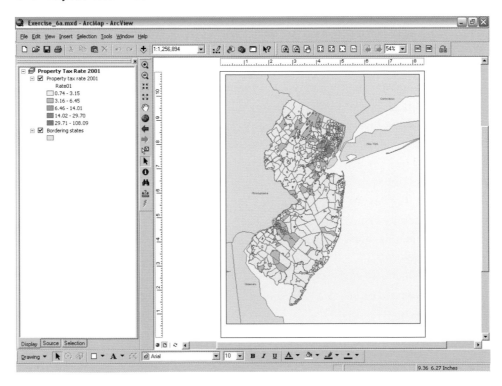

The map now appears to be placed on a page. The layout view allows you to see how a map will look if it is printed. A new toolbar—the *Layout* toolbar—appears in layout view.

In the map, the *Layout* toolbar is docked in the upper right. Your *Layout* toolbar may appear somewhere else.

If necessary, click the **Layout** toolbar, hold down the left mouse button, drag and dock the *Layout* toolbar above the map next to the *Standard* toolbar.

The state of New Jersey should nearly fill the map. If it appears zoomed out too far, while in *Layout View*, enter 1:1,100,000 in the map scale field. You may need to pan the map to the left. (Note: There are pan tools on both the *Standard* toolbar and the *Layout* toolbar. You can tell the name of a toolbar by undocking it.) Use the pan tool on the *Standard* toolbar to pan within the map. Using the pan tool on the *Layout* toolbar would move the map itself.

Question 1: Is a map scale of 1:1,100,000 larger or smaller than a map scale of 1: 2,000,000?

The next steps involve inserting cartographic elements from the insert menu, dragging them to an appropriate place on the map layout, and resizing them. Begin by adding a title to the map layout.

Step 3   Add a map title to a map layout

Click the **Insert** pull-down menu on the *Main Menu*.

Click **Title**.

A text box is inserted into the map layout containing some default text—in this case the name of your map document.

Enter the title, **Property Tax Rate by Municipality, New Jersey, 2001**.

Press Enter on your keyboard.

The *text box* containing the title is inserted into the map. It is surrounded by a bounded dashed blue box.

Right-click the text box.

Click **Properties** at the bottom of the context menu.

The text *Properties* dialog box opens.

Edit the label so "Property Tax Rate" is on the first line, "by Municipality" is on the second line, and "New Jersey, 2001" is on the third line. Your text properties dialog box should look like the graphic on the following page:

Step 4   Format a map title

Click the *Change Symbol* button in the lower right corner.

Click the *Size* pull-down menu and change the font size to **16**.

Click the **B** (bold) button to make the font bold.

Click *OK* to close the *Symbol Selector* dialog box.

Click *OK* again to close the *Properties* dialog box.

    The text box should still be highlighted. Move your cursor over the title, being careful not to click the mouse. Notice that the cursor changes to a four-arrowed rectangle.

Click anywhere on the text box and drag it so that it is at the top right of the map with some separation between the label and the top of the map.

Step 5   Add a north arrow to the map layout

Click the *Insert* pull-down menu.

Click *North Arrow*.

    The *North Arrow Selector* dialog box opens with a variety of north arrow styles to choose from.

Click the *ESRI North 8* symbol to select it.

Click *OK*.

    A north arrow is inserted in your map. (You may have to look hard to see it against the map background). Four blue square bounding boxes surround the north arrow.

Click the north arrow and drag it to a location on the bottom left of the map in the ocean between the small promontory at the southern end of New Jersey and Delaware. (You can refer to the map in step 7 if you are not clear on where to place the north arrow.)

Step 6   Add a scale bar to a map layout

Click the *Insert* pull-down menu.

Click *Scale Bar*.

The *Scale Bar Selector* dialog box opens with a variety of scale bar styles to choose from.

Question 2: What do you feel would be a good length for a scale bar in this map? Why? What standards help make a good scale bar?

Click the first type of scale bar: *Scale Line 1*.

Click *OK*.

The scale bar is inserted into the map layout. Eight blue squares bound the scale bar.

While highlighted, click the scale bar and drag it to the bottom right of the map.

Now you will adjust the size of the scale bar to represent exactly fifty miles.

Hover your cursor over the center blue bounding box on the right side of the scale bar. A two-headed arrow should appear.

Click on the center *blue bounding box* with the two-headed arrow.

Hold down the left mouse button.

Drag the center blue bounding box to the left to a location that you estimate will create a fifty-mile scale bar.

Note: If you have difficulty seeing the figures for the scale bar, you can zoom in using the *Zoom In* tool on the layout toolbar.

Release the left mouse button. You may have to repeat the process of dragging the center blue bounding box to the left or right if you over- or undershoot until you get the scale to represent exactly fifty miles.

Step 7   Add a legend to the map layout and format it

Click the *Insert* pull-down menu.

Click *Legend*.

The *Legend Wizard* opens. In the *Legend Wizard* there are two columns: *Map Layers* and *Legend Items*. The *Legend Wizard* prompts you to choose the layer(s) to be included in the legend. The *Map Layers* column lists all of the map layers in the active data frame. The *Legend Items* column lists layers that will be visible in the legend. You can click layers in the *Map Layer* column and move them into the *Legend Items* box by clicking the right arrow connecting the two boxes. Similarly you can move layers out of the *Legend Items* box with the left arrow.

Make sure *Property tax rate 2001* is in the *Legend Items* box. If not, click *Property tax rate 2001* and move it into the legend items box with the right arrow. Remove *Bordering states* from the *Legend Items* column.

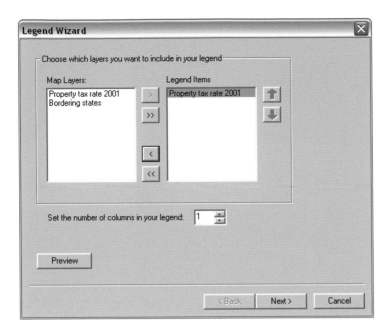

Click **Next** and delete the word *Legend* from the *Legend Title* box.

Click **Next** successively, accepting the defaults, until the legend is complete.

Click, hold down, and drag the legend to the bottom right corner above the scale bar. Resize the legend if necessary. Your screen should look like this:

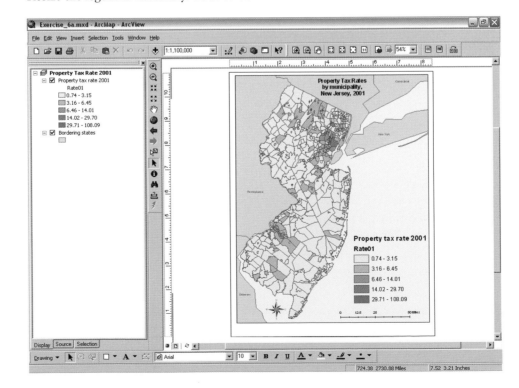

Step 8   Add a neatline to the map layout

Click the *Insert* pull-down menu.

Click *Neatline*.

Click the *Place around all elements* option button to select it.

Click *OK*.

> A neatline appears around all the map elements.
>
> Now you will learn to add map elements to a layout and adjust them to create good symbology. You will use data related to social equality in Camden and Burlington counties, New Jersey, the city of Camden, and Mount Laurel township.

Step 9   Work with layout elements

Navigate to the **TGAR\Part_3\Exercise_6** folder and open **Exercise_6b.mxd**.

When prompted, do not save changes to **Exercise_6a**.

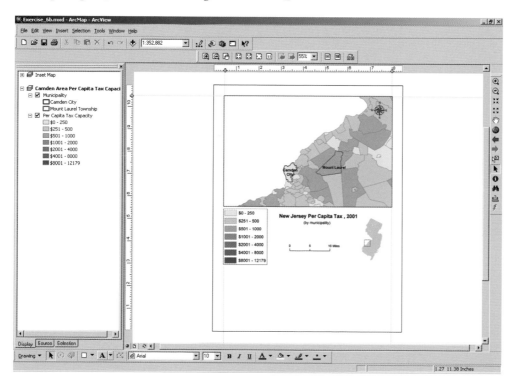

A map of New Jersey municipalities opens in layout view showing 2001 per capita taxes by municipality.

> The map already contains several map elements. However, the elements are out of place and need to be arranged before you print out a hard copy of the map. The north arrow is not necessary and you will delete it shortly. You will also add photos and text to enhance the map.

In this exercise, you will use the *Layout* toolbar to navigate in the layout view.

The layout zoom tools are very similar to tools on the *Tools* toolbar. However, the layout zoom tools are designed for page navigation, not map navigation. Be careful to use the layout zoom tools when zooming in or panning in *Layout View*.

Click on the north arrow and press the delete key to delete it.

Click and drag the *legend*, *title*, *subtitle*, *scale bar*, and *locator map* to the sides and off the page. The locator map is the very small map of New Jersey that shows where Camden and Burlington counties are located. (All of these elements are located in the white space below the map.)

After you have dragged the map elements off the map, your layout view should look like this:

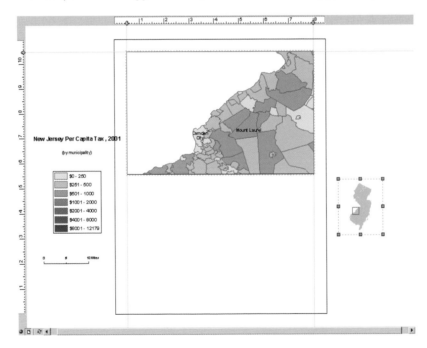

Dragging all the map elements off the map is good practice to give you a clean canvas to work with as you position each element in its final place.

Step 10   Use page guides to align map elements

Make sure the rulers are visible and set to inches. You can toggle the ruler visibility on and off from the *View* pull-down menu by clicking on rulers. To set the ruler units, right-click the ***ruler***, click *options*, click the *Layout View* tab and enter the desired units (inches in this case). Using your cursor, click the .5 inch mark on the bottom of the left ruler.

A blue guide appears in the data frame, creating a box for the *Camden Area Per Capita Tax Capacity* map to align to. If you miss the mark or want to try again, right-click on the guide and click *clear guide*.

Click the *Per Capita Tax Capacity map* to select it. Make sure the blue bounding boxes are visible.

Hover your cursor on the bottom center blue bounding box until a two-headed arrow appears. Click and drag the bottom line until it snaps to the guide you previously created.

Your map screen should look like this:

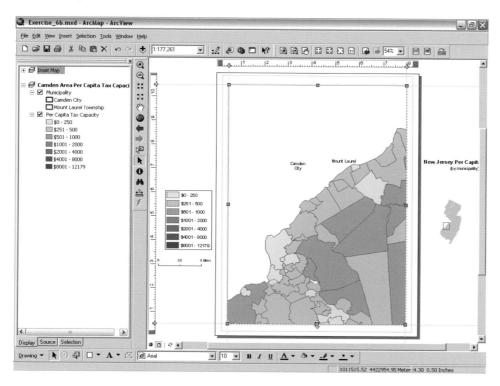

Unselect the *Per Capita Tax Capacity* map by clicking in the white space outside the page.

Click the label for Camden city and place the label in the center of Camden (outlined in red).

Click the label for Mount Laurel and place the label in the center of Mount Laurel (outlined in amethyst).

Step 11   Add a picture to a map layout

Click the *Insert* pull-down menu.

Click *Picture*.

Navigate to the **TGAR\Part_3\Exercise_6\Images** subfolder.

Click *Camden housing.jpg*.

Click *Open*.

A JPEG image of Camden housing opens.

Repeat this process to insert the **Mount_Laurel_housing** JPEG.

Resize each image to about 1.25 inches in height and two inches in width (use the rulers or image below for reference) and move each photo to the position as seen below.

Click in the white space outside the layout frame to unselect the images.

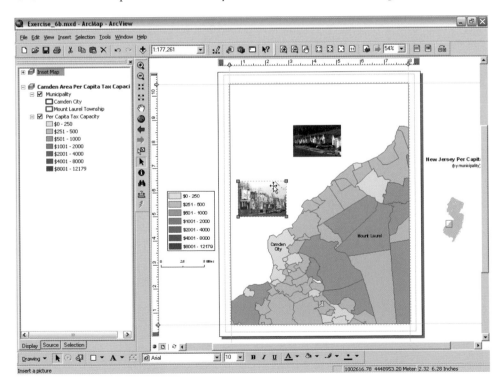

Question 3: Other than photographs, what are some other items you might want to include in a map layout?

Step 12   Use the Layout zoom tools to align the legend

Click the legend and drag it to the bottom right corner of the map as close to the border as possible until it snaps to the guides.

Click the *Layout* toolbar **Zoom In** tool 🔍 . (Make sure you are not using the *Tools* toolbar *Zoom In* tool 🔍 .)

Zoom in to the bottom right corner of the page until your map layout looks like the following image:

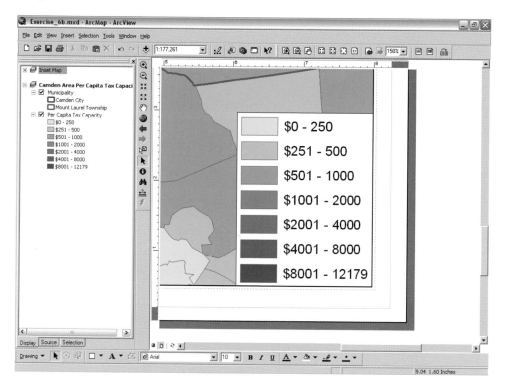

Click the **Select Elements** tool ▶ .

Right-click each guide. Then point to *Guides* and click to turn them off.

Notice that the legend covers the border of the map.

If the legend is not selected, click it.

Use the keyboard directional arrows to nudge the legend so that the border of the map can be seen (one click to the right and one click down of the directional arrows should be sufficient).

Click off of the page to unselect the legend.

Click the **Zoom Whole Page** button 🔳 to view the entire page.

The legend is now properly positioned, but you need to position other elements and make final changes to the map.

Step 13   Align the title and subtitle

Turn on a page guide at one inch from the top of the map.

Click and drag the title and subtitle to the top center of the map, leaving a one-inch margin from the top.

First click the title to highlight it.

On the keyboard, hold down the Shift key.

Click the subtitle text to also highlight it.

Click the map.

 All three elements should be highlighted.

Right-click the map.

Select *Align*.

Click *Align Center*.

 The title and subtitle should align in the center of the page. Your map should look like this:

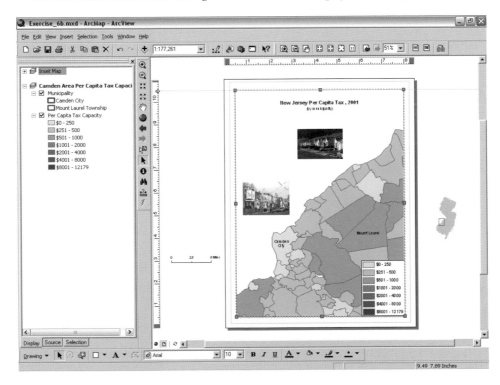

Step 14   Add text and leader lines to a map layout

Click the *Insert* pull-down menu.

Click *Text*.

A *text box* is inserted into the map. You may have to look hard to find it.

Click anywhere on the map. Then double-click the text box to bring up the *Text Properties* dialog box.

Enter the following text:

> Camden's housing stock includes
> many older multifamily units.

Click **OK**.

Click the text box and drag it below the Camden image.

Repeat the process and add the following text for the Mount Laurel image:

> Mount Laurel's housing stock includes
> many new single-family detached houses.

Click the text box and drag it below the Mount Laurel image.

Now you want to draw a leader line from the photograph to the text. You need to activate the *New Line* tool.

Click the **pull-down menu** next to the *New Rectangle* on the *Draw* toolbar.

Click the **New Line** tool from the selection box.

Click just below the text for the Camden photo.

Drag your mouse pointer to the middle of Camden on the map just above the label to draw a *leader line* from Camden to the picture.

Release the mouse, then double-click to end the line.

Repeat this process for Mount Laurel.

Step 15   Finish up and export your map as a PDF file

Click the scale bar and drag it to the lower left corner of the map.

Click the locator map and drag it to the upper left corner of the map. Use the keyboard directional arrows to slide it closer to the border. Let it snap to the corner.

Your final layout should look like this:

Click *File*.
Click *Export Map*.
Click the *pull-down menu* for *Save As Type*.
Select *PDF (*pdf)*.

Question 4: Why might you want to export a map as a PDF file?

Save your map in your **TGAR\MyWork** folder or another folder you specified for output.
Name your map **Camden and Mount Laurel region**.
Click *Save*.

If you are continuing with the next exercise, leave ArcMap open. Otherwise, click the *File* menu and click *Exit*. Click *No* if prompted to save your changes.

Answers to exercise 6 questions

Question 1 (step 2)

A map scale of 1: 2,000,000 is smaller than a map scale of 1:1,100,000. Remember, a map scale of 1:1 would be life size (very big), so the larger the denominator, the smaller the map scale.

Question 2 (step 6)

An appropriate length for a scale bar depends on the map size and context. It should be large enough to be visible, but not so large that it dominates the map. Generally, the length of the scale bar should be rounded off. Simple scale bars are as effective as elaborate ones.

Question 3 (step 11)

Data graphics and tables are often included in map layouts. Any image can be scanned into a standard image file format (JPEG, TIFF, or GIF) and inserted.

Question 4 (step 15)

PDF files are small files that can easily be sent by e-mail. They can contain both words and images (including map images). They reproduce color well. Most computers have software (Adobe® Reader®) to read PDF files, and for those that do not, such software is easily downloadable for free from the Web.

Your Turn

1. If you are continuing from Exercise_6b, navigate to the **TGAR\Part_3\Exercise_6\YourTurn** folder, open it, and open the **YourTurn_6.mxd** file. Don't save changes to **Exercise_6b**.

   Otherwise open ArcMap, navigate to the **TGAR\Part_3\Exercise_6\YourTurn** folder, open the folder, and open the *YourTurn_6.mxd* file.

2. A map opens showing New Jersey urbanization between 1980 and 2000. The symbology makes the map difficult to understand. You will improve the symbology.

3. Switch to the *Layout View*. The layout has been zoomed in to Camden and Mount Laurel.

4. Open both the Camden and Mount Laurel attribute tables so they are visible at the same time. Scroll to the right so that the population and density values are visible.

   Question 1: What was the population of the two cities in 1980? How did the population of the two cities change between 1980 and 2000?

   Question 2: How did the density of the two cities change between 1980 and 2000?

5. Close the tables and turn off Camden and Mount Laurel.

6. Turn off the labels for *County boundaries*. The visibility of labels is a toggle.

7. Use the *Zoom Whole Page* button to zoom to the whole page.

8. Use the layout *Zoom In* tool and page guides, as needed, to navigate to a location on the map where you can see transit routes. Throughout this exercise use these tools as needed.

9. Change the *Transit route* layer symbol. Choose the *Railroad* symbol. Make it *Medium Coral Light* (second row, second column) with a width of one point.

10. Change the *State line* symbol to Arterial Street, Gray 60%, .4 points wide.

11. Change the *Bordering states* symbol to Gray 10%.

12. Change the Ocean color to *Sodalite Blue*.

13. Zoom in around the Philadelphia urbanized area.

14. Notice the county labels are large bold numbers that conflict with the urban area labels. Change the *County boundaries* layer labels to show the county name, unbold them, and reduce the font size to 7 points. Move the urbanized area labels so that the county names are completely visible and not overlapping (you may need to pan around to find other labels overlapping).

15. Notice that the *Urbanization 1970* layer has a red symbol that conflicts with the red polygon symbol for Camden. Change the *Urbanization 1970* layer from the category symbol to a single symbol feature.

   Question 3: What would be an appropriate fill color, outline color, and outline width for the *Urbanization 1970* layer?

16. Symbolize the *Urbanization 1970* layer based on your answer to question 3.

17. Stretch the scale bar out to show twenty miles.

18. Place the scale in the middle of the ocean.

19. Zoom in to the legend in the upper left corner. There is an error. The word *Country* has been mistakenly written instead of *County*. Open the legend properties and correct the spelling to *County*.

20. Use the *Zoom Whole Page* button to zoom to the whole page.

21. Insert a title. Go to its properties. On the first line type "New Jersey:". On the second line type "Change in urbanized areas, 1970–1990". Keep the text left justified.

22. Change the title text to a Verdana font, size 12, bolded. Make sure the title is center aligned to the map and is positioned just above the map.

23. Insert the *urbpopdensity.jpg* image from the **Exercise_6\YourTurn\Images** folder.

24. Resize the JPEG to 3 inches wide and 2.25 inches high. Place it in the bottom right corner of the map so that it overlaps the right data frame border but not the bottom border line. Make sure the scale bar is still visible.

25. Insert the ESRI North 27 arrow, and place it above the scale bar.

26. Export your map as a PDF file and print it out.

27. Exit ArcMap. Do not save changes to **YourTurn_6**.

Answers to exercise 6 Your Turn questions

Question 1: Camden's population was almost five times as large as Mount Laurel's in 1980 (84,910 compared to 17,614). Between 1980 and 2000, Camden's population decreased slightly to 79,904, while Mount Laurel's more than doubled to 40,221.

Question 2: Camden was more than ten times as densely populated as Mount Laurel in 1980 (8,166 people per square mile in Camden, compared to only 806 people per square mile in Mount Laurel). By 2000, Camden's population density had decreased slightly to 7,684 people per square mile, while Mount Laurel's had more than doubled to 1,832 people per square mile.

Question 3: This is a matter of judgment, but the Urbanization 1970 layer should be a neutral color, the outline should probably be gray or black, and the outline width should not be too large. One appropriate combination would be Sahara Sand color, Gray 60% outline color, and .4 points outline width.

Bringing it all together in the Metro region

Learning objectives

Exercise 7 is the culminating exercise in *Think Globally, Act Regionally*. It is different from the other exercises you have completed. Exercises 1 through 6 used a step-by-step approach. Those six exercises told you exactly what to do to learn GIS operations using ArcMap. You explored topics that illustrate spatial analysis concepts discussed in this book. The Your Turn exercises at the end of each exercise required you to repeat the same operations on your own with different data and without the step-by-step handholding. Now you are ready to carry out an entire GIS analysis yourself. Exercise 7 describes four hypothetical regional planning problems and asks you to select one of them. It then requires you to use GIS to analyze the problem and produce a high-quality map with a layout consisting of one main and two smaller maps.

Exercise 7 provides a very rich dataset—data from Metro's regional land information system (RLIS) database that you read about in chapter 12—generously made available by Metro. You can choose from four scenarios related to regional planning and policy issues in the Portland region:

- regional urban growth management (exercise 7a)
- regional transportation planning (exercise 7b)
- regional environmental planning (exercise 7c)
- regional risk reduction and environmental education (exercise 7d)

For each of these scenarios, an initial ArcMap .mxd file opens with key layers from the Metro regional land information system (RLIS) database. Only a few layers are turned on to provide a framework for you to begin your work. Additional layers that are particularly relevant to the scenario are in the table of contents, but they are turned off.

Many more data layers for exercise 7 are stored in file subfolders within the exercise 7 folder. The subfolders are named and organized in such a way that you can find and add additional data layers you consider relevant to your analysis. Excellent metadata, created by Metro, accompanies each layer.

To create a layout with the main and smaller maps, you will need to create two additional data frames where you can add layers to use to create the two small maps. You will need to copy data layers from the opening data frame to these two data frames and may want to add additional layers from the exercise 7 subfolders to the opening map and the data frames you create.

Each of the scenarios in exercise 7 describes an important regional planning and policy topic and provides high-quality, real data relevant to the topic organized to be readily accessible. Each scenario describes a hypothetical planning and policy need for spatial analysis and data visualization using the starter set of spatial analysis and data visualization skills you have learned. Your job is to prepare one thoughtful map layout with a main map and smaller maps in a layout. Your layout should look similar to map 12.1 showing the Metro region.

Before you begin your analysis, you will need to explore the scenario and think carefully about what additional data you will need and what your final maps will be like. After you have explored the scenario and available data in the data folders, you should make a list of data you want to use, outline the layers you will add to each data frame, and sketch out what the final maps will look like. Since spatial analysis is an iterative process, your final map will reflect insights you gain in the course of the analysis.

Exercise 7 will work best if there is some meeting time in a computer lab with an instructor or teaching assistant present to help you get started and to help as questions arise, but it will also require you or groups of you and your fellow students to work on your own. It should take four to six hours to complete exercise 7. If you are able to devote more time to the exercise, you can complete a more thorough analysis and more polished map.

Enjoy.

Scenario 7a   Regional urban growth management

Exercise_7a involves regional urban growth management. Like many regions, the Portland metropolitan area is gaining population. You learned in chapter 12 that the population of the region is expected to increase by 720,000 in the fifty-year period from 1990–2040. Every city in the region is expected to gain population. The amount of urbanized land in the area will increase. Portland's 2040 Urban Growth Concept proposes containing almost all new development within a regional urban growth boundary. It envisions Portland remaining the region's employment and cultural hub. Regional centers outside Portland would be connected to Portland by high-capacity public transit and highways. Smaller town centers with local shopping and employment opportunities would connect to each regional center by road and public transit.

The **Exercise_7a.mxd** file opens twelve layers:

- Metro region
- Cities
- Counties
- Urban growth boundary
- Permits 1995–1998
- Parks
- Planning areas
- Zoning
- Vacant land
- Developed land
- Major rivers
- States

Three layers are turned on: *States*, *Major rivers*, and *Metro region*. Remember, you can add many other layers from the exercise 7 subfolders to this map or to new data frames you create.

Imagine that as the Metro planning director you have been asked to deliver a keynote address titled "Bringing it all together in the Metro region" to the American Planning Association (APA) National Convention. From past experience you anticipate having to answer questions about the governmental organization of the Portland region—how many cities there are within the Metro boundary and how many counties are entirely or partly within the Metro boundary. Urban planners from other metropolitan areas will want to know how much of the land within the urban growth boundary is developed and how much remains vacant (undeveloped). They will want to know how much parkland there is. Since a major objective of Metro is to contain development within the regional urban growth boundary, there are sure to be questions about how much building there has been recently, of what type, and where. The planners will be interested in how much land in the Metro region is zoned for different uses.

Prepare a map layout with one large map and two small maps. The large map should show government structure in the Portland region—the Metro boundary, cities within Metro, and counties that are at least partially within Metro. You can add additional layers you feel will contribute to the keynote address. The main map in your layout should have a legend, title, north arrow, scale bar, and at least one neatline. You may include other map elements such as visual images, charts, tables, and text. Optionally, you may include a locator map to show the location of the smaller maps in the layout.

The two small maps should show close ups of (a) developed and vacant land within an area near the urban growth boundary where a lot of development is occurring, and (b) an area where there is a lot of development near park land.

Prepare the map layout for your APA talk.

Scenario 7b   Regional transportation planning

Imagine that a nonprofit organization named "Citizens for Transportation Alternatives (CTA)" uses Metro data and GIS to propose multimodal regional transportation solutions for the Portland metropolitan region. Following Bertin's approach, CTA "uses vision to think" about carpooling, light rail, bus, and bicycling as alternatives to people driving alone in cars. As director of CTA, you are working on a five-year action plan. You want to identify areas that are presently underserved by transit alternatives and propose solutions.

Among the alternatives your group has endorsed are (a) extending existing light-rail lines and adding new transit stops, (b) adding bus routes and bus stops, (c) creating new park-and-ride locations, and (d) adding bicycle lanes to streets that do not already have them.

The **Exercise_7b.mxd** file opens zoomed in to one area in Portland. The table of contents contains seventeen layers:

- Metro region
- Transit centers
- Park-and-ride locations
- Light rail stops
- Light rail lines
- Portland hospitals
- Portland schools
- Major arterials
- Portland bike routes

- Portland bus lines
- Portland bus stops
- Portland streets
- Airports
- City boundaries
- Major rivers
- City of Portland
- States

Three layers related to transportation are turned on: *Portland streets*, *Light rail lines*, and *Light rail stops*. Two background layers are also turned on to provide context: *Major rivers* and *City of Portland*.

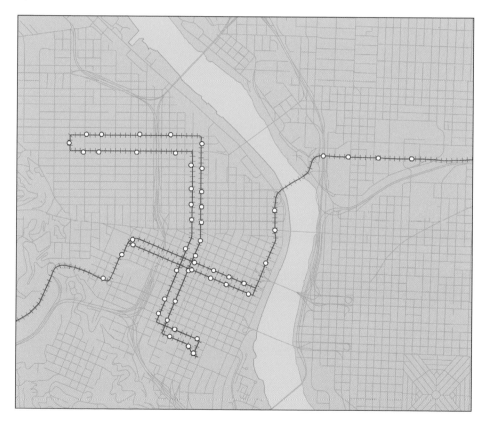

Prepare a map layout with one large map illustrating transportation infrastructure in Portland and two small maps illustrating alternative modes of transportation to the automobile. The main map should show some combination of (a) freeways, (b) major arterials, (c) other arterials, (d) light-rail lines, (e) light-rail stops, (f) transit centers, and (g) park-and-ride locations. Make sure you symbolize polygons, lines, and points in appropriate symbol types, sizes, and colors and that your layout has a legend, title, north arrow, scale bar, and neatline. You may include other map elements such as visual images, charts, tables, and text. Optionally, you may include a locator map to show the location of the features depicted in the smaller maps in the layout

The two small maps should focus on transportation in particular areas within Portland. For example, you might show (a) a portion of a light-rail line and several stops and then add layers showing how the stops are served by bus and bike routes, or (b) an area where you believe more park-and-ride locations should be added based on characteristics of the area.

Scenario 7c   Regional environmental planning

Exercise 7c involves regional environmental planning. Imagine that as the chief environmental planner for a citizens' urban planning organization named 1,000 Friends of Oregon, your job is to analyze conflicts between different types of land use and develop recommendations to promote sound policy to balance the built and natural environments. You are preparing a background report on Portland's regional environment.

The **Exercise_7c.mxd** file opens with a map of the Metro region. The table of contents contains thirteen layers:

- Metro boundary
- Rivers
- Streams
- Wetlands
- Floodplains
- Parks
- Forests
- Agriculture land
- Vacant land
- Developed land
- Cities
- Counties
- Digital orthophoto

Four layers are open: *Metro boundary*, *Rivers*, *Forests*, and *Agriculture land*.

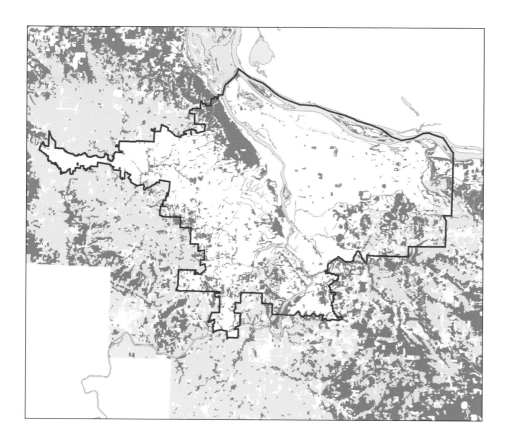

Create a map for your background report on conflicts between the natural and built environments in the Portland region that has one large map providing an overview of the Portland environment and two small maps showing specific areas where there are conflicts between the natural and built environments. Make sure you symbolize polygons, lines, and points in appropriate symbol types, sizes, and colors. Your main map should have a title, legend, north arrow, scale bar, and neatline. You may include other map elements such as visual images, charts, tables, and text. Optionally, you may include a locator map to show the location of the smaller maps in the layout.

Your small maps might show (a) an area where parks, wetlands, and agricultural land are near undeveloped land, but where many building permits have been issued recently, or (b) an area where you can see developed areas on the digital orthophoto near wetlands, streams, and parks.

Scenario 7d   Water-related risk management and environmental education

The topic for exercise 7d involves water resources. It requires analyzing both water-related risks (such as potential flood damage to houses and streets) and water-related opportunities (such as schools with bicycle paths leading to nearby wetlands where it would be feasible to start environmental education programs to teach elementary school children about wetlands and

transportation alternatives to automobiles). The **Exercise_7c.mxd** file opens with a map of the Rock Creek watershed. The table of contents contains nine layers:

- Schools
- Permits 1995–1998
- Bike routes
- Streets
- Streams
- Floodplains
- Rock Creek watershed
- Orthophoto
- Watersheds

Three layers are open: *Rock Creek watershed*, *streams*, and *watersheds*.

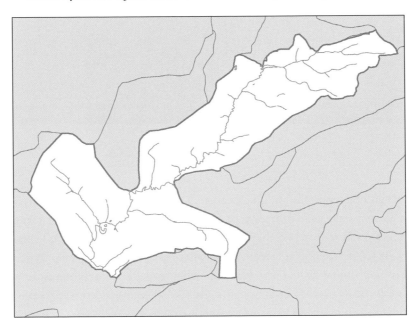

Imagine that you are a regional planner preparing a series of reports on watersheds titled "Thinking regionally about water: Problems and opportunities." Rather than address water-related issues on a city-by-city basis, the purpose of your studies is to help all the local governments in the region think about water-related problems and opportunities in terms of the natural setting in which they occur—watersheds. The first report in your series is on the Rock Creek watershed.

Prepare a main map showing key water-related feature in the Rock Creek watershed. You may include other map elements such as visual images, charts, tables, and text. Optionally, you may include a locator map to show the location of the smaller maps in the layout.

Then create two small maps. The first small map should illustrate water-related risks to property and streets. The second small map should show how wetlands in the Rock Creek watershed area might be used for an environmental education program.

One of the small maps can be zoomed in to one or more areas within the Rock Creek watershed where building permits have been issued near, or actually within, floodplains and where streets cross floodplains or streams in the Rock Creek watershed area. You might label major streets and symbolize them so local elected officials and citizens can clearly see how many problem streets there are and where they are located. You could use the digital orthophoto to show an image of the area. Creating buffers and measuring distances may help with your analysis.

For the second small map, imagine that a school district in the Rock Creek watershed area has identified wetlands as a recreational and teaching resource. Teachers in the district have developed an innovative program to teach selected elementary school students the relationship between stewardship of natural resources and alternative forms of transportation. They would like to have students bicycle to wetland areas near their schools. Teachers can teach about wetland ecology and explain how bicycling rather than dependence on automobiles can save nonrenewable resources and reduce pollution. The school district has a limited amount of money, so it needs to target schools near wetlands that have bicycle paths running from the school to the wetland. Prepare a second small map showing wetlands, schools, streets, and bicycle lanes to help them plan their program. Add appropriate data layers to do this project. You might create buffers around key wetlands in the Rock Creek area to help your research. Analyze which schools are closest to wetlands. Which have bicycle paths between the school and a wetland? In an era of scarce resources, which elementary schools should receive funding for the innovative program?

Like many spatial analysis problems, the amount of time to complete an analysis of any of the four scenarios above can vary enormously. When an analysis is as complete as time and your skill level permits, further analysis and refinement of the maps will still be possible. If class time allocated to this material is limited, you should be able to create good basic maps that adequately analyze and display results to any of the above scenarios in four to six hours of computer lab time (preferably working with other students and with an instructor or lab assistant present). If you have more time, you can produce more sophisticated analysis and more professional maps.

The data you have been working with in the *Think Globally, Act Regionally* exercises is representative of the kinds of data social scientists and public policy professionals work with. If you have completed *Think Globally, Act Regionally* as part of a semester-long course which covers additional GIS concepts and operations, the data in the book—particularly the RLIS data in this exercise—should provide plenty of material for additional course assignments. If you want to proceed further with GIS on your own, you can use this data to practice concepts and operations explained in documentation that comes with ArcGIS, academic GIS texts identified in the chapter 2 annotated bibliography, or any of the growing number of books teaching ArcGIS skills.

Congratulations, you are well on your way to doing spatial analysis!

References

Abbott, Carl. 2005. Personal communication with the author.

⸻. 2001. *Greater Portland: Urban life and landscape in the Pacific Northwest.* Philadelphia: University of Pennsylvania Press.

⸻. 2000. The capital of good planning: Metropolitan Portland since 1970. In *The American Planning Tradition: Culture and Policy,* ed. Robert Fishman. Washington, D.C.: Woodrow Wilson Center Press.

⸻. 1983. *Portland: Planning, politics, and growth in a twentieth century city.* Lincoln: University of Nebraska Press.

Abbot, Carl, Deborah Howe, and Sy Adler, eds. 1994. *Planning the oregon way: A twenty-year evaluation.* Corvallis, Ore.: Oregon State University Press.

Aldenderfer, Mark and Herbert D. G. Maschner, eds. 1996. *Anthropology, space, and geographic information systems.* Oxford: Oxford University Press.

Association of Bay Area Governments (ABAG). 2003. *Projections 2003.* Oakland, Calif.: ABAG.

Barth, Gunther Paul. 1988. *Instant cities: Urbanization and the rise of San Francisco and Denver.* Reprinted. Albuquerque: University of New Mexico Press.

Bartholomew, Keith. n.d. *Making the land use, transportation, air quality connection (LUTRAQ)—Freeways or communities. It's your choice.* Portland, Ore.: 1,000 Friends of Oregon.

Beatley, Timothy. 2000. *Green urbanism: Learning from European Cities.* Washington, D.C.: Island Press.

⸻. 1994. *Habitat conservation planning: Endangered species and urban growth.* Austin, Tex.: University of Texas Press.

Beatley, Timothy, David J. Brower, and Anna K. Schwab. 2002. *An introduction to coastal zone management.* Washington, D.C.: Island

Beatley, Timothy, and Stephen Wheeler. 2004. *The sustainable urban development reader.* London and New York: Routledge.

Bedient, Philip B., and Wayne C. Huber. 2002. *Hydrology and floodplain analysis.* 3rd ed. New York: Prentice Hall.

Bernhardsen, Tor. 2002. *Geographic information systems: An introduction.* 3rd ed. New York: John Wiley and Sons.

Bernick, Michael, and Robert Cervero. 1997. *Transit villages for the 21st century.* New York: McGraw-Hill.

Bertin, Jacques. 1967. Reprint 1983. *Semiology of graphics: Diagrams, networks, maps.* Translated by William J. Berg. Madison, Wis.: University of Wisconsin Press.

Bolstad, Paul. 2002. *GIS fundamentals.* White Bear Lake, Minn.: Eider Press.

Brail, Richard K., and Richard E. Klosterman, eds. 2001. *Planning support systems: Integrating geographic information systems, models, and visualization tools.* Redlands, Calif.: ESRI Press.

Brewer, Cynthia. 2005. *Designing better maps.* Redlands, Calif.: ESRI Press

———. 1994a. Color use guidelines for mapping and visualization. In *Visualization in modern cartography,* eds. A. M. MacEachren and D. R. F. Taylor. Tarrytown, N.Y.: Elsevier Science.

———. 1994b. Guidelines for use of the perceptual dimensions of color for mapping and visualization. In *Proceedings of the International Society for Optical Engineering (SPIE),* ed. Jan Bares, 54–63. San Jose, Calif.

Brewer, Cynthia, and Trudy A. Suchan. 2001. *Mapping census 2000: The geography of U.S. diversity.* Redlands, Calif. ESRI Press.

Bridenbaugh, Carl. 1938. *Cities in the wilderness.* New York: Ronald Press.

Brinton, Crane. 1963. *The shaping of modern thought.* New York: Prentice Hall.

Calthorpe Associates. 1997. *Making the connections: A summary of the LUTRAQ report.* Berkeley, Calif.: Calthorpe Associates.

Calthorpe, Peter. 1993. *The next American metropolis.* Princeton, N.J.: Princeton Architectural Press.

Calthorpe, Peter, and William Fulton. 2001. *The regional city: Planning for the end of sprawl.* Washington, D.C., Island Press.

Card, Stuart K., Jock D. Mackinlay, and Ben Schneiderman. 1999. *Readings in information visualization—Using vision to think.* San Francisco: Morgan Kaufmann.

Carson, Rachel. 1962. Reprinted 2002. *Silent spring.* New York: Mariner Books.

Cervero, Robert. 1991. Jobs-housing balance as public policy. *Urban Land.* 50 (10):10–14.

———. 1996. Jobs-housing balance revisited: Trends and impacts in the San Francisco Bay Area. *Journal of the American Planning Association.* Autumn: 492–511.

Chandler, Tertius. 1987. *Four thousand years of urban growth.* Lewiston, N.Y.: Edwin Mellen Press.

Chandler, Tertius, and Gerald Fox. 1974. *3000 years of urban growth.* New York: Academic Press.

Chrisman, Nicholas. 2001. *Exploring geographic information systems.* 2nd ed. New York: John Wiley and Sons.

Chudacoff, Howard P., and Judith E. Smith. 2005. *The evolution of American urban society.* New York: Prentice Hall.

Clark, Colin. 1957. Transport: Maker and breaker of cities. *Town Planning Review.* 28 (4): 237–250.

Clark, Rich, and Marc Maynard. 1998. Research methodology: Using online technology for secondary analysis of survey research data—'Act globally, think locally.' *Social Science Computer Review.* Special Issue. *State of the Art of Computing in the Social Sciences.* Spring: 58–71.

Clarke, Keith C. 2003. *Getting started with geographic information systems.* 4th ed. New York: Prentice Hall.

Cleveland, William. 1994. *The elements of graphing data.* Revised edition. Murray Hill, N.J.: AT&T Bell Labs.

———. *Visualizing data.* 1993. Murray Hill, N.J.: AT&T Bell Labs.

Cooper, C. David, and F. C. Alley. 2002. *Air pollution control.* 3rd ed. Prospect Heights, Ill.: Waveland Press.

Craig, William J., Trevor M. Harris, and Daniel Weiner. 2002. *Community participation and geographical information systems.* Boca Raton, Fla.: CRC Press.

Cronon, William. 1992. *Nature's metropolis: Chicago and the Great West.* New York: W. W. Norton.

Daniels, Roger. 2002. *Coming to America: A history of immigration and ethnicity in American life.* 2nd ed. New York: Perennial.

Davidoff, Paul. 1965. Advocacy and pluralism in planning. *American Institute of Planners Journal.* November: 277–295.

Davis, Kingsley. 1973. *Cities: Their origin, growth, and human impact.* San Francisco: W. H. Freeman.

———. 1965. The urbanization of the human population. *Scientific American.* September: 41–53.

DeGrove, John, and Deborah A. Miness. 1992. *The new frontier for land policy: Planning and growth management in the States.* Cambridge, Mass.: Lincoln Institute of Land Policy.

DeMers, Michael N. 2004. *Fundamentals of geographic information systems.* 3rd ed. New York: John Wiley and Sons.

———. 2001. *GIS modeling in raster.* New York: John Wiley and Sons.

Dent, Borden D. 1999. *Cartography: Thematic map design.* 5th ed. New York: McGraw-Hill.

Devlin, Keith. 1999. *InfoSense—Turning information into knowledge.* New York: W. H. Freeman and Company.

Ditmar, Hank, and Gloria Ohland. 2003. *The new transit town: Best practices in transit-oriented development.* Washington, D.C.: Island Press.

Domhoff, G. William. 1967. *Who rules America?* New York: McGraw-Hill.

Dowall, David. 1984. *The suburban squeeze.* Berkeley, Calif.: University of California Press.

Downing, Andrew Jackson. 1844. *A treatise on the theory and practice of landscape gardening adapted to North America.* New York and London: Wiley and Putnam.

Downs, Anthony, ed. 2004. *Growth management and affordable housing: Do they conflict?* Washington, D.C.: Brookings Institution Press.

———. 1992. *Stuck in traffic.* Washington, D.C. and Cambridge, Mass.: Brookings Institution Press and Lincoln Institute of Land Policy.

————. 1994. *New visions for metropolitan America*. Washington, D.C. and Cambridge, Mass.: Brooking Institution Press and Lincoln Institute of Land Policy.

————. 1989. The need for a new vision of metropolitan America. New York: Salomon Brothers. Reprinted in *The city reader*, 3rd ed., eds. Richard LeGates and Frederic Stout. 2003. New York and London: Routledge.

————. 1973. *Opening up the suburbs: An urban strategy for America*. New Haven: Yale University Press.

Duany, Andres, and Elizabeth Plater-Zyberk. 2001. *Suburban nation: The rise of sprawl and the decline of the American dream*. New York: North Point Press.

Forester, John. 1987. Planning in the face of conflict. *Journal of the American Planning Association*. Summer.

Forthingham, Stewart, Chris Brunsdon, and Martin Charlton. 2000. *Quantitative geography: Perspectives on spatial data analysis*. Thousand Oaks, Calif.: Sage.

Frankenberg, Erica, Chungmei Lee, and Gary Orfield. 2003. *A multiracial society with segregated schools: Are we losing the dream?* Cambridge: The Harvard Civil Rights Project.

Galster, George, Peter A. Tatian, Anna M. Santiago, Kathryn L. S. Pettit, and Robin E. Smith. 2003. *Why not in my backyard? Neighborhood impacts of deconcentrating assisted housing*. New Brunswick, N.J.: Center for Urban Policy Research. Rutgers University.

Geddes, Patrick. 1915. *Cities in evolution*. London: Williams and Norgate. Reprinted in *Early urban planning 1870–1940*, eds. Richard LeGates and Frederic Stout. 1998. London: Routledge/Thoemmes.

Gilbert, Alan, ed. 1996. *The mega-city in Latin America*. New York: United Nations University Press.

Golway, Terry. 1997. *The Irish in America*. New York: Hyperion books.

Goodchild, Michael. 1997. What is geographic information science? Santa Barbara. National Center For Geographic Information and Analysis.

Goodchild, Michael S., and David W. Rhind, eds. 1991. *Geographical information systems: Principles and applications*. London: Longman.

Gordon, Peter, and Harry Richardson. 2000. Defending suburban sprawl. *The Public Interest* no. 139: 65–71.

Gorr, Wilpen L., and Kristen S. Kurland. 2005. *GIS tutorial: Workbook for ArcView 9*. Redlands, Calif.: ESRI Press.

Hall, Peter. 2002. *Cities of tomorrow*. 3rd ed. London: Blackwell Publishing.

Harris, Robert L. 1996. *Information graphics: A comprehensive illustrated reference*. Atlanta: Management Graphics.

Hartman, Chester. 2002. *City for sale: The transformation of San Francisco*. Berkeley, California University of California Press.

Harvey, David. 1973. *Social justice and the city*. Johns Hopkins University Press. Baltimore, Md. Reissue edition Oxford. Basil Blackwell. 1992.

Heat-Moon, William Least. 1982. *Blue highways*. Boston: Back Bay Books.

Heywood, Ian, Sarah Cornelius, and Steve Carver. 2002. *An introduction to geographical information systems*. 2nd ed. New York: Prentice Hall.

Hoggan, Daniel H. 1996. *Computer-assisted floodplain hydrology and hydraulics*. New York: McGraw-Hill.

Holliday, J. S. 1981. *The world rushed in: The California Gold Rush experience*. New York: Simon and Schuster.

Howard, Ebenezer. 1898. *Tomorrow: The peaceful path to real reform*. London. Sonnenschein. Subsequently titled *Garden cities of tomorrow*. Reprinted in *Early urban planning*, eds. Richard LeGates and Frederic Stout. 1998. London: Routledge/ Thoemmes.

Huxhold, William E., Brian M. Fowler, and Brian Parr. 2004. *ArcGIS and the digital city*. Redlands, Calif.: ESRI Press.

International Union for Conservation of Nature and Natural Resources (IUCN). 2004. *IUCN red list of Threatened species*. www.iucnredlist.org.

Job-Center Housing Coalition. 2004. *Housing in your area*. www.jobcenterhousing.com/ area-sv.html.

Kain, J. F. 1968. Housing segregation, Negro employment, and metropolitan decentralization. *Quarterly Journal of Economics*. 82: 32–59.

Katz, Peter. 1994. *The new urbanism: Towards an architecture of community*. New York: McGraw-Hill.

Kay, Robert, and Jackie Alder. 1999. *Coastal planning and management*. London: Sponpress.

Kent, Jack. 1964. *The urban general plan*. San Francisco: Chandler.

Kirp, David. 1995. *Our town: race, housing, and the soul of Suburbia*. Rutgers: Rutgers University Press.

Knaap, Gerrit. 2000. The urban growth boundary in metropolitan Portland, Oregon: Research, rhetoric, and reality. American Planning Association Planning Advisory Service *PAS MEMO*. December.

Knaap, Gerrit, Richard Bolen, and Ethan Seltzer. 2004. Metro's regional land information system: The virtual key to Portland's growth management success. *American Planning Association Planning Advisory Service PAS MEMO*. May/June.

Knowles, Anne Kelly. 2002. *Past time past place: GIS for history*. Redlands, Calif.: ESRI Press.

Koch, Tom. 2005. *Cartographies of disease: Maps, mapping, and medicine*. Redlands, Calif.: ESRI Press.

Kozol, Jonathan. 1992. *Savage inequalities: Children in America's schools*. New York: Harper Perennial.

Krumholz, Norman, and John Forester. 1990. *Making equity planning work*. Philadelphia: Temple University Press.

Krumholz, Norman, and Pierre Clavel. 1994. *Reinventing cities: Equity planners tell their stories*. Philadelphia: Temple University Press.

Leccese, Michael, ed. 1999. *Charter of the new urbanism*. New York: McGraw-Hill.

LeGates, Richard. 1989. *Growing old gracefully: The Petaluma plan reaches middle age*. San Francisco: San Francisco State University Public Research Institute.

LeGates, Richard, and Frederic Stout, eds. 2003. *The city reader.* 3rd ed. New London and New York: Routledge.

Levine, Ned. 1996. Spatial statistics and GIS: Software tools to quantify spatial patterns. *Journal of the American Planning Association.* Summer: 381–391.

Lippmann, Walter. 1929. *A preface to morals.* New York: Macmillan.

Listoken, David. 1976. *Fair share housing allocation.* New Brunswick, N.J.: Center for Urban Policy Research. Rutgers University.

Lo, Fu-chen and Yue-man Yeung, eds. 1996. *Emerging world cities in Pacific Asia.* New York: United Nations University Press.

Logan, John. 2001. *Ethnic diversity grows, neighborhood integration lags behind.* Albany: Lewis Mumford Center.

Longley, Paul. 2000. Spatial analysis in the new millennium. *Annals of the Association of American Geographers.* March: 157–165.

Longley, Paul A., Michael F. Goodchild, David J. Maguire, and David W. Rhind. 2005. *Geographic information systems: Principles, techniques, management and applications.* 2nd ed. New York: John Wiley and Sons.

Madden, Janice. 2000. *Changes in income inequality within U.S. metropolitan areas.* Kalamazoo, Mich.: W. E. Upjohn Institute for Employment Research.

Marger, Martin. 2001. *Social inequality: Patterns and processes.* New York: McGraw-Hill.

Massey, Douglas S., and Nancy A. Denton. 1993. *American apartheid: Segregation and the making of the underclass.* Cambridge: Harvard University Press.

McCoy, Jill, and Kevin Johnston. 2001. *Using ArcGIS Spatial Analyst.* Redlands, Calif.: ESRI.

McHarg, Ian. 1969. *Design with nature.* Garden City: Doubleday and Company.

Meadows, Donella H., Dennis L. Meadows, Jorgen Randers, and William W. Behrens III. 1972. *The limits to growth: A report for the club of Rome's project on the predicament of mankind.* New York: Universe Books

Medoff, Peter, and Holly Sklar. 1994. *Streets of hope: The fall and rise of an urban neighborhood.* Boston: South End Press.

Melton, Hope. 1993. *Ghettos of the nineties: The consequences of concentrated poverty.* St. Paul, Minn.: Department of Planning and Economic Development.

Metro. 2004a. *The nature of 2040.* Portland, Ore.: Metro.

———. 2004b. *Protecting the nature of the region.* Portland, Ore.: Metro.

———. 2002. *UGB decision and map.* Portland, Ore.: Metro.

———. 2000. *Regional transportation plan.* Portland, Ore.: Metro.

———. 1997. *Regional framework plan.* Portland, Ore.: Metro.

———. 1992. *Charter.* Portland, Ore.: Metro.

Miller, David. 2002. *The regional governing of metropolitan America.* Boulder, Colo.: Westview Press.

Mills, C. Wright. 1956. *The power elite.* London and New York: Oxford University Press.

Mitchell, Andy. 2005. *The ESRI guide to GIS analysis, volume 2: Spatial measurements and statistics*. Redlands, Calif.: ESRI Press.

———. 1999. *The ESRI guide to GIS analysis, volume 1: Geographic patterns & relationships*. Redlands, Calif.: ESRI Press.

Monmonier, Mark. 1996. *How to lie with maps*. 2nd ed. Chicago and London: University of Chicago Press.

———. 1993. *Mapping it out: Expository cartography for the humanities and social sciences*. Chicago: University of Chicago Press.

Moore, Thomas. 1516. Reprinted 1997. *Utopia*. New York: Dover.

Myers, Dowell. 1992. *Analysis with local census data—Portraits of change*. Boston: Academic Press.

National Center for Geographic Information and Analysis (NCGIA). 2000. *Core curriculum in GIScience*. Santa Barbara: NCGIA.

New Jersey Department of Environmental Protection (NJDEP). Division of Publicly Funded Site Remediation. Site Remediation Program (SRP). 2001. *Known contaminated site list for New Jersey 2001*. www.state.nj.us/dep/gis/stateshp.html

Nyerges, Timothy, and Reg Golledge. 1997. *Asking geographic questions*. Santa Barbara: NCGIA.

Oakland, California, Community Economic Development Agency (CEDA). 2004. *Fourth annual small business symposium*. Oakland: Oakland CEDA.

O'Looney, John. 2000. *Beyond maps—GIS and decision making in local government*. Redlands, Calif.: ESRI Press.

Orfield, Myron. 2002. *American metropolitics: The new suburban reality*. Washington, D.C.: Brookings Institution Press.

———. 1999. *Metropolitics: A regional agenda for community and stability*. Washington, D.C.: Brookings Institution Press.

Orfield, Gary, and John T. Yun. 1999. *Resegregation in American schools*. Cambridge: The Harvard Civil Rights Project.

Orfield, Myron, and Thomas Luce. 2003. *New Jersey metropatterns*. Minneapolis: Ameregis.

Ormsby, Tim, Eileen Napoleon, Robert Burke, Carolyn Groessl, and Laura Feaster. 2004. *Getting to Know ArcGIS*. 2nd ed. Redlands, Calif.: ESRI Press.

Orshansky, Mollie. 1965. Counting the poor. Another look at the poverty profile. *Social Security Bulletin*. January: 3–29.

———. 1963. Children of the poor. *Social Security Bulletin*. July: 3–13.

Ortolano, Leonard. 1997. *Environmental regulation and impact assessment*. New York: John Wiley and Sons.

Ozawa, Connie, ed. 2004. *The Portland edge: Challenges and successes in growing communities*. Washington, D.C.: Island Press.

Parzen, Julia A., and Michael H. Kieschnick. 1993. *Credit where it's due: Development banking for communities*. Philadelphia: Temple University Press.

Peirce, Neal R. 1994. *Citistates: How urban America can prosper in a competitive world.* Santa Ana: Seven Locks Press.

Pemer, Mats. 2001. *Developing a sustainable compact city in Stockholm, Sweden.* Stockholm, Sweden: Strategic Department. Stockholm City Planning Department.

Peters, Alan, and Heather MacDonald. 2004. *Unlocking the census with GIS.* Redlands, Calif.: ESRI Press.

Pickles, John. 1994. *Ground truth: The social implications of geographic information systems.* New York: Guilford Press.

Playfair, William. 1786. *The commercial and political atlas.* London: J. DeBrett.

Polo, Marco. 1299. *The travels of Marco Polo.* A modern translation by Teresa Waugh from the Italian by Maria Bellonci. 1984. London: Sidgwick and Jackson.

Porter, Douglas, Barry Hogue, Terry Jill Lassar, Robert Lewis, Robert Narus, Paul O'Mara, Bruce Rips, David Salvesen, and Richard C. Ward. 1996. *Profiles in growth management: An assessment of current programs and guidelines for effective management.* Washington, D.C.: Urban Land Institute.

Porter, Douglas, Robert Dunphy, and David Salvesen. 2002. *Making smart growth work.* Washington, D.C.: Urban Institute.

Porter, Michael. 1995. The competitive advantage of the central city. *Harvard Business Review.* May/June.

Putnam, Robert. 2000. *Bowling alone.* New York: Simon and Schuster.

Putnam, Robert, and Lewis M. Feldstein. 2003. *Better together: Restoring the American community.* New York: Simon and Schuster.

Quine, Willard Van Orman. 1951. Two dogmas of empiricism. *Philosophical Review* 60: 20–43.

Rabinovitch, Leitman. 1996. Urban planning in Curitiba. *Scientific American* March: 46–63.

Rahm, Dianne. 2002. *Toxic waste and environmental policy in the 21st century United States.* Jefferson, N.C.: McFarland and Company.

Rakodi, Carole, ed. 1997. *The urban challenge in Africa: Growth and management of its large cities.* New York: United Nations University Press.

Reisner, Marc. 1993. *Cadillac desert: The American West and its disappearing water.* New York: Penguin.

Robinson, Arthur H., Joel L. Morrison, Phillip C. Muehrcke, A. Jon Kimerling, and Stephen C. Guptill. 1995. *Elements of cartography.* 6th ed. New York: John Wiley and Sons.

Roosevelt, Franklin D. 1957. Second inaugural address.

Sassen, Saskia. 1994. *Cities in a world economy.* Thousand Oaks, Calif.: Pine Forge Press.

Scott, J. Michael et al. 1993. *Gap analysis: A geographic approach to protection of biological diversity.* Wildlife monographs no. 123. *Supplement to the Journal of Wildlife Management.* January.

Scott, Mellior. 1985. *The San Francisco Bay Area. A metropolis in perspective.* 2nd ed. Berkeley: University of California Press.

Slocum, Terry A., Bruce B. McMaster, Fritz C. Kessler, and Hugh H. Howard. 2003. *Thematic cartography and geographic visualization.* 2nd ed. New York: Prentice Hall.

Spence, Jonathan D. 1994. *The memory palace of Mateo Ricci.* London and New York: Penguin.

Spirn, Anne Whiston. 1985. *The granite garden: Urban nature and human design.* New York: Basic Books.

Stein, Bruce A., Lynn S. Kutner, and Jonathan S. Adams, eds. 2000. *Precious heritage: The status of biodiversity in the United States.* New York: Oxford University Press.

Stevens, Stanley Smith. 1949. On the theory of scales of measurement. *Science.* 677–680.

Stevens, Wallace. 1990. *The collected poems of Wallace Stevens.* New York: Vintage Books.

Strunk, William Jr., and Elwyn Brook White. 2000. *The elements of style.* Needham Heights: Allyn Bacon.

Swift, Jonathan. 1711. Thoughts on various subjects.

Szasz, Andrew. 1994. *Ecopopulism: Toxic waste and the movement for environmental justice.* Minneapolis: University of Minnesota Press.

Taylor, Paul. 1999. Worlds of large cities: Pondering Castells' space of flows. *Third Word Planning Review* 21 (3): iii–x.

Tomlin, C. Dana. 1990. *Geographic information systems and cartographic modeling.* Englewood Cliffs: Prentice Hall.

Tufte, Edward R. 2003. *The cognitive style of PowerPoint.* Cheshire, Conn.: Graphics Press.

———. 2001. *The visual display of quantitative information.* 2nd ed. Cheshire, Conn.: Graphics Press.

———. 1997. *Visual explanations: Images and quantities, evidence and narrative.* Cheshire, Conn.: Graphics Press.

———. 1990. *Envisioning information.* Cheshire, Conn.: Graphics Press.

Tukey, John Wilder. 1977. *Exploratory data analysis.* Reading, Mass.: Addison-Wesley.

United Nations. 2004. *Urban agglomerations 2003.* New York: UN Department of Economic and Social Affairs. Population Division.

———. 2002. *World population prospects: The 2002 revision.* Highlights. New York: UN Department of Economic and Social Affairs. Population Division.

———. 2000. *World population prospects report.* New York: UN Department of Economic and Social Affairs. Population Division.

———. 1999. *World urbanization prospects: The 1999 revision.* New York: UN Department of Economic and Social Affairs. Population Division.

Unwin, David J. 1997. *Curriculum design for GIS.* Santa Barbara, Calif.: National Center for Geographic Information and Analysis.

U.S. Census. 2004. *Historical statistics of the United States 1790–1970.* Washington, D.C.: U.S. Government Printing Office.

———. 2002a. *Measuring America: The decennial censuses from 1790 to 2000.* Washington, D.C.: U.S. Government Printing Office.

———. 2002b. *The foreign born population 2000.* Washington, D.C.: U.S. Government Printing Office.

————. 2000a. *Census of population and housing.* Washington, D.C.: U.S. Government Printing Office.

————. 2000b. *Current population survey 1968 to 2000.* Washington, D.C.: U.S. Government Printing Office.

U.S. Department of Housing and Urban Development. 2000. *State of the nation's cities.* Washington, D.C.: U.S. Department of Housing and Urban Development.

U.S. Endangered Species Act (ESA). 1973. 16 USC s 1531 et seq.

U.S. Housing Act of 1949. Title V of PL 81–171. October 25, 1949.

Van der Ryn, Sim, and Stuart Cowan. 1996. *Ecological design.* Washington, D.C.: Island Press.

Ward, Michael, and John O'Loughlin, eds. 2002. Spatial methods in political science. *Political Analysis* Summer.

Weitz, Jerry. 2000. *Sprawl busting: State programs to control growth.* Chicago: Planners Press.

Wheeler, Stephen. 2004. *Planning for sustainability: Creating livable, equitable, and ecological communities.* London and New York: Routledge

Wilde, Oscar. 1895. Reprinted 1990. *The importance of being earnest.* Mineoloa, N.Y.: Dover Publications.

Wilson, William Julius. 1996. *When work disappears: The world of the new urban poor.* New York: Knopf.

————. 1987. *The truly disadvantaged.* Chicago: University of Chicago Press.

————. 1980. *The declining significance of race: Blacks and changing American institutions.* 2nd ed. Chicago: University of Chicago Press.

Winchester, Simon. 2002. *The map that changed the world: William Smith and the birth of modern geology.* New York: Perennial.

World Bank. 2004. *World development indicators 2004.* Washington, D.C.: World Bank.

————. 1984. *World development report: Infrastructure for development.* Oxford: Oxford University Press.

World Commission on Environment and Development (The Brundtland Commission). 1987. *Our common future.* New York: Oxford University Press.

Map credits

All maps in *Think Globally, Act Regionally,* with the exception of those noted with a different copyright holder, were created by students and staff employed by San Francisco State University working under the direction of the author, supported by U.S. National Science Foundation (NSF), Division of Undergraduate Education (DUE), Course, Curriculum and Laboratory Improvement-Educational Materials Development (CCLI-EMD) grant # DUE 0228878. Richard LeGates holds the copyright to these maps.

Every effort has been made to contact copyright holders for their permission to use data to create maps in this book. The publishers would be grateful to hear from any copyright holder who is not here acknowledged and will undertake to rectify any errors or omissions in future editions of this book.

Maps in this book may not be reproduced without express written permission of the copyright holder.

Following is copyright information for the maps that appear in this book:

Chapter 1
Map 1.1: San Francisco Bay Area with small maps of San Francisco and Contra Costa County © 2005 Richard LeGates. Created from data in 2000 U.S. Census of Population and Housing.

Map 1.2: Urban agglomerations with more than five million people, 2000 © 2005 Richard LeGates. Created from data in United Nations, *Urban agglomerations 2003* © 2003 United Nations Department of Economic and Social Affairs, Population Division.

Map 1.3a: Percent of population urban by country, 2003 © 2005 Richard LeGates. Created from data in World Bank, W*orld development indicators 2004* © 2004 World Bank.

Map 1.3b: Percentage change in the urban population by country, 2003 © 2005 Richard LeGates. Created from data in World Bank, *World development indicators 2004* © 2004 World Bank.

Map 1.4: Population size of selected European cities, 1750 © 2005 Richard LeGates. Created from data in Tertius Chandler and Gerald Fox, *3000 years of urban growth* © 1974 Academic Press.

Map 1.5: Percent of the population foreign born, San Francisco Bay Area, 2000 © 2005 Richard LeGates. Created from data in 2000 U.S. Census of Population and Housing.

Map 1.6a: Number of Asians/Pacific Islanders in San Francisco by census tract, 2000 © 2005 Richard LeGates. Created from data in 2000 U.S. Census of Population and Housing.

Map 1.6b: Number of Hispanics in San Francisco, 2000, by census tract © 2005 Richard LeGates. Created from data in 2000 U.S. Census of Population and Housing.

Map 1.7a: The five U.S. colonial cities with the largest populations, 1775 © 2005 Richard LeGates. Created from data in Howard P. Chudacoff and Judith E. Smith, *The evolution of American urban society,* sixth edition. © 2005, 2000, 1994, 1988, 1981 Pearson Education Inc.

Map 1.7b: Five cities with populations in 2000 similar to the five largest U.S. colonial cities in 1775 © 2005 Richard LeGates. Created from data in 2000 U.S. Census of Population and Housing.

Map 1.8: Balkanization of San Francisco Bay Area local government © 2005 Richard LeGates. Created from data in 2000 U.S. Census of Population and Housing.

Map 1.9: Urban sprawl in eastern Contra Costa County © 2005 Richard LeGates. Created from data in 2000 U.S. Census of Population and Housing.

Map 1.10a: Number of people age 16 and older who drive to work alone, selected Santa Clara County census tracts, 2000 © 2005 Richard LeGates. Created from data in 2000 U.S. Census of Population and Housing.

Map 1.10b: Number of people age 16 and older who carpool to work, selected Santa Clara County census tracts, 2000 © 2005 Richard LeGates. Created from data in 2000 U.S. Census of Population and Housing.

Map 1.11: Vacant lots in downtown Oakland, 2004 © 2005 Richard LeGates. Created from data in Oakland Office of Information Technology parcel database © 2004 Oakland Office of Information Technology.

Chapter 2

Map 2.1: Housing in San Francisco's South Bayshore neighborhood financially assisted by the San Francisco Redevelopment Agency © 2005 Richard LeGates. Created from San Francisco Redevelopment Agency data © 2004 San Francisco Redevelopment Agency.

Map 2.2a: San Francisco census tracts © 2005 Richard LeGates. Created from data in 2000 U.S. Census of Population and Housing.

Map 2.2b: San Francisco streets © 2005 Richard LeGates. Created from data in 2000 U.S. Census TIGER files.

Map 2.2c: Affordable housing units financially assisted by the San Francisco Redevelopment Agency © 2005 Richard LeGates. Created from San Francisco Redevelopment Agency data © San Francisco Redevelopment Agency 2004.

Map 2.2d: Affordable housing units financially assisted by the San Francisco Redevelopment Agency, census tracts, and streets © 2005 Richard LeGates. Created from San Francisco Redevelopment Agency data (affordable housing units) © 2004 San Francisco Redevelopment Agency; data in 2000 U.S. Census of Population and Housing; and 2000 U.S. Census TIGER files.

Chapter 3

Map 3.1a: Map with one layer (countries) © 2005 Richard LeGates. Created from data in ESRI Data and Maps 2003 © 2003 ESRI.

Map 3.1b: Map with two layers (countries and urban agglomerations with five to ten million people) © 2005 Richard LeGates. Created from data in ESRI Data and Maps 2003 © 2003 ESRI (countries) and © 2004 United Nations Department of Economic and Social Affairs, Population Division, *Urban agglomerations 2003 (urban agglomerations)*.

Map 3.1c: Map with three layers (countries, urban agglomerations with five to ten million people, and megacities with more than ten million people) © 2005 Richard LeGates. Created from data in ESRI Data and Maps 2003 © 2003 ESRI (countries) and © 2004 United Nations Department of Economic and Social Affairs, Population Division, *Urban agglomerations 2003 (urban agglomerations and megacities)*.

Map 3.2a: San Francisco Bay Area and Bay Area cities © 2005 Richard LeGates. Created from data in 2000 U.S. Census of Population and Housing.

Map 3.2b: San Francisco Bay Area zoomed to San Francisco County © 2005 Richard LeGates. Created from data in 2000 U.S. Census of Population and Housing.

Map 3.2c: San Francisco Bay Area zoomed out and panned left © Richard LeGates 2005. Created from data in 2000 U.S. Census of Population and Housing.

Map 3.3: San Francisco Bay Area residents age 16 and older who bicycled to work, 2000 © Richard LeGates 2005. Created from data in 2000 U.S. Census of Population and Housing.

Map 3.4: Land parcels in Oakland © 2005 Richard LeGates. Created from data in Oakland Office of Information Technology parcel database © 2004 Oakland Office of Information Technology.

Map 3.5: Elementary schools and historic fire areas in Contra Costa County © 2005 Richard LeGates. Created from data in U.S. Geological Survey Geographic Names Information System and California Department of Forestry and Fire Protection, *The changing California 2003 forest and range assessment.*

Map 3.6a: Single feature: Hamilton Family Center © 2005 Richard LeGates. Created from San Francisco Redevelopment Agency data © 2004 San Francisco Redevelopment Agency.

Map 3.6b: Multiple features of the same type: housing financially assisted by the San Francisco Redevelopment Agency © 2005 Richard LeGates. Created from San Francisco Redevelopment Agency data © 2004 San Francisco Redevelopment Agency.

Map 3.6c: Multiple features of different types: five kinds of affordable housing financially assisted by the San Francisco Redevelopment Agency © 2005 Richard LeGates. Created from San Francisco Redevelopment Agency data © 2004 San Francisco Redevelopment Agency.

Map 3.7: Proximity: housing financially assisted by the San Francisco Redevelopment Agency within one-quarter mile of San Francisco's Mission Street © Richard LeGates. Created from San Francisco Redevelopment Agency data © 2004 San Francisco Redevelopment Agency.

Map 3.8a: Clustering: world cities with 40,000 or more residents, 1850 © 2005 Richard LeGates. Created from data in Tertius Chandler and Gerald Fox, *3000 years of urban growth* © 1974 Academic Press.

Map 3.8b: Dispersal: Asian cities with 40,000 or more residents, 1850 © 2005 Richard LeGates. Created from data in Tertius Chandler and Gerald Fox, *3000 years of urban growth* © 1974 Academic Press.

Map 3.8c: Apparently random pattern: cities in North and South America with 40,000 or more residents, 1850 © 2005 Richard LeGates. Created from data in Tertius Chandler and Gerald Fox, *3000 years of urban growth* © 1974 Academic Press.

Map 3.8d: Cities in Contra Costa County (ordered pattern following highways) © 2005 Richard LeGates. Created from data in 2000 U.S. Census of Population and Housing.

Map 3.9: Dot density map of San Francisco African-American population, 2000 © 2005 Richard LeGates. Created from data in 2000 U.S. Census of Population and Housing.

Map 3.10: William Smith's geological map of England and Wales (1820). IRP/61-23C British Geological Survey © NERC. All rights reserved.

Map 3.11: A redrawing of John Snow's map of cholera in central London (1854). Copyright © 1983 Edward Tufte.

Map 3.12: The original London tube map created by Harry Beck (1933) © 1933 Transport for London.

Map 3.13: Charles Joseph Minard's map of Napoleon's Russian campaign (1861). Copyright © 1983 Edward Tufte.

Map 3.14: Greenbelt Alliance "Region at Risk" map © 1999 Greenbelt Alliance.

Map 3.15: Metro's map of the Portland, Oregon, region 2040 Growth Concept (2004) © 2004 Metro.

Map 3.16a: Uniform point symbols, South American cities © 2005 Richard LeGates. Created from data in ESRI Data and Maps 2003 © 2003 ESRI.

Map 3.16b: Graduated point symbols (five classes), South American cities © 2005 Richard LeGates. Created from data in ESRI Data and Maps 2003 © 2003 ESRI.

Map 3.17: California counties (unclassified) © 2005 Richard LeGates. Created from data in 2000 U.S. Census of Population and Housing.

Map 3.18a: Equal interval classification of California county populations, 2000 © 2005 Richard LeGates. Created from data in 2000 U.S. Census of Population and Housing.

Map 3.18b: Quantile classification of California county populations, 2000 © 2005 Richard LeGates. Created from data in 2000 U.S. Census of Population and Housing.

Map 3.18c: Natural breaks classification of California county populations, 2000 © 2005 Richard LeGates. Created from data in 2000 U.S. Census of Population and Housing.

Map 3.18d: Manual classification of California county populations, 2000 © 2005 Richard LeGates. Created from data in 2000 U.S. Census of Population and Housing.

Chapter 5

Map 5.1: Three views of Contra Costa County and environs: land use (main map); red-legged frog habitat (bottom left); regional ozone pollution (bottom right) © 2005 Richard LeGates. Created from data in California Department of Conservation Farmland Mapping and Monitoring Program © 1984–2004 California Department of Conservation (main map); California Gap Analysis Project (CA-GAP) (red-legged frog habitat); and California Air Resources Board 2000 ambient air quality databases (ozone pollution).

Map 5.2: Urbanization and prime farmland in eastern Contra Costa County, 2000 © 2005 Richard LeGates. Created from data in California Department of Conservation Farmland Mapping and Monitoring Program © 1984–2004 California Department of Conservation.

Map 5.3: Ozone pollution in Contra Costa County © 2005 Richard LeGates. Created from data in California Air Resources Board 2000 ambient air quality databases.

Map 5.4: Toxic release incidents in Contra Costa County © 2005 Richard LeGates. Hypothetical data based on 2003 U.S. Environmental Protection Agency Toxic Release Inventory.

Map 5.5: Prime California vole habitat in Contra Costa County © 2005 Richard LeGates. Created from data in California Gap Analysis Project (CA-GAP).

Map 5.6: Historic fire areas in Contra Costa County © 2005 Richard LeGates. Created from data in California Department of Forestry and Fire Protection, *The changing California 2003 forest and range assessment.*

Chapter 6

Map 6.1a: Vector image of land near Walnut Creek, California © 2005 Richard LeGates. Created from data in California Department of Conservation Farmland Mapping and Monitoring Program © 1984–2004 California Department of Conservation.

Map 6.1b: Raster image of land near Walnut Creek, California © 2005 Richard LeGates. Created from data in California Department of Conservation Farmland Mapping and Monitoring Program © 1984–2004 California Department of Conservation.

Map 6.2a: Suitability of Contra Costa County habitat for red-legged frogs © 2005 Richard LeGates. Created from data in California Gap Analysis Project (CA-GAP).

Map 6.2b: Area of detail © 2005 Richard LeGates. Created from data in California Gap Analysis Project (CA-GAP).

Map 6.3a: Raster dataset zones © 2005 Richard LeGates. Created from data in California Gap Analysis Project (CA-GAP).

Map 6.3b: Raster dataset region © 2005 Richard LeGates. Created from data in California Gap Analysis Project (CA-GAP).

Map 6.4: Digital elevation model (DEM) of San Francisco © 2005 Richard LeGates. Created from data in 2000 U.S. Census of Population and Housing.

Map 6.5a: Habitat suitability for San Francisco garter snake © 2005 Richard LeGates. Created from data in California Gap Analysis Project (CA-GAP).

Map 6.5b: Habitat suitability for California towhee © 2005 Richard LeGates. Created from data in California Gap Analysis Project (CA-GAP).

Map 6.6: Areas of Contra Costa County with habitat most suitable for two or more of four endangered species © 2005 Richard LeGates. Created from data in California Gap Analysis Project (CA-GAP).

Map 6.7: Vegetation types in Contra Costa County © 2005 Richard LeGates. Created from data in California Gap Analysis Project (CA-GAP).

Map 6.8: Variety of vegetation types in eastern Contra Costa County © 2005 Richard LeGates. Created from data in California Gap Analysis Project (CA-GAP).

Map 6.9: Contra Costa County watersheds © 2005 Richard LeGates. Created from data in California Department of Forestry and Fire Protection, *The changing California 2003 forest and range assessment.*

Chapter 7

Map 7.1: Straight line distance from Contra Costa County highways © 2005 Richard LeGates. Created from 2000 U.S. Census TIGER files.

Map 7.2: Thiessen polygons around Contra Costa County cities © 2005 Richard LeGates. Created from 2000 U.S. Census of Population and Housing.

Map 7.3: Kernel density of red-legged frogs in Contra Costa County © 2005 Richard LeGates. Created from data in California Gap Analysis Project (CA-GAP).

Map 7.4: Ozone sample sites © 2005 Richard LeGates. Created from data in California Air Resources Board 2000 ambient air quality databases.

Map 7.5: Statistical surface of interpolated ozone levels for Contra Costa County © 2005 Richard LeGates. Created from data from California Air Resources Board 2000 ambient air quality databases.

Map 7.6a: Prime Contra Costa County farmland, 1984 © 2005 Richard LeGates. Created from data in California Department of Conservation Farmland Mapping and Monitoring Program © 1984 California Department of Conservation.

Map 7.6b: Prime Contra Costa County farmland, 2000 © 2005 Richard LeGates. Created from data in California Department of Conservation Farmland Mapping and Monitoring Program © 2000 California Department of Conservation.

Map 7.6c: Prime Contra Costa County farmland lost between 1984–2000 © 2005 Richard LeGates. Created from data in California Department of Conservation Farmland Mapping and Monitoring Program © 1984, 2000 California Department of Conservation.

Chapter 8

Map accompanying figure 8.4 © 2005 Richard LeGates. Created from data in 2000 U.S. Census of Population and Housing.

Chapter 9

Map 9.1: Camden and Burlington counties, Camden (city), and Mount Laurel, New Jersey © 2005 Richard LeGates. Created from data in Myron Orfield and Thomas Luce, *New Jersey metropatterns* © 2003 Ameregis.

Map 9.2: Poor children under age 5 in Camden and Burlington counties © 2005 Richard LeGates. Created from data in Myron Orfield and Thomas Luce, *New Jersey metropatterns* © 2003 Ameregis.

Map 9.3: Median income: Camden and Burlington counties cities, 2000 © 2005 Richard LeGates. Created from data in Myron Orfield and Thomas Luce, *New Jersey metropatterns* © 2003 Ameregis.

Map 9.4: African-Americans in Mount Laurel © 2005 Richard LeGates. Created from data in Myron Orfield and Thomas Luce *New Jersey metropatterns* © 2003 Ameregis.

Map 9.5: Percentage of non-Asian minority students in Camden and Burlington counties' elementary schools, 2000 © 2005 Richard LeGates. Created from data in Myron Orfield and Thomas Luce, *New Jersey metropatterns* © 2003 Ameregis.

Map 9.6: African-Americans and primary schools in Mount Laurel © 2005 Richard LeGates. Created from data in Myron Orfield and Thomas Luce, *New Jersey metropatterns* © 2003 Ameregis.

Map 9.7: Known contaminated sites in Camden (city) with groundwater contamination (2001) and the percentage of the population non-white by census tract (2000) © 2005 Richard LeGates. Created from data in New Jersey Department of Environmental Protection, Division of Publicly Funded Site Remediation, Site Remediation Program, *Known contaminated sites in New Jersey, 2001 edition.*

Map 9.8: Per capita tax capacity: Camden and Burlington counties cities, 2000 © 2005 Richard LeGates. Created from data in Myron Orfield and Thomas Luce, *New Jersey metropatterns* © 2003 Ameregis.

Chapter 10

Map 10.1: Harry Beck's 1933 map of the London tube tells the truth by distorting reality © 1933 Transport for London.

Map 10.2a: The world in a Mercator projection © 2005 Richard LeGates. Created from data in ESRI Data and Maps 2003 © 2003 ESRI.

Map 10.2b: The world in a Robinson projection © 2005 Richard LeGates. Created from data in ESRI Data and Maps 2003 © 2003 ESRI.

Map 10.3a: San Francisco, showing land on the peninsula, Treasure Island, and the Farallone Islands © 2005 Richard LeGates. Created from data in 2000 U.S. Census of Population and Housing.

Map 10.3b: San Francisco, including underwater land owned by the city © 2005 Richard LeGates. Created from data in 2000 U.S. Census of Population and Housing.

Map 10.4: Crimes per 100,000 people, Camden and Burlington counties, 2000 © 2005 Richard LeGates. Created from data in Myron Orfield and Thomas Luce, *New Jersey metropatterns* © 2003 Ameregis.

Map 10.5: Monochromatic five-class grayscale color ramp showing the percentage of African-Americans in Camden census tracts © 2005 Richard LeGates. Created from data in Myron Orfield and Thomas Luce, *New Jersey metropatterns* © 2003 Ameregis.

Map 10.6: Cities in the British Isles in 1850 with a cyan (light blue) data frame and uniform point symbols © 2005 Richard LeGates. Created from data in Tertius Chandler and Gerald Fox, *3000 years of urban growth* © 1974 Academic Press.

Map 10.7: Population of cities in the British Isles in 1850 symbolized as graduated point symbols © 2005 Richard LeGates. Created from data in Tertius Chandler and Gerald Fox, *3000 years of urban growth* © 1974 Academic Press.

Map 10.8: World cities in 1850 symbolized using proportional symbols © 2005 Richard LeGates. Created from data in Tertius Chandler and Gerald Fox, *3000 years of urban growth* © 1974 Academic Press.

Map 10.9: Global cities and cities with more than five million people, 2000 © 2005 Richard LeGates. Created from data in United Nations, Department of Economic and Social Affairs, Population Division, *Urban agglomerations 2003* © 2003 United Nations (cities with more than five million people, 2000). Global cities were designated based on a classification by the Globalization and World Cities Study Group and Network based at Loughborough University in the United Kingdom.

Map 10.10: Camden roads, streets, and major arterials © 2005 Richard LeGates. Created from data in Myron Orfield and Thomas Luce, *New Jersey metropatterns* © 2003 Ameregis.

Map 10.11: Populations of Italian cities, 1850 © 2005 Richard LeGates. Created from data in Tertius Chandler and Gerald Fox, *3000 years of urban growth* © 1974 Academic Press.

Map 10.12: Municipalities in Camden and Burlington counties symbolized to call attention to Camden (city) and Mount Laurel © 2005 Richard LeGates. Created from data in Myron Orfield and Thomas Luce, *New Jersey metropatterns* © 2003 Ameregis.

Map 10.13: Toxic sites in Camden and Burlington counties © 2005 Richard LeGates. Created from data in New Jersey Department of Environmental Protection, Division of Publicly Funded Site Remediation, Site Remediation Program, *Known contaminated sites in New Jersey, 2001 edition.*

Map 10.14a: Dot density map of Mount Laurel's African-American population, using entire city as the area, 2000 © 2005 Richard LeGates. Created from data in Myron Orfield and Thomas Luce, *New Jersey metropatterns* © 2003 Ameregis.

Map 10.14b: Mount Laurel census blocks © 2005 Richard LeGates. Created from data in Myron Orfield and Thomas Luce, *New Jersey metropatterns* © 2003 Ameregis.

Map 10.14c: Dot density map of Mount Laurel's African-American population, using census blocks as the area, 2000 © 2005 Richard LeGates. Created from data in Myron Orfield and Thomas Luce, *New Jersey metropatterns* © 2003 Ameregis.

Map 10.14d: Dot density map of Mount Laurel's African-American population, with census block boundaries dissolved, 2000 © 2005 Richard LeGates. Created from data in Myron Orfield and Thomas Luce, *New Jersey metropatterns* © 2003 Ameregis.

Chapter 12

Map 12.1: Metro region, Portland, Oregon © 2005 Richard LeGates. Created from Metro Data Resource Center (Portland, Oregon) Regional Land Information System Lite data © 2004 Metro.

Map 12.2: Part of the Metro 2040 Growth Concept plan © 2004 Metro.

Map 12.3: Portland area transportation © 2005 Richard LeGates. Created from Metro Data Resource Center (Portland, Oregon) Regional Land Information System Lite data © 2004 Metro.

Map 12.4: Rock Creek watershed © 2005 Richard LeGates. Created from Metro Data Resource Center (Portland, Oregon) Regional Land Information System Lite data © 2004 Metro.

Data for many of the maps is in the public domain and available on the Web. Following is a listing of the Web sites for this data as of spring 2005. The Web sites are organized by the chapters where most maps based on the data are located, though some data layers from these sources are included in maps elsewhere in the book.

Chapters 1–3

United Nations urban agglomerations data
www.un.org/esa/population/publications/wup2003/2003urban_agglo.htm

U.S. Census demographic data: American FactFinder
factfinder.census.gov/home/saff/main.html?_lang=en

World Bank development indicators data
www.worldbank.org/data/wdi2005/index.html

Chapters 5–7

California Air Resources Board data
www.arb.ca.gov/homepage.htm

California Department of Conservation Farmland Mapping and Monitoring Program data
www.consrv.ca.gov/dlrp/FMMP

California Department of Forestry and Fire Protection 2003 forest and range assessment data
www.frap.cdf.ca.gov/assessment2003

California Gap Analysis Project (CA-GAP) data
www.biogeog.ucsb.edu/projects/gap/gap_home.html

U.S. Environmental Protection Agency Toxic Release Inventory data
www.epa.gov/tri

Chapters 9–11

New Jersey contaminated sites data: New Jersey Department of Environmental Protection, Division of Publicly Funded Site Remediation, Site Remediation Program
www.state.nj.us/dep/gis/stateshp.html

New Jersey Metropatterns data: Metropolitan Area Research Corporation
www.metroresearch.org

Chapter 12

Metro (Portland, Oregon) Regional Land Information System data
www.metro-region.org

Figure credits

All figures in *Think Globally, Act Regionally*, with the exception of those noted with a different copyright holder, were created by students and staff employed by San Francisco State University working under the direction of Richard LeGates, supported by U.S. National Science Foundation (NSF), Division of Undergraduate Education (DUE), Course, Curriculum and Laboratory Improvement-Educational Materials Development (CCLI-EMD) grant # DUE 0228878. Richard LeGates holds the copyright to these figures.

Every effort has been made to contact copyright holders for their permission to use data to create figures in this book. The publishers would be grateful to hear from any copyright holder who is not here acknowledged and will undertake to rectify any errors or omissions in future editions of this book.

Figures in this book may not be reproduced without express written permission of the copyright holder.

Following is copyright information for the figures that appear in this book:

Chapter 1
Figure 1.1a: Increase in city population © 2005 ESRI.

Figure 1.1b: Different levels of urbanization (two countries) © 2005 ESRI.

Figure 1.1c: Increase in city physical size (no increase in population) © 2005 ESRI.

Figure 1.2: Kingsley Davis's family of "S" curves representing the urbanization of four countries over time © 2005 ESRI.

Chapter 3
Figure 3.1: Historical city populations attribute table © 2005 Richard LeGates. Created from data in Tertius Chandler and Gerald Fox, *3000 years of urban growth* © 1974 Academic Press (population data for 1800 and 1850); Tertius Chandler, *Four thousand years of urban growth* © 1987 Edwin Mellen Press (population data for 1990 and 1950).

Figure 3.2: Attribute table of South American cities © 2005 Richard LeGates. Created from data in ESRI Data and Maps 2003 © 2003 ESRI.

Figure 3.3: Histogram of California county populations classified in five equal intervals © 2005 Richard LeGates. Created from data in U.S. Census of Population and Housing.

Chapter 4

Figure 4.1: Shaker chairs: the epitome of minimalism © 2005 Shaker Museum and Library.

Figure 4.2: A photograph of Contra Costa County hiking trails shows open space in a way that text and maps cannot © Brad Rovanpera.

Figure 4.3: Digital orthophoto of Portland, Oregon © 2005 Richard LeGates. Created from Metro Data Resource Center (Portland, Oregon). Regional Land Information System Lite data © 2004 Metro.

Figure 4.4: Bicycle routes superimposed over a digital orthophoto of Portland, Oregon © 2005 Richard LeGates. Created from Metro Data Resource Center (Portland, Oregon) Regional Land Information System Lite data © 2004 Metro.

Figure 4.5: Pie chart showing race and ethnicity of San Francisco Bay Area residents, 2000 © 2005 Richard LeGates. Created from data in 2000 U.S. Census of Population and Housing.

Figure 4.6: Bar chart showing tax capacity per capita: selected southern New Jersey municipalities, 2000 © 2005 Richard LeGates. Created from data in Myron Orfield and Thomas Luce, *New Jersey metropatterns* © 2003 Ameregis.

Figure 4.7: Histogram showing city population sizes in 1800 for world cities with populations of more than 11,000 © 2005 Richard LeGates. Created from data in Tertius Chandler and Gerald Fox *3000 years of urban growth* © 1974 Academic Press.

Figure 4.8: Line chart showing population size of London, England, 1750–2000 © 2005 Richard LeGates. Created from data in Tertius Chandler and Gerald Fox, *3000 years of urban growth* © 1974 Academic Press (population data for 1750, 1800, and 1850); Tertius Chandler, *Four thousand years of urban growth* © 1987 Edwin Mellen Press (population data for 1900 and 1950); and United Nations, *Urban agglomerations 2003* © 2003 United Nations Department of Economic and Social Affairs, Population Division (population data for 2000).

Chapter 6

Figure 6.1: Zoomed view of nine cells in a raster dataset grid representing area of detail in map 6.2b © 2005 Richard LeGates. Created from data in California Gap Analysis Project (CA-GAP).

Figure 6.2: Rows and columns in a raster dataset grid © 2005 Richard LeGates.

Figure 6.3: Variety of vegetation types in sixty-one Contra Costa County watersheds © 2005 Richard LeGates. Created from data in California Department of Forestry and Fire Protection. The changing California 2003 forest and range assessment.

Chapter 7

Figure 7.1: Raster cells with a source and straight line distance values © 2005 ESRI.

Figure 7.2: Cost-weighted distance raster © 2005 ESRI.

Figure 7.3: Hypothetical distribution of Bay Area Air Quality Management District ozone field monitoring sites © 2005 ESRI. Created from data in California Air Resources Board 2000 ambient air quality databases.

Figure 7.4: ArcGIS Spatial Analyst Raster Calculator © ESRI. Data shown is from California Department of Conservation Farmland Mapping and Monitoring Program © 1984–2004 California Department of Conservation.

Figure 7.5: Red-legged frog habitat suitability model © 2005 Richard LeGates. Created from data in California Gap Analysis Project (CA-GAP).

Chapter 8

Figure 8.1: Driving alone and carpooling in twelve southern Santa Clara County census tracts, 2000 © 2005 Richard LeGates. Created from data in 2000 U.S. Census of Population and Housing.

Figure 8.2: City population size: London, Paris, and Rome, 1750–2000 © 2005 Richard LeGates. Created from data in Tertius Chandler and Gerald Fox, *3000 years of urban growth* © 1974 Academic Press (population data for 1750, 1800, and 1850); Tertius Chandler, *Four thousand years of urban growth* © 1987 Edwin Mellen Press (population data for 1900 and 1950); and United Nations, *Urban agglomerations 2003* © 2003 United Nations Department of Economic and Social Affairs, Population Division (population data for 2000).

Figure 8.3: The relationship between percent urban and percent change in urban population for selected countries, 2003 © 2005 Richard LeGates. Created from data in World Bank, *World development indicators 2004* © 2004 World Bank.

Figure 8.4: Demographics of five San Francisco census tracts, 2000 © 2005 Richard LeGates. Created from data in 2000 U.S. Census of Population and Housing.

Figure 8.5: Area chart showing population of five global cities © 2005 Richard LeGates. Created from data in Tertius Chandler and Gerald Fox, *3000 years of urban growth* © 1974 Academic Press (population data for 1800 and 1850); Tertius Chandler, *Four thousand years of urban growth* © 1987 Edwin Mellen Press (population data for 1900 and 1950); and United Nations, *Urban agglomerations 2003* © 2003 United Nations Department of Economic and Social Affairs, Population Division (population data for 2000).

Chapter 10

Figure 10.1a: Vector GIS polygon representing precise borders of Contra Costa County farmland © 2005 Richard LeGates. Created from California Department of Conservation Farmland Mapping and Monitoring Program data © 1984–2004 California Department of Conservation.

Figure 10.1b: Vector GIS polygon representing simplified borders of Contra Costa County farmland © 2005 Richard LeGates. Created from California Department of Conservation Farmland Mapping and Monitoring Program data © 1984–2004 California Department of Conservation.

Figure 10.2: Mimetic point symbols © 2004 ESRI.

Figure 10.3: Hatched lines, dots, and cross-hatched lines © 2004 ESRI.

Chapter 11
Figure 11.1: "Gettysburg Address" PowerPoint slide © Peter Norvig.

Figure 11.2: *New York Times* graphic on people moving out of the U.S. Heartland © 2003 The New York Times Graphics.

Figure 11.3: Jacques Bertin's retinal variables © 2005 Richard LeGates. Based on concepts in Jacques Bertin, *Semiology of graphics: Diagrams, networks, maps.* Translated by William J. Berg © 1967 University of Wisconsin Press (reprint 1983).

Figure 11.4: Urbanization of three countries, with graphical elements identified © 2005 Richard LeGates. Created from data in World Bank, *World development indicators 2004* © 2004 World Bank.

Chapter 12
Figure 12.1: Metropolitan Area Express (MAX) light-rail train, Portland, Oregon © Bruce Forster.

Figure 12.2: Portland skyline with Mount Hood © Bruce Forster.

Data for many of the figures is in the public domain and available on the Web. Following is a listing of the Web sites for this data as of spring 2005. The Web sites are organized by the chapters where most figures based on the data are located, though some data layers from these sources are included in figures elsewhere in the book.

Chapters 1–4
Country urbanization data: World Bank development indicators
www.worldbank.org/data/wdi2005/index.html

New Jersey Metropatterns data: Metropolitan Area Research Corporation
www.metroresearch.org

Portland, Oregon digital orthophoto and bicycle routes: Metro (Portland, Oregon) Regional Land Information System data
www.metro-region.org

U.S. Census demographic data: American FactFinder
factfinder.census.gov/home/saff/main.html?_lang=en

World city population data: United Nations urban agglomerations
www.un.org/esa/population/publications/wup2003/2003urban_agglo.htm

Chapters 6–8
Contra Costa County endangered species data: California Gap Analysis Project (CA-GAP)
www.biogeog.ucsb.edu/projects/gap/gap_home.html

Contra Costa County vegetation data: California Department of Forestry and Fire Protection. The changing California 2003 forest and range assessment
www.frap.cdf.ca.gov/assessment2003

Chapters 10–11
Contra Costa County farmland data: California Department of Conservation Farmland Mapping and Monitoring Program
www.consrv.ca.gov/dlrp/FMMP

New Jersey Metropatterns data: Metropolitan Area Research Corporation
www.metroresearch.org

Chapter 12
Metro (Portland, Oregon) Regional Land Information System data
www.metro-region.org

Data credits

The exercise data on the *Think Globally, Act Regionally* CD-ROM was assembled from multiple sources by students employed by San Francisco State University working under the direction of the author, supported by U.S. National Science Foundation (NSF), Division of Undergraduate Education (DUE), Course, Curriculum and Laboratory Improvement-Educational Materials Development (CCLI-EMD) grant # DUE 0228878. ESRI holds the copyright to the CD-ROM. The exercises are for one-time use by purchasers of *Think Globally, Act Regionally*. None of the data on the *Think Globally, Act Regionally* CD-ROM may be reproduced, copied, sold, or used for any other purpose without express written permission of the original copyright holder(s). While every effort has been made to assure the accuracy of the data, the data is for academic purposes only. ESRI does not warrant the accuracy of the data.

Every effort has been made to contact copyright holders for their permission to use data to create maps in this book. The publishers would be grateful to hear from any copyright holder who is not here acknowledged and will undertake to rectify any errors or omissions in future editions of this book.

Following is copyright information for the exercise data on the *Think Globally, Act Regionally* CD-ROM:

Exercise 1

Countries 2000. ESRI Data and Maps 2004 © 2004 ESRI.

Cities 2000. ESRI Data and Maps 2004 © 2004 ESRI.

Global cities. ESRI Data and Maps © 2004 ESRI. Global cities were selected using criteria developed by the Globalization and World Cities Study Group and Network based at Loughborough University, United Kingdom.

World city populations in 1800. Tertius Chandler and Gerald Fox. *3000 years of urban growth* © 1974 Academic Press.

Exercise 1 Your Turn

Cities 2000. Tertius Chandler. *Four thousand years of urban growth* © 1987 Edwin Mellen Press.

Cities 1900. Tertius Chandler and Gerald Fox. *3000 years of urban growth* © 1974 Academic Press.

Cities 1850. Tertius Chandler and Gerald Fox. *3000 years of urban growth* © 1974 Academic Press.

Cities 1800. Tertius Chandler and Gerald Fox. *3000 years of urban growth* © 1974 Academic Press.

Canadian provinces. ESRI Data and Maps 2004 © 2004 ESRI.

USA states. ESRI Data and Maps 2004 © 2004 ESRI.

Countries 2000. ESRI Data and Maps 2004 © 2004 ESRI.

Exercise 2a

Bay Area cities 2000. 2000 U.S. Census of Population and Housing.

Bay Area tracts 2000. 2000 U.S. Census of Population and Housing.

Exercise 2b

S.F.R.A. housing © 2004 San Francisco Redevelopment Agency.

S.F. streets. 2000 U.S. Census TIGER files.

S.F. planning districts © 2004 San Francisco Planning Department.

S.F. tracts 2000. 2000 U.S. Census of Population and Housing.

S.F. block groups 2000. 2000 U.S. Census of Population and Housing.

Bay Area counties. 2000 U.S. Census of Population and Housing.

Exercise 2 Your Turn

Bay Area cities 2000. 2000 U.S. Census of Population and Housing.

City of Oakland. 2000 U.S. Census of Population and Housing.

Bay Area tracts 2000. 2000 U.S. Census of Population and Housing.

Exercise 3

Ozone sample points. California Air Resources Board 2000 ambient air quality databases.

Bay Area counties. 2000 U.S. Census of Population and Housing.

California counties. 2000 U.S. Census of Population and Housing.

Libraries. U.S. Geological Survey Geographic Names Information System (GNIS) 2004.

Cities. ESRI Data and Maps 2004 © 2004 ESRI.

Highways. 2000 U.S. Census TIGER files.

Farms2000 © 1984–2004 California Department of Conservation, Farmland Mapping and Monitoring Program.

Distance to libraries. U.S. Geological Survey Geographic Names Information System 2004.

Farm84_grid © 1984-2004 California Department of Conservation, Farmland Mapping and Monitoring Program.

Farms1984 © 1984–2004 California Department of Conservation, Farmland Mapping and Monitoring Program.

County_grid. 2000 U.S. Census of Population and Housing.

Exercise 3 Your Turn

County boundary. 2000 U.S. Census of Population and Housing.

Urban centers. 2000 U.S. Census of Population and Housing.

Redwood forests. California Gap Analysis Project (CA-GAP).

Hardwood forests. California Gap Analysis Project (CA-GAP).

Wetlands areas. California Gap Analysis Project (CA-GAP).

Vegetation types. California Gap Analysis Project (CA-GAP).

Ownership. California Resources Agency Legacy Project. Public and Conservation Lands (2003) data.

Bay Area counties. 2000 U.S. Census of Population and Housing.

Ozone sample points. California Air Resources Board 2000 ambient air quality databases.

Contra Costa County. 2000 U.S. Census of Population and Housing.

Exercise 4

Contra Costa County. 2000 U.S. Census of Population and Housing.

Frog sightings. Hypothetical data created by Richard LeGates.

Toxic release sites. U.S. Environmental Protection Agency Toxic Release Inventory.

Highways. 2000 U.S. Census TIGER files.

Rivers. U.S. Geological Survey in cooperation with U.S. Environmental Protection Agency.

Red-legged frog habitat. California Gap Analysis Project (CA-GAP).

Land cost. Hypothetical data created by Richard LeGates.

Highway distance. 2000 U.S. Census TIGER files.

River distance. U.S. Geological Survey in cooperation with U.S. Environmental Protection Agency.

Toxic distance. U.S. Environmental Protection Agency Toxic Release Inventory.

Bay Area counties. 2000 U.S. Census of Population and Housing.

Exercise 4 Your Turn

Contra Costa County. 2000 U.S. Census of Population and Housing.

Vole sightings. Hypothetical data created by Richard LeGates.

Vole habitat. California Gap Analysis Project (CA-GAP).

Land cost. Hypothetical data created by Richard LeGates.

Reclass of highways. 2000 U.S. Census TIGER files.

Reclass of rivers. U.S. Geological Survey in cooperation with U.S. Environmental Protection Agency.

Reclass of toxics. U.S. Environmental Protection Agency Toxic Release Inventory.

Bay Area counties. 2000 U.S. Census of Population and Housing.

Exercise 5a

Cities 1750. Tertius Chandler and Gerald Fox. *3000 years of urban growth* © 1974 Academic Press.

Cities 1600. Tertius Chandler and Gerald Fox. *3000 years of urban growth* © 1974 Academic Press.

Cities 1500. Tertius Chandler and Gerald Fox. *3000 years of urban growth* © 1974 Academic Press.

Countries. ESRI Data and Maps 2004 © 2004 ESRI.

Exercise 5b

New Jersey © 2003 Ameregis.

Camden © 2003 Ameregis.

Mount Laurel © 2003 Ameregis.

Exercise 5c

Elementary schools © 2003 Ameregis.

Mount Laurel © 2003 Ameregis.

Census blocks © 2003 Ameregis.

Camden, N.J. toxic sites. New Jersey Department of Environmental Protection, Division of Publicly Funded Site Remediation, Site Remediation Program. *Known contaminated sites in New Jersey, 2001 edition.*

Camden census blocks © 2003 Ameregis.

Camden city limits © 2003 Ameregis.

Percent African-American pop © 2003 Ameregis.

Exercise 5 Your Turn

Schools © 2003 Ameregis.

Burlington County © 2003 Ameregis.

Camden County © 2003 Ameregis.

Census blocks © 2003 Ameregis.

Exercise 6a

Property tax rate 2001 © 2003 Ameregis.

Bordering states © 2003 Ameregis.

Exercise 6b

Municipality © 2003 Ameregis.

Per capita tax capacity © 2003 Ameregis.

Exercise 6 Your Turn

Camden © 2003 Ameregis.

Mount Laurel © 2003 Ameregis.

State line © 2003 Ameregis.

County boundaries © 2003 Ameregis.

Transit route © 2003 Ameregis.

Inland water © 2003 Ameregis.

Urbanization 1970 © 2003 Ameregis.

Urbanization 1990 © 2003 Ameregis.

Water line © 2003 Ameregis.

New Jersey © 2003 Ameregis.

Bordering states © 2003 Ameregis.

Ocean © 2003 Ameregis.

Exercises 7a, b, and c
All data for exercise 7 © 2004 Metro.

Other credits

Tables, boxes, photos, histograms, and other material in *Think Globally, Act Regionally* may not be reproduced without express written permission of the copyright holder.

Every effort has been made to contact copyright holders for their permission to use all tables, boxes, photos, histograms, and other material that appear in this book. The publishers would be grateful to hear from any copyright holder who is not here acknowledged and will undertake to rectify any errors or omissions in future editions of this book.

Following is copyright and source information for the tables, boxes, photos, histograms, and other material that appear in this book:

Chapter 1

Photograph of San Francisco. Photodisc © 1999–2005 Getty Images, Inc.

Box 1.1: World population clock. U.S. Census Bureau.

Photograph of San Francisco's Chinatown. Photodisc © 1999–2005 Getty Images, Inc.

Photograph of traffic congestion. Photodisc © 1999–2005 Getty Images, Inc.

Chapter 2

Photograph of student at computer © 2005 Elmer Tosta.

Box 2.1: Five definitions of GIS. Adapted from Keith C. Clarke, *Getting started with geographic information systems,* fourth edition. © 2003 Prentice Hall

Box 2.2: Map projection considerations © 2005 Richard LeGates.

Table 2.1a: Attribute table using U.S. Census information on driving behavior in Santa Clara County census tracts. 2000 U.S. Census of Population and Housing.

Table 2.1b: Table of congestion index scores for Santa Clara County census tracts based on field observation. Hypothetical data.

Box 2.3: FGDC metadata standards © 2005 Richard LeGates using standards prepared by the Federal Geographic Data Committee.

Chapter 3

Box 3.1: Reporting what is contained within feature(s) © 2005 Richard LeGates.

Box 3.2: Operators for GIS queries © Richard LeGates.

Histogram showing population of Camden County, New Jersey, municipalities © Richard LeGates.

Chapter 5

Photograph of scenic Contra Costa County © 2005 Brad Rovanpera.

Photograph of Contra Costa County hiking trails © 2005 Brad Rovanpera.

Photograph of grassland habitat and encroaching urbanization © 2005 Brad Rovanpera.

Chapter 7

Photograph of student at computer © 2005 Richard LeGates.

Box 7.1: Calculating loss of prime farmland in Contra Costa County 1984–2000 © Richard LeGates. Created from data in California Department of Conservation Farmland Mapping and Monitoring Program © 1984–2004 California Department of Conservation.

Chapter 9

Photographs of housing stock in Camden and Mount Laurel, New Jersey. Reprinted courtesy of the *Courier-Post*, Cherry Hill, N.J.

Chapter 10

Box 10.1: ColorBrewer. Developed by Cynthia Brewer, associate professor of geography at Pennsylvania State University, with interface design and programming by Mark Harrower, assistant professor of geography at the University of Wisconsin, Madison.

Box 10.2: Symbolizing polygons with color © 2005 Richard LeGates.

Table 10.1: Map scale and equivalents measured on the earth's surface © 2005 Richard LeGates.

Box 10.3: What to include in map layouts © 2005 Richard LeGates.

Chapter 11

Photograph of students at computer © 2005 Richard LeGates.

Box 11.2: Selected concepts and principles in Tufte's "Theory of data graphics." Created by Richard LeGates from material in Edward C. Tufte, *The visual display of quantitative information*, second edition. © 2001 Edward Rolf Tufte.

Box 11:3: William Cleveland's elements of graphing data (selections). Created by Richard LeGates from material in William S. Cleveland, *The elements of graphing data* © 1994 AT&T.

Chapter 12

Box 12.1: Understanding the 2040 Growth Concept map. Created by Richard LeGates from information in *The nature of 2040* © 2005 Metro (Portland, Oregon).

Data license agreement

Important:

Read carefully before opening the sealed media package.

ENVIRONMENTAL SYSTEMS RESEARCH INSTITUTE, INC. (ESRI), IS WILLING TO LICENSE THE ENCLOSED DATA AND RELATED MATERIALS TO YOU ONLY UPON THE CONDITION THAT YOU ACCEPT ALL OF THE TERMS AND CONDITIONS CONTAINED IN THIS LICENSE AGREEMENT. PLEASE READ THE TERMS AND CONDITIONS CARE-FULLY BEFORE OPENING THE SEALED MEDIA PACKAGE. BY OPENING THE SEALED MEDIA PACKAGE, YOU ARE INDICATING YOUR ACCEPTANCE OF THE ESRI LICENSE AGREEMENT. IF YOU DO NOT AGREE TO THE TERMS AND CONDITIONS AS STATED, THEN ESRI IS UNWILLING TO LICENSE THE DATA AND RELATED MATERIALS TO YOU. IN SUCH EVENT, YOU SHOULD RETURN THE MEDIA PACKAGE WITH THE SEAL UNBROKEN AND ALL OTHER COMPONENTS TO ESRI.

ESRI License Agreement

This is a license agreement, and not an agreement for sale, between you (Licensee) and Environmental Systems Research Institute, Inc. (ESRI). This ESRI License Agreement (Agreement) gives Licensee certain limited rights to use the data and related materials (Data and Related Materials). All rights not specifically granted in this Agreement are reserved to ESRI and its Licensors.

Reservation of Ownership and Grant of License:

ESRI and its Licensors retain exclusive rights, title, and ownership to the copy of the Data and Related Materials licensed under this Agreement and, hereby, grant to Licensee a personal, non-exclusive, nontransferable, royalty-free, worldwide license to use the Data and Related Materials based on the terms and conditions of this Agreement. Licensee agrees to use reasonable effort to protect the Data and Related Materials from unauthorized use, reproduction, distribution, or publication.

Proprietary Rights and Copyright:

Licensee acknowledges that the Data and Related Materials are proprietary and confidential property of ESRI and its Licensors and are protected by United States copyright laws and applicable international copyright treaties and/or conventions.

Permitted Uses:

Licensee may install the Data and Related Materials onto permanent storage device(s) for Licensee's own internal use.

Licensee may make only one (1) copy of the original Data and Related Materials for archival purposes during the term of this Agreement unless the right to make additional copies is granted to Licensee in writing by ESRI.

Licensee may internally use the Data and Related Materials provided by ESRI for the stated purpose of GIS training and education.

Uses Not Permitted:
Licensee shall not sell, rent, lease, sublicense, lend, assign, time-share, or transfer, in whole or in part, or provide unlicensed Third Parties access to the Data and Related Materials or portions of the Data and Related Materials, any updates, or Licensee's rights under this Agreement. Licensee shall not remove or obscure any copyright or trademark notices of ESRI or its Licensors.

Term and Termination:
The license granted to Licensee by this Agreement shall commence upon the acceptance of this Agreement and shall continue until such time that Licensee elects in writing to discontinue use of the Data or Related Materials and terminates this Agreement. The Agreement shall automatically terminate without notice if Licensee fails to comply with any provision of this Agreement. Licensee shall then return to ESRI the Data and Related Materials. The parties hereby agree that all provisions that operate to protect the rights of ESRI and its Licensors shall remain in force should breach occur.

Disclaimer of Warranty:
THE DATA AND RELATED MATERIALS CONTAINED HEREIN ARE PROVIDED "AS-IS," WITHOUT WARRANTY OF ANY KIND, EITHER EXPRESS OR IMPLIED, INCLUDING, BUT NOT LIMITED TO, THE IMPLIED WARRANTIES OF MERCHANTABILITY, FITNESS FOR A PARTICULAR PURPOSE, OR NONINFRINGEMENT. ESRI does not warrant that the Data and Related Materials will meet Licensee's needs or expectations, that the use of the Data and Related Materials will be uninterrupted, or that all nonconformities, defects, or errors can or will be corrected. ESRI is not inviting reliance on the Data or Related Materials for commercial planning or analysis purposes, and Licensee should always check actual data.

Data Disclaimer:
The Data used herein has been derived from actual spatial or tabular information. In some cases, ESRI has manipulated and applied certain assumptions, analyses, and opinions to the Data solely for educational training purposes. Assumptions, analyses, opinions applied, and actual outcomes may vary. Again, ESRI is not inviting reliance on this Data, and the Licensee should always verify actual Data and exercise their own professional judgment when interpreting any outcomes.

Limitation of Liability:
ESRI shall not be liable for direct, indirect, special, incidental, or consequential damages related to Licensee's use of the Data and Related Materials, even if ESRI is advised of the possibility of such damage.

No Implied Waivers:
No failure or delay by ESRI or its Licensors in enforcing any right or remedy under this Agreement shall be construed as a waiver of any future or other exercise of such right or remedy by ESRI or its Licensors.

Order for Precedence:

Any conflict between the terms of this Agreement and any FAR, DFAR, purchase order, or other terms shall be resolved in favor of the terms expressed in this Agreement, subject to the government's minimum rights unless agreed otherwise.

Export Regulation:

Licensee acknowledges that this Agreement and the performance thereof are subject to compliance with any and all applicable United States laws, regulations, or orders relating to the export of data thereto. Licensee agrees to comply with all laws, regulations, and orders of the United States in regard to any export of such technical data.

Severability:

If any provision(s) of this Agreement shall be held to be invalid, illegal, or unenforceable by a court or other tribunal of competent jurisdiction, the validity, legality, and enforceability of the remaining provisions shall not in any way be affected or impaired thereby.

Governing Law:

This Agreement, entered into in the County of San Bernardino, shall be construed and enforced in accordance with and be governed by the laws of the United States of America and the State of California without reference to conflict of laws principles. The parties hereby consent to the personal jurisdiction of the courts of this county and waive their rights to change venue.

Entire Agreement:

The parties agree that this Agreement constitutes the sole and entire agreement of the parties as to the matter set forth herein and supersedes any previous agreements, understandings, and arrangements between the parties relating hereto.

Installing the software

Think Globally, Act Regionally includes one CD that contains the exercise data. The exercise data takes up about 370 megabytes of hard-disk space. The data installation process takes about five minutes.

Installing the data

Follow the steps below to install the exercise data. Do not copy the files directly from the CD to your hard drive. A direct file copy does not remove write-protection from the files, and this causes data editing exercises not to work. In addition, a direct file copy will not enable the automatic uninstall feature.

1. Put the data CD in your computer's CD drive. In your file browser, click the icon for your CD drive to see its contents. Double-click the Setup.exe file to begin.

2. Read the Welcome.

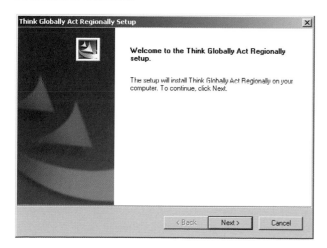

492

3. Click Next. Accept the default installation folder or click Browse and navigate to the drive or folder location where you want to install the data. If you choose an alternate location, please make note of it. The book's exercises direct you to C:\TGAR as the location where exercise data is installed. If the exercises are in another location, you will need to navigate to that location to find the exercise files.

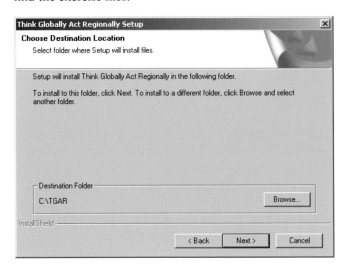

4. Click Next. The exercise data is installed on your computer in a folder called TGAR. When the installation is finished, you see the following message:

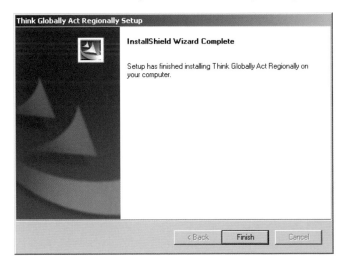

5. Click Finish.

Uninstalling the exercise data

To uninstall the exercise data from your computer, open your operating system's control panel and double-click the Add/Remove Programs icon. In the Add/Remove Programs dialog box, select the following entry and follow the prompts to remove it:

* Think Globally Act Regionally

Index

Books from

ESRI Press

Advanced Spatial Analysis: The CASA Book of GIS *1-58948-073-2*
ArcGIS and the Digital City: A Hands-on Approach for Local Government *1-58948-074-0*
ArcView GIS Means Business *1-879102-51-X*
A System for Survival: GIS and Sustainable Development *1-58948-052-X*
Beyond Maps: GIS and Decision Making in Local Government *1-879102-79-X*
Cartographica Extraordinaire: The Historical Map Transformed *1-58948-044-9*
Cartographies of Disease: Maps, Mapping, and Medicine *1-58948-120-8*
Children Map the World: Selections from the Barbara Petchenik Children's World Map Competition *1-58948-125-9*
Community Geography: GIS in Action *1-58948-023-6*
Community Geography: GIS in Action Teacher's Guide *1-58948-051-1*
Confronting Catastrophe: A GIS Handbook *1-58948-040-6*
Connecting Our World: GIS Web Services *1-58948-075-9*
Conservation Geography: Case Studies in GIS, Computer Mapping, and Activism *1-58948-024-4*
Designing Better Maps: A Guide for GIS Users *1-58948-089-9*
Designing Geodatabases: Case Studies in GIS Data Modeling *1-58948-021-X*
Disaster Response: GIS for Public Safety *1-879102-88-9*
Enterprise GIS for Energy Companies *1-879102-48-X*
Extending ArcView GIS (version 3.x edition) *1-879102-05-6*
Fun with GPS *1-58948-087-2*
Getting to Know ArcGIS Desktop, Second Edition Updated for ArcGIS 9 *1-58948-083-X*
Getting to Know ArcObjects: Programming ArcGIS with VBA *1-58948-018-X*
Getting to Know ArcView GIS (version 3.x edition) *1-879102-46-3*
GIS and Land Records: The ArcGIS Parcel Data Model *1-58948-077-5*
GIS for Everyone, Third Edition *1-58948-056-2*
GIS for Health Organizations *1-879102-65-X*
GIS for Landscape Architects *1-879102-64-1*
GIS for the Urban Environment *1-58948-082-1*
GIS for Water Management in Europe *1-58948-076-7*
GIS in Public Policy: Using Geographic Information for More Effective Government *1-879102-66-8*
GIS in Schools *1-879102-85-4*
GIS in Telecommunications *1-879102-86-2*
GIS Means Business, Volume II *1-58948-033-3*
GIS Tutorial: Workbook for ArcView 9 *1-58948-127-5*
GIS, Spatial Analysis, and Modeling *1-58948-130-5*
GIS Worlds: Creating Spatial Data Infrastructures *1-58948-122-4*
Hydrologic and Hydraulic Modeling Support with Geographic Information Systems *1-879102-80-3*
Integrating GIS and the Global Positioning System *1-879102-81-1*
Making Community Connections: The Orton Family Foundation Community Mapping Program *1-58948-071-6*
Managing Natural Resources with GIS *1-879102-53-6*
Mapping Census 2000: The Geography of U.S. Diversity *1-58948-014-7*
Mapping Our World: GIS Lessons for Educators, ArcView GIS 3.x Edition *1-58948-022-8*
Mapping Our World: GIS Lessons for Educators, ArcGIS Desktop Edition *1-58948-121-6*
Mapping the Future of America's National Parks: Stewardship through Geographic Information Systems *1-58948-080-5*
Mapping the News: Case Studies in GIS and Journalism *1-58948-072-4*
Marine Geography: GIS for the Oceans and Seas *1-58948-045-7*
Measuring Up: The Business Case for GIS *1-58948-088-0*
Modeling Our World: The ESRI Guide to Geodatabase Design *1-879102-62-5*
Past Time, Past Place: GIS for History *1-58948-032-5*

Continued on next page

When ordering, please mention book title and ISBN (number that follows each title)

Books from ESRI Press (continued)

Forthcoming titles from ESRI Press

Ask for ESRI Press titles at your local bookstore or order by calling 1-800-447-9778. You can also shop online at www.esri.com/esripress. Outside the United States, contact your local ESRI distributor.

ESRI Press titles are distributed to the trade by the following:

In North America, South America, Asia, and Australia:
Independent Publishers Group (IPG)
Telephone (United States): 1-800-888-4741 • Telephone (international): 312-337-0747
E-mail: frontdesk@ipgbook.com

In the United Kingdom, Europe, and the Middle East:
Transatlantic Publishers Group Ltd.
Telephone: 44 20 8849 8013 • Fax: 44 20 8849 5556 • E-mail: transatlantic.publishers@regusnet.com

ESRI Press • 380 New York Street • Redlands, California 92373-8100 • www.esri.com/esripress